NEW YORK STATE

Picture Research by Allis Wolfe

Partners in Progress
by
Robert W. Arnold III, Charlene Costanzo, David Fleming,
Daniel J. Herbeck, Thomas James McMenemy, Anne P. Marsh,
Joseph A. Porcello, and Gordon Wackett

Produced in cooperation with
The Business Council of New York State, Inc.
and
The New York State Museum Institute

Windsor Publications, Inc.
Northridge, California

NEW
YORK
STATE
GATEWAY TO AMERICA

DAVID M. ELLIS

Windsor Publications, Inc.—History Books Division
Managing Editor: Karen Story
Design Director: Alexander D'Anca

Staff for *New York State: Gateway to America*
Manuscript Editor: Nora Perren
Photo Editor: Susan L. Wells
Development Editor: Jerry Mosher
Assistant Director, Corporate Biographies: Phyllis Gray
Editor, Corporate Biographies: Brenda Berryhill
Production Editor, Corporate Biographies: Una FitzSimons
Senior Proofreader: Susan J. Muhler
Editorial Assistants: Didier Beauvoir, Thelma Fleischer, Kim Kievman, Michael Nugwynne, Kathy B. Peyser, Pat Pittman, Theresa Solis
Sales Representatives, Corporate Biographies: Marcia Cohen, Stephen Hung, Bill Joeks, Steve Nafe, Robert Ottenheimer, Robert Sadoski
Layout Artists, Corporate Biographies: Mari Catherine Preimesberger, S.L. Wells
Designer: Tom McTighe

Library of Congress Cataloging-in-Publication Data
Ellis, David Maldwyn.
New York, gateway to America / by David M. Ellis; Partners in progress by Robert W. Arnold III . . . et al.; produced in cooperation with the Business Council of New York State, Inc. and the New York State Museum Institute.—1st ed.
Bibliography:
Includes index.
ISBN: 0-89781-246-8
1. New York (State)—History. 2. New York (State)—Description and travel—Views.
3. New York (State)—Industries. I. Business Council of New York State. II. New York State Museum Institute. III. Title.
F119.E445 1988 87-36829 974.7--dc19 CIP

Windsor Publications, Inc.
Elliot Martin, Chairman of the Board
James L. Fish, III, Chief Operating Officer
Hal Silverman, Vice-President, Publisher

CONTENTS

For Carol
To celebrate the joys of over three decades together

INTRODUCTION

Diversity has always characterized the history of New York province and state as well as its communities. A combination of factors encouraged diversity: topography and resources; a heterogeneous population; and the amazing breadth and complexity of its economic activities.

Edmund Wilson, America's leading man of letters in this century, spent much of his later years at his ancestral home a few miles north of Rome, New York. He observed: "The country, magnificent and vast, has never been humanized as New England has: the landscape still overwhelms the people." Wilson's observation highlights the creative tension and uneasy balance between man and his environment. On one hand nature has been singularly kind to New York. The great harbor with its hundreds of miles of sheltered shoreline enabled Manhattan's merchants to capture the bulk of the coastal, transatlantic, and interior trades in the early decades of the 19th century. The Hudson, a tidal arm of the sea for more than 100 miles, and its Mohawk tributary provided the best gateway through the Appalachian barrier. On the other hand nature compelled New Yorkers to perform amazing feats of engineering and construction. Note the digging of the 363-mile-long Erie Canal through the wilderness, the spanning of the Hudson River in addition to tunnels under it, the construction of the St. Lawrence Seaway, and the harnessing of the Niagara and St. Lawrence rivers for electric power.

In 1975 the state legislature selected the beaver as the state animal, a choice more than casually appropriate. Like humans, beavers try to change and conquer their environment. The legislature, however, might just as easily have picked the bulldozer as a state symbol, because it forced phantasmagoric changes in our cities and countryside after World War II. One example may suffice. Robert Moses, perhaps the greatest builder since Ramses II, marked the landscape with airports, bridges, highways, parkways, and power plants.

Transportation has been the key to New York's development. The Hudson, turnpikes, canals, railroads, highways, and airlines forced each generation to make continual adjustments. Hardly had the canal system concentrated population in the urban corridor from Albany to Buffalo when businessmen and their political allies both within and outside that corridor promoted railroads, which captured the bulk of the freight and the passenger traffic. The widespread acceptance of automobiles and trucks after 1910 spelled trouble for the railroads, which lost almost all of their passenger and much of their freight business.

Almost every community developed a specialty, sometimes exploiting a resource such as lumber, sometimes relying upon the enterprise of an entrepreneur. Niagara Falls catered to honeymooners but also to heavy industry eager to utilize the waterpower of the Niagara River. The sanitaria of Saranac Lake attracted Robert Louis Stevenson and other victims of tuberculosis, but when medical science conquered that disease, businessmen sponsored winter sports and opened summer hotels. Because the Finger Lakes moderated the climate along their shores, farmers cultivated grapes, which in turn nourished wineries in that region.

The genius, inventiveness, and entrepreneurial skills and talents of individuals have located camera production (George Eastman) in Rochester, business machines (Thomas Watson) in the Binghamton area, and electrical devices (Charles Steinmetz) in Schenectady. The people who have acquired skills, shown imagination, and demonstrated a capacity for hard work have always constituted the greatest resource.

No other state has had so mixed a population as New York, with the possible exception of California after 1960. Director General William Kieft in 1643 reported that 18 languages were spoken in New Amsterdam. The relative tolerance shown by the Dutch and their successors, the English, was codified in the state constitution of 1777, which guaranteed religious toleration and provided for the separation of church and state.

New Yorkers have usually gone beyond a passive toleration of differences; many have taken pride in diversity whether ethnic, religious, or racial. St. John de Crevecoeur, the French settler who wrote graceful sketches of frontier life in Rockland County just before the American Revolution, noted, "Here individuals of all nations are melted into a new race of men . . . "

Politicians, too, have boasted about the ethnic diversity of the Empire State and "balanced the ticket" so that each party slate usually has representatives of the major religious groups plus a black and Italo-American. Quite often candidates for mayor of New York City and governor will first take the "three I" tour, a whirlwind visit to Ireland, Italy, and Israel. St. Patrick's Day in New York City and a number of upstate centers has become a community festival involving many more people than the descendants from Old Erin. The upsurge of black conciousness in the 1960s stimulated the revival of ethnicity among Jews, Italians, and other groups.

Sometimes overlooked are the Yankees, those enterprising New Englanders who swept into every corner of the state after the Revolution and who dominated the commercial, cultural, and financial life of the Empire State for the rest of the 19th century. Beginning in the 1840s a torrent of Irish and Germans rapidly became the major elements of the urban population for the latter half of that century. Thereafter newcomers from Italy, Russia (mostly Jews and Poles), and other parts of southern and eastern Europe outnumbered the immigrants from northwestern Europe.

After World War I Congress reduced the influx of immigrants, especially those from southern and eastern Europe. This legislation, however, did little to curb immigration to the Empire State; it merely changed the geographical origins of newcomers. Job opportunities during the two World Wars and the booms of the 1920s and after 1945 attracted blacks from the Southern states, where the boll weevil and the cotton picker displaced thousands of sharecroppers, until by 1970 blacks constituted about 13 percent of the state's population, three-fourths of them in the metropolis. In 1940 Puerto Ricans had a small beachhead in Manhattan, but the prosperous times during the next three decades and cheap air fares led hundreds of thousands of these American citizens to leave their overpopulated island. Other Hispanics joined this northern flight: Cubans fleeing from Castro's tyranny; the Haitians, Dominicans, and other Caribbean islanders, from poverty; Central Americans, from civil war. Today Spanish is the mother tongue of more than a million and a half New Yorkers.

Assimilation has accompanied immigration at a different rate for various groups. Recently interfaith marriages, a sensitive index of acculturation, have steadily mounted, to the dismay

of Jewish rabbis, Catholic priests, and Protestant ministers. For each community—Dutch, Huguenots, Palatine Germans—that has vanished, newer groups have sprung up, adding fresh colors to the warp and woof of the demographic pattern. Our capacity to tolerate significant differences in social institutions, national backgrounds, and economic status has impressed foreign observers and kept our society remarkably open to fresh talents. Clifford Wharton, who administered the State University of New York during the first half of the 1980s, is black; Edward Koch, Jewish, is mayor of New York City; Mario Cuomo, who occupies the governor's mansion, boasts of his Italian descent.

New Yorkers have pursued the Almighty Dollar with wholehearted fervor and enviable success since the Dutch founded two trading posts on the Hudson River. The English, who captured New Netherland to plug up a hole in their mercantilist system, expanded trade. Yankee invaders bore witness to the Protestant ethic of getting ahead. Consider the value system expressed by John Brown of Providence, Rhode Island, who purchased a large tract near Old Forge in the Adirondacks. In 1798 he visited his tract and divided it into eight townships, bearing the names Industry, Enterprise, Perseverance, Unanimity, Frugality, Sobriety, Economy, and Regularity. Despite this high-sounding nomenclature his settlement failed to attract settlers.

For a century and a half after 1820, New York led all other states in foreign trade, domestic commerce, manufacturing, finance, transportation, and even the arts. Only recently has California seized the lead in population and manufacturing.

Conviviality has characterized the lusty transient society that grew up in the seaport, canal centers, and village crossroads. William Dean Howells declared that nothing was more characteristic of New York City in 1895 than "the eating and drinking constantly going on in the restaurants and hotels, of every quality, and the innumerable saloons." Upstaters also appreciated good food and drink. Saratoga Springs gave us potato chips; Buffalo immortalized chicken wings; and Phelps, near Rochester, has the largest sauerkraut factory.

With all their getting and spending, New Yorkers have also displayed a social conscience and a sense of compassion. Allan Nevins, distinguished historian, observed that no other metropolis has produced so many leaders of humanitarian societies as New York. Upstate became a nursery of reform movements as well as strange cults and communities before the Civil War. In 1848 the embattled women met at Seneca Falls and drew up a declaration of women's rights. Some reformers attacked Demon Rum; others established settlement houses to aid the needy. The National Association for the Advancement of Colored People emerged from meetings of white and black leaders in Niagara Falls in 1910.

Of course these achievements were offset by criminals (Murder Incorporated in the 1940s in Brooklyn and the Loomis Gang in central New York during the 1860s), social pathology such as draft riots in the Civil War, and eccentric personalities (John Brown and Amelia Bloomer). If New Yorkers had achievements galore, they also had their share of shortcomings.

Change—constant, uprooting, unremitting—has transformed New York since the fire of 1776 consumed a third of Manhattan's buildings and Indian-Tory raids devastated the Mohawk Valley. But did not the countryside so lovingly depicted by Grandma Moses enjoy stability and cherish traditional values? Not really. Half of the cultivated acreage of 1880 has gone back to pasture, forest, or underbrush. Cheap wheat from the Genesee Valley and the Lake States undercut wheat growers in the Schoharie Valley after the Erie Canal was built. Dairy farmers shifted production from cheese and butter to fluid milk because of western competition and the coming of railroads with refrigerator cars.

If thousands of farms were abandoned, many of them were bought by city-dwellers eager to secure a summer home or a place from which to commute to a job miles away. Vacationers, tourists, sportsmen, and families swarmed into every corner of the state: the Hamptons on Long Island; the Adirondacks with its lakes and peaks; the ethnic resorts in the Catskills; and the lovely villages of the Finger Lakes region.

Each generation has found it necessary to make thousands of adjustments because of the influx of newcomers, the rise and collapse of manufacturing plants and modes of transportation, and the shifting values of a cosmopolitan society. For many these changes brought pain and heartache as old neighborhoods lost their cohesion and some villages withered away. For even more people these changes brought opportunity and accomplishment. On the whole New Yorkers have not spent too much time lamenting change but have made plans for a brighter future. John Jay Chapman, American essayist, observed: "The present in New York is so powerful that the past is lost." He was referring to New York City, but his observation applies equally well to the entire Empire State.

As a student of New York State's history for half a century, I am indebted to the writings and insights of hundreds of historians inside and outside academic walls. Many thanks. I would also like to thank many librarians, especially those at the Hamilton College Library, for manifold favors.

David M. Ellis

Dutch and English in the Hudson Valley 1609-1763

Edmund Wilson, America's leading man of letters, observed in 1971 that in New York "the landscape still overwhelms the people." Two-thirds of the state's land mass consists of upland regions including the Adirondacks in the northeast and the Catskills and the Allegheny Plateau or Appalachian Uplands rolling gently across the southern and southwestern parts of the state. Each generation of New Yorkers has sought routes through or around these barriers, which have formed a backdrop to the unfolding drama of exploration, settlement, and transportation.

Every corner of the state presented obstacles as well as opportunities to travelers and pioneers. In the west Niagara Falls blocked navigation between Lake Ontario and Lake Erie. To the north Indians and traders dared to shoot the rapids of the St. Lawrence River, but ships had to wait for canals and the Seaway. Challenged by these obstacles of varying magnitude, New Yorkers refashioned their environment by prodigious feats of engineering and construction. Novelists, songsters, and historians have celebrated the upstaters who dug the Erie Canal through 363 miles of wilderness, a stupendous achievement. Later generations displayed equal engineering prowess by erecting Brooklyn Bridge across the East River, by tunneling under the Hudson River, and by spanning the Hudson and the Narrows with bridges praised for their engineering and admired for their design. Within the past half century New Yorkers have harnessed the turbulent waters of the Niagara and St. Lawrence with dams and powerhouses. Pictures from satellites have given us three-dimensional views of New York's landscape. Most noticeable are the rugged Adirondacks, which geologically belong to the Canadian Highlands. Perhaps the oldest mountains in the world, these mountains emerged from the primordial sea millions of years before the Rockies took shape. Mount Marcy, 5,344 feet above sea level, is the highest

among the 46 peaks more than 4,000 feet high. The advancing and retreating glaciers wore down scores of peaks and studded this region with hundreds of lakes by depositing moraines across the valleys. The New York State Forest Preserve of almost 2.5 million acres is the largest state park in the lower 48 states, and since 1894 the state constitution has protected this preserve by the "forever wild" clause in that document.

The Catskill Mountains belong to the Appalachian chain. Once a plain, this region was pushed upward only to have its peaks rounded off by water, wind, and ice. The peaks, approximately 3,000 feet high, do not form parallel ridges like those in the Adirondacks. Because of its proximity to New York City, the Catskill region annually attracts hundreds of thousands of visitors who throng its resorts and fill hundreds of motels. West of the Catskills the Allegheny Plateau extends southward to New Jersey and westward all the way to Lake Erie, embracing about a third of the state's surface.

Some 50 million years ago the Hudson River carved a channel from the Great Lakes to the sea. Ten million years ago the channel became deeper and extended well out to sea beyond Sandy Hook. According to geologists, the last ice age—about 20,000 years ago—cut its way

Page 14: The pristine beauty of this scene of the Sacandega River in Hamilton County is not unlike what drew early explorers and settlers into New York and the New World. Photo by Daniel E. Wray

Page 15: One of the earliest extant American landscapes, Van Bergen Overmantle, attributed to John Heaton, was originally a panel over the fireplace of the parlor in the Van Bergen homestead. Rich in detail, it offers a comprehensive view of a Hudson Valley Dutch farm around 1733. Martin Van Bergen, the builder of the manor house, is depicted in his long coat, "knickerbocker" breeches, and white stockings. Courtesy, New York State Historical Association, Cooperstown

Right: In 1664 New York City, New Amsterdam, consisted of a cluster of canals and streets, surrounded by a protective wall. Two gates guarded the city, a land gate near the western part of the settlement, and a water gate, shown here, at Wall and Pearl streets. Courtesy, Picture Collection, The Branch Libraries, The New York Public Library

through the Highlands, carving an even deeper channel through the solid rock below. One can see evidence of these mighty forces today by observing the Hudson near the city of Newburgh. Stretching eastward for 118 miles from the Upper Bay of New York Harbor lies Long Island, whose shores attracted Yankee settlers and whalers. The Gulf Stream warms its shores and provides a growing season of 220 days. Two glacial deposits—Harbor Hill Moraine and the Ronkonkoma Moraine—left a rich soil, which farmers and suburban dwellers till with success.

New York enjoys abundant resources of water, although the metropolis experiences periodic shortages because of occasional droughts upriver and leaky pipes in the city. An arm of the sea with salt in the water as far as Newburgh, the Hudson is tidal as far north as Albany, where oceangoing vessels discharge and take on cargo. The Indians called the Hudson "the water-that-flows-two-ways." The Mohawk, its principal tributary, carried a torrent of glacial water that accumulated along the southern front of the glacier. When the glacier retreated northward, this water formed another channel down the St. Lawrence Valley. About half of Lake Ontario (193 miles long and 53 miles wide) lies within the state's borders. In addition to the water coming down the Niagara River, Lake Ontario catches much water from the south. The Genesee River, originating in Pennsylvania, laid down vast amounts of alluvia along its valley, probably the most fertile soils in the state. The Oswego River drains most of the Finger Lakes, of which Seneca and Cayuga are the largest. It also carries the water of Oneida Lake to Lake Ontario at Oswego. Another important river, the Black, passes Watertown after draining much of the western Adirondacks.

The Susquehanna and its northern tributaries (Unadilla, Chenango, Chemung, and Canisteo) carried logs, wheat, and other frontier products to markets in Pennsylvania and in Baltimore. The watershed of the Delaware River, whose channel forms the border between New York

This engraving of Englishman Henry Hudson, by E.G. Wilhams & Bros., shows the explorer who discovered the river now bearing his name while searching for a shortcut to China. Courtesy, The New-York Historical Society, New York City

and Pennsylvania for several miles, provides New York City with much of its drinking water.

The Hudson-Mohawk route provided a water-level corridor for settlers, travelers, and immigrants heading for the great interior. They took passage on Hudson River steamboats to Albany, stepped into stagecoaches heading west, or climbed aboard canal packets at Schenectady. By 1840 railroad cars were beginning to steal passengers by offering speedy travel in winter as well as summer. Naturally, the Thomas E. Dewey Thruway after World War II followed the same route from Albany to Buffalo. Three-quarters of the state's population has clustered within an urban area 25 miles wide, stretching from Buffalo to Albany, then cutting south at right angles to metropolitan New York. Conversely, the nine-tenths of the state lying outside this band is generally sparsely settled.

The web of waterways interlacing the landscape provided an ideal homeland for nomadic hunters who followed the caribou and other animals feeding on the vegetation that grew up behind the retreating glacier. The ancestors of our Native Americans, more familiarly known as Indians, crossed the Bering Sea sometime between 25,000 and 12,000 B.C., spread south through the Rocky Mountains and across the treeless plains, and filtered into the Northeast by 7,000 B.C. Gradually they developed a more mature and sophisticated culture, adding bows and arrows to their early weapons such as javelins and stone axes. The women molded soft clay into pots that eased the task of cooking. Separate collars above the necks of pots exhibited varied designs, sometimes rectangular, sometimes castellated. No one knows precisely when the Indians began to raise corn, the most important crop ever grown in New York.

When Henry Hudson and Samuel de Champlain explored New York in 1609, they found two major groups, the Algonkians and Iroquois, who differed mainly in language. The Algonkians built their villages in the Hudson and Schoharie valleys or on Long Island. Iroquoian tribes migrated to New York sometime in the 13th and 14th centuries from the interior and pushed the Algonkians farther east and north. Food shortages and enemies drove the Senecas into southwestern New York. Allied tribes or possibly offshoots of the Senecas or Hurons, the latter living north of Lake Ontario, formed the other Indian tribes in New York—Cayugas, Onondagas, Oneidas, and Mohawks.

The five Iroquois tribes in central and western New York formed the Confederacy of the Five Nations about 1570. Legends tell us that Hiawatha, an Onondaga, who was appalled by the continuous warfare among the tribes, accepted the message of peace preached by a former

Right: This engraving of E Tow O Koam *by John Farber shows the "King of the River Nation" in New York State in 1710. Courtesy, New York State Library*

Far right: Making wampum beads, which the Indians used for adornment, trade, and tribute, was Long Island's first industry. They were made of whelk shells and in the seventeenth century were used by settlers for money. The Europeans gave the Indians sophisticated iron tools with which to fashion the beads, replacing the stone implements they had been using. Courtesy, Suffolk County Historical Society, gift of Roy Latham

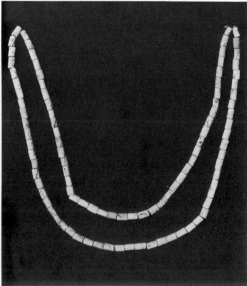

Huron, Deganawidah. Together they won over the Mohawks, then the Oneidas and Cayugas, to the concept of a league. To secure the assent of Atatarbo, the wily chief of the Onondagas, they placed that tribe in charge of the sacred council fire. The Seneca nation became the Keeper of the Western Door; the Mohawk nation, Keeper of the Eastern Door. The Oneida and Cayuga nations became "younger brothers," as did the Tuscaroras, an Iroquois tribe that fled from North Carolina in 1714 and became the sixth nation.

Each of the nations elected chiefs or sachems who attended the governing council of the confederacy, which was skillfully organized to preserve the balance of power. Because each nation had one vote and all decisions required unanimity, each nation was actually equal. The purpose of the league was to ban war among the six nations, a prohibition observed with few exceptions. Each tribe, however, reserved the right to fight outside tribes. Ironically the ideal of universal peace turned into a justification for the annihilation of neighboring tribes who refused to accept the overlordship of the Iroquois. The league exploited its central position on the waterways and terrorized enemies as far west as Illinois and as far south as Virginia; it also sent raiding parties to the outskirts of Montreal. The Iroquois chiefs displayed cunning as well as bravery by playing off the British from the French in their contest for New World empire. If one remembers that the New York Iroquois probably had a maximum of 20,000 people, including 4,000 warriors, one must marvel at their ability to dominate most of the province for well over a century. In contrast the Algonkians, numbering approximately the same, rapidly lost their power because of disease, "firewater," and warfare.

The Iroquois lived in approximately 70 to 80 small villages surrounded by clearings. Because the Indians moved their villages every decade or so when game and fish in the neighborhood were exhausted, they have left us many hundreds of sites. The family included a father, mother, and her children but also those of her brothers and sisters, which meant that each child regarded his cousins (our sense) as brothers and sisters. Women owned the real estate, did the planting and harvesting, and gave their family name to the children. Each of the Five or Six Nations had at least three clans—Bear, Wolf, and Turtle, each of which had political as well as ceremonial duties. Each clan had a governing council that sent delegates to the tribal council.

Every Iroquois thus felt a close identification by blood, marriage, or association to almost everyone in the village. This interlocking system of relationships gave each individual a sense of belonging. The welfare of the group took precedence over that of the individual.

Near Owasco Lake and the city of Auburn one can see a restored village, 300 feet long and 120 feet wide, surrounded by a palisade of sapling poles. The palisade kept out animals—wolves, raccoons, skunks, and bears. Each of the two longhouses housed about 120 persons. Sheets of elm bark covered the frame of the longhouse, which included many compartments for the nuclear family of father, mother, and children. Adults slept on corn-husk mats laid on the ground; the children crawled into bark-lined bunks.

The rhythm of the seasons determined the time patterns of the Indians. Each season had its appropriate festival such as the Green Corn Festival in September, which was followed by the Harvest Festival. After the spring planting the clan set aside time for dancing, prayers, and the burning of tobacco. The Indians worshiped nature as the giver and taker of life.

The French sent dozens of friars and priests to convert the Indians to Christianity. The English paid less attention to the beliefs of the Iroquois. Many Indians obviously resented the intrusion of Europeans into their communal life, because the white men attacked their myths and beliefs as superstition. Father Isaac Jogues was the first of several martyrs who met death after torture by the natives.

Below right: Albany was chartered as a city in 1686, when it ranked as the chief colonial fur trading center. It was first settled by Henry Hudson in 1609 and grew slowly, containing only 25 cabins and about 100 people by 1643. In 1754 Albany hosted the Albany Congress, a meeting that laid the groundwork for revolutionary organization a decade later. Almost by accident, it became the state capital in 1794. Courtesy, Picture Collection, The Branch Libraries, The New York Public Library

Below: Twenty-two years before the Declaration of Independence, a plan to unify the colonies was presented to an intercolonial council by Benjamin Franklin. The meeting took place in the Stadt Huys, or "Hall of Independence," shown here, that stood at Broadway and Hudson avenues in Albany until well into the nineteenth century. Courtesy, Picture Collection, The Branch Libraries, The New York Public Library

Following the Revolutionary War, Handsome Lake, a Seneca, arose from his despondency and rallied his fellow tribesmen by preaching a new religion, a mixture of old beliefs and some elements of Christianity. A victim of alcoholism, Handsome Lake campaigned against strong drink, which obviously was causing degradation and ill health. Moreover, he urged warriors to join the women in plowing, cultivating, and harvesting the crops. Today the New Religion of Handsome Lake has enrolled at least a third of the Indians living on the nine reservations in New York.

The Indians, who had shown skill as traders before the arrival of Hudson, soon discovered the advantages of guns, strouds (blankets), iron kettles, and other imports. Liquor held a peculiar attraction, despite its devastating effects. At first the French in Montreal assigned to the Hurons the role of middlemen between the city and the tribes bordering the Great Lakes. The Mohawks took advantage of their location near Fort Orange, where the Dutch traded with the Indians for decades after the English conquest of New Netherland. The Mohawks and other Iroquois followed every stream in search of beaver, with the result that the supply ran low. Hard pressed for pelts, the Iroquois bands began to intercept brigades bringing western furs down the Ottawa River to Montreal. They destroyed the villages of Huronia, driving hundreds of inhabitants into the snow and cold of the winter of 1649. Next they pounced on the Neutrals, the Eries, and other tribes around Lake Erie.

The French defended their western trade by setting up fur posts on the Upper Great Lakes, where they could collect the furs and guard the brigades with soldiers. The French struck the Mohawk and Seneca villages in the 1680s and established a post at Niagara. In 1701 the Five Nations signed a treaty of friendship with France, complaining that the British had failed to defend them against raids.

City officials in Albany regulated Indian affairs until the middle of the 18th century. Their regulations brought some order in the fur trade, but the Dutch traders, not the Indians, derived most of the benefits. Thereafter Sir William Johnson, a landholder and trader, took charge of

Below: Fort Frederick stood guard over Albany from 1676 to 1789. Originally made of wood, it was rebuilt of stone between 1702 and 1735. Despite its apparent defensive importance, its 21 guns never fired in battle. Courtesy, Picture Collection, The Branch Libraries, The New York Public Library

Indian affairs for the purpose of enlisting Iroquois aid against the French. The British founded a fort at Oswego in order to attract the trade of western Indians.

Approximately 9,000 of the 40,000 Indians living in New York State in 1980 made their homes on reservations. Several hundred Mohawks live in Brooklyn, and many of the men weld girders of new skyscrapers and bridges. During the past decade Indians have demanded more rights and have brought suit against local and state governments, claiming that fraud and illegality tainted the treaties of land cession in the 1790s.

The first contact between the natives and white invaders took place in 1524 when the Italian navigator Giovanni da Verrazano, in the service of France, sailed into New York Harbor and observed the natives "clothed with the feathers of birds of various colors." Not until 1609, however, did New York Indians face a serious invasion of their territory, for in that year Champlain from the north and Hudson from the south probed far into the interior. Paddling south on Lake Champlain, the famous French explorer and two musketeers accompanied a band of northern Indians to the vicinity of Ticonderoga, where they ran into a band of Mohawks. Dumbfounded by the bullets that killed a chief and several warriors, the Mohawks fled into the forest. The French, however, paid dearly for this victory, because the Mohawks, smarting from their losses, established friendly relations with the Dutch and their successors, the English, who supplied them with guns and bought their furs.

In 1609 the Dutch East India Company employed Hudson, an English navigator, to find a water passage to the Orient around Siberia. When ice blocked his ship's progress, Hudson turned west and in September sailed his tiny *Half Moon* up the harbor, past the Palisades and Highlands, to the vicinity of modern Albany. Natives paddled canoes to his ship, seeking to exchange beaver and mink skins for European goods, especially guns and whiskey. Hudson's reports of his voyage and his cargo of furs spurred several other Dutch captains to visit the Hudson Valley.

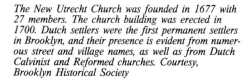

The New Utrecht Church was founded in 1677 with 27 members. The church building was erected in 1700. Dutch settlers were the first permanent settlers in Brooklyn, and their presence is evident from numerous street and village names, as well as from Dutch Calvinist and Reformed churches. Courtesy, Brooklyn Historical Society

The Purchase of Manhattan

Peter Minuit's purchase of Manhattan Island from the Indians for $24 of beads is one of the best-known stories in our history. Documentary evidence is scanty, but it does seem to confirm that Minuit was actually director general of New Netherland at the time of the purchase shortly after May 11, 1626. There is no evidence that Minuit or his agent used beads to buy the island. One historian has estimated that if someone had placed the $24 at 6 percent compound interest, the amount by 1986 would reach $31 billion.

Robert Juet, the keeper of Henry Hudson's log, discovered an older map on which the navigator had written "Mannahata." The Algonkian name Mahican or Manecan is the probable source for this name.

In 1624 the Dutch West India Company, chartered three years earlier with a monopoly of Dutch trade in the Americas, sent a boatload of 30 French-speaking Protestants (Walloons), who founded the first permanent settlement at Fort Orange (near future Albany). The next year the Dutch set up their headquarters at Fort Amsterdam on Manhattan's southern tip. Originally the company directors expected to set up an outpost or two made up of traders, clerks, soldiers, and farmers who would work for the company. It quickly became apparent that the colony would never enjoy a vigorous growth in trade or population. When the English captured New Netherland in 1664, only 8,000 white settlers lived in the vast region between the Connecticut and Delaware rivers. Why did this region, today the home of more than 20 million Americans, attract so few inhabitants?

First of all, the Dutch homeland enjoyed a burgeoning economy, probably the most prosperous in the world, a large degree of individual freedom including religious toleration, and a stable government. Because few Dutch wanted to emigrate, the company had to recruit settlers from other countries, thus giving the colony from the start a cosmopolitan flavor so characteristic of its future. Second, the company preferred to seek trade and riches in Brazil, Africa, and the West Indies instead of investing funds and manpower in the Hudson Valley. Third, the fur trade required only a handful of traders to deal with the Indians. Fourth, the Algonkians, at first quite friendly, became restless, because some Dutch mistreated them and because the Dutch favored their enemies, the Iroquois. When Governor William Kieft massacred the inhabitants of one village for failure to pay taxes, the Indians retaliated by killing hundreds of settlers in the outskirts of New Amsterdam. For a time Dutch families cowered behind a fortified embankment and trench built across lower Manhattan. Later the path behind the embankment became Wall Street.

Another depressing factor was the land system, which discouraged farmers from settling in the colony. In 1629 the directors decided to rely more on individual enterprise than on a company monopoly of production and distribution. They awarded tracts of land, called patroonships, to any of the company shareholders who would settle 50 persons on a tract. Only one patroonship, Rensselaerswyck, lasted; the others were stillborn. Killiaen Van Rensselaer, a diamond merchant, secured a tract on both sides of the Hudson that included about 750,000 acres in modern Albany and Rensselaer counties. Although he worked hard to develop his holdings and attracted more than 200 tenant farmers, many drifted away. Much more successful than the patroon system was the offer in 1640 of 200 acres to anyone who would bring more than five adults.

Killaen Van Rensselaer, an Amsterdam diamond and gold merchant, was an officer of the Dutch West India Company. He was most responsible for instituting a system of land grants in order to make the colony of New Netherland self sufficient, and to create a supply base for the company's growing merchant marine. Rensselaerswyck near Fort Orange, the future site of Albany, was the only grant to succeed. Rensselaer ruled it as an absentee landlord, and his tenants held perpetual leaseholds. Courtesy, The New-York Historical Society, New York City

Last, a series of weak and incompetent governors quarreled with settlers, who wanted lower taxes, more representation, and better protection against the Indians. Peter Stuyvesant, 1647-1664, brought integrity to the office as well as a testy temperament. With an army of only 70 soldiers, Stuyvesant put down an Indian revolt and slowed the Yankee advances along both sides of Long Island. Stuyvesant secured an army of more than 600 men to conquer New Sweden on the Delaware River. An autocrat by nature, Stuyvesant had to grant much self-government to towns settled by New Englanders. In 1664 the old soldier at first declared he would fight the English invaders, but he grudgingly yielded to the appeal for surrender made by 90 leading citizens.

A miniature New Amsterdam with more than 300 buildings emerged at the southern point of Manhattan Island. One can see a splendid reconstruction of this village of some 1,300 inhabitants in the Museum of the City of New York. The skyline with its waterfront, church, and houses, as well as the canal down the center of today's Broad Street, reminded the residents of Old Holland. Within the fort's walls were several buildings: the governor's brick house, barracks, company storehouses, a jail, a Dutch Reformed church. The weighmaster on a pier on the East River recorded every item imported or exported. Many merchants built houses similar to that of the governor with its spacious garden and gabled roof facing the street.

The Dutch left their mark on our architecture, food, language, place-names, and folklore. Modern New Yorkers still eat crullers, cookies, and coleslaw. Terms like stoop and boss punctuate our speech. Hundreds of localities, streams, and hills bear Dutch names. Note Brooklyn, named after Breukelen, and Yonkers, derived from Adriaen Van der Donck. Many streams entering the Hudson still bear the term kill, the Dutch word for creek. Wyck (district or town), bush (forest), dorp (village), vliet (stream) are only a few surviving Dutch names. Few fans rooting for the Knickerbocker basketball team know that this name comes from the pseudonym used by Washington Irving, whose *History of New York* caricatured the Dutch as lazy and superstitious as well as addicted to strong liquor.

Above: This early engraving of New Amsterdam was first published by Joost Hartgers in Amsterdam in 1651. The view shows a settlement with about 30 houses, a mill, and a five-bastioned fort. Courtesy, Prints Division, Stokes Collection, New York Public Library

Right: The First Saint Peter's Church was built in Albany under an edict of the British royal government to provide a place of worship for British officers and other Anglicans. It was located in such a way as to provide it the protection of Fort Frederick's guns. Courtesy, Picture Collection, The Branch Libraries, The New York Public Library

King Charles II of England gave his brother James, Duke of York and Albany, a vast tract including the land between the Connecticut and Delaware rivers, to mention the most important section. As proprietor, James had the right to make laws, levy taxes, appoint officials, and grant land. This autocratic power, however, was tempered by distance, neglect, local resistance, and rising tensions in England.

The terms of surrender limited the victor's power. Any resident had the right to remain or leave the colony, retain all property, and worship, as he pleased. James appointed Colonel Richard Nicolls as the first governor, a man who showed patience and sensitivity. In 1665 Nicolls met with delegates from Long Island and promulgated the so-called Duke's Laws for the purpose of mollifying Yankee settlers on Long Island and in the towns of Westchester County. Although the new code granted trial by jury, freedom of religion, and election of local officials in these towns, it said nothing about a colonial assembly with power to make laws and tax. When governors under the proprietorship, 1664-1685, imposed taxes, merchants, landowners, and freemen protested vigorously. In 1683 Governor Thomas Dongan, following instructions from James, called a group of delegates to frame a "Charter of Liberties and Privileges" that authorized an elected assembly and a bill of rights. James, however, revoked this charter upon his accession to the throne in 1685.

This action angered New Yorkers, who were feeling the sting of hard times, the threat of French invasion, and the loss of provincial identity. Just at this time James set up the Dominion of New England, which included New York and the northern colonies and had its capital in Boston. Adding to the turmoil were rumblings of an uprising against James. When King James

Edmund Andros was commissioned by Charles II of England to receive New York from the Dutch under the treaty of Westminster, July 24, 1674. Andros went on to serve James II, Duke of York, for whom New York was named, and to act as governor of the short-lived and very unpopular attempt to consolidate New York and the New England colonies. Courtesy, The New-York Historical Society, New York City

II fled to France, a Boston mob jailed Edmund Andros, the abrasive governor of the Dominion. Not to be outdone, New Yorkers stormed the jail and seized power. Their leader, Jacob Leisler, favored a more representative government and called for an elected assembly, which in turn placed power in the hands of Leisler.

The new monarchs, William III and his wife, Mary II, sent out Colonel Henry Sloughter to restore royal authority. When Leisler balked at turning over the keys to the fort to an underling of Sloughter, the commander at once arrested him, tried him for treason, and had him hanged. Leisler dead became Leisler the martyr, whose memory became a rallying cry for his followers, chiefly Dutch, artisans, and farmers who detested the elite in the governor's circle.

After 1691 an elected assembly shared or often competed with the governors for power over taxation, appointments, and legislation. New Yorkers learned the art of effective government by debating issues, making compromises, and producing leaders. Although most leaders were drawn from the upper class of merchants, landlords, and lawyers, these men had to listen to the wishes of farmers, artisans, and shopkeepers. Approximately half of the adult men could vote, a much broader electorate than in mother England.

The colony grew sluggishly and in 1750 had only 75,000 people. The rate of growth picked up thereafter, but the population did not exceed 175,000 when the Sons of Liberty chased Governor Sloughter out of New York. The great majority of New Yorkers lived within a dozen miles of the Hudson River, Long Island Sound, and the Atlantic Ocean. New York City had

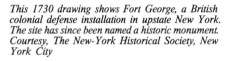

This 1730 drawing shows Fort George, a British colonial defense installation in upstate New York. The site has since been named a historic monument. Courtesy, The New-York Historical Society, New York City

some 13,000 residents in 1756, many more than the 4,000 living in Albany, the only other chartered city.

St. Jean de Crevecoeur, who had a farm on the west bank of the lower Hudson, wrote around 1770 that the "American" was a "new man" shaped by free institutions, a mixture of nationalities, and a stimulating environment. He declared: "Here individuals of all nations are melted into a new race of men."

Approximately 20,000 blacks lived in New York, most of them slaves who served as house servants or field hands, especially on the farms of Dutch residents. They probably received slightly better treatment than slaves in most other colonies but not enough to warrant praise. As usual, Quakers made the first efforts at assistance by opening schools and by urging the end of slavery. In 1741 Manhattan citizens became hysterical when individuals spread rumors that blacks had set fire to several buildings. The authorities rounded up 100 or more blacks, burned 13, hanged another 13, and exiled 70 more.

People of English descent constituted about half of the population. Their greatest concentration was in the Yankee towns on Long Island. Other English came directly from England as officials, soldiers, craftsmen, and traders. Although the Dutch language persisted for many years, especially in the Kingston and Albany areas, the young people gradually learned English, the language of the courts, the government, and trade. The small Scottish contingent included such figures as Robert Livingston and Cadwallader Colden. The Scotch-Irish had several communities in Ulster County, where the important Clinton family achieved prominence during and after the Revolution. William Johnson, perhaps the most famous colonial New Yorker, hailed from the Emerald Isle.

Encouragement given for People to remove and settle in the Province of New-York in America.

THe Honourable *George Clarke*, Efq. Lieut. Governour and Commander in chief of the Province of *New-York*, Hath upon the Petition of Mr. *Lauchline Campbell* from *Ifla, North-Britain*, promifed to grant him Thirty thoufand Acres of Land at the *Wood-Creek*, free of all Charges excepting the Survey and the King's Quit-Rent, which is about one Shilling and Nine Pence Farthing *Sterling* for each hundred Acres. *And alfo*, To grant to thirty Families already landed here Lands in proportion to each Family, from five hundred Acres unto one Hundred and Fifty only paying the Survey and the King's Quit-Rent. And all *Proteftants* that incline to come and fettle in this Colony may have Lands granted them from the Crown for three Pounds *Sterling* per hundred Acres and paying the yearly Quit-Rent.

Dated in New-York this 4th Day of December, 1738.   GEORGE CLARKE.

Printed by *William Bradford*, Printer to the King's moft Excellent Majefty for the Province of *New-York*, 1738.

Although the British Colonies in North America were wealthy in land resources, they needed labor and population to make the land productive and secure. Colonies continuously advertised for new settlers from the Old World. Courtesy, The New-York Historical Society, New York City

Ten ships with more than 2,500 Germans on board arrived in 1710, the largest single contingent of immigrants up to that time. Fleeing from the rampaging armies of the French king, Louis XIV, refugees from the Palatinate crowded into London. The British government sent these Palatine Germans to New York in order to make naval stores for the royal navy. The plan failed but the Palatines remained, some taking up farms near Rhinebeck and on Livingston Manor. A few hundred, lured by false rumors of free land, settled in the Schoharie Valley. When Albany landlords claimed their land, some moved to Pennsylvania, others agreed to buy their tracts, and others accepted the offer of Governor Robert Hunter of free land in the Mohawk Valley.

The heterogeneous population spawned a variety of denominations, although New Yorkers took religion more lightly than did the Puritans of New England. In 1776, according to one scholar, the Dutch Reformed led with 81 churches, followed by 61 Presbyterian. There were 30 Anglican (Episcopal) congregations, 26 Quaker, 22 Lutheran, and 16 Baptist. No Roman Catholic parish took form, but one Jewish congregation emerged. The governors promoted the Church of England, the established church in the counties of Westchester, New York, Queens, and Richmond. Presbyterians challenged the Anglicans when the latter sought sole control of King's College on Manhattan Island and agitated for a resident bishop. During the Revolutionary War Anglican clergymen usually backed the royalist cause, whereas the rebels sometimes earned the name of "Presbyterian party."

New York remained a wilderness except for occasional clearings and the settled communities along the lower Hudson and on Long Island. Small farms of 100 to 200 acres were the prevailing units. Even the manor lords, chiefly on the east bank of the Hudson, divided their tracts into small farms.

No other colony had a land system featuring so many large tracts where more than 6,000 tenant farmers lived. These baronial estates—about 30 in number—enclosed more than 2 million acres of land. Six manors—Scarsdale, Cortlandt, Philipsburg, Pelham, Fordham, and Morrisania—covered half of Westchester County. The landed aristocrats favored renting their farms rather than selling the land outright. Tenancy did have its advantages even for tenants: no down payment, and free rent for several years; low rent usually payable in winter wheat; proximity to gristmills and sawmills operated by the landlord. Leases varied; some were forever, some for the lifetimes of two or three persons listed in the contract. Tenants on Van Rensselaer Manor received perpetual leases, in effect, a warrantee deed except for some nuisance fees such as delivering four fat hens and working a day or two with wagon and team for the landlord. Most galling of all were the quarter-sales, which required the payment of a fourth of the sale price if the tenant disposed of his farm. If tenants took a lease on Livingston Manor, the conditions were more onerous. After the death of the two persons named, usually a man and his wife, the farm passed back to the Livingstons. No wonder the tenants denounced the leasehold system, which smacked of Old World feudalism. Tenants also charged that the landlords acquired their tracts by bribe or gift and claimed that the tenants made the land valuable by clearing the trees and tilling the soil. Actually the tenants were not an oppressed peasantry tied to the land. They could and did move at will. They could sell their improvements to newcomers. The Van Cortlandts and other landlords developed their holdings by building roads, mills, and landings. Most landlords treated their tenants fairly, probably less from a sense of *noblesse oblige* than because of the shortage of immigrants.

The landed elite shared power with the rising merchants; in fact, they were often engaged in trade. As in England, a mansion with broad acres conveyed a bit more status than trade. Whatever their origin, the wealthy merged into one class through intermarriage, business associations, and political alliances. Distinctive in their clothing imported from the better shops in London or from local imitators, their homes furnished with imported furniture and china, the aristocrats prided themselves on their genteel manners and conspicuous hospitality. During the early years some rough-and-ready "new men" of plebian background acquired wealth and status, but the doors to the charmed circle of grandees gradually closed as the 18th century progressed.

A strong middle class of freehold farmers, artisans, and lesser merchants emerged and challenged the pretensions of the elite. Occasionally they backed candidates who defeated a De Lancey or other aristocrat.

Farmers produced for the market because of the splendid transportation provided by the Hudson River. Of course they supplied or produced much of their own food, fuel, tools, and clothing. A farmer had to be a lumberjack and a rough carpenter, and some had additional skills such as leather tanning and shoemaking. His wife was equally skilled, spinning thread, weaving yarn, baking bread, and preserving food, not to mention joining her husband in harvesting or sugaring off maple syrup. Girls copied their mother; boys watched or helped their father. Moreover, families exchanged labor and goods. Sometimes groups would join forces to raise a barn, burn off a tract of trees, and harvest the crops.

Artisans were important in the countryside and in town. These men made or fixed tools and furniture that the average person could not handle. Thus the blacksmith fashioned horseshoes, nails, and the like. Coopers made barrels; hatters made hats; cobblers made shoes. Peddlers piled their carts high with trinkets, ribbons, needles, scissors, and tinware. Sometimes no money changed hands, because the farmer paid for his goods with furs, potash, and lodging. Inns sprang up at river landings, crossroads, and villages. Here men traded horses and made deals while relaxing with a drink or two. Judges on circuit held court in taverns whose proprietor was often a leading figure in the community. A New York tavern posted these rules:

Four pence a night for Bed
Six pence with Supper
No more than five to sleep in one bed
No boots to be worn in bed

New York lagged behind New England in formal education, and probably half of the children never saw the inside of a schoolhouse. However, children picked up skills in their homes, workshops, stores, and farms. Ministers and schoolmasters set up schools to which the more enlightened farmers and artisans sent their children. The elite found tutors among clergymen or ladies of genteel accomplishments. Only New York and Albany had secondary schools, and a mere handful of young men attended college: Yale or the College of New Jersey (Princeton), both under Calvinist control. In 1754 King's College, now Columbia University, received its charter.

Mammon outranked culture in the eyes of almost all New Yorkers. Nevertheless New York City achieved a modest level of cultural activity. If Philadelphia was first with its philosophical society, public library, hospital, and medical school, New York was second. If Boston published many more books than New York, this output was mostly theological. New York and Philadelphia published works on politics, law, education, social science, and literature that reflected the varied interests of an increasingly secular society.

The Dutch brought with them a strong tradition of painting, and even before 1700 Albany merchants hired limners to paint their portraits. By mid-century New York attracted three artists of merit—John Wollaston, Benjamin West, and John Singleton Copley—the last two moving on to distinguished careers in London. Lack of patronage and some disapproval by the clergy discouraged the occasional troupes that attempted to stage plays in the colony.

New York's splendid harbor and extensive waterways made it the key to control of North America, a vital prize in the imperial struggle between England and France. Each country sought to control the routes leading to the heartland, the region between the Great Lakes and the Gulf of Mexico. The British government stationed four independent companies of regular British troops in New York, the only continental colony so favored.

England fought two wars with France between 1689 and 1713, but New York played a minor role in each. Fur traders in Albany favored prudent neutrality in order not to disturb their profitable trade with the Indians and also with French merchants in Montreal. The French, who had succeeded in winning Iroquois neutrality in 1701, were reluctant to provoke them to warfare. Although England and France signed a peace treaty in 1713, both countries continued preparations for defense and the eventual death struggle. The British fortified Oswego, and the

This painting by John Wollaston shows Sir William Johnson, Mohawk Valley Indian trader and commissary for New York for Indian Affairs. Johnson convinced the Iroquois to join him in the King George War (1740-1748). As an officer in that war, Johnson led New York, New England, and Iroquois troops into battle. In 1763 the colonists negotiated a peace treaty with the Indians. Courtesy, Albany Institute of History & Art

French built Crown Point on Lake Champlain. During King George's War, 1744-1748, a French party killed and captured more than 100 inhabitants at Saratoga. The pioneers north of Albany fell back to the shelter of that city.

Meanwhile William Johnson had established a store near the present site of Amsterdam, where he won the trust and affection of the Iroquois by fair dealing and genuine friendship. Johnson favored an aggressive policy against the French, a stand that brought him into conflict with the Dutch traders. Cajoling the Indians with gifts provided by himself and with endless palaver, Johnson won them over to the British side. In 1755 he led a force of 3,500 colonials and 400 Indians to the southern shore of Lake George, where he halted a French army. For this victory the grateful Crown knighted him, made him a baronet, and appointed him superintendent of Indian affairs in the north.

Prior to 1758 the French stung the British with defeat after defeat, but thereafter the tide turned because of the energetic leadership of William Pitt. In 1759 Sir William Johnson captured Fort Niagara and Lord Jeffrey Amherst drove the French out of Fort Ticonderoga. Soon Quebec fell to General James Wolfe, ending French power in North America.

New Yorkers in common with other colonists looked seaward more than westward. They regarded England as their defender, and their markets were in the mother country and the West Indies. They took pride in the rights of Englishmen, hailed Magna Carta, and admired William Shakespeare. In 1763 it looked as though the victorious British Empire would last for centuries.

Below the surface, however, a new society was emerging in New York as well as in the other colonies whose interests were coming into conflict with those of the Crown. In New York, outside pressures—the French and Indian threats, New England claims to the eastern border, the running battle for more autonomy from royal authority—had helped mold together the quarrelsome factions within the province. Moreover the silver chain of rivers and lakes linked New York City with the backcountry.

Had New Yorkers by 1763 fashioned a sense of community and overarching patriotism transcending the sectional disputes, the class structure, and heterogeneous population? One can advance a weak and tentative "Yes." Whether they lived in town or countryside, New Yorkers pursued gain with zeal and some success. Prominent lawyer William Livingston observed: "Neighbors have told us in an insulting Tone, that the Art of getting Money, is the highest improvement we can pretend to . . . " Another characteristic was a widespread toleration toward differences in ethnic origins and religious beliefs. An offshoot of urban Amsterdam, New Yorkers imitated the cosmopolitan culture of that great metropolis, and the landed grandees sedulously copied the manners of English lords.

Theodore Roosevelt as an exuberant young man wrote several volumes extolling frontiersmen, but he also dashed off a history of the city where he was born. Although historians today have dug far deeper into the sources of state history, they can still profit from his comment, perhaps more penetrating than he was aware. In 1891 he wrote, "The most important lesson taught by the history of New York City is the lesson of Americanism." In microcosm colonial New York, metropolis and province, was predicting the major features of the great republic of the future.

King Hendrick, an Iroquois leader, was slain while fighting the French in colonial warfare on September 6, 1755. Courtesy, New York State Library

REVOLUTIONARY COCKPIT 1763-1789

No colonists celebrated British victory more fervidly than New Yorkers. Citizens hailed William Pitt as the architect of victory, and they drank toasts to George III, the young and popular king of 22 years of age. New Yorkers took pride in their British citizenship, for which they had fought and bled on many battlefields.

Victory, however gratifying, created as many problems as it solved. How should Great Britain solve the Western problem involving Indians, fur trade, and land speculation? How should Parliament strengthen the navigation acts that previous ministries had failed to enforce? How much of the tremendous war debt and the substantial cost of defending the frontiers should Americans pay? Any attempt to solve these problems would undoubtedly require imperial interference with American rights and freedom. The colonists, always excepting the blacks, enjoyed the greatest freedom of any people in the world including England itself. They could speak, print journals, and hold meetings with practically no restraints. Moreover, large numbers of white adult males (about half in New York) could vote for members of the assembly. When the Crown began to tighten the old imperial system by imposing more taxes and regulating trade more strictly, the colonists first sulked, then raised their voices in protest.

Even before the war was over, Pontiac had stirred up the Indians west of the Appalachians and captured several posts. To quiet the Indians the king issued a proclamation in late 1763 that banned white men from buying land or settling west of the crest of these mountains and required fur traders to obtain a license. These requirements enraged settlers, land speculators, and fur traders. Neither the British government nor the Indians, however, were able to hold back these vigorous groups. In 1768 Sir William Johnson called a conference at Fort Stanwix, where over 2,000 Indians gorged themselves on dozens of barbecued oxen. They agreed to a boundary line running south from Fort Stanwix to the Unadilla River, down that stream to the point where it joins the Susquehanna, then south and west. This treaty opened up a large area, but it was not large enough to satisfy speculators and settlers.

In 1760 William Pitt ordered officials to enforce the Molasses or Sugar Act of 1733, which had placed a prohibitive duty on molasses coming from the French and Spanish West Indies. The British ministers and local officials had previously winked at merchants who smuggled molasses into colonial ports. Pitt's new order directed royal custom collectors to enforce the law by securing writs of assistance, court orders granting them power to enter any building in search of contraband. These regulations hit merchants in their pocketbooks and branded respectable merchants as criminals. In 1764 Parliament passed a new Sugar Act, providing for strict enforcement. In October the New York Assembly petitioned Parliament to repeal this law, stating: "Exemption from burthen of ungranted, involuntary taxes must be the grand principle of every free state." Conceding that Parliament could regulate trade, the colonists denied Parliament could lay taxes inside the colonies.

Prime Minister George Grenville had little use for these fine distinctions and decided to call the bluff of British subjects in America. He had Parliament impose a stamp tax on legal documents such as deeds and contracts, newspapers (each issue), liquor licenses, playing cards, and many other items. Worse still, admiralty courts would try offenders, who could no longer rely upon sympathetic juries. If the government had deliberately set out to stir up vocal and influential groups—lawyers, land speculators, printers, tavern keepers—it could not have done a better job.

Some grumblers urged merchants to boycott English imports, and this movement spread rapidly when colonists learned of the proposed Stamp Act. In October 1765 delegates from several colonies met in New York and declared that taxation without consent of representatives violated the rights of the king's subjects. A group of middle-class New Yorkers organized to thwart the Stamp Act. Led by shipmaster Isaac Sears, a howling mob gathered outside Fort George, where the stamps were stored. The crowd burned the carriage of Acting Governor Cadwallader Colden, who delivered the stamps to the mayor and announced that no more attempts to collect the tax would be made. Meanwhile a group of men called the Sons of Liberty

Right: In New York, The Sons of Liberty formed the nucleus of the American revolutionary movement. The name Sons of Liberty was adopted from an anti-Stamp Act speech in 1765. Courtesy, The New-York Historical Society, New York City

Page 32: In this engraving aptly titled Sacred to Patriotism, *Cornelius Tiebout surrounds George Washington with symbols of the Republic. A public promenade that replaced Fort George at the Battery following the Revolution, and New York's harbor appear in the background. Courtesy, Fraunces Tavern Museum, New York City*

ADVERTISEMENT.

THE Members of the Affociation of the Sons of Liberty, are requefted to meet at the City-Hall, at one o'Clock, To-morrow, (being Friday) on Bufinefs of the utmoft Importance ;—And every other Friend to the Liberties, and Trade of America, are hereby moft cordially invited, to meet at the fame Time and Place.   *The Committee of the Affociation.*

Thurfday, NEW-YORK, 16th December, 1773.

appeared in New York, drawn from the ranks of shopkeepers and artisans but usually led by merchants and lawyers.

In Great Britain merchants whose exports had slumped petitioned Parliament to repeal the Stamp Act. Parliament listened to this appeal and agreed. When the news reached New York, crowds of beer-drinking citizens thronged the streets and cheered the name of Pitt. Tensions kept rising, however. In December 1765 General Thomas Gage asked the New York assembly to make provision for quartering his troops and supplying them with food, including free beer and rum. The assembly reluctantly agreed, but, showing an unusual gesture toward temperance, it left out the provision for free beer. Lord Hillsborough, the new secretary for the colonies, suspended the assembly, an action that further antagonized New Yorkers.

In June 1767 Lord Charles Townshend, Chancellor of the Exchequer and notorious for his extravagant rhetoric, placed heavy duties on imports, such as paint, lead, paper, glass, and tea. He also tightened the collection of customs and provided for the payment of governors' salaries from the new revenue. If a governor did not have to ask an assembly for money for his salary, he would be more likely to follow instructions from London. New Yorkers followed Bostonians with mass meetings to protest the Townshend Duties. Merchants threatened another boycott unless Townshend rescinded these duties. During the next year imports to New York plummeted to one-seventh. Pinched by the boycott, London merchants urged the British government to lift these duties.

Various other issues led to more bickering. The Quartering Act, the suspension of the assembly, and the Townshend Acts inspired fiery broadsides and speeches. Governor Colden threw Alexander McDougall into jail for his broadside criticizing the assembly for agreeing to the Quartering Act in late 1769. The Sons of Liberty erected a Liberty Pole as a symbol of defiance, a gesture immediately grasped by the British soldiers, who cut down the pole. Taunts and jeers led to a riot on Golden Hill in which several citizens and soldiers suffered serious wounds. Some New Yorkers claimed that the first blood of the Revolution was shed in New York, but the Boston Massacre in 1770 in which five citizens lost their lives dwarfed this episode.

Parliament repealed in 1770 all the duties except that on tea, an action that satisfied most New Yorkers. Although radicals continued their agitation, most colonists welcomed a lull in the stormy relations with the motherland. Some began to worry more about the Sons of Liberty, who acted like bullies above the law.

This 1805 view of old Broadway, looking south from Maiden Lane, depicts a historic site in Albany. Here, in the covered market place, citizens were summoned by drumbeat in May of 1775 to enlist and equip troops for an American army of independence. By the end of May, five companies of militia were formed, financial aid was collected and forwarded to Boston, and Fort Frederick was surrendered by the British with the firing of a single gun. Courtesy, Picture Collection, The Branch Libraries, The New York Public Library

*An Englishman by birth, Thomas Paine was a charismatic Revolutionary figure. This 1793 portrait of him by George Romney shows Paine with two of his most critical works—*The Rights of Man *and* Common Sense. *Courtesy, The New-York Historical Society, New York City*

The British government upset the truce in 1773 by granting to the bankrupt British East India Company the right to send tea to the American colonies by paying a low duty of three penny a pound. This concession enabled the company to undersell rivals, even those who smuggled in tea from Holland. Furthermore, the company picked its own agents to handle the tea, bypassing the regular merchants, who naturally joined forces with the Sons of Liberty. This radical group called for a boycott of goods from England. Their warning to shipmasters not to land tea in New York led one prudent captain to turn back. When a merchant tried to sneak in a shipload, the Sons of Liberty copied the example of the Boston radicals by disguising themselves as Indians and dumping the tea into the harbor.

The British government punished Massachusetts by imposing the Intolerable or Coercive Acts, one of which closed the port of Boston until citizens paid for the tea. Another act limited local and provincial self-government in Massachusetts by virtually repealing its charter. Alarmed by these measures, citizens in New York formed a committee to deal with the situation. They sent delegates to the First Continental Congress, which met in October 1774 in Philadelphia. It formed the Continental Association, which urged a boycott of imports and exports. The conservative New York delegates, however, refused to approve this action, but voters in various towns and cities elected committees to enforce the association. Out of this network of committees, which the more militant citizens dominated, the revolutionary government emerged.

On April 19, 1775, British troops fired upon militiamen in Lexington, Massachusetts. The news spread like wildfire across the countryside and reached New York City four days later. Immediately citizens seized 600 army muskets. Upriver, patriots, the name often used to designate persons opposed to the British government, took steps to rid their districts of Loyalists. Ethan Allen, a Vermonter, led a group of Green Mountain Boys and captured Fort Ticonderoga.

The beleaguered British garrison in Boston needed help, so the British forces in New York City took ship for that city. Local committees moved into the vacuum of power, and when Governor William Tryon fled, the Provincial Congress called for the establishment of a new government.

Events were in the saddle, forcing New Yorkers to take thought of their future including the possibility of independence, an idea abhorrent to many citizens. Several times the Provincial Congress denied any intent or desire for independence. The slashing prose of Thomas Paine's *Common Sense* pushed many to consider the prospect of cutting off all ties with the Crown.

George Washington's successful retreat from Brooklyn Heights is considered one of the most remarkable achievements of military history. Totally surrounded by enemy troops, Washington led the American army to safety across the East River, landing near a pond at what is now First Avenue and 30th Street. From Grafton, The American Revolution, *1975*

A committee of the Provincial Congress on May 27, 1776, declared: "It hath become absolutely necessary for the good people of this Colony to institute a new and regular form of internal government and police."

In order to add more legitimacy, the county committees arranged for a new election for a Fourth Provincial Congress, which promptly established a new government.

Meanwhile, the Second Continental Congress had met and begun to discuss the issue of independence. When this Congress adopted the Declaration of Independence on July 4, New York delegates abstained. Shortly thereafter the Fourth Provincial Congress met at White Plains and approved the Declaration on July 9. No doubt many citizens felt uneasy about the way their early protests had severed the ties with the British Empire. An able and determined minority had outmaneuvered the partisans of George III and the moderates, some indifferent, some vacillating, depending on the fortunes of war.

The Revolutionary War in New York was more than a rebellion against imperial controls; it was also a civil war among citizens as well as a clash between Indians and settlers. Because nearly a third of all military engagements took place within the state's borders, few sections escaped some destruction. Flames, perhaps set by patriots such as Nathan Hale, burned down a third of the buildings on Manhattan Island. Blackened timbers and abandoned fields marked the Mohawk Valley.

The war left us a rich legacy of stirring events, colorful personalities, and deeds of infamy as well as daring. Who can forget the gallantry of that arch-traitor Benedict Arnold? Who cannot repeat the final words of Nathan Hale, memorized by generations of schoolchildren? Those who never read Walter Edmonds' *Drums Along the Mohawk* have undoubtedly seen the motion-picture version. The surrender of General John Burgoyne in 1777 at Saratoga made Edward S. Creasy's list of the "fifteen decisive battles of the world from Marathon to Waterloo."

George Washington's Newburgh headquarters were located on the west side of the Hudson River, about 50 miles north of New York City. This painting by an anonymous artist probably dates from 1886 or later. Courtesy, Albany Institute of History & Art

On April 13, 1776, George Washington came to New York City, where the populace greeted him with cheers and the ringing of church bells. Two months later observers on Sandy Hook watched 130 ships bring in 10,000 soldiers under the command of Sir William Howe. Each week thereafter more ships brought more troops to Staten Island until Howe had 31,000 professional soldiers, including more than 8,000 German mercenaries. To counter this formidable force, Washington had 28,000 men, few of them trained, many without arms, and large numbers down with camp fever. The British fleet under the command of Admiral Richard Howe, an older brother of the general, could move regiments around the vast harbor. Washington lacked this mobility and had other worries: an untrained army and inexperienced officers, the threat of a British invasion from Canada, and a good portion of his army in an exposed position on Long Island. General Howe landed 20,000 men on Long Island beginning on August 22 and prepared to attack the American army entrenched behind Brooklyn Heights. Four days later Howe, while feigning an attack on the American center and right wing, led a sweeping movement that rolled up the American left flank. The next morning Howe smashed the force of General John Sullivan and threatened the breastworks on Brooklyn Heights. Washington rushed to the scene and immediately saw the danger to his disorganized soldiers. Skillfully and calmly, Washington withdrew his forces in the dead of night to Manhattan Island. The British made feelers to the Americans for peace negotiations and invited representatives from the Continental Congress to meet with the Howe brothers on September 6. The meeting proved fruitless, largely because the Americans would not accept the condition that Congress revoke the Declaration of Independence.

Meanwhile Washington, hoping to retain control of Manhattan Island, was regrouping his disorganized regiments. On September 15 General Howe sent his army to Kip's Bay on the East River side of the island and almost cut off the Americans who were scrambling up the western side to the hilly land around Harlem Heights. The next day the Americans threw back Howe's advance force, but Washington realized that his position was desperate. Howe tried to outflank the American army by ferrying his troops to the mainland north of Long Island Sound. Washington also marched north to the vicinity of White Plains. Howe captured a key hill, but Washington had averted disaster. He crossed the Hudson River to New Jersey, leaving many of his men stranded on Manhattan Island.

The situation looked grim for Washington, who had lost New York City as well as thousands of soldiers who were killed, wounded, and captured. Washington, who had already earned the nickname of "Old Fox," realized that the only strategy was to avoid a climactic battle. The Patriots could afford to give up land, hoping that in time the British would become tired of chasing their elusive foe. What the British had to avoid was getting bogged down in the vast hinterland, where militiamen and farmers could cut their communications, demoralize the redcoats with sniper fire, and destory their morale by guerrilla warfare.

A victory in the north partially offset the grievous losses around New York City. The British had ordered Guy Carleton, Governor of Canada, to move south on Lake Champlain and on to the upper Hudson Valley. Benedict Arnold, American chief, saw that his task was to delay Carleton's advance until winter stopped him.

The Americans had a flotilla of three schooners and a sloop on Lake Champlain. Carleton was assembling a fleet at the north end of the lake in order to protect his small boats laden with troops. Whoever controlled the water would eventually control the forts at Ticonderoga and Crown Point. In Skenesboro (Whitehall today), Arnold built more vessels at a furious speed, using raw timber from the forest. When news of his activity filtered back to the coastal towns of New England, scores of carpenters and sailmakers marched to Arnold's aid. They built row-galleys, 70 feet long and 18 feet wide, which had two short masts, each boat capable of carrying 80 men and several guns. Dozens of flat-bottomed gondolas were also hammered together.

Powder horns in the eighteenth century are meticulously decorated. This one, which dates from 1758, shows Hudson River scenes, Albany, Saratoga, Fort Edward, and Fort Ticonderoga. The other side depicts a leaf design with flowers and ducks. Leaves and flowers, as well as small animals, were common adornments on furniture and other surfaces in the period. Courtesy, Albany Institute of History & Art

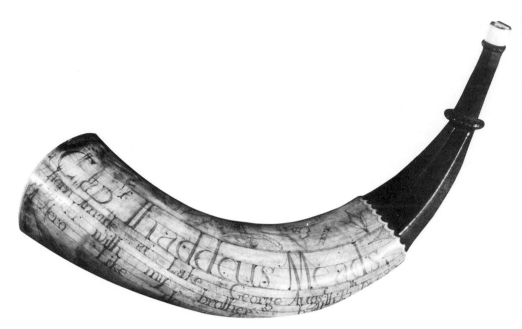

On October 10 the British sailed south toward the American fleet anchored off Valcour Island near the present city of Plattsburgh. A sharp battle took place, each side inflicting heavy losses. Carleton had the edge in guns and experienced gunners and sailors. Arnold realized his desperate situation and sneaked out through the night fog. With muffled oars his men rowed all night to put miles of blue water between them and the British.

Carleton felt chagrin at daybreak on finding that the Americans had fled. At once he raised his sails to chase his quarry. By noon he began to catch up with vessels crippled during the fight. Some American skippers beached and burned their boats. Arnold lost 11 of his 16 vessels and also command of the lake. Crown Point fell on November 1, without a struggle. But Fort Ticonderoga had a garrison of 9,000 men who might withstand a siege for several weeks. Carleton, however, turned back, no doubt influenced by the frosty nights and shorter days. Arnold thus succeeded in thwarting Carleton's campaign and making more difficult Burgoyne's thrust in the following year.

Burgoyne returned to London in November 1776. There "Gentleman Johnny" plunged into the social whirl, joined the king on hunting excursions, and lost large sums at the gaming tables. He did put together a plan for invading America from the north, using the water route of Lake Champlain-Lake George to the upper Hudson. Another force would strike south from Oswego and join Burgoyne in the Albany area. Howe was to send a force north to Albany. If the British controlled these water lines, they could isolate New England from the other colonies.

Burgoyne had many influential friends who helped him secure the command of the expedition heading south from Canada. Lord George Germain, the colonial Secretary, preferred Burgoyne over Carleton, whom he hated. Historians have long debated whether Germain forgot to send orders to Howe, thus causing Burgoyne's expedition to be left without aid during the next autumn. Actually Howe did receive a copy of Burgoyne's orders, which noted that Burgoyne should effect a "junction" at Albany with forces from the south. Moreover Germain did approve of Howe's plan to send most of his soldiers to Philadelphia. Howe did not sail for Philadelphia until after he learned Burgoyne had taken Fort Ticonderoga, the main stronghold between Montreal and Albany.

On July 6 Burgoyne captured Fort Ti by placing guns on Mount Defiance overlooking the fort. He had approximately 3,700 German soldiers and the same number of British regulars, including famous Irish, Scottish, and Welsh regiments. But Burgoyne had serious problems, among them a shortage of Indian scouts and a scarcity of horses, which he needed as mounts for his Brunswick dragoons. Worst of all, he burdened his train with 138 pieces of artillery. Even though New York had a large number of Loyalists, few of them came to Burgoyne's assistance.

The garrison in Fort Ti fled during the night over a swaying bridge of boats to the Vermont side. Four hundred and fifty men carried the women, wounded, and ill to small boats and rowed south to Skenesboro. Burgoyne sent troops to pursue the Americans and broke their formations at Hubbardton. The American flotilla managed to reach Skenesboro a scant two hours before their pursuers, then fled south through the forest toward Fort Edward. Burgoyne decided to change his plans, which called for him to row south to the base of Lake George and then use the old military road to Fort Edward. Burgoyne chose to head south from Skenesboro, a shorter route but one blocked by forest and swamps.

Philip Schuyler, commander of the American forces, recruited axmen to fell trees over a trail and to roll huge boulders into Wood Creek in order to block passage by boats. Luckily, torrential rains raised the level of the creek and turned the valley into a swamp. Burgoyne's engineers worked steadily cutting log obstructions, but the army advanced at the rate of about one mile a day. His progress was slowed by his heavy guns and 20 wagons full of china, wine, and dress uniforms.

During the Revolutionary War, Nathan Hale, a New York school teacher, volunteered for a spying mission behind British lines. Hale is shown here on his way to be executed, flanked by a guard of British redcoats. Courtesy, The New-York Historical Society, New York City

The British army finally reached the Hudson River and pushed south. Because his supplies were running low, on August 13 Burgoyne sent soldiers to capture foodstuffs and horses in the Bennington area of Vermont. He sent a raiding party composed mainly of Germans up the Walloomsac Valley. Four miles from Bennington a brigade of Americans had taken a position, their leader the brave and testy John Stark of New Hampshire. Each hour more militiamen drifted into the American lines, and Colonel Friedrich Baum, outnumbered and apprehensive, sent a courier to Burgoyne asking for assistance. As the Americans charged the British position, a stray bullet by chance ignited the ammunition wagon, which blew up and demoralized the German soldiers. A bullet cut down Baum, and most of his men surrendered. Meanwhile the relief party sent by Burgoyne met dozens of fleeing soldiers, behind whom were American snipers.

Joseph Brant
1743-1807

Isabel Thompson Kelsay in her biography (1984) of Joseph Brant claims, "He was the most famous American Indian who ever lived." Born in a bark hut, Brant achieved prominence in the worlds of red men and white men, meeting George III, George Washington, and other luminaries of his day. The young Mohawk attracted the attention of Sir William Johnson, who took him at the age of 13 on a raid against the French. In 1761 Brant attended a school run by Eleazer Wheelock, the founder of Dartmouth College. An excellent scholar, Brant became a Christian, joined the Anglican church, and translated the Book of Common Prayer and parts of the Bible into the Mohawk language.

During the Revolution, Brant sided with the Loyalists and the Johnson family. The British made him a captain. He organized the ambush of Herkimer's expedition at Oriskany, and he led raids on Cherry Valley and other settlements. Sometimes called "Monster Brant," he was usually merciful in warfare, although some of his braves occasionally got out of hand.

After the Revolution, Brant with many other Mohawks settled in Canada on a tract granted by the British government. He tried without success to persuade the American government to pay the Mohawks for their land in New York. Finally, in 1797, New York State signed a treaty with the Mohawks awarding them $1,000 for their land claims.

Son of a Mohawk chieftain, Joseph Brant became a protege of Sir William Johnson, Indian agent for the British government in New York. This portrait of Brant by Ezra Ames was the last one ever done. Brant was also painted by Romney, Stuart, and Peale. Courtesy, New York State Historical Association, Cooperstown

The British turned around and retreated. The Bennington campaign cost Burgoyne almost 600 men killed or wounded, while the Americans lost only 14 dead and 42 wounded. News of this victory encouraged more settlers to join the militia assembling below Saratoga.

Colonel Barry St. Leger headed the small force that moved south from Oswego toward the Mohawk Valley, which some Tories claimed had hundreds of secret allies ready to fight for the Crown. He led 340 soldiers (100 Germans, 200 British regulars, 40 artillerymen) and 1,000 or more Indians under Joseph Brant, a Mohawk chief, plus assorted Tories (Sir John Johnson with his contingent of 133 Royal Greens and the rangers under Colonel John Butler). Johnson, Butler, and Brant, who grew up in the Mohawk Valley, knew every path, ford, and settlement.

News that St. Leger had reached Fort Stanwix on August 3 sent a shock wave through the frontier settlements. General Nicholas Herkimer, the American commander, called out the militia of Tryon County to meet at Fort Dayton (near present-day Herkimer). Almost 600 men flocked to the colors and marched west, followed by dozens of oxcarts filled with supplies for Fort Stanwix. Near Oriskany the wagon road dipped into a deep ravine where Brant's Indians and Butler's Tories poured a deadly fire from ambush. A hail of bullets smashed Herkimer's leg and killed his horse. After six hours of bloody battle both sides withdrew, the Americans having suffered the greater losses.

Although the British had turned back Herkimer's force, they could not capitalize on their victory. Several Indian chiefs had been killed, and Brant's Indians, whose camp had been raided by the Fort Stanwix garrison during the battle at Oriskany, melted away. St. Leger was making slow progress in building enfilading trenches to approach the fort. Meanwhile Philip Schuyler had dispatched Benedict Arnold with 900 men to bring relief to Fort Stanwix. When St. Leger heard of Arnold's approach, he ordered a withdrawal from the siege. His men panicked and raced to Oneida Lake, scattering along the trail clothing, guns, and supplies. The Patriots had saved the Mohawk Valley. True, Herkimer died of his wound, but the hated Tories had also been bloodied.

Revolutionary war hero General Horatio Gates was named president of the Board of War in November 1777. He was a voice for strengthening the power of the Continental Congress as early as 1783. Courtesy, New York State Library

In mid-September Burgoyne crossed to the west bank of the Hudson at old Saratoga (now Schuylerville) and dragged his heavy guns toward Albany. Facing him was General Horatio Gates, a former officer in the British army, who had taken over command from Schuyler. Known as "Granny" for his fussy mannerisms, Gates knew how to organize an army and what not to do. He placed his men, reinforced each day by more volunteers, behind fortifications at Bemis Heights. Burgoyne had two choices: attack or retreat. In fact he had only one choice, because retreat would probably result in a rout. Twice his redcoats and German soldiers stormed the American defenses; twice they fell back with heavy losses. On October 9 Burgoyne began his retreat and on October 17, after consulting his senior officers, offered to surrender. Gates accepted and graciously granted Burgoyne the honors accorded to defeated officers.

Victory had consequences far beyond the borders of New York. Up and down the seaboard Americans cheered lustily, because they recognized the strategic significance and also because it offset the loss of Philadelphia to Howe. In Britain defeat shocked the public, and officials sent feelers to the Americans offering to repeal the tea duty and the Intolerable Acts. In fact they hinted at self-government similar to that enjoyed before 1763. But this offer came too late.

In Paris Benjamin Franklin was skillfully maneuvering to secure a formal alliance with France, whose officials saw a wonderful opportunity to get revenge for its smashing defeat in the Seven Years' War. Louis XVI quietly signed this treaty guaranteeing more funds and supplies plus the open assistance of the French army and navy. This alliance led Great Britain to break off relations with France, which also meant eventual war with Spain, a close ally of France. Within New York the British had to withdraw to the lower Hudson.

Bands of Tories and Indians continued to ravage the frontier settlements. In 1778 at Cherry Valley, Indians killed 40 survivors of the raids, and this spread terror throughout the state. The next year Washington ordered General James Clinton to strike at the Onondaga villages, which he did. Clinton then moved his troops from Canajoharie to Otsego Lake, where he built a dam at the outlet to raise the water level. Cutting through the dam, Clinton's flotilla of rafts and boats rode the flood crest to the Susquehanna River. At Tioga Clinton joined General John Sullivan, and together they marched to the Genesee Valley, where they burned the Seneca villages. Although the Senecas had to move to the shelter of Fort Niagara, they continued to send roving bands. The last battle of the Revolution on New York soil took place near Herkimer in 1781, when 400 Patriots forced a larger group of British and Indians to retreat.

Meanwhile Arnold, whose egotism outmatched his bravery, negotiated to surrender West Point to the British. Some Americans accidentally captured Major John Andre, a British officer

Philip Schuyler was a major general in the Continental Army. After planning an attack on Canada he was forced to retire from active duty due to illness. Courtesy, Albany Institute of History & Art, gift of Mrs. Charles Hamlin

Facing page: Young Major Andre is shown here just before his execution. Andre was the British go-between in Benedict Arnold's plot to betray American forces during the Revolutionary War. Arnold was warned of Andre's capture and escaped behind British lines. Courtesy, The New York Historical Society, New York City

who was carrying messages from Arnold to Sir Henry Clinton. Andre met death as a spy with courage and dignity. Arnold escaped to the British lines, his name thereafter a synonym for traitor.

The British recognized American independence on September 3, 1783. Patriots lit bonfires and fired cannon. On November 25 the Americans, headed by George Washington and George Clinton, led a victory march and parade followed by regiments and citizens. The departing British had cut the halyards to the flagpole, but an American sailor climbed the greased pole and replaced the Union Jack with the Stars and Stripes.

New Yorkers were well prepared for independence because of their long experience in electing representatives and debating public issues. How well would they use this skill in the tempestuous days of freedom when enemy troops held the seaport and a good share of the population remained loyal to George III?

On July 9, 1776, soldiers in the Continental army in New York City had listened to the reading of the Declaration of Independence. We can safely assume that the ideals phrased so felicitously by Thomas Jefferson expressed their beliefs and aspirations. Note that the Declaration was included in the first state constitution.

Right: John Jay was involved in public service since the Revolutionary period, both for New York State and the United States. A close associate of Alexander Hamilton, Jay wrote five of the Federalist *with Hamilton and James Madison. John Jay was the first Chief Justice of the Supreme Court and served as governor of New York State from 1795 until 1801. Courtesy, Albany Institute of History & Art*

Facing page: This portrait of George Clinton by Ezra Ames (1768-1836) established the artist's reputation. He later painted the images of many figures involved in the building of the Erie Canal and the nation's first railroads. Courtesy, New York State Historical Association, Cooperstown

Born on the British West Indies island of Nevis, Alexander Hamilton adopted New York as his home. In 1787 he was one of three New Yorkers chosen to attend the Constitutional Convention at Philadelphia. After the convention, Hamilton collaborated with John Jay and James Madison in writing a brilliant series of essays in support of the constitution, known collectively as The Federalist. *Courtesy, The New-York Historical Society, New York City*

The Convention of the Representatives of the State of New York, formerly the Provincial Congress, appointed a committee on August 1 to formulate a constitution. John Jay, a conservative lawyer and later Chief Justice of the United States, had a major hand in writing this document. Like many other state constitutions, New York's clipped the power of the governor. Henceforth he had to share his appointive and veto powers with commissions that included legislators. The requirements for voting and holding office were quite liberal, especially when compared with European standards, because approximately two-thirds of adult white males could vote for members of the assembly. To vote for governor and senator, one had to meet higher property qualifications. Freedom of religion and separation of church and state were also guaranteed.

In 1777 voters elected as their first governor George Clinton, who served six terms until

1795. Clinton defeated Philip Schuyler, who felt that Clinton came from a family unworthy of such a high office. He conceded that Clinton had ability, courage, and patriotism. Actually Clinton sprang from good farmer stock, but he had no pretensions of high social status. Washington, incidentally, thought well enough of Clinton to join him in a land partnership.

At first Clinton spent most of his efforts recruiting militia, securing supplies, and protecting the borders. A passionate hater of Tories, Clinton urged the legislature to strip them of their property and sell their land. Active Tories felt the full brunt of his hatred. The confiscation of Tory lands in the lower Hudson Valley led to a sharp reduction in the number of tenant farmers. The legislature also took ownership of land owned by the Crown and sold it to speculators who upheld the cause of independence. They in turn sold small tracts to settlers. The repeal of primogeniture and entail, under which manors and large estates passed to the eldest son, helped loosen the old leasehold system. For example, when Stephen Van Rensselaer died in 1839, his estate had to pass equally to both of his sons.

On the whole the Revolution created a more open and democratic society by reducing the

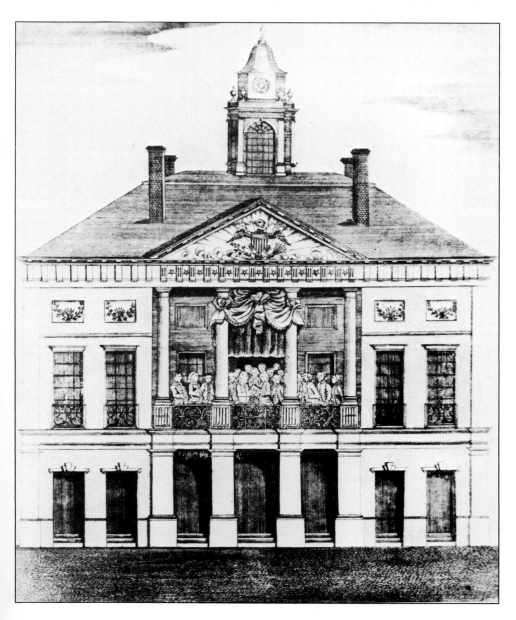

After the ratification of the constitution, New York's old City Hall was remodeled to accommodate the needs of the new Federal government. In 1788 it emerged as one of the largest and most elegant buildings on the continent, boasting native marble, woods, iron work, draperies, and patriotic friezes. Congress met there on March 4, 1789, and from the Wall Street gallery, George Washington was inaugurated on April 30, 1789. Courtesy, Fraunces Tavern Museum, New York

Trinity Church was founded by English Royal charter in 1697. The first Trinity Church was destroyed in the great fire of 1776. A second building was completed in 1790. There were special pews for the United States President, New York State governor and members of Congress. In 1841 the second Trinity Church was taken down and replaced by the present structure, completed in 1846. Courtesy, New York State Library

power of the landed elite and changing the land system as well as disestablishing the Church of England. Clinton and Jay favored a reform of the criminal code and a ban on the importation of more slaves. Jay crusaded for the abolition of slaves within the state, a drastic reform avoided by Clinton, whose Ulster County neighbors often owned a slave or two. The flight of Tories —over 10 percent of the population—and the broadening of the electorate meant greater opportunities for ordinary men to advance in politics and business. The elite lost their majority in the assembly and state senate when "new men" from the farming and artisan class took their seats. George Clinton and Alexander Hamilton, political enemies, are good examples of "new men."

Clinton quarreled with many groups besides the elite. He disturbed some conservatives by approving a limited issue of paper money. But Clinton was no radical agrarian and opponent of property rights. He put down antirenters and he opposed Shays' Rebellion in Massachusetts. He denounced the Green Mountain Boys, who defied New York sheriffs and rejected the land claims of New Yorkers. Clinton realized that he could not put down the Vermonters against the opposition of the other New England states, so he and the legislature recognized Vermont's independence in 1790.

The opponents of Clinton gradually coalesced around Hamilton, Jay, and the Livingstons.

Erasmus Hall is the second oldest high school in America. It was built in 1786 by the townspeople of Flatbush, on land donated by the Dutch Reformed Church. Contributors to the project included both Alexander Hamilton and Aaron Burr. Courtesy, New York State Library

This group advocated a stronger central government that could protect American rights on the high seas, secure favorable trade treaties, and settle interstate disputes. Clinton, however, adhered to the states' rights position. Why throw off British interference only to exchange it for other outside officials even if they were Americans? Clinton upheld the Articles of Confederation, in which New York alone could tax and make laws for its citizens.

During the war the legislature granted the Continental Congress power to collect revenues from duties on imports. Once the war was over, New York ended this concession, largely because it needed the money for its own activities. New York did not place duties on American goods reaching the state, but it did impose duties on foreign goods entering the state through New Jersey and Connecticut. Most foreign vessels brought goods to Manhattan merchants, who then distributed them up and down the seaboard and into the interior. Merchants paid duties to New

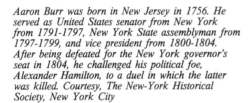

Aaron Burr was born in New Jersey in 1756. He served as United States senator from New York from 1791-1797, New York State assemblyman from 1797-1799, and vice president from 1800-1804. After being defeated for the New York governor's seat in 1804, he challenged his political foe, Alexander Hamilton, to a duel in which the latter was killed. Courtesy, The New-York Historical Society, New York City

York on these goods and passed along this tax to the consumers in other states, who complained with some justification. Hamilton urged unsuccessfully that New York grant Congress a 5 percent impost, but Clinton opposed it. Clinton was afraid that the loss of this revenue would force him to place higher taxes on land.

In 1787 delegates from 12 states met in Philadelphia to revise the Articles of Confederation. New York sent three delegates—Robert Yates, John Lansing, and Alexander Hamilton—to do just that. Only Hamilton favored a strong national government and he was the only delegate to sign the final document, the other two having gone home on legal business. The new Constitution gave the proposed government control over commerce within the country and with foreign nations. Congress had the crucial power to lay and collect taxes. States could not issue paper money, make treaties, or impair the obligation of contract.

A vigorous debate took place over ratification, which required the approval of only nine states to go into effect. This requirement was a revolutionary act, because it overruled the confederation's requirement for unanimity for any amendment. Clinton opposed ratification, because the document did not include a Bill of Rights. Jay and Hamilton made brilliant speeches and Jay, Hamilton, and James Madison wrote perceptive essays, later published as *The Federalist*. When the votes were tallied, opponents or Anti-Federalists had elected 46 delegates. The pro-Constitution Federalists won only 19 seats, almost all from the area of greater New York City.

If the Federalists were weak in numbers, they were strong in talent. Hamilton, Jay, Robert R. Livingston, James Duane, and others outshone the delegates opposed to the Constitution. Jay patiently reassured those who were worried about the lack of a Bill of Rights, telling them that he would work hard for the inclusion of such amendments.

One by one states ratified the Constitution, and each step made the Anti-Federalists more uneasy. Could New York survive if left outside the Union? Would the seaport, lower Hudson Valley, and Long Island break away and join the new government? By the time Virginia ratified as number 10, it became evident that New York had to approve the new document. The debate shifted to possible conditions, with most moderate Clintonians and Federalists agreeing to include a Bill of Rights. On July 26 the Poughkeepsie Convention, by 30 to 27, voted approval "in full confidence" that the other states would consider amendments.

Even opponents lost their suspicions when the benefits of the new government became apparent. New York became the first capital, temporarily to be sure, but still representing recognition of its status. On April 30, 1789, New Yorkers heartily celebrated the inauguration of Washington as first president. Citizens joined the parade that wound its way to Federal Hall, where Chancellor Robert R. Livingston administered the oath of office. Washington selected several New Yorkers for prominent positions, among them John Jay as first chief justice and Alexander Hamilton as secretary of the treasury.

New Yorkers had followed a zigzag course from 1763 to 1789. At first they had led the resistance against the Sugar Act and the Quartering Act, but by 1776 they lagged well behind other colonists in severing ties with the mother country. During the war New York became the major battlefield and suffered the greatest losses in population and property. Appropriately, New Yorkers in the postwar years received the most benefits. The defeat of the Iroquois opened up a vast hinterland in central and western New York where tens of thousands of migrants created a greater New England. Growers of wheat from this hinterland and cotton from the South found the merchants of New York City the main markets for these products, which were distributed to Europe and the West Indies, and along the coast.

In 1783 Washington visited upstate, admired the beauty of Lake George, and predicted that the countryside, interlaced with rivers and lakes, would become "the seat of empire." A practical man with a keen sense for land values, Washington purchased a tract near Fort Stanwix, so confident was he of the future growth of New York.

THE RISE OF THE EMPIRE STATE 1790-1830

New York grew at a spectacular pace in the period after the Revolution and by 1820 led all states in population, foreign and domestic commerce, transportation, banking, and manufacturing. Proudly grasping the title of Empire State, it grew faster than all other Northeastern states in all four decades. These achievements were a glowing testimonial to individual enterprise plus a judicious admixture of public promotion, notably the Erie Canal. Pioneers and workers of both sexes, merchants, shipowners and captains, speculators in land and business, artisans, and professional men created the Empire State. (Who coined this phrase is still unknown).

Whereas in 1785 three out of four New Yorkers lived within a dozen miles of tidal waters, by 1820 approximately the same percentage lived well away from the Hudson River and Atlantic Ocean. Who, at the conclave at Fort Stanwix in 1768, would have predicted that a half century later a majority of New Yorkers would be living on the Indian side of the famous treaty line?

New Yorkers remained primarily rural dwellers; fewer than 15 percent lived in centers of more than 3,000 people. Growth was slow in the old river ports between New York City and Albany after 1810, with the loss of the exuberance that characterized the turnpike boom. Albany and Troy, the latter a Yankee outpost, grew steadily because of the traffic on the Hudson River and Erie Canal. The urban pattern of upstate is clearly discernible by 1830.

The population of state and metropolis more nearly reflected the ethnic background of the nation between 1790 and 1830 than at any other time before or after this period. Persons of English origin constituted the great majority. Timothy Dwight, president of Yale, estimated that in 1820 more than 60 percent of the state's inhabitants stemmed from New England.

Southern New England, especially Connecticut, was likened to a "hive" throwing off "its annual swarms of intelligent, industrious, and enterprising settlers, the best qualified of any in the world, to subdue and civilize the wilderness . . . " This observation was made in 1788 by Elkanah Watson, Albany merchant and later the founder of the county-fair movement. Although land hunger was the compelling reason for the Yankee flight west, exhausted soils, large families, and perhaps prying neighbors provided other incentives. Even more persuasive were the letters from relatives and comments from returning neighbors who reported upon the fertile soil, the rising land values, and their success in farming and trade in New York State. The stay-at-homes

Population of New York State and New York City, 1790-1830

State and metropolis grew at approximately the same pace between 1790 and 1830.

Year	New York State	New York City
1790	340,120	33,131
1800	589,051	60,489
1810	959,049	96,373
1820	1,372,812	123,706
1830	1,918,608	202,580

grew increasingly restive. Would not a move west prove better not only for them but particularly for their children?

A mania for land speculation swept New York after the Revolution. The Empire State offered the choicest and most varied opportunities: Manhattan real estate but also village lots at inland crossroads and the outlets of rivers and lakes; lands formerly belonging to Loyalists and the Crown; and vast tracts of backcountry west and north of Fort Stanwix. In 1786 New York settled its dispute with Massachusetts over land claims in central and western New York, yielding to its eastern neighbor all the land west of Seneca Lake and 10 townships near present-day Binghamton. New York received title to the land east of Seneca Lake plus political sovereignty over the entire area from Fort Stanwix to Lake Erie.

The state reserved for Revolutionary War veterans a tract of more than 1.5 million acres in 28 townships in central New York. This Military Tract covered the area east of Seneca Lake to about Cazenovia and from the neighborhood of Syracuse to south of Ithaca. Note the classical names that a state official sprinkled over this tract: Cato, Romulus, Sempronius, and Cicero. These names amused a generation of foreign travelers.

Wealthy families along the seaboard and in northern Europe caught the land fever, a term later used by Carl Carmer in his novel describing the life of Charles Williamson, a land agent. Poorly drained lowlands often proved a breeding ground for mosquitoes and malaria. Merchants in New York, Philadelphia, Boston, and Albany coveted land so feverishly that some migrated to the frontier, where they built a mansion in the midst of their tracts. Farmers, shopkeepers, and artisans caught the fever because they yearned for cheap land and village lots. Bargain prices and future profits excited the cupidity of scores of Europeans: Lord William Pulteney of Bath; canny Dutch bankers; emigres from France. Few Americans could resist the frenzy when Robert Morris, the "financier of the Revolution," was buying and selling millions of acres, and Washington was dabbling in upstate real estate.

Clearly, land prices would rise and did soar in the long run, although in the short run violent swings took place, depending on the business cycle, wars, and the opening of new tracts. The shrewd and lucky ones made fortunes; the rash and unlucky faced bankruptcy. What most speculators failed to take into account was the cost of carrying land: interest on loans; taxes; expenses such as surveys and roads; selling costs; and the free credit offered to early settlers.

One obstacle, namely Indian claims, stood in the way before speculators could guarantee clear title. By 1790 land jobbers, in cooperation with state and sometimes federal officials, had negotiated treaties for most of the land as far as the Genesee River, and during the next decade they acquired title to almost all the land west of the river. In negotiations lubricated with barrels of rum, the demoralized Indians gave up their hunting grounds through a combination of coercion, corruption, and chicanery.

Massachusetts, the owner of 6 million acres west of Seneca Lake, sold the land to Oliver Phelps and Nathaniel Gorham, two speculators with excellent political connections. The price was cheap—three cents an acre—which they expected to pay for with rising land values. Few settlers, however, had ready cash when they applied for land at the P and G land office in Canandaigua. Strapped for cash, Phelps and Gorham turned back the western two-thirds to Massachusetts in order to keep the eastern section, which they sold to Robert Morris for eight cents an acre. Morris felt confident that he could persuade his European friends to buy land, so confident, indeed, that he also bought the western tract from Massachusetts.

Morris had guessed correctly, because he sold a million acres to Sir William Pulteney and other English capitalists for a handsome profit. Pulteney believed that he could charge premium

The early Dutch settlement at Albany consisted of but one single street, skirting the river bank. A number of old Dutch buildings of red and yellow brick still stood in 1818, bearing the year of their origin above the second floor windows in huge iron numerals. The stepped design of the roof was typical of Dutch colonial construction. Courtesy, The New-York Historical Society, New York City

This watercolor drawing was the work of Archibald Robertson, who came to New York in 1791, and with his brother Alexander opened the Columbian Academy of Painting. Of note in this picture is the large building in the center. It is the Government House at the foot of Broadway facing Bowling Green. The structure was the residence of New York Governor George Clinton. Courtesy, The New-York Historical Society, New York City

prices if he provided such improvements as roads, mills, and taverns. He hired Charles Williamson as his agent, who made many improvements, including a racetrack and an opera house at Bath. Despite his Scottish origins, Williamson spent lavishly—more than a million dollars, a sum far greater than the revenues. Pulteney fired him.

Morris also sold in excess of 2.5 million acres west of the Genesee River to a group of Amsterdam bankers who formed the Holland Land Company. They hired Joseph Ellicott to lay out the tracts, build roads, and open offices. The company agents gradually sold the land until the 1830s, when they liquidated their investment, netting a modest return. Morris had retained a 500,000-acre reserve embracing the finest alluvial soils along the Genesee River. A sheriff's sale stripped him of this tract when he failed to pay his creditors. Morris ended up in debtors' prison, a fate not uncommon for many speculators.

Northern New York also experienced a land boom. In 1791 Alexander MacComb, who formed a syndicate of speculators, bought about 4 million acres for about eight cents an acre. He resold a huge chunk in the Black River basin to William Constable and another tract to a group of Belgian capitalists and refugees from Revolutionary France. Samuel Ogden founded Ogdensburg in 1801 and enticed a considerable number of Vermonters to sleigh across Lake Champlain and follow the "winter road" to the mouth of the St. Regis River. David Parish, descendant of a German and English mercantile family, bought 200,000 acres in 1808 from Gouverneur Morris, prominent patriot who served as ambassador to France. Parish added to his holdings and in 1811 moved to the St. Lawrence Valley, where he built roads, forges, and piers. Investors north of Fort Stanwix could not match the success of capitalists who acquired fertile land in the Finger Lakes region, the Genesee Valley, and along the Great Lakes. The Adirondacks remained a wilderness area until well after the Civil War.

These speculators stimulated the peopling of western and northern New York by making improvements, especially roads that enabled settlers to bring their household goods by sleigh or wagon. Their advertisements in newspapers lured Yankees who had lost hope after years of drudgery cultivating thin soils in rock-strewn fields. Dozens of speculators moved to the frontier, hoping to carve out a baronial estate. James and William Wadsworth established a social and political bailiwick in Geneseo, where the gentry in greencoats chased the fox. Oliver Phelps moved to Canandaigua and Zephaniah Platt of Dutchess County founded Plattsburgh on Lake Champlain. Scores of speculators left their family names on towns and villages in central, western, and northern New York. Even the Holland Land Company left its Dutch names and architectural monuments in Adam Mappa Hall in Barneveld (Trenton), Lorenzo, the Jan Lincklaen mansion in Cazenovia, and the company land office in Batavia, the Roman name for Holland's inhabitants.

During the 1790s the number of westering Yankees increased each year until it became a flood. By the turn of the century pioneers had passed beyond the Military Tract and were invading the Pulteney tract. Soon they were crossing the Genesee River in search of good and cheap land offered by the Holland Land Company. By 1812 more than 200,000 people lived in western New York, at least a tenth of them west of the Genesee River.

The exodus alarmed such pillars of New England society as Timothy Dwight, who warned that a society destitute of church, school, and culture would revert to barbarism. He was not entirely wrong. Another Yankee, the Reverend John Taylor, who toured the Black River country

Citizen Edmund Genet was a political functionary in Revolutionary France who was implicated in a clumsy attempt at extortion involving American government officials. The incident almost started a war between the United States and France. Courtesy, New York State Library

Advice and Reflections of Judge William Cooper from *A Guide in the Wilderness*

I began with the disadvantage of a small capital, and the encumbrance of a large family, and yet I have already settled more acres than any man in America. There are forty thousand souls now holding, directly or indirectly, under me, and I trust that no one amongst so many can justly impute to me any act resembling oppression. I am now descending into the vale of life, and I must acknowledge that I look back with self complacency upon what I have done . . .

In May, 1786, I opened the sales of 40,000 acres, which in sixteen days were all taken up by the poorest order of men. I soon after established a store, and went to live among them, and continued to do so till 1790, when I brought on my family. For the ensuing four years the scarcity of provisions was a serious calamity; the country was mountainous, and there were neither roads nor bridges. But the greatest discouragement was in the extreme poverty of the people, none of whom had the means of clearing more than a small spot in the midst of the thick and lofty woods, so that their grain grew chiefly in the shade; their maize did not ripen, their wheat was blasted, and the little they did gather they had no mill to grind within twenty miles distance; not one in twenty had a horse, and the way lay through rapid streams, across swamps or over bogs. They had neither provisions to take with them nor money to purchase them; nor if they had, were any to be found on their way.

The King family was prominent in Revolutionary America, both in Massachusetts and New York. Rufus King, shown here, represented Massachusetts at the Constitutional Convention. He soon married Mary Alsop, a daughter of a New York merchant, and moved to New York. There he served in the state assembly and as senator from the state in the federal congress. Courtesy, Society for the Preservation of Long Island Antiquities

in 1802, described life around Remsen in these terms: "This is a broken society. The people are very ignorant and very wicked . . . " But Taylor also observed: "There is no complaining of hard times, but everyone is cheerful and contented for they all foresee that in a few years they will have a great plenty of worldly goods . . . "

The Yankees swept into the valleys, uplands, and villages in almost every section of New York. They submerged the Dutch communities along the Hudson and the German villages in the Mohawk and Schoharie valleys. They gained control of the city council of Albany and passed an ordinance that required the Dutch burghers to cut off their long rainspouts on their houses. They greatly outnumbered the immigrants from Pennsylvania and New Jersey who were pushing up the Delaware and Susquehanna valleys. A good example is William Cooper, father of the novelist, who moved from Burlington, New Jersey, to Otsego County in 1785 and began to sell his own lands and those of some associates. No one can verify and few resist the story of Penn Yan on Keuka Lake, which supposedly got its name as the place where newcomers from Pennsylvania met the Yankees from New England.

The Yankee impact affected every aspect of business, religion, politics, and culture. Yankees opened shops and kept the ledgers; they organized churches and academies; they kept school, perhaps more skillfully than Ichabod Crane. Yankee families in Manhattan—Macy, Low, Fish, Morgan, to mention only a few—dominated the mercantile and shipping world. In education Gideon Hawley was the father of the district-school law establishing neighborhood schools. The outstanding members of the Whig and Democratic parties usually stemmed from New England, the notable exceptions being Martin Van Buren and De Witt Clinton. Rufus King, one of the first two United States senators from New York, was a newcomer from Massachusetts.

Cheap transportation was the key to New York's growth. The natural waterways carried the bulk of freight and most of the passenger traffic. Wooden sailing vessels reigned supreme on the high seas. Although monthly service from New York to Liverpool began in 1817, the overwhelming majority of ship captains followed no fixed route or regular schedule. One-masted sloops slowly gave way to two-masted schooners in the coastal trade. Gradually square-rigged ships, brigs, and three-masted vessels appeared.

Small sloops dominated the Hudson River even after August 1807, when Robert Fulton's

Left: In this drawing, artist J. Evers depicts the bustling Fly market on Front Street in about 1816. This scene, as many others, was preserved by D.T. Valentine, whose manuals of New York City were published between 1846 and 1870. Courtesy, General Research Division, The New York Public Library

Left: Robert Fulton was born in Pennsylvania, in a town that now bears his name, in 1765. Fulton had a career as an artisan, civil engineer, and inventor. Of course, he is best known for his pioneering efforts in steam navigation in New York. Courtesy, New York State Library

Right: Albany, on the west bank of the Hudson River, remained a small municipality until the completion of the Erie Canal in 1825. Then, like other towns along the canal's route, it mushroomed in size and commercial possibilities. Albany's population increased fivefold within four years of the canal's completion. Courtesy, The New-York Historical Society, New York City

Right: Several powerful mills, some for grinding corn, one for cutting limestone, and a very large one for sawing timber, are seen on the approach to this Adirondack village. There were also kilns for making charcoal from wood to sell to local smiths. Courtesy, The New-York Historical Society, New York City

steamboat belched black smoke on its maiden journey to Albany. The *North River Steamboat of Clermont* soon became known as the *Clermont.* Passengers who had spent three to nine days on sloops rushed to board steamboats, which soon were covering that distance in slightly more than 24 hours. The legislature granted Fulton a monopoly of steam navigation on state waters, and he naturally charged high rates. Nevertheless, the number of steamboats grew steadily, because passengers loved the speed and regularity of these vessels. After 1809, when the first steamboat appeared on Lake Champlain, entrepreneurs launched vessels on the other large upstate lakes.

Farmers after the Revolution used so-called roads that were little more than traces "underbrushed" through the wilderness. A ride in a cart or wagon was at best uncomfortable, at worst hazardous. The spring rains made passage through mud holes and quagmires a test of endurance for oxen or horses and of patience for teamsters. Farmers generally preferred to sleigh their wheat and potash to Albany, because sleighs moved twice as fast as wagons and because they could use frozen lakes and rivers as roadways.

Local overseers of highways had neither funds nor the skill to build all-weather highways for through traffic. The need for better roads increased as interior communities grew. Merchants, landowners, and farmers clamored for better transportation, and to meet the demand the legislature granted private corporations the right to charge tolls if they built a turnpike. In the decade following 1797, the legislature granted charters to 88 turnpike and bridge companies, which built about 900 miles of roadway. In 1821 the Empire State could boast of 4,000 miles of turnpikes linking its communities. Albany, the turnpike and staging capital of the state, had two trunk roads (present-day routes 5 and 20) to the west, a road to Lebanon Springs and other points in New England, and the Albany Post Road coming up from New York City. Utica also became a turnpike center, with eight daily stage lines running east and west and half that number going north and south in 1830.

Turnpikes cut the cost of freighting, speeded up traffic, and opened up tracts away from navigable rivers. In wagons and stagecoaches, peddlers, itinerant craftsmen, and thousands of pioneers paraded along the turnpikes stopping for food, drink, and rest at taverns that dotted the route every mile or so. The staging companies provided work for thousands of teamsters, drivers, hostlers, porters, and agents.

The "knights of the road" have received little attention from novelists and historians who have romanticized the boatmen. With a little imagination one can hear the driver blowing his horn as his galloping team swept into a village and can picture him pulling up his steaming horses before the inn. Stablemen led the horses to the barn before replacing them with fresh animals. The driver, the envy of small boys, took off his greatcoat, strode into the barroom, and regaled the locals with gossip and stories. Passengers rushed to the dining room for a meal or a drink. At the command of All Aboard, they hastened to their seats for another two or three hours of "excruciating jolting."

Turnpikes and rivers in most seasons did not provide cheap and reliable transportation for freight. Frontiersmen piled produce on rafts and arks and rode the crest of the spring freshets on rivers. Merchants in the Hudson River ports became alarmed that the western trade would reach markets in Montreal, Philadelphia, and Baltimore unless New York improved the Mohawk River and constructed a canal.

Above: James Eights departed from his usual Albany subjects to create this view of western New York. Shown here is Rochester's Acquaduct Bridge in 1823. Courtesy, Albany Institute of History & Art

Left: In the early nineteenth century, Little Falls was described as the most romantic and beautiful of the thousands of glens, hamlets, and waterfalls in this area of the state. Its beauty made it a natural subject for J. Milbert's lithographs of his travels around New York. Courtesy, The New-York Historical Society, New York City

In 1792 the legislature accepted Governor Clinton's recommendation and incorporated the Western Inland Lock Navigation Company to build a canal around Little Falls and a channel in the marshy ground between the Mohawk and Wood Creek. High tolls and rotting locks hampered its success, although boats of 10 tons' burden could use the canal. Nothing was done about the Great Falls at Cohoes, which forced boats to discharge their cargo at Schenectady.

In 1816 De Witt Clinton drafted his famous memorial citing the need for "cheapness, celerity, certainty, and safety in the transportation of commodities." The next year the legislature authorized the construction of a canal of more than 360 miles through the wilderness to Lake Erie. Could the canal commissioners overcome the lack of trained engineers, dig a channel through swamps and gorges, and build scores of locks? They could and they did.

Shrewdly the commissioners chose the middle section running west of Little Falls to the region beyond Onondaga Lake as their first undertaking. This hundred miles required no locks, the ditch following the contour of the land. The commissioners gave out contracts to farmers

Dubbed "Clinton's Big Ditch" by its detractors, the Erie Canal opened New York to the commerce of the expanding Midwest. This picture shows the process of excavation for the canal at Lockport, New York. Courtesy, Prints Division, The New York Public Library

along the route, who hired axmen to fell trees and clear the underbrush. The farmers often used their own plows to scoop out a ditch 4 feet deep and 40 feet wide on the surface. The contractors and farmers showed great versatility in developing new wheelbarrows, stump pullers, and plows equipped with knives to cut roots and brush.

Tremendous obstacles stood in the way of the canal commissioners. They had to build aqueducts across the Mohawk River east of Schenectady and one across the Genesee River. The ooze of the Montezuma Swamp kept filling the ditch until they carved out the ditch in the frozen earth and wrapped it with logs. They conquered the limestone ridge at Lockport by building a double set of locks and then blasting a channel with explosives.

No wonder that citizens celebrated the opening of the canal in October 1825 with fireworks, endless toasts and odes, and a cannon serenade, all the way from Buffalo to New York and back. No one misunderstood the symbolism when Governor De Witt Clinton poured a keg of Lake Erie water into New York Harbor.

The Erie Canal lived up to all the expectations of its promoters. Freight charges fell dramatically while tolls opened a cornucopia of revenue that converted most naysayers into ad-

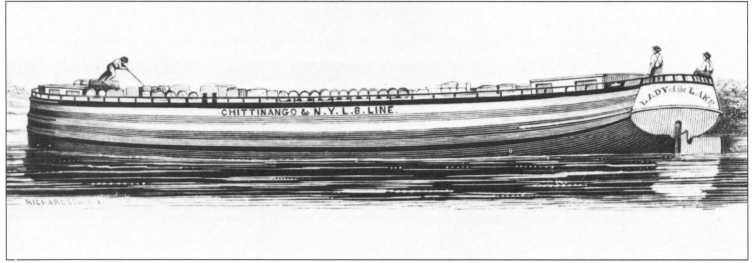

Left and below: Opened on October 26, 1825, the Erie Canal was destined to become the most important transportation artery of its era. Courtesy, Prints Division, The New York Public Library

vocates, especially in sections of the state to the north and south of "Clinton's Ditch." In the 1830s the legislature voted to enlarge the Erie to the depth of seven feet and to build several feeders and branches such as the Chenango, Oswego, and Black River canals. Farmers west of Rome shipped ever-greater amounts of wheat and lumber products eastward, undercutting farmers in eastern New York, who shifted over to dairying. Cities along the canal grew explosively, but villages along the Cherry Valley turnpike lost through traffic; and stagecoach centers such as Auburn, Geneva, and Geneseo had to content themselves with a slow, orderly growth or even stagnation. Thousands of persons, most from New England, others from Europe, took passage on packets in their migration to the Middle West. What better testimonial to the success of the Erie Canal was given than the rush by Pennsylvania, Maryland, and other states to imitate the canal system of New York?

Most New Yorkers derived their livelihood from the land and the forest. Farmers looked upon the forest not only for fencing, fuel, and cabins but also for ready cash. Those near major rivers cut down trees and floated log rafts to market. Those farther back from the river burned huge tracts, scraped together the ashes, ran water through them, and boiled the lye in kettles. The black salts left were potash and pearlash, if refined, both useful in fertilizers and soap. In 1791 pearlash was the chief export of Whitestown on the upper Mohawk. Potash rivaled wheat as the state's chief export.

Almost overnight upstate farmers became transformed into commercial farmers, because they were exposed to the market. Far from seeking self-sufficiency, the pioneers worked desperately to escape the penury and drudgery of trying to produce everything for their own needs.

Above: After several years of harassment by both British and French ships on the high seas, James Madison declared war on Great Britain in 1812. British superiority at sea made the frigate Fulton, shown here, a boon to the United States. Courtesy, Prints Division, The New York Public Library

Right: The Battle of Plattsburgh took place on September 11, 1814. Young American naval officers maneuvered superior British forces into a significant defeat that gave the United States control of Lake Champlain and forced the British to retreat to Canada. Courtesy, New York State Library

The export markets grew rapidly, owing to foreign demand in warring Europe and in the West Indies. During the period from 1792 to 1815, England and France were locked in a death struggle. Whenever it suited either power to interfere with American trade, they did so, a practice that made orderly marketing difficult. When farm prices fell, land values collapsed. Debt-ridden farmers could not meet their payments, which in turn brought down some merchants and landowners. The embargo of 1807-1809 and the War of 1812 paralyzed shipping and disrupted marketing. The postwar boom ended in the panic of 1819 which ruined thousands.

The domestic market, however, was much more important than the foreign market. The needs of tens of thousands of newcomers streaming past the farms, villages, and country stores seemed endless: oxen and horses, hay and oats, tools, and shelter. The care and nurture of these families provided work for land agents, lawyers, surveyors, innkeepers, storekeepers, and blacksmiths. Many newcomers had modest amounts of cash with which to survive the first years of clearing their tracts.

The New Englanders sought to reconstitute the economy and social institutions of their upbringing with squares, churches, schools, and taverns. Hugh White from Middletown, Connecticut, settled about three miles west of Old Fort Schuyler (Utica). In 1792 Francis Adriaen Van der Kemp, a Dutch exile who settled in Barneveld, north of Utica, described the rapidity with which White reproduced all the comforts of his hometown.

He enjoys that exquisite gratification of being the creator of his own fortune, and placing all his children in an independent situation. Judge White resided in Connecticut in the year 1785. He made a journey to the western part of this State; made a purchase of the land he now lives on; moved thither in 1786 with his five sons, built a log house and barn; went the next year for his wife and remaining children . . . In 1788 he constructed a saw and grist mill; possessed in the fourth year all which he wanted for his convenience, ease and comfort in abundance; built in the fifth year a convenient frame house and substantial barn, and is now encircled by a number of respectable families . . .

One can repeat White's story many times if one reads the accounts of pioneers collected by Orsamus Turner's histories of western New York. Novelists, historians, and orators have vied in celebrating the courage, endurance, and resourcefulness of the pioneers. Van der Kemp rhapsodized over the life of his neighbors. In 1795 he spoke to a newly formed agricultural society: "What pleasure; what raptures we enjoy in contemplation of a cleared, fenced acre of the first crop of corn, wheat or grass, that ever covered that spot, since the creation!" His climax had the pioneers shouting: "I too am a free American."

Corn proved the most valuable crop in feeding both the family and the livestock and poultry, although wheat brought in more hard cash. Wheat yields in eastern New York declined because of constant cropping and the infestation of Hessian fly, smut, and grasshoppers. The completion of the Erie Canal to Rochester in 1823 speedily shifted the center of wheat production to the Genesee Valley, which became known as the Granary of America. Meanwhile animal husbandry was making headway, if only because of the excellent pastures and meadows. Butter making developed in Orange County; Herkimer County specialized in cheese. Sheep raising received a boost when Chancellor Robert Livingston put imported Merino rams on display. The rams rapidly improved the wool of the stunted native sheep, and the wool found a ready market in the textile mills of Dutchess and Oneida counties.

Livingston estimated that the average farm in 1813 had eight horses or four horses and an equal number of oxen. In addition the farm had about 10 cows and 6 yearlings, and 25 sheep and swine. One must figure into the real income of farm families the value of foodstuffs, clothing, and tools created by members. Equally important was the formation of capital goods such as barns, fences, houses, and cleared land.

Above: This detailed Plan of the City of New York *was engraved by P.R. Maverick around 1798. The city's natural and protected harbor, located strategically between Maine and Florida, helped to propel her to preeminence in American commerce. Courtesy, Prints Division, The New York Public Library*

Above: This domestic scene from the Alexander Anderson Scrap Book *shows daily life before the industrial revolution. At the dawn of the nineteenth century home and work were inseparable for most families. Courtesy, Prints Division, The New York Public Library*

Above, left: Robert Livingston was one of many politically prominent figures to be painted by Ezra Ames. Livingston accompanied James Monroe, at the behest of Thomas Jefferson in 1803, to France to buy the port of New Orleans. The mission resulted in the purchase of the entire Louisiana Territory. Courtesy, Albany Institute of History & Art

The general level of agriculture was low: farmers burned trees and wore out their fields. The shortage of labor drove them to exploit the ample resources of timber and soil. A few gentlemen farmers who read about the scientific agriculture in England began to experiment with new crops and adopt improvements such as fertilizing their fields. Even the most retrograde farmer had to admit that treating fields with gypsum (lime) and planting clover produced startling yields. Robert Livingston and Elkanah Watson publicized new agricultural methods at fairs and meetings of agricultural societies. Watson helped found scores of county agricultural societies that sponsored fairs where men and women could compete for prizes for the best sheep, potatoes, and quilts. Jethro Wood invented the cast-iron plow, which soon outmoded the wooden plow. Despite these changes most farmers continued their slovenly practices.

The imperial reach of New York City stretched across the high seas and far into the interior. Many factors contributed to the rise of the seaport to primacy by 1815 and, a decade later, to unrivaled supremacy. First of all, Manhattan merchants captured a large portion of the coastal trade, which naturally gravitated to its splendid harbor, strategically located midway between Maine and Florida. Shippers showed enterprise in getting a stranglehold on the cotton export trade, the most important in the nineteenth century. Ships sailed from Charleston, Savannah, and New Orleans for Liverpool and other European ports, and they often returned to New York with cargoes of textiles, hardware, and luxuries for wholesale houses. The vessels, generally owned by New Yorkers, would take some imports and other goods to their Southern customers before once again carrying cotton to Europe. Much cotton came directly to New York before reshipment to New England, upstate, or Europe. The remarkable growth of the upstate hinterland before the completion of the Erie Canal enriched hundreds of businessmen. Of course the canal greatly enlarged this area to include the states bordering the Great Lakes.

New Yorkers also seized a gargantuan share of the transatlantic trade. In fact, over half of all imports, measured by value, reached this nation through New York Harbor during the century following 1815. New York prices were generally the lowest, because of low shipping charges, cheap credit, and the auction law requiring all goods up for sale to go to the highest bidder. New York also offered the best services: frequent sailings, marine insurance, and plenty of cheap labor. New York City gradually elbowed Philadelphia aside as the nation's financial capital with such developments as the opening of the New York Stock Exchange in 1817. Moreover, the thousands of immigrants from New England stimulated all phases of its mercantile, shipping, and financial life.

This engraving by M. Dubourg, after a sketch by J. Milbert, shows a Methodist Camp meeting in a dense oak forest. People traveled great distances to attend the meeting, bringing beds, essential household utensils, and large pieces of canvas for tents. The meeting lasted one month. Courtesy, The New-York Historical Society, New York City

At first glance we tend to dismiss a village of 500 as unimportant economically. Multiply that village by several hundred and we have impressive numbers. Most villages in microcosm provided the same functions as the metropolis. Townspeople in Canandaigua, the largest village west of Utica between 1800 and 1820, were part of the commercial nexus linking them with New York and even London. In 1811 Canandaigua had 120 handsome houses around its square and boasted an academy and courthouse. Visitors could patronize six stores, six taverns, two tanning yards, two distilleries, six doctors, and six lawyers. Only Schenectady received a city charter (1798), joining Albany and New York as a city.

Prior to 1830 craftsmen made their products by hand with the assistance of power by wind, water, or animals. The apprenticeship system for training the young to become master workmen broke down because of the influx of immigrants, the division of work into simple operations, and court decisions against unions. The shift from hand tools to complex powered machinery

Officially opened in 1795, Union College is one of the nation's oldest institutions of higher education. Situated on the Mohawk River in Schenectady, Union owed its founding to popular agitation for higher education during the early years of the republic. Courtesy, Prints Division, The New York Public Library

had emerged in England but developed slowly. As late as 1820 only 10,000 persons worked in factories in New York State. Tiny textile mills sprang up along streams in central New York, and a cluster of gristmills crowded the Genesee River in Rochester.

Pioneers and their families had more time for church, school, and cultural activities after the first decade of frontier living. The overwhelming majority had a Protestant background, although only a minority belonged to churches. In 1825 New York City had only 3 Roman Catholic churches, compared with Presbyterians with 22, Episcopalians with 18, Baptists with 14, and Methodists and Dutch Reformed with 13 each. The Methodists and Baptists, who preached at every crossroads and street corner, made the largest gains, but their churches were often small congregations.

Governor John Jay pushed for the passage of more lenient laws in regard to the punishment of criminals. The legislature ended the whipping of criminals and reduced the number of capital crimes to three. Prisons were scandalous institutions where hardened criminals mixed with youthful offenders, the mentally ill, and indigent men and women of every age all crammed into close quarters. Thomas Eddy, a Quaker businessman, advocated prison reforms as well as free schools for children. In 1816 the state built a prison at Auburn where each prisoner had a separate cell. During the daylight hours prisoners worked in silence with other prisoners. In 1824 the New York House of Refuge was established, the first reformatory in the United States.

The Revolutionary War disorganized the weak educational system of colonial New York. In 1782 the prospect of imminent peace prompted Governor Clinton to recommend a University of the State of New York under the direction of a Board of Regents. It supervised the entire educational field and approved the establishment of secondary schools and colleges. The Regents advocated a public school system to the legislature, but progress was slow. Nevertheless, by 1799 it had established 1,352 grammar schools, educating about 60,000 students. Churches and reformers also encouraged the formation of schools. In 1805 Thomas Eddy organized the Free School Society in New York City, which enrolled more than 5,000 students in the next two decades.

The school-district law of 1812 was a seminal act that enabled New York State to catch up with New England. Appropriately, it was a transplanted Yankee, Gideon Hawley, who traversed the state tirelessly encouraging rural neighborhoods to set up district schools. Each district elected three trustees to build a school, hire a teacher, and collect taxes. By 1828 some 442,000 children were attending schools in 8,298 districts.

A later age has cast a rosy glow around the little red schoolhouse. Obviously thousands, even tens of thousands of youngsters learned how to read, write, and do sums. A few graduates attended academies and colleges, becoming ministers, lawyers, doctors, and teachers. A closer look reveals that the usual schoolhouse was a shabby building with no blackboards, books, or even toilets. Moreover, the teachers were often inexperienced young people and sometimes cruel masters who had to handle children of every age.

The few who pursued their education beyond the elementary level attended academies in the larger villages and towns. Here they could study the Latin and Greek necessary for college entrance, modern languages, English literature, and natural sciences. A handful entered college, probably half of them planning to enter the ministry. Columbia College emerged from the chrysalis of King's College. Union College in Schenectady received its charter in 1795; Hamilton, in 1812; Hobart, in 1824. The influx of New Englanders meant that New York attracted many graduates of Harvard, Yale, Brown, and other colleges.

New York State assumed national leadership in literature during the first quarter of the nineteenth century because of the talent of Washington Irving and James Fenimore Cooper. Irving quarried colonial folklore and left us memorable characters such as Ichabod Crane and Rip Van Winkle. Cooper mixed social criticism into his stirring tales of pioneering. His characters Natty Bumppo, woodsman, and Uncas, Indian chief, gave European readers their image of American frontier and Indian life. More realistic in his depiction of American life was James Kirke Paulding, who also displayed a virulent nationalism.

New Yorkers, notably Hamilton and Jay, enjoyed high office under President Washington, and in 1795 the Federalists elected their candidate, Jay, as governor. Jay proved to be an efficient administrator, but the Anti-Federalists disliked his stand against France, whose slogan of liberty, equality, and fraternity disturbed good conservatives. When the Federalists in Congress passed the Sedition Act making it a crime to write anything critical of Congress or the president, Jedediah Peck, Otsego County farmer, attacked the law as violating the Bill of Rights. Judge William Cooper, a staunch Federalist, put Peck in jail, arousing a storm of protest. Peck won his release.

The Anti-Federalists rallied behind Thomas Jefferson in the campaign of 1800 and in the next year put George Clinton back in the governor's chair for his seventh term. The Anti-Federalists began to call themselves Democratic Republicans, a title that in a few years was shortened to Democrats. Meanwhile Aaron Burr, a political foe of Hamilton, challenged him to a duel, claiming that Hamilton had blackened his character. Near Weehawken, New Jersey, on July 11, 1804, Burr shot and killed Hamilton.

Daniel D. Tompkins replaced Clinton as leader of the Democratic-Republicans. He became governor in 1807 and held that office until 1817, a period in which the United States conducted trade embargoes against Great Britain and entered the War of 1812. An ardent patriot, Tompkins organized and financed the militia despite the lukewarm support of the Federalists.

New York had the dubious distinction of providing the battlefields and inland waters for more military engagements than any other state. Both sides conducted raids on each other, the Americans burning York (Toronto) and the British burning Buffalo. In 1814 the militia invaded Canada, inflicting heavy losses on the British at Lundy's Lane west of Niagara Falls. Temporary peace in Europe in 1814 permitted the British to dispatch 10,000 professional soldiers to Montreal for an invasion along Lake Champlain. Facing them were 1,500 militiamen and a fleet of 14 gunboats under the command of Captain Thomas Macdonough. Macdonough skillfully swung his vessels back and forth in order to bring both sets of guns to bear on the British ships. After hours of battle the British withdrew, leaving several ships adrift. The invading army retreated to Montreal.

The Federalist party had split into warring factions, one of which joined the Democratic group backing De Witt Clinton for governor. His smashing victory enabled him to push the Erie Canal, but his arrogant behavior offended so many individuals that he did not dare to run for a third term in 1822. But when Martin Van Buren and his allies forced Clinton off the canal board, a firestorm swept the state. Taking advantage of this outcry, Clinton ran again in 1824 and won, a victory allowing him to preside over the opening of the canal.

James Fenimore Cooper was born in New Jersey in 1789, and lived in New York State for most of his life. Cooper distinguished himself as a novelist, historian, and social critic. Although he never completed his education, having been expelled from Yale for some impropriety, it does not seem to have deterred him from creating the first authentic American literature. Courtesy, New York State Library

The Code Duello

Dueling became popular during the first third of the 19th century. It appealed to the upper class, which was becoming alarmed by the great amount of violence that took place not only on the frontier but also on the streets of New York. Philip Hone, mayor of New York, reported seeing William Cullen Bryant, the poet of peaceful pastoral scenes, horsewhip a rival on the street. Upstaters also settled arguments with fisticuffs. In 1799 William Cooper pummeled a political rival, James Cochran. Ten years later, Cooper, it was rumored, met his death as a result of a scuffle outside Lewis' Tavern in Albany.

Nearly everyone has heard of the duel between Alexander Hamilton and Aaron Burr, men of national stature. Few have heard that De Witt Clinton, the father of the Erie Canal, likewise engaged in a duel with John Swartwout, Burr's henchman. Both were political rivals, and when Clinton called Swartwout "a liar, a scoundrel and a villain," he received a challenge. Clinton accepted, and the duelists fired three times without injury. After each ex-change the second asked Swartwout, "Are you satisfied?" Each time Swartwout said no and insisted on an apology. On the fourth exchange Clinton wounded his challenger in the right leg, which required the attending surgeon to take out the ball.

Clinton offered to shake hands, but Swartwout refused. On the fifth exchange Clinton wounded his foe in the left leg, but Swartwout insisted on continuing. Clinton walked away without apologizing.

The death of Hamilton shocked New Yorkers and other Americans. In Albany Eliphalet Nott, a Presbyterian minister, mounted the pulpit of the North Dutch Church and charged that his listeners, like other citizens, were guilty of Hamilton's death. Solemnly he declared, "I cannot forgive you, my brethren, who till this late hour have been silent whilst successive murders were committed." His indictment included ministers, public prosecutors, judges, governors, and the public. The sermon had tremendous impact and elevated Nott to national prominence. It led to his selection as president of Union College in Schenectady, a post he held for 62 years, the longest tenure of any college president in American history. The wide dissemina-

DeWitt Clinton was the youngest politician of the Clinton family to reach considerable acclaim as a mayor of the City of New York, and as the governor of the state in 1816. It was under his governorship that the legislature was convinced to vote to build the Erie Canal with taxpayer money. Ezra Ames painted this portrait of Clinton in 1818. Courtesy, Albany Institute of History & Art

tion of Nott's sermon pressed jurors and judges to enforce the new antidueling law of 1803, which held all participants, including seconds and surgeons, guilty of murder if a fatality resulted.

A large number of distinguished citizens met in Albany in 1821 to consider a revision of the constitution. Chancellor James Kent led a company of diehard Federalists who opposed granting the vote to more citizens. Militant Democrats, however, wanted universal manhood suffrage. Martin Van Buren, who led the largest delegation of Democratic-Republicans, steered a middle course, urging that owners of personal property and freeholders should vote. Van Buren's allies won, and the result was that 84 percent of adult white males could vote for governor, roughly doubling the suffrage. Blacks had to meet higher property qualifications, however.

The maze of factional feuding and personality rivalries in New York politics has baffled observers. In addition eruptions of ideology and reform have complicated political developments. In 1826 a whirlwind of Anti-Masonic feeling swept the western part of the state because many believed that the fraternal order had caused the murder of William Morgan, a printer who had written an expose. This third party won several seats in the assembly and attacked the Albany Regency, a label pasted on Van Buren and his allies, as a conspiracy against the public. Thurlow Weed, a Rochester publisher, saw that if he could combine the Anti-Masons and the National Republicans, he could unseat Van Buren. Weed failed in his early effort to upset Van Buren and Andrew Jackson, who were running for governor and president in 1828, but he later helped

organize the Whig party and still later the Republican party. Hardly had Van Buren taken the oath of office as governor when Andrew Jackson invited him to become secretary of state. Van Buren accepted and climbed another rung on the political ladder in his successful quest to become the first New Yorker to win the presidency.

Meanwhile, New York had taken steps to end slavery, the Federalists pushing through a law in 1799 providing for gradual emancipation. The act of 1817 declared that every Negro born before July 4, 1799, should be free after July 4, 1827.

New Yorkers could look back with pride upon their achievements in many fields of activity. The pioneers conquered the wilderness and transformed large portions of the state into a smiling countryside of freeholding farmers. Entrepreneurs and politicians built a network of turnpikes and that miracle of the age, the Erie Canal. Merchants in the seaport and their upstate allies captured the lion's share of the coastal and transatlantic trade as well as a stranglehold on the two largest exports, cotton and wheat. They had formed parties and produced political leaders of national stature.

If these accomplishments arose primarily from the business acumen and political skill of citizens, other achievements bespoke humanitarian and cultural concerns: the end of slavery and the education of thousands of children. In short they were seeking to establish a democratic commonwealth in which the liberal principles of the Revolution would come to fruition.

Left: John Jacob Astor was born in Germany in 1763. He made a fortune as an immigrant fur trader and died the richest man in America in 1848. Astor also left his mark by contributing to social and cultural causes to improve the lives of the city's poor. His special projects included the Children's Aid Society, for which he founded training schools for indigent boys, and various free public libraries. Courtesy, New York State Library

Facing page: Stephen Van Rensselaer III served as a general in the War of 1812. His forces were defeated because a New York militia group refused to cross out of state. This was a continuing problem in the war, when it was never possible to field the requisite number of men in an all-out national effort to win a victory. Gilbert Stuart painted this portrait in 1795. Courtesy, Albany Institute of History & Art

GROWTH, REFORM, AND CONTROVERSIES 1830-1860

The transformation of New York from an 18th century to a 19th century society was accomplished largely during the period from 1830 to 1860. An explosive urbanization took place, accompanied by the most massive influx of immigrants in state history. Furthermore, a new class structure was emerging. Whereas the merchant, artisan, and farmer were the most characteristic citizens in 1830, three decades later the railroad promoter (Erastus Corning) and financier (J.P. Morgan) rivaled the merchant, while workers, male and female, had almost submerged the class of artisans.

In 1830 wealthy merchants and their allies dominated not only the economy but also the political system, which actually had no formal organization. Local parties mouthed the debates between Democrats and Whigs in Congress. By the Civil War the merchant elite had retreated from local government, where the boss or career politician was emerging as kingpin and local issues had become paramount. Meanwhile, city and local governments had taken over the functions of fire fighting, policing, education, and charity, which previously had been handled by private charity, volunteer organizations, and civic service such as working on roads.

The fairly homogeneous population of 1830 shared a consensus as to the proper role of government. For example, few disputed that one of the functions of government was to assist economic developments such as the Erie Canal and aid other transportation enterprises. After 1830, new ideas as well as more than a million immigrants had arrived in the state, including advocates of Adam Smith's laissez-faire doctrine but also exponents of socialism.

The Catholic majority in many cities had somewhat different goals than the Protestants in the countryside. Workers displayed class consciousness, organized unions, and demanded the 10-hour day, all anathema to entrepreneurs. When old Knickerbocker families were not making snide comments about the *nouveau riche,* they expressed shock at the uncouth behavior of Irish mobs brawling in the streets. The rise of political machines disturbed members of the old aristocracy. In 1857 George Templeton Strong confided to his diary, "Heaven be praised for all its mercies. The legislature of the state of New York has adjourned." Despite these antagonistic forces, the Empire State lurched forward, becoming an essential building block in the progress of the United States.

The Empire State doubled its 1830 population (1,913,131) in the next three decades, keeping

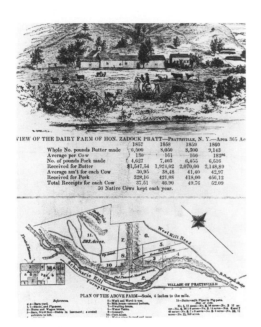

VIEW OF THE DAIRY FARM OF HON. ZADOCK PRATT—Prattsville, N. Y.—Area 365 Ac

Above: Zadock Pratt hoped to sell his 365- acre farm by circulating this broadside in around 1860. Courtesy, The New-York Historical Society, New York City

Above, right: This engraving of Wall Street in 1832 by C. Burton appeared in the New York Mirror. *Among the banks and insurance companies that lined the street were the Bank of America, Dry Dock Bank, The Bank of New York, and the New York Insurance Company. Courtesy, The New-York Historical Society, New York City*

Page 74: Wall Street, half past two o'clock October 13, 1857, by James H. Cafferty and Charles B. Rosenberg, portrays the panic which ensued on Wall Street after banks suspended specie payments. Commodore Vanderbilt is shown in the center wearing a light coat. Courtesy, Museum of the City of New York

pace with the national increase. This growth was all the more remarkable because New York was losing hundreds of thousands of its residents. In 1860, 867,032 former New Yorkers were living in other states, especially those bordering the Great Lakes.

Metropolitan New York—the five counties that were to make up Greater New York in 1898—contained more than a quarter of the state population, but residents in "new New York," the area west of Rome, totaled about half of the population. Furthermore the urban corridor—Manhattan, Albany, Buffalo—had attracted three out of four inhabitants. By 1860 metropolitan New York rivaled London and Paris as a commercial and financial center. New York County with 814,000 people and Brooklyn with another 267,000 formed the inner core of the seaport, the meeting place for the three major trade routes: North Atlantic, coastal, and Hudson-Erie Canal.

The second urban cluster centered in Albany, state capital but also terminus for steamboats, a canal, and railroads. Albany leaders looked with alarm at the brash tactics of those from Troy who challenged Albany (62,367) for control of the canal traffic from the west and north and sought its rail connections up the Mohawk Valley, east to New England, and down to New York City. Schenectady lagged far behind Albany and Troy, because it lost its position as entrepot for traffic coming down the Mohawk River, as the canal boats passed by the warehouses of the old Dutch river port. To be sure, its leaders did bid for railroad business to Albany, Saratoga, and the West; however, through trains treated Schenectady as another way station.

Rochester, Syracuse, and Utica became important regional markets but secured only a fraction of canal and railroad freight passing east and west. Each city also began to develop a manufacturing base: Rochester in flour milling; Syracuse in preparing salt for market; Utica in textiles. The river ports on the west shore of the Hudson—Newburgh, Catskill—lost momentum after their turnpike links to the interior withered into local roads. Kingston, terminus of the Delaware and Hudson Canal after 1828, brought Pennsylvania coal to markets such as steel mills in Troy. Villages on the east shore grew slowly as regional centers, but Hudson, founded by Nantucket whalers, continued to send its vessels all the way to the Antarctic and the Bering Sea.

Citizens in the Southern Tier of counties bordering Pennsylvania complained of neglect and demanded state aid for canal connections and for a railroad line from the Hudson River to Lake Erie. The Erie Railroad, which had opened its line to Dunkirk by 1851, did not make Binghamton and Elmira into major cities. Turnpike centers away from the canal—Batavia, Bath,

Cazenovia, Geneva, Canandaigua—made valiant efforts to secure rail connections, only to find that the lucrative freight traffic from the interior was passing them by. The hinterlands of northern centers such as Watertown and Ogdensburg expanded slowly, but Oswego grew fairly rapidly, because its flour mills attracted wheat shipments passing through the Welland Canal and then using the Oswego Canal to Syracuse.

Heavy immigration of young adults from northwestern Europe accounted for most of the population growth. Many newcomers brought their children with them and encouraged relatives to settle in America. Offsetting this massive increase was the rising death rate, especially in New York City and other urban centers where cholera, tuberculosis, and children's diseases struck with deadly force upon immigrant families living in cramped quarters lacking sanitary facilities. Sharing their poverty and high rate of illness were the blacks, who had received emancipation in New York State by 1828 only to face increasing competition for jobs on the wharves and as domestics from the flood of Irish immigrants.

Above: The Mohawk and Hudson River Railroad was the nation's first, running from Albany to Schenectady. Courtesy, Albany Institute of History & Art, gift of Vera Adams Carver

Left: The design motifs on this Franklin type stove indicate that it was probably made in Pennsylvania or New Jersey, although the marking on it says Albany. It was used for heating and was manufactured around 1820. Courtesy, Albany Institute of History & Art, Institute Purchase

Above: Rich deposits of lead were found in Rossie on the Parish family's land. The early yield of the mines was very rich. However, expenses were very high and the mines ceased operation in about 1840. Shown here is a picture of a working mine as drawn by Salathiel Ellis. Courtesy, The New-York Historical Society, New York City

Below, right: David Parish acquired some 200,000 acres of land in Jefferson and St. Lawrence counties in 1808. During the next fifty years, his family developed the property. In 1838 artist Salathiel Ellis was commissioned to draw a set of views of their property and enterprises. Shown here is a view of the blast furnace. Courtesy, The New-York Historical Society, New York City

Below: The S-shaped columns on the middle section of this four-column parlor stove are an adaption of contemporary furniture designs that were popular in the 1840s. Courtesy, Albany Institute of History & Art, Institute Purchase

Immigrants transformed cities, predominantly composed of native stock as late as 1830, into "foreign cities" in which the foreign born listed in the census of 1855 constituted a majority in New York City, Albany, and Buffalo. The other canal cities had almost as large a proportion of their inhabitants born abroad. The Irish formed the largest group in New York City and Albany, but the Germans outnumbered them in Rochester and Buffalo. The latter city had 30,000 Germans in its population of 74,000 in 1855.

Many Irish were tenants on the estates of English landlords, but an even greater number were landless laborers called cotters. In 1845 a blight in Ireland struck the potato plants, the chief source of food. Tens of thousands starved during the next five years, and disease took an even greater number suffering from malnutrition. News spread through the countryside that in America men could find work digging canals and laying railroad ties, and Irish girls could become servants in the houses of wealthy residents.

The Irish backed their clergy and political allies when Protestants attacked the Roman Catholic church and citizens complained about Irish violence. American workmen charged that the immigrants undercut their wages. The Irish, who had already learned political skills in their successful campaign for Catholic emancipation in Ireland, joined the Democratic party, which had welcomed immigrants as voters. The Irish regarded the Whigs and later the Republicans with suspicion because of their nativist attitude, their flirtation with prohibition and abolition, and their aristocratic leadership.

The German immigration swelled in the 1850s until it came close to the Irish flood. Poor crops, high birth rates, and conscription of young men stimulated emigration. When Germans heard about political freedom and economic opportunities in the United States, they made their way to seaports to take passage to New York. Many Germans had important skills, whether in making pianos (Steinway) or instruments (Bausch) or operating breweries. Among the Germans were several thousand Jews, who soon entered retailing, the manufacture of clothing, and the professions.

If the larger cities became crowded with Irish, German, and British immigrants, the countryside remained a stronghold of the old native stock. The descendants of New Englanders and the colonial population gradually forgot their earlier differences and formed a common front against the new urban culture, especially that emerging in the metropolis. Actually many immigrants and particularly their children were becoming "Americanized" with rapidity. The school, workplace, newspapers, political rallies, sports, and recreation kept eroding the nationality consciousness of newcomers. In fact Irish-Americanism was emerging, an ethnic subculture quite different from that in Ireland but not identical with old-line Americanism. Signs reading "No

Irish Need Apply" and attacks on the Irish as priest-ridden, violent, and ignorant slowed the progress of assimilation.

Urban-rural tension was matched in many cities by the clash between middle-class Protestants and working-class Catholics over the observance of the Sabbath, the regulation of drinking, and the level of education. Many workers resented Protestant control of banks and factories, their claims to higher offices in government, and their thinly veiled disdain for the newcomers. The sharpest cleavage grew up between metropolitan New York and upstate, each feuding over apportionment of legislative seats, taxation, and licensing of beverages. Of course, immigrants had their own internecine quarrels. German Roman Catholics did not like to take orders from Irish bishops. Immigrants from England, Scotland, and Wales who inherited a distaste for Irish troublemakers in the Old Country followed the lead of the native-stock Americans who welcomed them as allies against the Irish and Germans. On the other hand, some American-born workers hated their poor conditions and the arrogance of some employers so much that they identified with workers no matter what their origin.

Improvements in New York's transportation, already the envy of other states, guaranteed the cheapest rates and the most diversified service on land and water. The golden age of sail, steamboats, and canal boats, however, was clearly on the wane as the iron horse and the iron steamships overtook their rivals.

On the high seas the wooden sailing vessels reigned supreme, despite the challenge of iron steamships beginning about mid-century. United States tonnage by 1860 exceeded 5.35 million tons, almost on a par with that of Great Britain, the mistress of the seas. American ships dominated the passenger traffic across the North Atlantic, the export trade in cotton and wheat, the import trade, and the "far trades" with California and the Far East. Mercantile houses near South Street in lower Manhattan handled most imports of cotton goods and woolens from England, lace and silk from France, and linens from Ireland. In New York Harbor the seasoned British steel industry undersold American iron and steel mills that found their best markets in railroads, bridges, and farm implements.

The East River yards, founded and operated by New Englanders, rivaled those fringing the shoreline from Maine to Cape Cod. In 1856 New Yorkers acclaimed the launching of the *Ocean Monarch*, registering 2,145 tons, the largest wooden ship afloat. The clipper ship, that remarkable combination of grace and utility, represented the epitome of the age of sail.

In fact America's love affair with the clipper ship handicapped this nation in the race for supremacy on the high seas, because the British, lacking ample supplies of timber, forged ahead in designing marine engines and constructed tramp steamers as well as liners.

The panic of 1857 ended a decade-long boom in American shipbuilding and ship operation. The boom was powered by the famous gold rush to California and the diversion of many British and French ships to the Black Sea during the Crimean War. Before there was time for the depression to end, the Civil War dealt a deadly blow to shipping by disrupting the export of cotton and unleashing Confederate raiders on the sea lanes. In desperation, hundreds of ship-owners shifted their registry to the British flag to avoid capture or destruction.

The canal era passed its peak in the 1850s, although the Civil War gave canal shippers a temporary boost in business. The spectacular success of the Erie Canal stimulated a rash of projects to link other regions to the main route. Even before the Erie opened in 1825, the legislature had authorized three canals: Champlain, Oswego, and Finger Lakes, each utilizing natural waterways in part. In addition a group of private investors built the Delaware and Hudson canal from Port Jervis, close by Pennsylvania coalfields, to Kingston, and by 1829 this canal was sending tons of coal to markets in New York and other cities.

During the 1830s each region sought a branch canal, and politicians vied with one another in logrolling projects through the legislature. After many surveys and much bickering over terminals, the state built the Black River Canal from Rome to Lyons Falls. This undertaking, begun in 1839 and completed in 1855, required the construction of 109 locks in 35 miles. Like most other branch canals, this one did not meet operating expenses (think of all those lock tenders), much less paying anything on the original cost. The Chemung Canal opened a channel from Seneca Lake to the Susquehanna River in the hope of diverting freight from the southern tier of counties. In 1833 the legislature authorized the Chenango Canal, to connect Binghamton with Utica. Four years later boats were carrying coal to central New York, and within the next decade Utica entrepreneurs decided to erect textile mills. The most audacious and economically the most questionable was the project from Rochester up the Genesee Valley to Olean on the Allegheny River. However, by the time of its completion the state found it useless to connect the canal with the river by locks, because Pennsylvania failed to make improvements in the river and, by 1851, rail service had become available.

Canal traffic kept increasing, but important shifts were taking place in the origin of freight and its composition. Prior to 1835 the Erie served producers within the state, but thereafter

This 1890 view of the Hudson River and the gentle hills in Greene County near Athens, New York, is the work of G.K. Nedwick. Nedwick was a German citizen who lived with his American wife and children in the area. Courtesy, Albany Institute of History & Art

an increasing amount of traffic originating west of Buffalo began to move over the Erie until 1847, when it passed that originating within the state. During the 1840s the speedy railroad trains had little trouble enticing passengers from the packets, which offered cramped quarters, voracious mosquitoes, and life-threatening low bridges. During the next decade trains captured almost all freight except eastbound lumber and wheat.

Canal policy or, more broadly speaking, internal improvements, aroused more controversy and inspired more rhetoric than the regulation of alcoholic beverages or the expansion of slavery. The Whigs ardently supported canals, the enlargement of the Erie to a depth of seven feet in 1835, and subsidies for railroads. Their leader, Samuel Ruggles, piloted a $40-million package through the legislature, only to see it founder during the near bankruptcy of the state during the depression following the panic of 1837. The Democrats divided over this issue, the Barn-burner wing demanding retrenchment, the Hunker wing supporting state aid. The Barnburners, (likened to farmers who burned their barns to get rid of rats), rode the wave of public disenchantment with expensive projects and placed in the new Constitution of 1846 severe limitations on expenditures unless approved by referenda. During the 1850s the Whigs and the Hunkers, (politicians accused of "hunkering" for patronage), devised legal end runs around these constitutional barriers.

A large number of vessels plied the waters of rivers and lakes. For example, 9,000-plus schooners, barks, brigantines, and brigs cleared the harbor of Buffalo in 1855. Shipping on Lake Ontario, although stimulated by the completion of the Welland Canal in 1831, trailed behind Lake Erie. The Hudson River won the admiration of even the most critical English visitors, who compared it favorably with the storied Rhine. Francis Trollope declared, "How I weep for my friends at home—they will never see it!" After the Supreme Court in its decision *Gibbons v. Ogden*

This painting by little known artist J.M. Evans depicts Poughkeepsie in about 1870 from a western point across the Hudson River. Courtesy, New York State Historical Association, Cooperstown

Above: This watercolor by J. Regan of a landing near Albany in about 1852 shows passengers and freight awaiting loading on the two-day boats for a trip to New York. With time to spare, some passengers stopped for a meal in the Weldon's House where James Weldon served oysters and other delectables. Courtesy, Albany Institute of History & Art, gift of Ledyard Cogswell, Jr.

Right: Brooklyn depended on its volunteer fire company beginning in 1785, until 1869, when the first professional fire company was formed. The development of pumping engines supplied the city with water for sanitation, fire, and domestic needs. Shown here is Fire Engine Company No. 13 in 1848. Courtesy, Brooklyn Historical Society, Print Collection

broke the Livingston steamboat monopoly, competition increased until the rival lines arranged agreements about fares and service. By 1840 more than 100 steamboats were making trips from New York to Albany every 24 hours, a few occasionally risking boiler explosions when captains challenged each other for the best times. The bulk of freight passed down the river on barges, rafts, and canal boats, some pushed by steamboats and tugs.

Long Island Sound likewise had its network of ferry boats and steamboats. A major development took place in 1847 when the Fall River Line opened service from New York to the Massachusetts port from which trains carried passengers to Boston.

Commodore Cornelius Vanderbilt earned his title during the Age of Sail and carried it over into the Golden Age of Railroads after 1860 when he secured control of the New York Central Railroad and increased his fortune made in shipping many times over. A Staten Island farm boy, Vanderbilt became a boatman, then a captain of a steamboat; he operated steamboats on the Hudson River and to the Isthmus of Nicaragua before he entered the railroad field—after the age of 65. The lad who quit school at the age of 11 amassed a fortune of more than $100 million.

New York kept its industrial supremacy, measured by value of output, number of workers, or diversity of production. The Empire State had three obvious advantages: a growing home market, a superb transportation system, and plenty of cheap labor. In addition it attracted skilled artisans such as shipbuilders from New England, furniture makers from Germany, and steelworkers from England. New York City had the greatest pool of capital of any U.S. city and good connections with the money kings of London. State and local governments were eager to assist with internal improvements for businessmen and favorable charters for corporations. More intangible but very significant was the business climate in which dynamic individuals could thrive and the accumulation of money was regarded with favor.

The shift of manufacture from the home or shop to the factory took place rather slowly and at a different pace in various branches of industry. As late as 1850 most goods were still made by hand, and only a few workers performed their work in factories. Quite often the key figure was the merchant who knew how to buy and sell products and learned how to organize

production. Sometimes he would take out to farm families cotton and wool for spinning and weaving.

The first factories appeared in the textile industry: tiny factories doing a single task such as carding wool. Gradually the factories grew larger, adopting more complicated machinery and steam engines powered by coal. Domestic manufacture—home crafts—was undercut by cheap factory-made goods, and after mid-century most farm housewives put their spinning wheels in the attic. These women did not get much of a rest, however, because most of them became dairymaids, churning butter and milking cows seven days a week.

The forges and furnaces gradually grew in size and complexity. By 1855 some 34,000 workers were making steel and iron products. Troy, for example, took second place only to Pittsburgh as a steel center. Henry Burden of Troy made a machine that produced a horseshoe every four seconds.

New York became the leading leather-producing state. The largest tanneries sprang up in the Catskills where tanners softened rawhides in vats of hemlock or oak bark. Hides were imported from South America as well as from the Western states and territories. The invention of the sewing machine speeded the rise of shoe and clothing industries.

The production of prepared foods and beverages—by slaughterhouses, breweries, distilleries, flour mills, and sugar refineries—led any other branch of manufacture in value. Sugar refineries clustered in New York Harbor, whereas saltmaking grew up around the salt springs near Syracuse. Flour milling centered at Rochester, but during the 1850s Buffalo began to challenge

Above: This cookstove was patented in 1852. It was fueled through a side door and had four boiling holes and a large cast iron oven. The stove was designed by foundry operator, Peter Clute, in Schenectady. Courtesy, Albany Institute of History & Art, Institute Purchase

Left: The newly invented sewing machine spurred the rapid development of factories to produce ready-made clothing. Shown here is W.S. & C.H. Thomson's, a skirt manufacturer. Courtesy, Library of Congress

its neighbor and, after the Civil War, to outstrip it. Every city had its slaughterhouses, but the largest ones arose near the largest markets: New York City, Buffalo, and Albany.

New York rivaled Pennsylvania in the production of lumber because of the fine stands of white pine in the Adirondacks, Catskills, and Alleghenies. Small sawmills sprang up along most streams and served the locality. Larger mills grew up in towns such as Glens Falls, Watertown, and Ogdensburg. Much of the Adirondack lumber reached Albany, where it was loaded on barges destined for New York City. The demand for lumber for homes, stores, factories, and railroads was insatiable, an appetite matched by that of steamboats and locomotives for fuel.

The status of artisans steadily deteriorated during this period, partly because of the influx of aliens, the breakdown of the apprentice system, and the invention of machinery. Furthermore employers fought unions in the courts and subdivided work into several minor operations that could be handled by women and children.

Workers tried to form unions and to secure a 10-hour day, but with modest success. Unions lacked skilled leaders, funds, and a unified work force. The recurrent panics led to high unemployment, which in turn caused workers to accept almost any wage.

Horace Greeley estimated that in 1845 better than two out of three New York City residents lived on hardly more than one dollar per week per person. The average laborer earned about $200 a year, and most working women earned less than two dollars a week. On the other hand, dozens of agencies, mostly private but some public, sought to take care of the needy and unfortunate.

Pauperism increased upstate as well as in the metropolis. Whereas in 1823 public poor relief was granted to 22,111 individuals, in 1855 the number had soared to 204,000, although population had only doubled. Most paupers lived in the cities and most were foreign born, two facts carefully noted by native-stock folk in the countryside.

Almost all counties had poorhouses set up under the report of the Yates Commission of 1824, the first comprehensive survey of poor relief in the nation. County government designed poorhouses in such a way that few individuals would apply for admission. A committee of

Above: The hop crop in New York was a significant product for many local and statewide breweries. Shown here is a depiction of hop-picking as drawn by Arthur Lumley in 1867. From Harper's Weekly, *1867*

Below: The Arba Read Steamer was the first engine in New York State, outside of New York City. It was delivered, ready for service, in May 1860. Courtesy, New York State Library

the state senate in 1856 described them as "badly-constructed, ill-arranged, ill-warmed and ill-ventilated, the rooms crowded with inmates; and the air, particularly in the sleeping departments, is very noxious, and to visitors, almost insufferable."

Few poorhouses had medical facilities, and they housed all types—men and women, young and old, diseased and healthy, sane and insane. The staff, overwhelmed by their problems and understaffed, neglected their charges. No wonder individuals believed that going to the poorhouse was probably a ticket to the cemetery.

Two societies, one rich and one poor, similar to those in England described by Charles Dickens, had also emerged in New York. Visitors hailed the progress, the mansions, theaters, and fancy restaurants of the metropolis; a few explored the teeming slums filled with criminals,

Below: The first Albany brewery was established in 1661. The brewery shown here, the Quinn and Nolan Ale Brewing Co., was in operation from 1845 to 1917. Courtesy, Albany Institute of History & Art

the downtrodden, and derelicts. Both portraits were true as far as they went. What they neglected to bring to the foreground was the growing middle class. Ambitious newcomers noted that American society did reward a considerable number who worked hard and chased the Almighty Dollar.

New York in 1830 was overwhelmingly Protestant in religious affiliation, but during the next three decades Roman Catholics increased rapidly and became the largest single group of Christians. One authority estimated that in New York City in 1855 approximately 45 percent of regular worshipers were Catholics, a figure that was not much lower in the larger cities upstate. The countryside, however, remained a stronghold of evangelical Protestants, who also enrolled most of the urban middle and upper classes.

Most Protestants belonged to seven denominations: Methodist-Episcopal, Baptist, Presbyterian, Congregational, Protestant-Episcopal, Dutch Reformed, and Lutheran. All believed in the divinely inspired Bible, a moral law undergirding God's universe, and the duty of morally responsible individuals to perform good works. They approved of revivals as an acceptable means of transforming individuals from a state of sin to one of grace.

The "burned-over district" is the term generally applied to the region of central and western

Above: The King's County poorhouse was established in 1830 and by the 1850s consisted of the almshouse, hospital, and insane asylum. Later it became the county's major hospital. From Stiles, A History of King's County, Including Brooklyn, *1884*

Churches, like this Baptist church in Grafton shown here around 1890, were not only religious centers, but social centers as well. Courtesy, New York State Library

New York where religious enthusiasts converted tens of thousands of followers and spawned several new sects. The most significant development took place in Oneida County in 1825-1826, when a group of evangelists led by Charles Grandison Finney set in motion the most important religious awakening in the first half of the 19th century. Finney declared that the regeneration of the individual should and would lead to the reformation of society.

New York was also the birthplace of many new religions. Joseph Smith of Palmyra founded the Church of Jesus Christ of Latter-day Saints (Mormons), which today has millions of members throughout the world. Smith asserted that the angel Moroni told him to dig up the Golden Plates of a new Bible, the Book of Mormon, which described the history of America from its settlement by one of the tribes that wandered away from the Tower of Babel.

William Miller of Hampton in Washington County preached his message that the world was coming to an end. Thousands of followers waited expectantly in 1843 for the final hour of doom. Nothing happened. Miller's followers, however, regrouped and formed the Adventist churches, one worshiping on Sunday, the other on Saturday, the seventh day of creation. Near Rochester in the village of Hydeville two young girls, Margaret and Kate Fox, reported that they could hear noises at night and that they had held communications with the dead by snapping their fingers. Although the girls later confessed that they had been fooling everyone, thousands of Americans and English remained convinced that they could receive messages from the dead by means of mediums. The Spiritualist movement attracted tens of thousands of followers in the 1850s and impressed scores of individuals, such as Horace Greeley, in educated circles. Lily

Dale, a camp meeting ground in Chautauqua County, remains the headquarters of the Spiritualist movement.

In 1848 John Humphrey Noyes moved from Putney, Vermont, to Oneida in central New York, where he established a community famous throughout the western world for its experiment in communal living. Asserting they were living in a state of perfection and therefore without sin, the followers of Noyes shared property, work, and sexual partners. The community disbanded after 30 years because of outside criticisms, internal dissent, and the failing powers of Noyes.

Individuals and communities suffered from many evils, among them intemperance, poverty, inequality of women, and the like. The evangelists attacked Demon Rum, an obvious threat to health, family stability, and community welfare. They organized hundreds of local societies whose members pledged themselves to avoid drunkenness and some to abstain from all alcoholic beverages. Temperance advocates turned to local and state governments, asking them to regulate the sale of beverages by higher license fees and, in the 1850s, by prohibition. Horace Greeley

Above: Born in New Hampshire in 1811, Horace Greeley was a renowned newspaper editor and social reformer. In 1872 he was defeated for the presidency when he ran against Ulysses S. Grant. Courtesy, New York State

Left: Built in the 1820s, Sing Sing was a fearsome name to New York's underworld. Guards at the 1,000-cell fortress enforced severe discipline in the cells, at various shops, and at the nearby marble quarries. A small women's prison with nearly 100 cells stood nearby. The quarters for prison staff were all done in marble. Courtesy, New York State Library

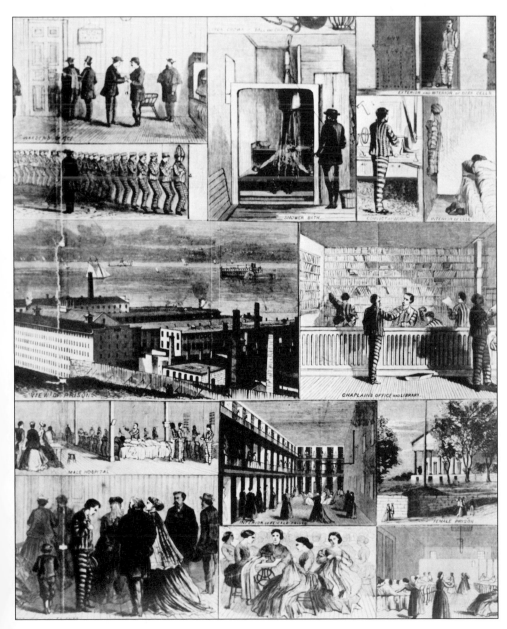

Above: In 1839 Gerrit Smith helped organize the Liberty Party, formed by moderate abolitionists loyal to the Union, and opposed to secession. The party played a pivotal role in the elections of 1844 and 1848. In 1859 Smith supported John Brown's plan to instigate a slave rebellion in Virginia, a plan which led to disaster for Brown and the nation, presaging the Civil War that enveloped the nation two years later. Courtesy, New York State Library

Above, right: Columbia University was founded as King's College in 1754. Despite its close affiliation to Trinity Church (its first class of eight students met in the church's schoolyard), the school mandated freedom of religion for faculty and students. Columbia moved to its present site on the Morningside campus in 1897. Courtesy, New York State Library

Above: Medical school was an unattainable dream for women before the middle of the nineteenth century. The first American woman to break the barrier for medical training and practice was Elizabeth Blackwell. She began practicing in a dispensary facing Tomkins Square Park in New York City, and later moved to 3rd Street. The New York infirmary and medical college for women evolved from her efforts. Courtesy, Library of Congress

and the Whigs pushed through a prohibition law in 1855, but the residents of the large cities, particularly Irish and German immigrants, openly defied this statute, which was declared unconstitutional in 1933. Temperance won many converts, and a number of local governments placed some restrictions on the sale of beverages.

New Yorkers took an active role in the fight for women's rights. Elizabeth Cady Stanton and Susan B. Anthony became famous throughout the country for their crusade for equal rights. Stanton helped organize the famous convention at Seneca Falls in July 1848 when the delegates drew up their list of grievances. At first these resolutions and agitation aroused much scorn and derision.

Children hooted and chanted refrains when women appeared in public wearing bloomers, a costume designed by Elizabeth Smith Miller, daughter of the famous abolitionist Gerrit Smith. Although the women had no success in winning the vote, they did secure the "Earnings Bill" of 1860, which legalized married women's right to the property they had inherited or earned. Moreover, wives were to receive a life interest in one-third of the real estate upon the death of their husbands in the state.

A handful of women pioneered in education and the professions. Elmira College in 1855 and Vassar a decade later opened their doors to women exclusively. Cornell University in 1865 became the first collegiate institution to admit men and women. Elizabeth Blackwell received her degree at the Geneva medical college and became the first woman to practice medicine in the country.

Central New Yorkers took a leading role in the fight to limit and abolish slavery. The Oneida Institution of Arts and Sciences in Whitesboro not only had the first student antislavery society but also welcomed more than a score of blacks as students. In 1835 Utica hosted the first state antislavery society, a meeting that shocked and enraged the establishment figures in the city, who chased the delegates from the church in which they were meeting. The delegates adjourned to the home of Gerrit Smith, who lived some 30 miles west of Utica. Abolitionists as such attracted a very small following, but they did influence a much larger group to oppose the expansion of slavery. The Free Soil party in 1848 nominated ex-President Martin Van Buren for president and split the Democratic vote, thus depriving that party of its usual victory. The crusaders managed to create a vigorous antislavery faction in both parties, and the new Republican party endorsed the stand of no expansion of slavery in the territories.

The foes of slavery kept the issue before the public by petitions to Congress, meetings, and journals, and by obstructing federal officials who were returning fugitive slaves. A stirring incident took place in Syracuse in 1851 when a mob took Jerry McHenry, a runaway slave, from a jail where the federal marshal had put him behind bars. The Reverend Samuel May, a Unitarian minister, and Gerrit Smith helped organize the Jerry Rescue. Jerry was spirited away to Canada, moving from station to station on the Underground Railroad.

Many New Yorkers took steps to aid criminals, the mentally ill, the blind, and the needy. More popular was the crusade for free public schools. Parents had to pay tuition, usually a small fee, to the district school, which received most of its support from the neighborhood and small grants from the state. Parents could avoid this fee if they signed a pauper's oath, but many families had too much pride to sign it. Furthermore some parents kept their children at home, because they needed their help on the farm or their earnings in the store or on the street. Reform-

Above: Bellevue opened in 1815 as an almshouse and penitentiary as well as a hospital. Paupers and prisoners were moved to Blackwell's Island in 1848, and in 1861 the hospital opened a medical college. Courtesy, General Research Division, The New York Public Library

Left: New Yorker Martin Van Buren served as Andrew Jackson's vice president, and as his successor beat a field of four political opponents in the election of 1836. Unfortunately for Van Buren, the financial panic of 1837 was blamed on him and cut short a promising political career. He was defeated for the presidency in 1840. Courtesy, Albany Institute of History & Art

Below: In the nineteenth century it was thought that small children did not need much attention. It was not unusual for a class of nearly one hundred six- and seven-year olds to be "taught" in one room. Courtesy, The New-York Historical Society, New York City

The *Caroline* Affair and Alexander McLeod

Buffalo and Rochester newspapers in January 1838 printed sketches of an American ship, the *Caroline*, poised on the brink of Niagara Falls, its crew yelling in terror. The newspapers called for war with Great Britain, which they asserted had sent the crew to destruction. Actually the *Caroline* sank before reaching the falls. Furthermore, only one American, not the 22 reported in the Washington *National Intelligencer,* had died.

A group of Canadians organized a rebellion in 1837 led by William Lyon Mackenzie, a Scottish-born journalist. The rebels claimed that the royal governor had blocked the will of the people in the legislature. Many Americans shouted their approval of the rebels, who were following the example of the Sons of Liberty. Besides, some wanted revenge against Britain, whose forces a quarter century earlier had burned Buffalo in the War of 1812.

The rebellion fizzled out and Mackenzie fled to the safety of Buffalo, where he set up headquarters at the Eagle Tavern. President Martin Van Buren urged Americans to suspend judgment and remain neutral until his diplomats could determine the facts and make the proper protests. Mackenzie seized Navy Island, a tiny spot above the falls but on the Canadian side of the Niagara River. William Wells of Buffalo, the owner of the *Caroline,* took supplies and reinforcements to the small force of rebels.

The British sent a hand-picked group of men to row across the river and set the *Caroline* on fire. The body of Amos Durfee, a Buffalo resident, was found the next morning on the wharf. The 3,000 people following his funeral cortege believed that Durfee had been killed by the raiders.

Van Buren called a cabinet meeting and ordered General Winfield Scott to take charge of the local militia. Gradually tempers cooled and the diplomats took over. Most Americans turned to other issues such as the severe depression.

However, in 1840 Alexander McLeod, an obscure Canadian who had served as an undercover agent for a Canadian sheriff, visited Buffalo. There he wandered from bar to bar. The more he drank, the more he boasted about his exploits, including the sinking of the *Caroline.* Word reached the Erie County sheriff that a Canadian was bragging about how he killed a Yankee. The sheriff jailed McLeod and charged him with the murder of Durfee.

Once again an uproar shattered the calm on both sides of the Atlantic. President William Henry Harrison had hardly taken office and appointed Daniel Webster his secretary of state before the McLeod case came before him. Like Van Buren, he sought to cool the controversy. But John Henry Palmerston, the bellicose foreign secretary, ordered the British ambassador to leave Washington if New York convicted McLeod. Palmerston held McLeod was only following the orders of Colonel Allan MacNab and did not come under local or state courts.

Webster, who was known and respected among British officialdom, tried to shift the case to the Supreme Court, but Governor William Seward rejected the request. Seward, however, agreed to move the trial to Utica, away from the heated atmosphere of Lockport, the county seat of Niagara County. Only a handful of citizens attended the trial, despite the presence of distinguished counsel on both sides. Joshua Spencer, an able criminal lawyer who had been retained by Webster, produced witness after witness who testified that McLeod was miles away on the night of the murder. Spencer shattered the testimony of prosecution witnesses whose reputation for veracity was no better than McLeod's. In less than 20 minutes the jury found McLeod not guilty.

As a result of these incidents Congress passed a law transferring cases involving international affairs out of state courts. The two nations soon negotiated the Webster-Ashburton Treaty in order to settle the Maine border. McLeod? He received a hero's welcome in Canada but almost immediately vanished from sight. Since 1840 our relations with Canada have seldom been marred by serious disagreements.

ers called for free schooling as a basic right, but some taxpayers and conservatives dissented. The debate raged on for years, and though the advocates won a popular referendum in 1849, it was later repealed. Finally the legislature in 1867 provided free public education for all children, but parents could keep their children out of school.

The larger cities also supported free public high schools, which gradually replaced the earlier academies. Each religious denomination established a college where its young men could be trained for the clergy and professions. In addition professional schools sprang up to train doctors, lawyers, and ministers. West Point (1802) and Rensselaer Polytechnic Institute (1825) in Troy provided engineering training.

During this period New York led the nation in music, arts, and the theater, but New England

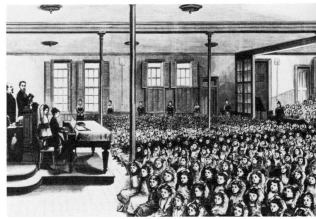

Left: The Catskill Mountain House was famous during the late nineteenth century as a scenic retreat and was a resort for landscape artists and people absorbed by the dramatic beauty of nature. It was described at the time of its greatest popularity as being "too near heaven!" Courtesy, New York State Library

Above: In the late nineteenth century, New York City school students were publicly examined annually. The results were used for evaluation of teachers and principals, in order to grant raises or tenure. This practice rapidly led to a rigid educational system, where the entire year was focused on rote memorization by hundreds of students for these annual exams. Courtesy, Library of Congress

Below: The one-room schoolhouse was a feature of many New York State towns well into the twentieth century. Shown here is the Grafton Center School around 1886. Wesley Howard was the teacher. Courtesy, New York State Library

dominated literature. Nevertheless two New York authors—Herman Melville and Walt Whitman—ranked with the best. Melville's books on the South Seas have won the acclaim of critics, although the general public found them difficult to understand. Whitman, a Long Island boy who worked as a carpenter, a teacher, and an editor, praised the common man in a style that was vigorous and fresh.

So many artists painted landscapes of the Catskills and the Hudson Valley that they became known as the Hudson River School. Thomas Cole and Fredrick Church, who moved to that region, enjoyed popular as well as critical praise.

Like most metropolitan centers New York attracted musical talents from many countries, with Germans and Italians the most numerous. Probably the most notable event was the tour of Jenny Lind, the "Swedish nightingale," who captivated thousands from Battery Park in Manhattan to Niagara Falls. In 1842 the Philharmonic Society of New York began to give symphony concerts.

*Above: Artist William Sidney Mount's favorite sub-
ject was rural life in Setauket and Stony Brook,
Long Island. This painting, done around 1840, is
titled* Eel Spearing at Setauket. *Courtesy, New York
State Historical Association, Cooperstown*

*Below: Thomas Cole is considered the father of the Hud-
son River school of painting. He was born in England in 1818 and emigrated to New York in 1825, moving from the city in 1826 to Catskill. Cole's pictures
are characterized by dramatic intensity and rich use
of color to delineate details of nature. Courtesy,
Albany Institute of History & Art*

Politics mirrored the turmoil caused by the expanding but volatile economy, the flood of
immigrants, the ferment of reform, and the rise of political machines. Martin Van Buren overshadowed other Democrats in the 1830s, becoming governor in 1829, vice-president in 1833,
and president in 1837. The Democrats continued their factionalism, however, one wing handing
out patronage and bank charters with abandon, the other extolling states' rights and retrenchment.
William Learned Marcy, senator and governor, expressed the viewpoint of the first group in
the memorable phrase " . . . to the victors belong the spoils of the enemy."

Meanwhile Thurlow Weed was assiduously melding together the remnants of the Anti-
Masonic party with the National Republicans, chiefly the followers of John Quincy Adams.
In 1834 this coalition took the name of Whigs, charging that "King" Andrew Jackson had
usurped executive power. Naturally the Whigs blamed the panic of 1837 upon the Democrats,
and the next year the Whigs elected William Seward as governor and two years later blocked
Van Buren's bid for another term in the White House. The Whigs soon paid a heavy price
for their prodigal spending for internal improvements, which almost bankrupted the state. The
Democrats got control of the legislature and governor's office, and in 1844 drafted Silas Wright,
a distinguished United States senator, for the gubernatorial race.

Even before their victory the Democrats split into two factions, the Barnburners, advocates
of retrenchment and enemies of Southern domination of their party, and the Hunkers, a more
pragmatic faction who "hunkered" for patronage and were willing to cooperate with Southern
kingmakers. Governor Wright had trouble pleasing both factions and offended many tenant

Jenny Lind, dubbed the "Swedish Nightingale" by P.T. Barnum, was booked into Castle Garden and publicized as a unique and amazing extravaganza. Lind's first American appearance on September 11, 1850, is depicted here in this Nathaniel Currier print. Courtesy, Prints Division, Eno Collection, The New York Public Library

farmers in eastern New York who were refusing to pay rent to landlords. When violence erupted, Wright put down the antirenters firmly. He failed to win a second term, partly because of the anger of the antirenters but mainly because of the treachery of the Hunkers.

National issues spilled over into state politics. When a group of antislavery congressmen proposed the Wilmot Proviso, which called for no slavery in any territory acquired from Mexico as a result of the Mexican War, the Barnburners tried to have the state Democratic convention endorse this stand. Failing to get their way, the Barnburners set up another convention to send delegates to the national Democratic convention. Although offered half the seats, the Barnburners stalked out and organized a national convention in Buffalo calling for the exclusion of slavery from any Western territory. They endorsed Van Buren for president and adopted the name of Free Soil party. The Free Soilers attracted some Conscience Whigs and other reformers, but they had no chance of winning. They took comfort in winning more votes than the regular Democrats and throwing the state's electoral votes to the Whigs, who put Zachary Taylor in the White House with Millard Fillmore of New York as his vice-president.

The slavery issue in one form or another broke out each year. In 1850 Fillmore, who inherited the presidency, threw his support behind the Compromise of 1850, which admitted California as a free state but also imposed a strong fugitive-slave law. Weed and Seward opposed this compromise, because they feared the antislavery Whigs would desert the party. When the next Whig convention in New York approved the Wilmot Proviso, the followers of Fillmore bolted. They received the name of Silver-Grays, because Gideon Granger, their leader, had a shock of iron-gray hair. Because of this opposition to him within the Empire State, Fillmore failed to receive the Whig nomination in 1852. The Democrats, temporarily exhausted by years of

THIS TICKET

ENTITLES THE HOLDER TO A

$7 SEAT,

AT

M'LLE JENNY LIND'S

Grand Concert.

FRIDAY,

November 29, 1850.

The other Ticket is to be
given up at the Door, but this
should be retained.

P. T. Barnum

Van Norden & Amerman, Pr. 60 Wm. St. N. Y

Above: P.T. Barnum established a precedent for later impresarios when he charged $225 for a seat in Castle Garden at the opening concert of Jenny Lind. Courtesy, Prints Division, Eno Collection, The New York Public Library

Right: William Learned Marcy coined the phrase "to the victors belong the spoils" during a congressional debate in 1831. He also served as secretary of war during the Mexican War under President James K. Polk. Courtesy, Albany Institute of History & Art, on permanent loan from the City of Albany

infighting, revived and swept both state and nation.

In 1854 Congress passed the Kansas-Nebraska Act, which allowed slavery in those territories closed to slavery ever since the Missouri Compromise of 1820. This act created a whirlwind of protests by antislavery people in both parties. Many left their old allegiances and joined the newly formed Republican party. The Whig party crumbled into fragments, a large portion drifting toward the Republicans. Free Soilers and Barnburners also tended to move the Republican party. Some Whigs joined the Native American party (Know-Nothings), who even ran Fillmore for president in the election of 1856.

Weed was using all his skills to bring the Whigs into the Republican camp, which he accomplished at a meeting in Syracuse on September 26, 1855. The new party attracted several important editors: Greeley of the *Tribune;* Henry Raymond of the *Times;* and William Cullen Bryant of the *Evening Post.* Henry Ward Beecher, the leading Protestant preacher of the period, also backed the Republicans.

Although the Republicans captured the state government, including the governorship in 1856, the Democrats, badly fractured as usual, ruled New York City. Fernando Wood, a colorful scamp, defeated the Tammany candidate for mayor in an election marred by fistfights and fraudulent votes. The victorious Republicans in Albany saw opportunities for spoils by getting control

of the New York City police and other functions. The Republicans combined with Tammany Hall to unseat Wood, but in the next election Wood staged a comeback. He denounced antislavery groups, a stand popular among Irish immigrants who feared that freed slaves might come north and compete with them for jobs.

It looked as though Seward had a head start on the Republican nomination for president in 1860. To be sure, an ungainly frontier lawyer, Abraham Lincoln, had won national attention for his homespun speech in his debates with Stephen A. Douglas. Behind Seward were the shrewd Weed and Governor Edwin Morgan; missing, however, was Greeley, who felt neglected by his former partners. On the first ballot Seward had a commanding lead, but he made no further gains as Lincoln passed him on the third ballot. Seward's defeat caused Weed to break into tears, but he was partly mollified when Lincoln appointed Seward secretary of state.

Confusion marked the 1860 election, in which the Republicans won the state by offering some pragmatic planks—protective tariff, free homesteads, and land grants to railroads—as well as their crusade against slavery in the territories. Weed, however, enjoyed sweet revenge by blocking Greeley's bid to become United States senator.

A vast and complicated urban society had developed by 1860 along the Hudson River and Erie Canal. The most notable achievement was the rapid development of the transportation system upon which the burgeoning national economy rested. If the countryside with its "finished civilization" seemed less exposed to the waves of foreign immigrants and ups and downs of the business cycle, it was willy-nilly more a participant in than a spectator at the upheaval transforming the cities.

One can find much to criticize in the Empire State in this period: bigotry, poverty approaching the worst in Europe, crass materialism, and exploitation of the helpless. On the other hand, reformers established agencies, public and private, that partially mitigated the harshness and rigors of the capitalistic economy. Furthermore the broad suffrage and the rise of professional politicians provided a safety valve for the kind of incendiary conditions that erupted in the European revolutions of 1830 and 1848.

Old stock and immigrants were being fused together into "that busy, stirring, populous go-ahead New York State" that Lady Emmeline Stuart-Wortley, English traveler and wife of a baron, observed in 1849.

Above: During the 1850s, the controversy over slavery accelerated, fueled by the Fugitive Slave Act and the publication of Harriet Beecher Stowe's expose of slave life. Anti-slavery lectures and fairs drew crowds in Northern cities, towns, and villages. Courtesy, Schomburg Center for Research in Black Culture, The New York Public Library

Left: The financial panic of October 1857 was greeted with great agitation on Wall Street. The event was to have broad national repercussions. It gave the new Republican party an issue other than slavery upon which to base its campaign from 1859 to 1860, when Lincoln ran for the presidency. Courtesy, Picture Collection, The Branch Libraries, The New York Public Library

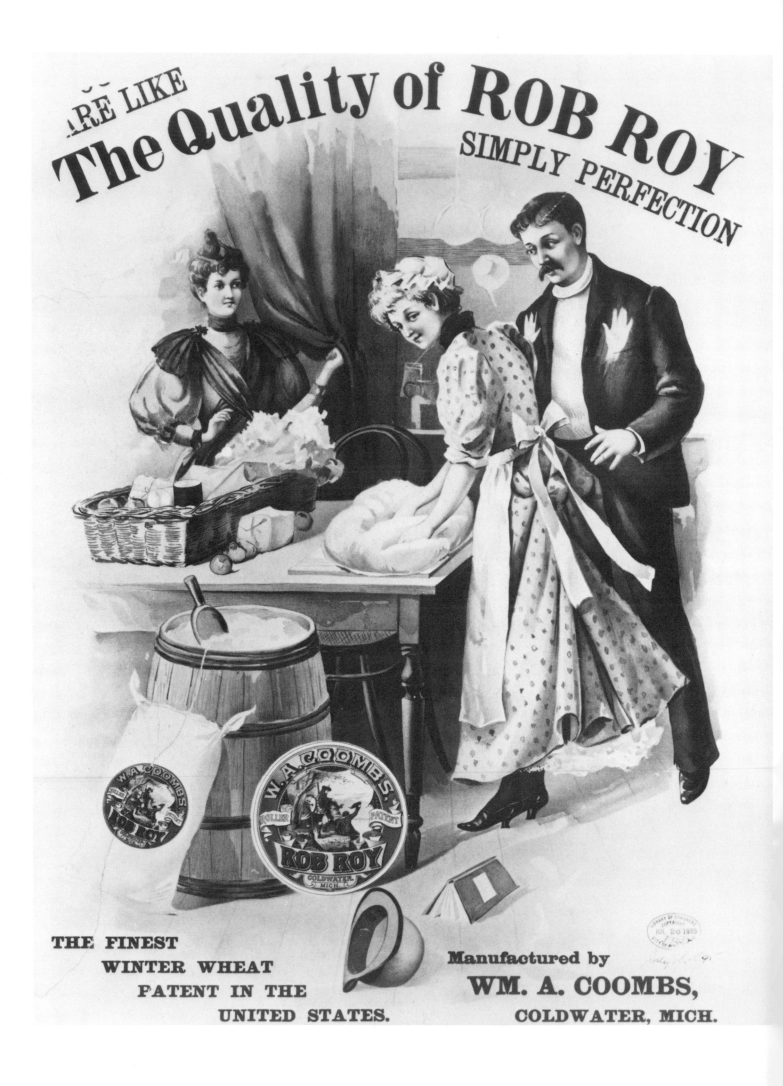

INDUSTRIALIZATION AND URBANIZATION 1860-1893

The rapid growth of cities and the economy that was clearly visible before the Civil War transformed the Empire State in the postwar period. Rather than an upheaval, this transformation was more of an expansion of the earlier phases of the industrial revolution, in which machine power was applied to new processes of manufacture and the thickening web of transportation. Furthermore the decline of prices stimulated the use of laborsaving machines on the farms and in factories. A second-rank nation in 1860, well behind Great Britain in output, the United States, paced by the Empire State, could boast three decades later an output larger than that of England, France, and Germany combined. The actual rate of growth per capita, however, was approximately the same as that in the countries of northwestern Europe.

Neither state nor metropolis had any near rivals in population. Rural townships, however, showed little or no gain—actually, absolute losses in many cases. The Civil War had a devastating effect upon growth with the loss of 53,114 men in the camps and on the battlefields as well as a decline in the birthrate and a falloff of immigration. During the 1880s nearly every rural township suffered a decline, because young people were moving to the cities and to the West. No wonder editors and farm leaders bewailed the growing number of abandoned farms and the decline of open country churches.

By contrast, New York City's share of the population by 1890 had risen to 45 percent. This development was often noted with alarm in the constitutional convention of 1894 when upstaters and Republicans wrote clauses in the new version designed to prevent the metropolitan area from ever securing a majority of the seats in the senate or assembly. Buffalo displaced Albany-Troy from second place. Syracuse passed Troy, the latter no longer able to compete with iron and steel cities of the Middle West.

The foreign born constituted about a fourth of the population in 1890, especially in the urban corridor. Irish and Germans composed about a third each of the solid majority born abroad or of foreign parentage. New York City and Brooklyn had the highest concentration of foreign born and foreign stock among the larger cities. Ira Rosenwaike, an expert on the state's population, estimated that 60 percent of all persons over 12 were born outside the United States. In 1890 the presence of 64,000 Italians and 100,000 Slavs from eastern Europe among the 1.5 million total of foreign born foretold the oncoming wave of immigrants.

Population of New York State and New York City, 1860-1890

Year	New York State	New York City*
1860	3,880,735	1,174,779
1870	4,382,759	1,478,103
1880	5,082,871	1,991,698
1890	6,003,174	2,507,414

*Figures cover the same territory for all years listed

Above: After the Civil War, women workers were often hired by industry to perform their traditional skills in a new setting. Courtesy, General Research Division, The New York Public Library

Right: Shown here is a portrait of Gardner Hollis, a Civil War soldier from New York. Irish and German immigrants made up a significant part of the New York contingent. Courtesy, New York State Historical Association, Cooperstown

Far right: Noble Lads of Brooklyn was actually a recruiting poster for the Union Army. It echoes a bravado that would soon turn to more realistic ideas on this—the bloodiest war in American history, the final cost included 500,000 American dead. Courtesy, New York State Library

Page 96: Traces of the servant's floured handprints on her master's jacket was a favorite motif used in advertisements during the late nineteenth century. Courtesy, Library of Congress

Ethnic and racial groups were not spread out across the state evenly. French Canadians moved into the North Country, Swedish furniture workers settled in Jamestown, Welsh farmers and craftsmen had several outposts in Oneida County, Polish immigrants contributed to Buffalo's rapid growth. In 1890 about 10 percent of the population of New York City was Jewish, the earlier German Jews outnumbered by those from Poland (Russia) and Galicia (Austria-Hungary). The small sector (one to two percent) of blacks did not increase, because of an extremely high death rate and low immigration from the Southern states before 1890.

Politics became more of a business than a game or a vehicle for ideology. Each party subscribed to the prevailing belief in individualism that later generations labeled as Social Darwinism. It was claimed that people joined the natural aristocracy of talent because of their hard work, ability, and virtue. The process of natural selection winnowed out the inferior and weak while the able rose to the top and reaped the rewards of success. The duty of government was to maintain order and protect property, not to regulate business or interfere with the free market. Poverty, to be sure, would persist, but rich men acting as stewards of God's bounty would extend aid to the poor. This doctrine received the blessing of many clergy and the support of many intellectuals. The guardians of the law enshrined it in their interpretation of the Fourteenth Amend-

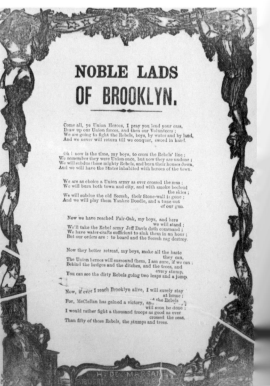

NOBLE LADS OF BROOKLYN.

Come all, ye Union Heroes, I pray you lend your ears,
Draw up our Union forces, and then our Volunteers ;
We are going to fight the Rebels, boys, by water and by land,
And we never will return till we conquer, sword in hand.

Oh ! now is the time, my boys, to cross the Rebels' line ;
We remember they were Union once, but now they are undone ;
We will subdue those mighty Rebels, and burn their houses down,
And we will have the States inhabited with heroes of the town.

We are as choice a Union army as ever crossed the seas ;
We will burn both town and city, and with smoke becloud the skies ;
We will subdue the old Secesh, their Stone-wall is gone ;
And we will play them Yankee Doodle, and a tune out of our gun.

Now we have reached Fair-Oak, my boys, and here we will stand ;
We'll take the Rebel army Jeff Davis doth command ;
We have water-crafts sufficient to sink them in an hour ;
But our orders are : to board and the Secesh rag destroy.

Now they better retreat, my boys, make all the haste they can,
The Union heroes will surround them, I am sure, if we can ;
Behind the hedges and the ditches, and the trees, and every stump,
You can see the dirty Rebels going two leaps and a jump.

Now, if ever I reach Brooklyn alive, I will surely stay at home ;
For, McClellan has gained a victory, and the Rebels will soon be done ;
I would rather fight a thousand troops as good as ever crossed the seas,
Than fifty of those Rebels, the stumps and trees.

ment. The novels of Horatio Alger carried the message to hundreds of thousands of readers.

The Democrats, who had dominated the federal and state government before the Civil War, were able to elect only one president, Grover Cleveland, in the years between 1860 and 1912. The Republicans, however, though generally victorious, won by the narrowest margins between 1872 and 1892.

On May 14, 1861, Colonel Elmer Ellsworth was shot by a Confederate tavern keeper when Ellsworth tore down a Confederate flag. "Remember Ellsworth" became the slogan for New York troops who were honoring the first Union officer slain in the conflict. After the first burst of patriotic fervor had receded, partisan sniping resumed. The Republicans, a minority group, rallied to their standard a group of War Democrats and usually called their ticket the Union party. Most Democrats favored defending the Union but criticized the drastic measures taken by Lincoln, such as suspending habeas corpus and conducting arbitrary arrests.

In 1862 the Democrats temporarily suspended their factionalism and nominated Horatio Seymour for governor, who defeated the Republican candidate. Seymour opposed the conscription act that Congress passed in March 1863. The draft not only had several defects, notably permitting wealthy men to hire substitutes and to buy exemptions, but also suffered from mismanagement. For example, a large number of New Yorkers had volunteered in 1861, but the federal officials did not take that into account in assigning draft quotas. Fortified with a weekend of drinking and incitement, a mob burned the homes of abolitionists, lynched several blacks, and sacked stores. After three days of riots, federal troops restored order.

The election of 1864 revolved almost exclusively around national issues. The Republicans devoted a great deal of effort to permitting the soldiers to vote by proxy, and they nominated Reuben Fenton for governor because of his political skill and his reputation as "the friend of the soldier." The Republicans carried the state for both Lincoln and Fenton in a very close contest that was decided by the soldier vote.

The Fenton Republicans found that victory had deprived them of their planks. They felt compelled to develop a positive program of their own if only to hold together their wartime coalition and incidentally to secure control of large chunks of New York City government. Therefore they took significant steps in the fields of urban safety, public health, housing standards, and popular education. In short, they faced up to the urgent problems arising from urbanization and industrialization.

Shown here is Thomas McIntyre Hose #3 of West Troy (Watervliet) built in 1876. The driver is Matthew Lawlor. Courtesy, New York State Library

Their first move was to propose a "paid fire department" in New York City, an innovation that only a handful of American cities had adopted. Any reform, however, would tread on the toes of the Democratic party, which relied on the fire laddies to get out the vote. No less a figure than William Marcy Tweed graduated from organizing the "Americus" fire company to ward heeler and "Boss." The voluntary system was marked by many evils: inefficiency; high insurance rates; brawling between rival companies; looting by members of the companies. After much bickering and maneuvering, the legislature accepted the appointment of a board of fire commissioners to be appointed by the governor, and Fenton promptly packed it with Radical Republicans. Although the new system did not reduce rates of insurance, it did make the department more efficient and eventually more professional.

Public health was the second problem attacked by the legislature. In 1865 New York City was regarded by many experts as the "filthiest city in the western world." More than 30,000 horses deposited their waste on streets already teeming with the refuse of slaughterhouses and the garbage of families. Contracts to clean the streets were handed out to political agents who seldom did the job and appointed friends to "no show" positions. New York's death rate was much higher than that of London or Philadelphia. In addition, some studies showed that over half the dwellers in tenements were ill. Many Radical Republicans were more interested in capturing control of the proposed Metropolitan Board of Health than in fostering good health, but the Metropolitan Health Law that emerged was a landmark in public-health legislation. The threat of a cholera epidemic was a major factor in securing passage of this legislation. The dwellers in the cities from Albany to Buffalo realized that the law was necessary, because cholera might spread along the canal as it had in 1832.

Radical Republicans made some gestures to workingmen. Groups in Utica, Rochester, Buffalo, and of course New York sent petitions to the legislature asking passage of an eight-hour day. A weak law appeared in 1867, and the executive branch failed to enforce it. More successful was the attempt to regulate housing that from all accounts included "pestilential hells" and repulsive plague spots. The legislature called for ventilation of every sleeping room in new buildings and a transom in old structures. It also required fire escapes and at least one toilet for every 20 persons. Unfortunately this law passed to the administration of the city under the new constitution of 1870, and enforcement became sporadic at best.

The Radical Republicans infused new life into the educational program. They sponsored a charter for Cornell University, a nonsectarian institution, and awarded it the land grant provided by the Morrill Act for agricultural and mechanical education. Four more normal schools were created to complement those at Oswego and Albany. Most important was the law of 1867 that provided enough funds to eliminate the levying of tuition at public schools.

Next the Republicans urged the granting of suffrage to adult male blacks on the same basis as whites. If passed, the bill would guarantee the Republicans another 10,000 votes, a decisive margin in close elections. The Democrats vehemently opposed this measure for obvious reasons, but they also intensified prevailing prejudice about black "inferiority." The debate became heated until the results from elections in Ohio, Pennsylvania, and other states came in. Clearly many Northerners—probably a majority—opposed equality for blacks. When the New York Republicans lost the next election by a large majority, they also lost their zeal for reform and relied more closely on federal patronage and business support.

In this lithograph D.W. Moody shows a modern city whose distant roots are hardly discernible. Syracuse was first settled as a trading post by Ephraim Webster in 1786. It is the fourth largest city in New York State, and an important industrial and trade center. Courtesy, New York State Historical Association, Cooperstown

Camping was a popular and common leisure time activity. Lakes and ponds were favored sites as shown in this camping expedition to Shaver Lake.
Courtesy, New York State Library

The boss system was firmly established by the 1870s in both parties. Tammany Hall, led by William Marcy Tweed, epitomized the urban machine. He handed out jobs, favors, and bags of coal to followers, who reciprocated by voting for his candidates "early and often." Democrats cultivated Irish support by twisting the tail of the British lion, curbing the prohibitionists, and checking enemies of the Roman Catholic church. The Republicans, who marshaled people of British stock, cloaked themselves in the mantle of patriotism against the rebels and Copperheads. After Fenton lost the leadership of the party, Roscoe Conkling of Utica controlled it until 1881, when he resigned his seat in the United States Senate. Thereafter Thomas C. Platt of Oswego took command. Elihu Root, later an outstanding United States senator and member of Theodore Roosevelt's cabinet, declared that during the last two decades of the 19th century "Mr. Platt ruled the state . . . It was not the governor, it was not the legislature; it was not any elected officers, it was Mr. Platt." His critics charged that Platt made corrupt deals with the railroads, insurance companies, and other corporations.

In 1869 Tweed dominated the state government with his minion, John Hoffman, in the governor's chair while his lieutenants ruled the assembly and senate. Tweed greased the palms of both Republicans and Democrats to secure a new city charter that ended the state commissions regulating the police and other functions. His blatant corruption aroused several critics, among them Samuel J. Tilden, who quietly amassed information against Tweed until the revelations of the *New York Times* caused Tilden to make an open break. Thomas Nast in his cartoons depicted Tweed as a bloated spoilsman. Although the reformers destroyed the Tweed ring, they failed to put many in jail. Tweed fled abroad, was extradited and tried, and died in prison

Unfortunately Tweed was typical of his era. Witness the corrupt members of President Grant's cabinet, the legislators in Albany, and the buccaneering tactics of Jay Gould and Daniel Drew.

The Democratic party elected a series of able governors—Tilden, Grover Cleveland, David B. Hill—in the period between 1875 and 1895. Tilden, a brilliant lawyer and calculating politician, earned a reputation as a reformer as well, although he left few important legacies. Like most other leaders of his generation, he believed that government might properly encourage transportation but should not attack property rights and redistribute wealth. Perhaps his major accomplishment was his investigation of the canal ring, a bipartisan group that awarded contracts to insiders in return for kickbacks.

Conkling, Republican boss, took more interest in national affairs than in state politics. He helped to elect Grant president on two occasions, and in return Grant allowed Conkling to fill about 7,000 government jobs in New York State. For example, he appointed his crony, Chester A. Arthur, to manage the New York Custom House. President Rutherford B. Hayes, however, favored civil-service reform, which automatically brought him into a pitched battle with Conkling. Hayes fired Arthur and, after a titanic battle, forced through his own appointee.

The next Republican president, James Garfield, became embroiled in a similar fight with Conkling. Conkling lost. These feuds among the Republicans carried over into state nominations and campaigns and helped Cleveland to win a smashing victory in his race for governor in 1882. Of course Cleveland's reputation for integrity and honesty added to his appeal. "The Big

Party Factionalism in the Gilded Age

"No thank you, I don't engage in criminal practice" was the stinging answer of Roscoe Conkling to emissaries of James G. Blaine in 1884 when Blaine sought the aid of his fellow Republican in his race for the presidency. Conkling no doubt savored the opportunity to strike back at Blaine, who had attacked Conkling on the floor of the United States Senate as "a grandiloquent swell" with "his majestic, supereminent, over powering turkey gobbler strut."

Contemporaries and historians alike have found few policy differences between Blaine and Conkling, each priding himself on his loyalty to the Grand Old Party (GOP). A spectacular and persuasive speaker, Conkling had emerged as a leading Radical Republican opposing the reconstruction policies of President Andrew Johnson. Conkling pushed forward Ulysses S. Grant as Republican candidate in 1868, who defeated Horatio Seymour, Conkling's brother-in-law in Utica. Gratefully, President Grant gave Conkling sole authority over the federal patronage in New York, which controlled some 7,000 federal jobs.

Conkling, however, could not resist planting his barbs under the skin of his enemies, a company that kept growing rapidly. Prominent among them was Blaine, whose magnetic personality won him millions of devoted followers, derisively called Half-Breeds by the Stalwarts backing Grant and Conkling. Corruption in the Grant Administration led to demands for reform and Conkling could not stop the nomination of Rutherford B. Hayes, who advocated civil-service reform. In 1880 the Republicans, led by Conkling, chose James Garfield over Conkling as their candidate. When Garfield appointed Blaine

James G. Blaine

Roscoe Conkling

secretary of state and placed an enemy of Conkling in charge of the New York Custom House, Conkling resigned his Senate seat. Imagine his surprise and fury when the Republican legislators, formerly his servants, refused to reelect him.

Factionalism also splintered the Democratic party. Samuel Tilden helped to topple Boss Tweed of Tammany Hall, an action that helped him win the governorship in 1874 and secure the presidential nomination two years later. Meanwhile, in Buffalo, Grover Cleveland was rising step by step from ward supervisor to mayor and on to the governorship in 1882. Tammany Hall had failed to check his steady rise.

The contest between Blaine and Cleveland for president became one of the closest and most scurrilous in American history. The Democrats hit hard at Blaine's shady deals, which were exposed and publicized. The Republicans retaliated by charging that Cleveland had fathered a child out of wedlock, a charge that Cleveland did not deny.

Why did Blaine lose New York by the hairline margin of 1,149 votes out of a total of more than a million? Many contemporaries and historians assign the loss to the statement of the Reverend Samuel Burchard accusing the Democratic party of representing "Rum, Romanism and Rebellion." Blaine himself is said to have remarked, "I should have carried New York by 10,000 if the weather had been clear on election day and Dr. Burchard had been doing missionary work in Asia Minor or Cochin China." Actually Blaine ran well in Irish-American wards, and Tammany Hall threw some votes from Cleveland to Blaine.

Blaine lost most of the Mugwump or Reform Republicans, who could not stomach his unsavory connections with corporations. Although Democrats lambasted Blaine for attending a banquet at Delmonico's restaurant hosted by Jay Gould and 200 other tycoons, this action shifted few if any votes. The Prohibition party ran its spellbinder, John P. St. John, and he collected 25,000 votes, almost all drained off from the Republicans. Most tantalizing was the role of Conkling, who refused to campaign for Blaine. Clearly many of his followers stayed home on election day or even voted for Cleveland, who had also grown up in Oneida County. Cleveland took the county by 19 votes, quite a drop from its usual Republican majority of more than 1,900. Did Conkling square accounts with Blaine, who had upset his presidential hopes in 1880 and ridiculed him on the floor of the Senate? Maybe so.

One," as Cleveland was known in Albany because of his bulk, supported civil-service reform, which young Theodore Roosevelt was also advocating in the assembly. The two men cooperated in forcing through such a law in 1882. When Cleveland made his successful campaign for president in 1884, some Republican reformers backed him over James G. Blaine, Republican candidate and spoilsman, but Roosevelt swallowed hard and made speeches for Blaine.

The politics of New York City mirrored the growing complexity of forces transforming the economy of the metropolis. Merchants, dominant since colonial days, were still the prevailing force in politics, although factions had arisen within that group. After the Tweed Ring was smashed, upper-crust merchants, called Swallowtails for their fancy frock coats, rushed to fill the vacuum, and every mayor between 1872 and 1886 was a merchant. Tammany Hall felt obliged to endorse a merchant for the top spot in order to present a respectable front. The Swallowtails, however, also had their factions, such as aggressive Protestants who favored planks to aid women, children, and the needy. Another group advocated low taxes; therefore they called for less government activity.

Theodore Roosevelt in his splendid autobiography made his famous but somewhat inaccurate observation that he, unlike most of his blue-blood friends, entered politics in order to join the governing class. Actually, several men of wealth and status ran for office, and in 1889 Roosevelt was complaining to Henry Cabot Lodge that he could not match the pocketbooks of other candidates.

The campaign for mayor in 1886 was one of the most exciting events in American municipal history. Challenging the establishment was Henry George, whose seminal book, *Progress and Poverty,* had converted tens of thousands to the program of the single tax, under which the government would capture the economic rent of land. The Democrats put up a manufacturer and philanthropist, Abraham S. Hewitt, while the Republicans nominated Roosevelt, the exuberant young "swell." A wide variety of labor, reform, and radical groups rallied behind George, who campaigned strenuously and effectively. Tammany Hall may have padded the election tallies in order to count out George, who ran strongly among second-generation Irish, Germans, and Jews.

This thrust by labor alarmed conservatives, whose candidate, Roosevelt, came in a poor third. The chieftains of Tammany Hall learned a lesson, namely, to borrow some planks from new third parties. Like most other third parties, the George coalition soon disintegrated into its warring factions. Samuel Gompers, the leader of the Cigar Workers Union and a founding father of the American Federation of Labor, abandoned the idea of a labor party and adopted the policy of rewarding friends and punishing enemies.

David B. Hill inherited the governor's office in January 1885 when Cleveland resigned to prepare for his higher post in Washington. Hill delighted in power, and he skillfully pressed the levers by offering various groups patronage and recognition. "I am a Democrat" was his war cry, which meant to his party faithful that he opposed Cleveland's flirtation with civil-service reform. A native of Elmira, Hill formed an alliance with Tammany Hall, which was ruled by John Kelly until 1886 and thereafter by Richard Croker. He cultivated labor by urging safety devices in factories and by designating the first Monday in September as Labor Day. Hill covertly encouraged the temperance forces to run an independent ticket, knowing that out of every 100 voters they collected the Republicans would lose 90. In addition he could secure contributions from breweries, distilleries, and saloonkeepers by openly blocking the drys. The Republicans tried to embarrass Hill by passing reform bills, knowing Hill would veto them. For example, Hill vetoed bills providing for a secret ballot and penalties for persons buying votes.

The long-standing feud between Hill and Cleveland made it difficult for the Democrats to present a united front against the Republicans. The Democrats outraged many citizens by seating one of their party members in a disputed election for the state senate. Because the Democrats

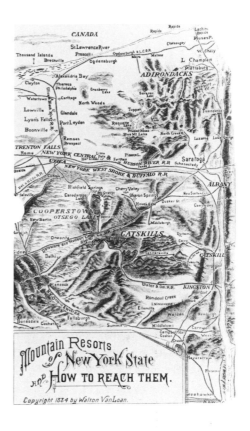

Above: The rapid industrialization and urbanization of post-Civil War America created a large urban middle class who wanted a summer retreat from the rigors of the city. Catskill mountain resorts began to proliferate in response to this new and growing market. Courtesy, Picture Collection, The Branch Libraries, The New York Public Library

Below: This quiet family portrait taken near Cooperstown, New York, around 1890 shows the rich use of decorative treatments typical of Victorian interior design. Courtesy, New York State Historical Association, Cooperstown

Above: The first home for the Grand Central Terminal was built in 1871 for the New York and Harlem, New York and New Haven, and New York Central railroads. It was enlarged and redesigned in 1899 by C.P.R. Gilbert. The most recent terminal building had been the pearl of Park Avenue architecture, until it was dwarfed by the massive edifice of the Pan Am Building. Courtesy, New York State Library

Below: Carriages were the primary means of local transportation in Upstate New York until the early 1900s. Vehicles, such as the one shown here, were used to carry passengers from New York Central Station at Canajoharie to camping sites beside Otsego Lake. Courtesy, New York State Historical Association, Cooperstown

were in power in 1893 when a panic precipitated the worst depression in American history except for that of the 1930s, they received the blame even if they had inherited a wobbly economy from the Republicans. To add to their troubles, the Reverend Charles Parkhurst in New York City charged in his sermons that Tammany Hall was in alliance with vice and crime. An investigation by the state legislature revealed that Croker's henchmen collected fees from prostitutes, saloonkeepers, and criminals. This combination of factors created a groundswell of outrage against the Democrats, who had lost control of their numerical advantage during the previous 20 years. As a result the Republican party became the dominant party in the Empire State and also the nation for the next 15 years.

The state took some early steps toward conservation, beginning in 1885 when the legislature authorized the establishment of a state forest preserve in the Adirondacks and voted funds for a park at Niagara Falls. Additional steps were taken, until in 1894 the constitutional convention of that year included the famous clause providing that some state land in the Adirondacks and the Catskills should be kept "forever wild."

On balance both parties failed to address the problems created by the rapid industrialization and urbanization. The legislators of New York followed the hands-off policy that prevailed among party bosses, intellectuals, and the public at large. Nevertheless breakthroughs did take place in labor legislation, conservation, and especially in the reform of the civil service.

The railroad clearly dominated almost every aspect of the economy and became an outstanding issue in politics. The tripling of track mileage in the three decades after 1860 tied most villages and many farmers more closely to urban markets. Undercut by Wisconsin butter and cheese, many farmers shipped fluid milk to the cities.

Coney Island

"The lungs of the great city" was the phrase used by an English visitor in 1881 to describe Coney Island. Wealthy New Yorkers as early as 1829 had boarded the ferry to the six-mile strip of sand in southern Brooklyn. Small hotels sprang up, and during the 1840s various notables—Edgar Allan Poe, P.T. Barnum, Henry Clay—joined the rich families for outings at Coney Island.

After the Civil War many more New Yorkers, including those of lesser means, discovered the resort, which could be reached by five railways. For some, the ocean was the main attraction; for others, the entertainment was the drawing card. Children loved the merry-go-round and flying swings; young men tested their aim in shooting galleries. All enjoyed the military bands and dance orchestras. Of course, Coney Island had its raffish side: bearded ladies, shell games, fortune-tellers, and even ladies of uncertain virtue.

Promoters built huge hotels and vied with one another in offering gargantuan meals. The Sea Beach Palace could seat 15,000 visitors at one time. By 1882 the resort attracted more than 5 million persons in one season. During the next decade or two, promoters established Steeplechase Park, with its exotic buildings and fast racetrack. In 1905 Dreamland opened, its tower ringed with a million electric lights.

After World War I the subway reached Coney Island and so did millions of people on hot weekends and holidays. Where else could you have a vacation for a nickel! After World War II Coney Island had become down-at-the-heels and could not compete with Jones Beach and newer resorts accessible by automobile. More recently, the old resort has made a partial comeback, because officials have checked the worst pollution and a more permanent population has taken up residence. By a strange quirk of events, a considerable number of refugees from Soviet Russia have established their homes in Brighton Beach.

Coney Island was the precursor of Disneyland, Great Adventure, and other such parks. If Saratoga gave us potato chips and Buffalo made chicken wings famous, Coney Island popularized the hot dog.

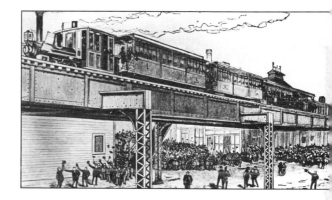

Above: The Elevated railroad, or "El," improved Brooklyn's rapid transit and boosted real estate development. In the first year of its operation, 2,000 new homes were built along its route. Shown here is the opening day of the elevated railroad in 1887. Courtesy, Brooklyn Historical Society

Below: In the 1880s, group picnics were a favorite pastime among the young. Shown here is a dinner group at Rose Lawn on Otsego Lake. The lake was a popular picnic spot because guests could row and sail and enjoy the eighteen-mile steamer trip around the lake. Courtesy, New York State Historical Association, Cooperstown

The New York Central and Erie railroads, which had taken form as systems by 1860, were joined by new systems: the Lehigh Valley, the Delaware, Lackawanna and Western, and the Delaware and Hudson running north from the Pennsylvania coalfields to the urban corridor. The iron horse penetrated all sections of the state, from Long Island with its beaches to the vastness of the Adirondacks, where the last lengthy line was completed in 1892 from Herkimer to Malone.

The 1980s have witnessed gigantic contests between entrepreneurs skilled in the art of taking over other companies by leverage buyouts and the use of "junk bonds." Similar high jinks by financial pirates took place a century ago when Jay Gould, Daniel Drew, and Jim Fiske looted companies by issuing watered stock. William H. Vanderbilt, the able son of the Commodore, did not endear himself to his contemporaries when he stated, "The public be damned."

Buffalo became one of the three railroad centers not only as a transshipment point for downlake traffic but also as the gateway to the West. Each major seaboard city—New York, Philadelphia, Baltimore, and even Boston and New Orleans—sought rail connections with Chicago,

Right: This 1887 painting of Albany's State and Pearl streets recalls the earlier work of artist James Eights. The painting serves as an interesting record of nineteenth-century merchandising. Courtesy, Albany Institute of History & Art

Bottom: The riverboat cabin was the model for American passenger cars. The spaciousness of the American railroad car seemed strange to European visitors who were accustomed to more intimate compartments. Shown here is the Delaware and Hudson Railroad in around 1900. Courtesy, New York State Historical Association, Cooperstown

Below: Port Jefferson owed its growth and early economic success to shipbuilding on its shore. This made it a natural depot for the new rail lines shown here as they were in 1878. Courtesy, The Brooklyn Public Library, Brooklyn Collection

the center of the grain trade of the Middle West. Each railroad engaged in rate wars to keep its share or, in the case of a new line such as the Baltimore and Ohio, to capture a portion of the grain trade. After several exhausting battles, the trunk lines in 1877 signed an agreement that granted Philadelphia and Baltimore lower rates than the basic rate from Chicago to New York or Boston. The grain exporters of New York City exploded in anger but the railroads serving New York insisted they had no choice because the metropolis enjoyed lower ocean rates and better services than the other ports.

The Delaware and Hudson became the third-most-important system after the Central and Erie systems. It fought the Erie railroad for control of the Albany and Susquehanna, which had completed a line to Binghamton in 1869. Each railroad hired bands of thugs to seize the right of way, as well as bribing judges and legislators. The Delaware and Hudson won and constructed a northern extension along the western shore of Lake Champlain to Plattsburgh. The headquarters of this railroad in Albany has become the head office of the State University of New York.

Canal tonnage, mostly wheat and lumber, reached its peak about 1870, then began to decline. During the 1870s railroads slashed rates in order to grab more traffic. Despite the repeal of tolls the Erie continued to lose freight and by the 1890s was handling only a quarter of the grain arriving at Albany. Meanwhile most lateral canals lost almost all their freight to the expanding rail network, with the result that the state abandoned the Genesee Valley, Chemung, Keuka, and Chenango canals.

Gas and electrical utilities not only provided power for manufacturing and commercial establishments but also made life safer and more comfortable for urban dwellers. Thomas Edison had a leading role in developing new methods of generating electricity and also in transmitting power. In 1882 he built the Pearl Street Station in lower Manhattan, amazing the first customers and envious onlookers with the clean and brighter means of illumination. Soon dozens of overhead wires draped streets, until Edison developed a modular system of underground electricity distribution. Genius though he was, Edison clung to his direct current until George Westinghouse, an upstate engineer, demonstrated the superiority of alternating current. Edison organized the Edison General Electric Company in 1889 and soon opened a plant in Schenectady to manufacture equipment, the nucleus for the famous General Electric Company of the future.

A movement to consolidate various plants got under way in New York and other cities, largely to take advantage of the obvious efficiency of having one company serving one area and also to put an end to cutthroat competition. Consolidated Edison today is the result of the combination and merger of more than 170 individual companies.

Clearly the foremost industrial state, New York outdistanced all others in the variety of firms, the number of gainfully employed, and the value added to raw materials. The reasons for its paramount position are by now familiar: excellent transportation; an abundance of labor, including the highest skills; entrepreneurs of great drive; a massive market within the state and the Northeast; an ample supply of capital and credit; a government willing to foster business.

The rapid development of manufacturing in the two decades before the Civil War slowed during that conflict when hundreds of thousands of men left shops, factories, and farms for camps and battlefields. A shortage of cotton forced textile mills to run on short schedules, but demands

Above: The Cropsey mansion stood on the corner of 84th Street and Bay Street in the New Utrecht Section of Brooklyn. It was built in 1887 and served as a home for several generations of the Cropsey family, whose roots date back to the Dutch settlement during the seventeenth century. Courtesy, Picture Collection, The Branch Libraries, The New York Public Library

Left: In the late nineteenth and early twentieth centuries, Saratoga Springs was the playground of newly-made millionaires. Many of the old hotels, such as the Grand Union Hotel shown here, graced the tree-lined streets of the town. Courtesy, Picture Collection, The Branch Libraries, The New York Public Library

for uniforms and blankets kept the woolen mills running overtime. Railroad construction fell off because of the lack of capital and immigrant labor, but railroad traffic increased sharply.

The processing of raw materials and foodstuffs constituted the most important industries. Flour milling in 1860 was number one if measured by value of product. Rochester by virtue of its waterpower and proximity to the Genesee Valley held top position, but when wheat growing moved west, it lost first rank. Buffalo, however, rose to national leadership because of the arrival at that port of western wheat, which was milled in that city before moving on to the expanding markets of the Northeast.

Clothing and its many allied industries became the dominant industry by 1880, whether measured in number employed or the value of manufactures. The sewing machine, the Civil War demand for uniforms, and the influx of immigrants greatly stimulated this industry. By 1880 the manufacture of women's clothing, which before the war had been largely made by housewives or seamstresses, had risen to second place. At first Irish and English formed most of the work force, but in the 1880s the Germans, including Jewish tailors and businessmen, had taken the leadership in this industry.

Leather goods, chiefly boots and shoes, became an important industry in many cities. Textile mills flourished in Oneida County and Cohoes while Troy had an allied industry, the making of shirts and collars. Tradition has it that Mrs. Hannah Lord Montague, a housewife, cut the dirty collars off her husband's shirts in order to avoid washing the whole garment. Ebenezer Brown began the manufacture of detachable collars in 1829. During the Civil War women organized their own union, carried on a strike, and contributed $1,000 to the Troy Iron Moulders Association, which included their husbands and sons.

The making of machines involved the metallurgical trades, such as the forges and foundries found in most cities. Elisha Otis of Yonkers developed the first elevator, an invention necessary before skyscrapers could be built. Near Buffalo steel mills utilized the iron ore from the Mesabi Range in Minnesota and coal from Pennsylvania.

Printing and publishing, well established before the Civil War, expanded as New York City became the center of many national journals and periodicals as well as book publishing. To keep the price of their magazines down, publishers sold a great deal of advertising to stores, patent-medicine companies, and sellers of such standard products as soap.

New York City was, in the words of Samuel Gompers, "the cradle of the modern American labor movement." Printers and cigar workers formed stable labor unions in the 1850s, especially among German immigrants. In the 1870s workers in the building trades and on the railroads organized and carried on strikes, with little permanent success. The large corporations had too much bargaining power to surrender to the demands of the weak unions. Furthermore employers could always recruit foreign workers as strikebreakers. Nevertheless there were frequent instances of labor unrest. Between 1885 and 1891 over a half-million workers participated in more than 20,000 strikes.

Unemployment stalked the urban scene, especially during the hard times after the panics of 1873 and 1893. Those lucky enough to find work faced hazards in the workplace. Child labor was a disgrace, and employers easily circumvented efforts to ban it. Charles Brace, founder of the Children's Aid Society, secured a compulsory-school-attendance law for children under 14, but school officials were afraid to enforce it. Moreover many parents needed the meager sums earned by youngsters. Jeremy Felt, the historian of child labor in New York State, estimated that more than 200,000 children were at work in the decade of the 1880s.

In agriculture the shift to dairying increased in tempo throughout the state. New York led

Below, left: Like other early photographers of rural America and New York, James West was a chronicler of the varieties of everyday life in his home town. Shown here is the Scriven Shirt Shop in Grafton, New York, in 1890. The young women working at making men's shirts were typical of the trade at the time. Courtesy, New York State Library

Below: The proliferation of factory-made products in the post-Civil War era gave birth to a new industry—advertising. Many products previously manufactured by women at home were marketed in national advertising campaigns such as this one for laundry soap. Courtesy, Library of Congress

Right: One of the most famous patent medicines of the nineteenth century was Lydia Pinkham's Vegetable Compound. It was advertised in women's magazines such as Godey's Ladies' Book. *It contained various roots, seeds, and 15 to 20 percent alcohol, which Pinkham insisted was only a solvent and preservative. Many competing products contained even more alcohol. Pinkham's compound grossed $200,000 per year at the height of its popularity. Courtesy, Landauer Collection, The New-York Historical Society, New York City*

Right: Mechanization revolutionized American agriculture. International Harvester, one of the largest manufacturers in the world, was at the forefront of producing sophisticated farm equipment. Shown here is a 1913 engine and plow used on an upstate New York farm. Courtesy, New York State Historical Association, Cooperstown

Below: Recalling the European roots of many settlers in upstate New York is this sleepy country lane. It was the main street of Berlin, New York, as photographed by James E. West. Courtesy, New York State Library

the nation in the production of cheese, butter, and fluid milk. Farmers along the railroad lines sent their milk to the expanding urban markets. Central New York farmers specialized in the production of cheese. Jesse Williams, a farmer near Rome, took in the milk of his neighbors in 1851 and started the first cheese factory. Dozens of factories sprang up in the area from Little Falls to Rome.

Although wheat output fell by over half, it remained an important crop in the state. Barley became even more important because of the demands of breweries and their customers. Horticulture centered in the fruit belt south of Lake Ontario, where the lake moderated the climate. Grapes were grown in the western Finger Lakes and Chautauqua County, regions whose climate was moderated by nearby water.

Agricultural improvements spread fairly rapidly as better harrows, plows, and mowing machines were produced. The census of 1890 showed New York State had the highest investment in farm equipment. Agricultural education, however, made slow progress. Although Cornell University received the land grant for the promotion of agricultural education, few students enrolled in the tiny department before 1888, when Liberty Hyde Bailey arrived and spurred development.

Farm life showed little change before the 20th century, when the automobile and truck revolutionized the rural way of life. Farmers and villagers lived in wooden frame houses, which Grandma Moses depicted in her paintings of the hill country east of Albany. The colored prints of Currier & Ives also give us some idea of the sports, diversions, celebrations, and farm activities in this period.

The family gathered in the kitchen for meals, the parlor being reserved for Sunday visitors, weddings, and funerals. Cast-iron stoves heated the houses and kerosene lamps lighted the kitchen; candles were used to light the way to the bedrooms. Housewives cooked the meals on a wood or coal stove and if lucky had a son or husband who would pump the water from the well and bring it to the kitchen. About 10 percent of the farmhouses had plumbing, and the backhouse with its mail-order catalogue was a fixture.

The typical farm ran to slightly under 100 acres, and after 1880 the acreage of improved land slowly fell because of the abandonment of fields and even farms in hilly areas. Farm life, however, had its attractions, which were vividly recalled by Agnes Sneller in her splendid *A Vanished World,* her recollections of her youth in Cicero township near Syracuse. She wrote, "I know now that we lived in a world of extraordinary beauty. The farm tools and machines had a music of their own; the click of hoes in springtime; the swish of a scythe in the deep grass of the fence corners; the sound of a mower traveling across a meadow, and most beautiful of all, the melody of the reaper at work on the harvest . . . "

The Empire State could not boast of many major literary figures in the third quarter of the century, compared with earlier luminaries such as Cooper, Irving, Melville, and Whitman. To be sure, Whitman lived on for many years, but his epoch-making *Leaves of Grass* had appeared before 1860. New York City, the national center of publishing, attracted many authors in search of publishers and excitement. Boston, however, remained the literary capital until the 1880s, when William Dean Howells took up residence in New York City, a symbolic move registering the end of the flowering of New England.

Of course there were many scribblers of uncertain talent but popular acclaim. Not many today read Horatio Alger's novels of young men leaving the countryside for the metropolis and

Above: After the Civil War, new household appliances began to crowd the marketplace. The cast-iron stove served at least a dual purpose—first to cook meals more efficiently than before, and also to heat rooms. The stove was usually located in the kitchen near a central chimney. It was fueled by coal or wood and created a dusty air quality. Courtesy, Landauer Collection, The New-York Historical Society, New York City

Left: The fight for female suffrage led many men to ridicule the results of such a "preposterous notion." This Currier and Ives print of 1869 shows a future where women appear in men's clothing, assume men's work roles, and even force men to do such "obviously female" tasks as tending to infants and doing the family wash or cooking! Courtesy, The New-York Historical Society, New York City

*John Heyl Vincent (right) and Lewis Miller (left) were the founders of the Chautauqua Movement.
From Cirker,* Dictionary of American Portraits, Dover, *1967*

The Chautauqua Movement

Every summer more than 50,000 visitors travel to Chautauqua Lake for study and recreation, for art and athletics, and for music and inspiration. More than 10,000 residents crowd the gingerbread cottages and Victorian-style hotels shaded by lovely trees. The beautiful lake provides an idyllic setting for the concerts, lectures, and dramatics offered throughout the summer months.

It all began when John Heyl Vincent, a Methodist minister, and Lewis Miller, a businessman, decided to improve the quality of Sunday School teaching. They selected an old camp-meeting ground on the lake shore in 1873 and planned their program. Vincent, the editor of a Methodist journal, told his readers of his new venture, and they responded with enthusiasm. At least 2,000, a figure soon doubled, showed up at the first meeting to attend classes taught by 142 teachers.

At first most visitors lived in boarding-houses in villages around the lake, where they were picked up each morning by steamers. Soon a large campus developed with scores of cottages around the large lecture hall, still the heart of Chautauqua. The Hall of Philosophy, distinguished by large Grecian columns, hosted scores of seminars. Students could walk around a miniature Jerusalem and walk through a large-scale representation of Palestine with the names of localities mentioned in the Bible.

Chautauqua gradually shifted from a predominantly religious emphasis to more secular interests such as concerts, plays, and art exhibits. In 1878 Vincent set up the Chautauqua Literary and Scientific Circle, which concentrated on "great books." Thousands rushed to join this program, which in another four years enrolled more than 180,000 persons.

Chautauqua pioneered in various forms of adult education. Its lakeside campus is sometimes called the first summer school. Its program on "great books" was later adopted by the University of Chicago and other colleges. In 1893 the Redpath Lyceum Bureau, a completely independent agency, organized a traveling Chautauqua that sponsored concerts, plays, and lectures. During the 1920s perhaps as many as 10 million Americans attended these traveling Chautauquas.

Page 115: French sculptor Frederic Auguste Bartholdi created this modern colossus that has become a symbol of freedom and prosperity to millions of immigrants since it first appeared in New York harbor in 1886. In her right hand she holds a torch, in her left, a tablet representing the Declaration of Independence, bearing the date of its proclamation, July 4, 1776. Courtesy, The New York State Department of Economic Development

Below: The stately Victorian-era Albany capitol building blends well with the sleek line of the futuristic state office buildings nearby at the Empire State Plaza. Courtesy, New York State Library

making it. Even fewer read the score or so of novels churned out by Marietta Holley of Watertown, whose Samantha series delighted thousands of readers. More lasting were the works on nature written by John Burroughs at Slabsides, his Catskill retreat. Philander Deming of Albany revealed to the public the harsh realities of life in the Adirondacks in his short stories.

The opening gun of a new era was sounded in 1887 when two novels appeared, one devoted to metropolitan life, the other analyzing upstaters. Henry Cuyler Bunney wrote *The Story of a New York House* and treated urban life with perception. Harold Frederic launched his career with *Seth's Brother's Wife,* the first of several works devoted to Mohawk Valley themes. His masterpiece, *The Damnation of Theron Ware,* won for him international stature as well as the accolades of the London literary set, of which he was an established member.

Left: During its early construction the capitol building in Albany provided jobs for local laborers. A daily procession of 200 railroad cars were drawn by draft horses to haul away clay deposits, and returned laden with massive blocks of white Maine granite. Courtesy, New York State Library

Next page: Work began on the New York State capitol building in Albany in 1867. It was not completed for thirty years, and cost $25,000,000. Today the structure borders the northern edge of the Empire State Plaza. Courtesy, New York State Library

Below: New York offered ballet performances in the nineteenth century. However, it was not until the twentieth century that the American Ballet Theatre and other companies were established, bringing the city to the forefront of ballet training. Courtesy, General Research Division, The New York Public Library

The Empire State became the center of journalism if only because of the metropolis, but upstate also had newspapers of more than regional merit. The *New York Times* won fame for helping bring down the Tweed Ring. In 1883 the *New York World* was purchased by Joseph Pulitzer of St. Louis, who transformed it into a sensational paper leavened, however, by sound foreign news and editorials advocating reform.

In painting, music, and theater, New York City held the lead, because wealthy businessmen became patrons of the arts. They needed paintings and sculpture to place in the new chateaus on upper Fifth Avenue. Architects had a field day imitating architectural styles from the days

of ancient Greece to post-Renaissance. Upstaters also constructed impressive mansions on the Main Street of their community.

Obviously, New Yorkers did not establish the good society in this period of rampant individualism and unbridled capitalism. The corruption in both government and business, the exploitation of women, children, and immigrants, and the contrast between ostentatious wealth and grinding poverty stand forth as glaring defects.

On the other hand, entrepreneurs were building a mature industrial economy, and politicians, however vulgar and selfish they appear to later generations, did improve education, establish parks, and protect public health. The cities continued to assimilate millions of newcomers pouring in from the countryside and Europe. A few leaders of national stature emerged, and a considerable number of reformers raised their voices against contemporary evils. Furthermore, a few tentative steps were taken toward a more humane society.

In 1886 New York Harbor was graced with the Statue of Liberty, a symbol of freedom and opportunity. Millions of the "huddled masses" of Europe voted with their feet to pass through the "golden door" into the Empire State.

Difficulties with engineering plans, casualties, and bickering on the part of politicians made many doubt that the Brooklyn Bridge would ever be completed. When it was, it became not only a marvel of great beauty, but a tremendous boon to the working class on both sides of the East River. Shown here is a bird's eye view of the bridge in 1883. Courtesy, The Brooklyn Historical Society

THE PROGRESSIVE ERA 1894-1920

Increasing complexity marked the urbanized society of the Empire State as it entered the twentieth century. Industrialization continued apace but a new threat appeared: the consolidation of corporations into giant trusts. Urban transportation underwent massive changes with the expansion of trolleys and interurbans, the construction of subways in New York City, and the popularization of the Model T Ford upstate. Millions of immigrants swarmed into the state from eastern and southern Europe, adding to the diversity of cultures and stimulating a demand for Americanization of the newcomers.

Taking credit for the good times after the depression of the 1890s, the Republicans normally won control of the federal and state governments. Their hold was loosened, however, by the split between the progressive and conservative wings of the GOP in 1912. Progressives in both parties, led by Theodore Roosevelt, Charles Evans Hughes, and the emerging Alfred E. Smith, promoted an impressive list of laws intended to ease the condition of women, children, and workers; to promote the expansion of democracy with measures such as the direct primary and women's suffrage; and to regulate Big Business by busting and regulating the trusts.

Reforms and improvements did not just happen. Rather they were the result of concerted efforts by thousands of reformers—many of them from the upper class, others from unions, and still others from religious groups. Intellectuals and journalists kept up a drumbeat of agitation, so much so that Theodore Roosevelt, himself responsible for much of the agitation, dubbed them "muckrakers." The rough edges of industrial and urban society stirred the conscience of many and inspired them to support legislation and to promote humanitarian activities.

Typical of the progressive spirit was the founding of the Henry Street Settlement in 1893, an oasis of humanitarian concern on the Lower East Side. Lillian D. Wald, a young nurse, found a great need for nurses to visit young mothers in the tenements. Following the example of Toynbee Hall in London and Jane Addams' Hull House in Chicago, the Henry Street Settlement in lower Manhattan kept expanding its health services and recreation and educational activities. Wald prodded President Theodore Roosevelt to call the National Children's Conference in the White House, which advanced the cause of children throughout the country. Herbert H. Lehman, Eleanor Roosevelt, and Senator Robert Wagner, who sparked the reforms of the New Deal, received some of their early training or inspiration from the programs of the Henry

Right: Charles Evans Hughes was the tenth Chief Justice of the Supreme Court. Hughes spent his earlier years as an academic and jurist. In 1916 he ran unsuccessfully for the presidency against Woodrow Wilson. Hughes served as New York State governor from 1906 to 1910. Courtesy, New York State Library

Far right: Alfred E. Smith was a popular New York City politician and Democratic party power broker, who made an unsuccessful run for the presidency in 1928. He was the first Roman Catholic to do so. Smith was raised on the Lower East Side of New York City and completed an eighth grade education in his parish school. Courtesy, New York State Library

Below: Tenement labor was a frequent subject for photographer Lewis W. Hine. Hine was a contributor to such journals as Survey *and* McClures, *which publicized sweatshop conditions. Here we see workers making flowers in a tenement room. Courtesy, The Jacob A. Riis Collection, Museum of the City of New York*

Population of New York State and New York City 1890-1920

Year	New York State	New York City
1890	6,003,174	2,507,414
1900	7,268,894	3,437,202
1910	9,113,614	4,766,883
1920	10,385,227	5,620,048

Street Settlement and similar agencies.

Population rose from approximately 6 million in 1890 to nearly 10.4 million in 1920. Most growth took place in urban centers, but hundreds of rural townships, especially in the Southern Tier and along the foothills of the Adirondacks, lost population.

The greatest growth took place in New York City and the suburbs surrounding it. Cities, however, grew at uneven rates, some benefiting from breakthroughs or inventions and some experiencing the collapse of earlier industries. Schenectady, the home of General Electric, and Niagara Falls, the site of cheap electricity, grew explosively. Some smaller cities—Jamestown, Corning, Geneva, Watertown, Binghamton—doubled in size, while other centers—Troy, Cohoes, Oswego, Hudson, Kingston—stagnated.

European villages and cities disgorged more millions of emigrants, who entered this country through Ellis Island in New York Harbor. After 1890, when Germans and Irish dominated, Italians, Poles, and Russians (chiefly Jews) had become the leading groups. In Italy times were hard, taxes heavy, land unavailable, and jobs scarce. When American contractors needed workers to build railroads, subways, and buildings, they sent padrones to recruit men in southern Italy and Sicily. At first most men had no intention of staying in the New World and made several

Left: Lewis W. Hine had a special interest in child laborers and often testified at legislative hearings on their behalf. In this 1906 photograph, Hine shows newsboys about to go out into a snowstorm to sell their papers. Photo by Lewis W. Hine, courtesy, Local History and Genealogy Division, The New York Public Library

Page 120: The area near the shore line of the southeast Bronx on Long Island Sound was used as an amusement and recreation area early in the century. Clason Point Park, shown here around 1909, had dance halls, rides, swimming facilities, and a ferry to the North Beach in Queens. Photo by Joseph F. Hefele

Above: This photograph of a colored lithograph done by Lewis Bradley depicts Oswego, New York, in about 1853. It is on the site of the earliest English trading post on the Great Lakes, a post that was founded in 1722. When the Erie Canal was extended to Buffalo, Oswego lost some of its importance as a Great Lakes port. Courtesy, New York State Historical Association, Cooperstown

Facing page: In 1900 southern blacks began a slow and steady migration to the north. Harlem began to take shape as a black community around 1910. The white reaction to the "Negro Invasion" of Harlem precipitated a real estate race war, in which white realtors attempted to buy up property to prevent black tenancy, and black investors bought up white buildings for the purpose of evicting white tenants and replacing them with blacks. Courtesy, The New York Public Library, Schomburg Center for Research in Black Culture

trips across the Atlantic before bringing over their families. In Russia the government intensified its persecution of minorities who lived in the western provinces from Finland to Bessarabia. Anti-Jewish riots set in motion waves of refugees who looked to New York as the promised city. Roman Catholic Poles met discrimination and sometimes persecution by the Czarist government, which harassed the restive nationalists in its Polish provinces. Meanwhile industrial America was expanding rapidly, with steel mills and flour mills in Buffalo, chemicals in Syracuse, textiles in Utica, and cameras in Rochester.

Blacks had been a declining proportion of the state's population for more than a century because of the influx of Europeans. This trend changed in World War I when immigration ceased and when blacks from Virginia and other Southern states moved north, the precursors of a mighty wave of the future. In 1920 the black population reached 200,000, of whom three out of four lived in the metropolis.

In 1890 approximately half of the New York State population stemmed from foreign stock, divided about evenly between those born abroad and those of foreign parentage. Professor Albert

Street peddling was a way of pursuing the American dream of economic success without the need for great capital. Indeed, many general store and department store moguls got their start as peddlers. Courtesy, Local History and Genealogy Division, The New York Public Library

Parker has estimated that 38 percent of the remaining people derived from New England origin and that only 8 percent came from pre-Revolutionary stock. Blacks constituted a little over one percent.

Dr. Parker has also made estimates of the religious composition, finding that Roman Catholic composed 30 percent of the population, Jews 4 percent, and Protestants 32 percent. Among the Protestants, Methodists claimed the most members at 11 percent, followed by Presbyterian Congregationalists at 8 percent, and Baptists and Episcopalians at 6 percent each. The various branches of Lutherans totaled about 5 percent. About a fourth of the population had no affiliation with any church or temple.

How open was American society to the newcomers? Some scholars challenged the Horatio Alger myth of rags to riches, pointing out that large numbers of immigrants failed to climb out of the pit of poverty. The streets of gold turned out to be mean streets fringed by tenements and the breadwinners fell victim to disease, unemployment, and accidents. All true. Yet the myth seemed to be shared by many thousands because it did have considerable basis in reality. Hard work and merit did open doors for immigrants in Poughkeepsie, Buffalo, and New York City, according to several serious studies by scholars.

Professor Thomas Kessner studied Jewish and Italian immigrants in New York City in the period between 1880 and 1915, and recorded his findings in *The Golden Door*. The census of 1920 showed that 803,000 persons born in Italy lived in New York City. Private estimates

Upon arriving in America, an Italian immigrant is said to have written home that not only were the streets not paved with gold, but they were not paved at all! As shown in this 1910 photo by Lewis W. Hine, the labor of immigrants was needed to pave the streets, lay the rails, build the bridges, and work in the mines. Courtesy, Local History and Genealogy Division, The New York Public Library

of Jewish population in 1925 ran to 1,713,000, the great majority of them immigrants.

Kessner's most important finding was that both groups improved their lot and rose out of the manual-labor class at the rate of approximately 37 percent in two separate decades. He found that Russian Jews rose faster than Italians, which is understandable because of their higher literacy and urban skills. Even though these two groups arrived at the same time, a major difference existed from the outset. The Jews came as families and permanent settlers; the Italian males came to work, save money, and return to their native village to settle down or perhaps return to America for another chance to earn money. The Jews had no intention of going back to Czarist Russia, where the government and the populace vied in displaying anti-Semitism. The Jewish background in tailoring gave many a headstart in the clothing trades, which were flourishing in the garment district of Manhattan. By 1905 about half of the Jewish immigrants had reached such white-collar positions as office worker, retailer, manufacturer, and professional.

The Italian family, famous for its strength in the homeland, survived the separation from male workers in America, proved resilient under stress, and provided a warm nest for children, who were expected to remain under the watchful eye of the mother.

Italians often started stores, bakeries, and small construction firms, which could always use another pair of hands. Unlike the Jews, the Italian peasants did not have a history of pushing young men to become professionals, nor did they witness examples of peasants climbing to the top ranks of government or business.

Both Italians and Jews lived in neighborhoods sometimes called ghettos. Whereas the European ghetto walled people in, the neighborhood in New York often launched newcomers to careers outside its boundaries. When the immigrant arrived, he found in the ghetto friends, ethnic restaurants, clubs, and churches. A network of relatives and friends got him a job, found him a boardinghouse, and introduced him to American sports.

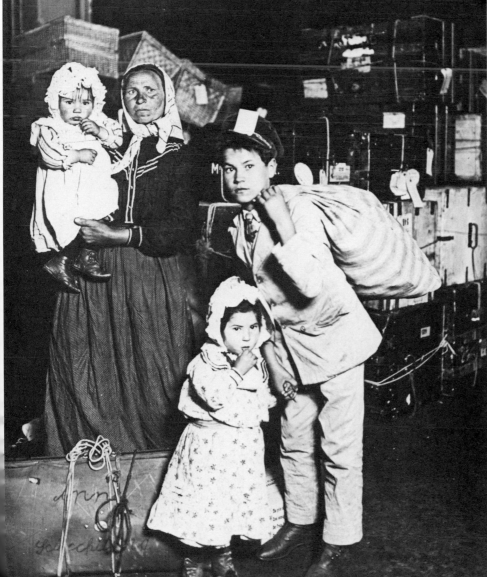

Above: Contract laborers working on jobs requiring temporary housing at the job site were often housed in crude, makeshift, crowded spaces. In this 1912 photo, Lewis W. Hine shows the bunkhouse where workers lived while working on the New York Barge Canal. Courtesy, The New York Public Library, Local History and Genealogy Division

Above, left: Lewis W. Hine left a record of work and home life among New York City's recent immigrants early in the twentieth century. Here he recorded an Italian family having supper in their Lower East Side home. Courtesy, The New York Public Library, Local History and Genealogy Division

Left: Lewis W. Hine captured the dismay of this Italian immigrant family at Ellis Island whose baggage had been misplaced. Courtesy, The New York Public Library, Local History and Genealogy Division

Facing page: Many immigrants brought well-honed skills with them to America. Here Lewis W. Hine captured the pride and concentration of an Italian craftsman in 1930. Courtesy, The New York Public Library, Local History and Genealogy Division

Economic success did not always bring happiness, however. The Italians, like the Germans and Irish before them, looked back on the old country with affection and nostalgia. Those who did attempt to reestablish a home found that World War I and other events disrupted the old way of life. Some could echo the words of Thomas Wolfe, who left Asheville, North Carolina, for a bohemian life in Greenwich Village: "You can't go home again." Abraham Cahan, founder of the *Jewish Daily Forward,* expressed it equally well in *The Rise of David Levinsky,* with "Such is the tragedy of my success, such is the tragedy of my success."

A common theme in many novels written by immigrants or their children was the clash between generations. Many children rejected the standards and authority of their parents in their effort to become 100 percent Americans. Some contested parental authority, a shocking position among Italians. Most traumatic of all was marriage to persons of a different religion or nationality. *Abie's Irish Rose,* a Broadway success for years, evoked much laughter, but people could sense the pathos and heartache underneath.

The economy continued its rapid growth, manufacturing challenging commerce for top position. As late as 1880 merchants included most of the richest men in the state, and commercial establishments dominated towns, cities, and the metropolis. Transportation, a close ally of commerce, generated a large number of railroad kings such as the Vanderbilts, Goulds, and Harrimans. The vertically integrated manufacturing firm, however, was expanding rapidly and indeed, after 1897, explosively. In 1901 J. Pierpont Morgan prodded several big steel companies into a consolidation, the United States Steel Company, the first billion-dollar corporation in the world.

In the early twentieth century, classes were sex segregated, and parents of girls often objected to the sexes even mingling at arrival and dismissal times. Many schools built entrances marked "boys" and "girls" at this time. Courtesy, The New York Public Library, Local History and Genealogy Division

High Society

A new upper class was gradually emerging, a mixture of the mercantile and landed gentry and the new elite of money and power. From all over the nation men of wealth and power gravitated to New York City and its environs, the center of finance, culture, and influence. The newcomers included oil kings (Rockefeller), mining tycoons (Hearst), railroad barons (Harriman, Gould), and steel magnates (Carnegie, Frick). The *nouveau riche* built mansions on Fifth Avenue and bullied their way into society, despite the disdain of some old families whose wealth had evaporated. These newcomers made up in wealth what they lacked in background and manners. Many of them stemmed from British or German stock. In 1900 more than 55 percent of brokers, wholesalers, and professional men in New York City were the sons of parents born in the United States, Canada, and Great Britain. Germans, a category including a good number of Jews, contributed 19 percent and the Irish another 10 percent.

The new elite excluded "outsiders" by a variety of means. Many bought estates along the Hudson and on Long Island. There were some 600 estates on the North Shore of Long Island. Glen Cove peninsula, on the northern tip of Long Island, was J.P. Morgan country. Here his yacht, *Corsair,* rode at anchor along with several craft owned by Morgan relatives. Nearby was the estate of George Baker, the president of the First National Bank and the largest stockholder of United States Steel and American Telephone and Telegraph. Several magnates of Standard Oil, notably Charles Platt and Stephen C. Harkness, acquired land nearby. Near Westbury, Henry Phipps, partner of Andrew Carnegie, surrounded himself with children and grandchildren. Among other millionaires were Claus Spreckels (sugar), Henry Payne Whitney (oil), Ogden Mills (minerals).

This 1848 painting by John Wilson depicts a wealth of detail of life on State Street in Albany. The buildings on the left side of the picture were owned by the Douws, a Dutch family dating back to the seventeenth century. Courtesy, Albany Institute of History & Art

The mansion of Frank W. Woolworth in Glen Cove had 62 rooms; that of Charles Tiffany, 82 rooms. Otto Kahn (banker) built a railroad in Cold Spring Harbor to carry the stone and earth needed to landscape the site for his mansion. The South Shore of Long Island also had its estates, although they were less numerous.

The wealthy also developed other enclaves, on both sides of the Hudson River. John D. Rockefeller had an elegant estate at Pocantico Hills near Tarrytown. Tuxedo Park across the Hudson was the country home of Edward Harriman and other millionaires. The Vanderbilt Mansion, now a National Historic Site, is situated close to the family home of Franklin D. Roosevelt at Hyde Park.

Men of wealth and power organized clubs where they could lunch or dine with their peers. Some clubs stressed ancestral ties; others appealed to persons of similar cultural interests such as music, museums, and theater. Women also had their clubs, some emphasizing their early origins. The Daughters of the American Revolution had chapters in most cities throughout the state. Boarding schools sprang up, especially in New England, where the elite could send their children. Most cities also had country day schools, attended by children of wealthy families, that gave special attention to preparation for colleges of academic excellence and social prestige. For example, the Utica Country Day School was established in 1921.

The public was alternately envious and repelled, fascinated and disgusted by the social pretensions of society. The "yellow press" of William Randolph Hearst and Joseph Pulitzer, neither of whom had a chance of becoming an insider, delighted in describing the ostentatious display of wealth and the domestic foibles of the elite. The formation of the Four Hundred in 1892 attracted attention and laughter, but it also caused many heartaches among social climbers and old gentry who did not find their names on the list drawn up by Mrs. William Astor and her social mentor, Ward McAllister. Because the Astor ballroom could accommodate 400 individuals, it automatically fixed the number of those eligible for invitations to her balls.

Above: The proliferation of inventions for washing clothes in the nineteenth century stimulated an interesting reaction. Here, Mrs. Partington's washing machine touted as the "cheapest and best" is actually her own prowess at the washboard! Courtesy, Landauer Collection, The New-York Historical Society, New York City

Right: The manufactures of Otsego County were numerous and included flour, lumber, cotton and woolen goods, leather and iron. By the mid-nineteenth century they exceeded $1.1 million in sales. Shown here is the Phoenix Mill around 1890. Courtesy, New York State Historical Association, Cooperstown

The consolidation of trusts and the public reaction to their formation are familiar stories to most readers. Therefore we shall make only a few observations as to their special impact upon New York State. If Morgan and associates had a major role in arranging these combinations, other New Yorkers likewise took the lead in opposing monopolies. President Theodore Roosevelt denounced the big trusts and helped bust several of them. Some New York firms became giants. General Electric, for example, developed out of the purchase by Thomas A. Edison of a vacant locomotive plant in Schenectady, where he began to manufacture Mazda lamps. Subsequently it expanded its activities to make turbines. The International Business Machines Company in the Binghamton area and Eastman Kodak in Rochester also became giant corporations famous for their research and marketing skills.

New York State, interestingly, had relatively fewer trusts than most other industrial states, because the typical firm as well as the leading manufactures in this state—textiles, clothing, printing and publishing, boots and shoes—were small in size and employed few workers.

Electricity became the main source of power, and steam plants using coal produced most of the power. The large hydroelectric plants on the Niagara River, however, symbolized the

new age of electricity. Because it was difficult to transmit electricity for any distance, generating plants were located near large cities where railroads could bring in the coal and the companies could transmit their power to local customers. New York State became the leading producer of electrical machines such as turbines. It ranked third in automobiles and automobile parts, which were concentrated in the Buffalo area.

Clothing remained the most important industry, measured in value of output both in 1890 and 1930, with women's clothing rising to top rank and men's standing at number three in 1930. By that date printing and publishing had climbed to second place because of the growing demand for newspapers, periodicals, and books.

The electric railway revolutionized urban transport by offering speedy and frequent service. Speculators in real estate worked closely with politicians in determining the routes that radiated out from the central business district. Many citizens became commuters by buying houses that were erected in the outskirts. Streetcar companies often established resorts and parks on the outskirts of town.

Above: This picture shows Lord & Taylor's elegant restaurant, The Mandarin Room, as it looked in 1914, the year the store opened. Courtesy, The New York Public Library Picture Collection, The Branch Libraries

Left: The invention of the sewing machine revolutionized the production of clothing. Shown here are the latest ready-made styles offered in 1900 at Bundy and Crittendon's of Cooperstown, New York. Courtesy, New York State Historical Association, Cooperstown

Above: With the popularity of electric powered trolley lines, few cities escaped the growth of prolific veins of track. Shown here is the excavation for the Cooperstown Branch Trolley in around 1900. Courtesy, The New-York Historical Society, New York City

Below: Urban Trolley lines derived their power from massive electric power stations. Shown here, in 1901, is the Cooperstown Power House. Courtesy, New York State Historical Association, Cooperstown

By 1900 interurbans were beginning to link neighboring communities such as Utica and Rome, Newburgh and Walden, Dunkirk and Fredonia. Within a few years more than 100 companies had built in excess of 4,000 miles of track, some paralleling railroad lines, some penetrating new areas. By World War I a hardy individual could board a car in Oneonta, ride to Little Falls, switch to another line, and after several changes ride to Buffalo. If he were sufficiently hardy, he could ride all the way to Chicago.

The craze for electric railways attracted not only serious investors but also speculators who looted some companies and mismanaged them. The collapse of electric railways, however, came about not so much because of mismanagement but because of automobiles and buses. As early as 1915 the state had 255,000 registered vehicles, a figure that more than doubled in the next five years. Henry Ford's Model T was not only durable but also cheap enough for the average family to afford. Other improvements came rapidly, such as the self-starter, balloon tires, and the closed chassis. The more reliable automobiles became, the more popular they grew.

Good roads were as much the cause as the result of the automobile revolution. Various bicyclist clubs actually led the early fight for good roads, but motorists soon joined the clamor. Mud in the spring, snow in the winter, and dust in the summer made travel hazardous and unpleasant. The first roads built by towns and cities were macadamized, that is, composed of several layers of stone that were rolled.

Resentment against the overweening power of the railroads to fix rates sparked the drive to rehabilitate the canal system, which by 1890 had almost collapsed. Businessmen and exporters in New York City argued that a barge canal would force the trunk-line railroads to cut rates to New York City and insure its commercial supremacy. In 1903 a large majority of citizens

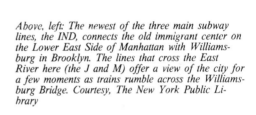

Above: Subway excavation on Lenox Avenue and 113th Street paved the way for subway service to the center of Harlem. In 1901 this was a newly developing middle-class area of the city. The current number three line that runs along these tracks is the only subway line to terminate in uptown Manhattan, in Harlem, at 148th Street. Courtesy, The New York Public Library Schomburg Center for Research in Black Culture

Above, left: The newest of the three main subway lines, the IND, connects the old immigrant center on the Lower East Side of Manhattan with Williamsburg in Brooklyn. The lines that cross the East River here (the J and M) offer a view of the city for a few moments as trains rumble across the Williamsburg Bridge. Courtesy, The New York Public Library

Left: Public street transportation had its start with horsedrawn vehicles. These were followed by cable cars attached by grips to an underground cable. Late in the nineteenth century, cars powered by an overhead copper wire like the Cooperstown Branch Trolley, shown here, enabled trolleys to traverse both city and intercity routes. Courtesy, New York State Historical Association, Cooperstown

Below: In the early days of the automobile, family portraits often included the family car. Shown here is Martin Moakler and family with their prize possession. Courtesy, New York State Historical Association, Cooperstown

Right:: America's love affair with the automobile coupled with a good camera buff made a picture like this an irresistible target. These cars were being shown at the local fairgrounds near Cooperstown in 1912. Courtesy, New York State Historical Association, Cooperstown

Facing page: In 1917 plowing was still done by horsepower. Shown here is the New York State Agricultural School in Farmingdale, L.I., in 1917. Courtesy, National Archives

Below: Samuel F.B. Morse developed the telegraph into a commercial venture after 1836. By 1861, the United States was crisscrossed with telegraph lines. By the turn of the century, cables crossed the Atlantic Ocean, facilitating communication with Europe in a matter of minutes. Photo by Byron, courtesy, Museum of the City of New York, Byron Collection

Right: New York's fertile Mohawk Valley has success-fully produced oats, corn, barley, wheat, hops, and potatoes. Shown here is a cornfield in Hartwich, New York, in 1914. Courtesy, New York State Historical Association, Cooperstown

Right: Between 1849 and the Volstead Act, hops was a major product in the Mohawk Valley region. It was usually picked by women and children who were followed by men to carry the bags of produce. By 1879 New York produced 21,628,931 pounds of hops on 39,000 acres. Shown here are hops pickers in Otsego County in 1902. Courtesy, New York State Historical Association, Cooperstown

voted for the creation of the New York State Barge Canal which deepened and widened the Erie Canal, whose route was also abandoned in several places. For example, the barge canal used the Mohawk River east of Herkimer, and it also utilized Oneida Lake east of Syracuse. The Barge Canal opened in 1918 but never lived up to the claims of its sponsors. The other canals—Champlain, Oswego, Cayuga, and Seneca—operated at a loss.

Agriculture and rural life did not change dramatically before 1920, because few farmers had yet bought a car or truck and utility companies did not extend power lines to farms. Nevertheless farming was becoming more commercial and more specialized. Milk production rose, even as the total land under cultivation contracted.

The demand for fluid milk soared because of increased population, the expanding rail net work, and public confidence in the purity of milk. The development of the glass bottle went hand in hand with the pasteurization of milk. The cheese factories began to decline because of Wisconsin competition and largely because farmers could make more money selling fluid milk to market.

Greater New York, 1898

The creation of Greater New York was "marked last night by perhaps the biggest, noisiest, and most hilarious New Year's celebration that Manhattan Island has ever known." So stated the *New York Tribune* on January 1, 1898. Thousands stumped through the heavy snow to see City Hall lit up by searchlights and fireworks. Steamboats and tugs blew their whistles, and the chimes of Old Trinity Church rang out the old year. The charter consolidated the five boroughs—The Bronx, Brooklyn, Queens, Richmond, and Manhattan—into the City of New York. A board of 65 aldermen was to form the legislative body; the mayor, comptroller, and president of the board of aldermen, together with the borough presidents, would constitute the board of estimate and apportionment in charge of the budget.

Two men, Andrew Haswell Green and Thomas C. Platt, were largely responsible for bringing about this epoch-making event. Green, a civic leader for four decades, had advocated this measure since 1868. He had restored city finances after Tweed's collapse, pushed the construction of the Brooklyn Bridge, and preserved Central Park from spoilsmen. Green argued that consolidation would help business, lower taxes, promote health, and improve police services. Most of the business elite favored consolidation, believing that it would knit the region's diverse units into a coherent transportation system.

Platt's motives were somewhat more pragmatic. As boss of the Republican party, he hoped the legislature would secure more control over municipal agencies. Furthermore he would win the title of "Father of Greater New York," which in turn would win for him the gratitude of the mercantile establishment. He might even have hoped to turn Greater New York into

a bastion for Republicans like Philadelphia and Chicago. During the 1890s the Republicans often won a majority of the votes in New York and Brooklyn.

Citizens of Brooklyn, however, formed the hard core of the opposition. Led by prominent Protestant clergymen, they declared that wicked Manhattan would swallow up the God-fearing community of Brooklyn famous for its churches and Sunday School parade. Platt, however, twisted the arms of Republican legislators and browbeat Governor Levi P. Morton, a Republican, to approve the measure.

The Democrats elected Robert Van Wyck as the first mayor of Greater New York, because the Republicans and independents could not agree on a candidate. Three years later the Republicans accepted a partnership with the independents and elected Seth Low as mayor. Several times in the future this coalition of Republicans, independents, and reformers was able to unseat or defeat the Democratic candidate.

Milk dealers in New York City formed an association to bring order to milk marketing and also to keep prices low for farmers, not for consumers. Dairymen cried monopoly and formed the Dairymen's League in 1907, conducting successful strikes in 1916 and 1919. In Albany representatives from rural counties carried on a thorough investigation of the industry and established the Department of Farms and Markets to supervise milk marketing and to assist farmers in learning about agricultural research. In 1904 the state founded the College of Agriculture at Cornell University under the direction of Liberty Hyde Bailey, who encouraged the appointment of agricultural experts or county agents who could pass on to working farmers the latest findings in research.

Lawn tennis was introduced to the United States from England in the 1870s. It was considered to be "a proper activity for young ladies" although no lady would think of serving overhand. On a summer day in 1888 the Daikin family of Cherry Valley, New York, had as much fun jumping over the net as they did in playing the game. Courtesy, New York State Historical Association, Cooperstown

Alfred H. Smiley first visited Mohonk Lake in 1869. Over the next fifty years he and his brother Albert acquired 7,500 acres of land in the New Paltz area. Today, this idyllic resort continues to be operated by descendants of the Smiley family. Courtesy, The New York Public Library Picture Collection, The Branch Libraries

Above: Early in this century, many little girls looked forward to dancing around the Maypole. Shown here is a May Day celebration at the Maples house in 1905 in Cooperstown, New York. Courtesy, New York State Historical Association, Cooperstown

Above: Although women's work was never done, they could lighten the tedium of some chores by gathering in congenial groups to sew, knit, and embroider. Shown here are three generations of the Olcott and Dakin family in the 1880s in their Cooperstown home. Courtesy, New York State Historical Association, Cooperstown

Below: In response to the deteriorating and exploitative conditions in many industries that employed women, middle class progressives formed the National Women's Trade Union League in 1903. The New York chapter was chartered in 1904. Courtesy, Library of Congress

The New York State Farm Bureau Federation was promoted by the county agents throughout the state. Although the Grange (Patrons of Husbandry) was primarily a social society, it did bring farmers together, and some chapters actively promoted measures designed to aid agriculture. In addition, the Dairymen's League provided dairymen with more bargaining power in negotiating prices of their products. In 1920 the three societies sponsored GLF (Grange, League, Federation), and Howard E. Babcock, principal founder of the Farm Bureau Federation, took command. The new agency performed several functions such as cooperative purchasing of feed, seeds, and gasoline.

During the last two decades of the 19th century, reformers played an increasingly important

Right: This New York City family found employment by making suspenders in their tenement home. Photo by Lewis W. Hine, courtesy, George Eastman Collection

Right, center: In the nineteenth and early twentieth centuries, orphanages and hospitals were generally thought to be the responsibility of churches and other charitable organizations. Shown here is an orphanage located in Cooperstown, New York, as it was in 1916. Courtesy, New York State Historical Association, Cooperstown

Right, below: During the Progressive Era, 1900-1914, many new industries arose that required little capital and unskilled labor. The women shown here were finishing pants in their tenement home. Courtesy, The Jacob A. Riis Collection, Museum of the City of New York

Below: Immigrant families in areas like New York City's Lower East Side provided garment manufacturers with a labor pool for a piecework cottage industry. Transport was often the responsibility of children; they moved the "bundles" before school in the morning. Courtesy, The New York Public Library, Local History and Genealogy Division

role in challenging the doctrines of laissez-faire. Walter Rauschenbusch of the Rochester Theological Seminary preached the social gospel, that is, applied Christianity. He and a growing number of churchmen urged old-age pensions, income tax, better housing, a ban on child labor, and government ownership of railroads. When Jacob Riis in 1890 published *How The Other Half Lives,* it was like a searchlight illuminating the squalor of the slums. A spirited writer and a brilliant photographer, Riis shocked the complacent middle class, and his book stirred the conscience of many wealthy citizens, including Theodore Roosevelt. Harriet Townsend, a founder of the Buffalo Women's Educational and Industrial Union, preached "organized mother love" as the goal of their society. It sought to educate immigrant women, provide legal services for domestics, and promote better health facilities.

Journalists exposed industrial abuses and political corruption. They described the plight of women working at dangerous jobs and at night, they deplored sweatshops, they condemned consumer fraud such as tainted meat and dangerous drugs. Some government studies provided ammunition for reformers. In 1894 Carroll D. Wright, United States Commissioner of Labor, estimated that New York City slums contained 360,000 dwellers. Many tenements were firetraps, and thousands lived in shanties, cellars, and sheds. Rats scurried through the garbage piled up in the streets and alleys. The homeless wandered about the streets, scavenging garbage pails and sleeping in cheap lodging houses if they had 10 or 15 cents. If penniless, they slumped in doorways, alleys, or railroad stations.

The seamy side of urban life attracted the attention of writers and artists. Stephen Crane wrote *Maggie: A Girl Of The Streets* in 1896. Artists painted scenes of alleys, tenements, and derelicts, thus becoming known as the Ash Can School.

The danger to the health and well-being of American mothers was a rallying cry for reformers trying to curtail abusive and exploitative work conditions. Courtesy, Schlesinger Library

The Progressives were a heterogeneous group agitating for hundreds of reforms, each of which had its core of dedicated advocates. In New York State social justice became the main concern, and by 1912 most Progressives favored workmen's compensation, insurance for health, accidents and unemployment, old-age pensions, the eight-hour day, and a ban on child labor. Organized labor joined forces with middle-class reformers on several issues—but not on all. Both favored consumer leagues and aid to women workers, who formed 23 percent of the work force in 1900.

The slums of New York had a greater density of population than those of London so graphically described by Charles Dickens and other writers. The *New York Tribune* in July 1899 printed this lurid description of a block on the Lower East Side:

. . . Huge malodorous "barracks" . . .
fronted these streets. In these blocks is said to have been the most overcrowded
spot in the world . . . Every room at one time was a workshop as well as a
sleeping and living apartment . . . factories honeycombed them all . . .

Above: This drawing of urban life was commissioned by the Russell Sage Foundation. Russell Sage and other foundations were active in helping new immigrants become acculturated to American life. Courtesy, The New York Public Library, General Research Division

Top: Before Central Park was built, 59th Street was the border between New York City's center of fashion on Fifth Avenue and the Squatter's City that extended almost to Mount Morris Park in Harlem. In this mini-city of tin and wood shacks lived more than 5,000 squatters. Courtesy, The New York Public Library, General Research Division

Right: Along with Jacob Riis and other progressive muckrakers, Lewis W. Hine was particularly disturbed by the conditions of tenement housing. He used his camera to expose and combat these conditions. Courtesy, The New York Public Library, Local History and Genealogy Division

The Bronx County Courthouse, shown here in 1909, is now a United States landmark. Photo by Joseph F. Hefele, courtesy, New York State Library

Lawrence Veiller, a prominent social worker, made a cardboard model of one block of 39 tenements housing 2,781 inhabitants and sharing 248 water closets. He marked tenements where individuals had criminal records and where there was tuberculosis, child mortality, and the like. The exhibit was a hit at the Paris Exposition of 1900, where many influential Americans could see the links between slums, disease, and crime. Governor Roosevelt and many other political figures were convinced that tenements needed regulation, and in 1901, the legislature outlawed the notorious "dumbbell" tenement because of its lack of light and air. The law also required toilets in each apartment as well as fire escapes for each building.

Both parties contained a growing number of members favoring a few or several progressive reforms. Tammany chieftains Alfred E. Smith and Robert Wagner endorsed many labor bills, especially after their service in the investigation of factories following the fire in the Triangle

The Triangle Fire

Late Saturday afternoon on March 25, 1911, New Yorkers in Washington Square on Manhattan Island could see smoke curling out of the windows of the Asch building a block away. The top three floors of the 10-story building housed the Triangle Shirtwaist Company, which employed more than 500 workers, mostly women but some of them girls 14 years of age. They had been working overtime cutting and sewing "Gibson Girl" blouses.

No one knows how or why a fire broke out on the eighth floor of the supposedly fireproof building. Cutters, however, were inveterate smokers and perhaps one dropped his cigarette or match in the waste material under the table. When flames shot up, workers threw pails of water on the oil-soaked refuse but to no avail. A workman reached for a fire hose only to find it rotted.

The workers rushed for the elevators and the two exits. A good number managed to escape down the Greene Street stairs, but those who raced to the Washington Street exit found the door locked, a point disputed in a later trial. The firm had ordered women to use the Greene Street stairway, where managers could make a random search of handbags to check on thefts of lace. The panic-stricken workers pressed so hard against the door, which opened inward, that it could not be opened. When Louis Brown finally got the door open, many workers tumbled down the dark stairs. Meanwhile the operators of the two elevators, each holding 15, moved up and down the shafts.

A telephone call alerted people on the 10th floor who escaped to the roof, where they climbed up ladders to the New York University building next door. Those trapped on the ninth floor received no warning, but smoke and flames made them

Above: The threat of fire was an ever present danger. Cooperstown, like other small towns, prided itself on keeping the most modern firefighting equipment to cope with the danger. Courtesy, New York State Historical Association, Cooperstown

Left: This fire on Cannon Place in Troy, New York, took place on December 13, 1893. Winter was an especially difficult time to fight fires because of icicles that routinely formed. Courtesy, New York State Library

aware of their peril. Some broke a window in the rear and began a hazardous descent on a rickety ladder. They had to drop from the last rung into a courtyard. Only 20 made it before the ladder collapsed under the weight, tumbling several persons to their death. The elevators kept running and took on women whose clothes and hair were aflame. Joseph Zito, an operator, reported hearing the thud of bodies hitting the roof of his elevator. Sarah Cammerstein jumped from the ninth floor to the roof of an elevator at the seventh floor and rode down to the lobby.

The Triangle fire caused the death of 146 individuals. Some 250,000 mourners watched a parade of workers forming a parade up Fifth Avenue that took four hours to pass them. The City and the State set up committees to investigate the tragedy. State Senator Robert F. Wagner and Assembly Speaker Alfred E. Smith, both Tammany politicians, joined other members in visiting 1,836 factories and tenements throughout the state. The commission looked into many matters besides fire hazards, such as sanitary conditions, child labor, and disease. Public demand resulted in a drastic reorganization of the state department of labor and 33 new labor laws, which author Leon Stein called the "golden era in remedial factory legislation."

Theodore Roosevelt, champion of the Progressive Movement, is shown here speaking before a meeting of the Women's Suffrage Association at his family home in Sagamore Hill, Long Island. Courtesy, Sagamore Hill National Historic Site

Shirtwaist Company. Republican Charles Evans Hughes, an outstanding governor, 1907-1910, fought hard for the direct primary and for regulation of the insurance industry and electric utilities.

Boss Tom Platt ruled the Republican party with an iron hand clothed in a velvet glove, thus earning the title "The Easy Boss." He held court every Sunday morning in the lobby of the Fifth Avenue Hotel, and party leaders came to take orders and ask for favors. His corner was called the Amen Corner because visitors generally followed Platt's decisions. Although Platt allowed his henchmen considerable leeway, on gut issues he demanded and got strict obedience.

Platt chose the Republican nominees, making sure, however, that the candidates could win. In 1894 Levi P. Morton ran against Governor David Hill and won handily by exploiting the hard times that had taken place under the Cleveland Administration. The Republicans handed out canal contracts to insiders and appointed unsavory lobbyists such as Louis Payn as the commissioner of insurance. By 1898 criticism had become an uproar, and Platt realized that he had to deflect rebellion among the voters by presenting a new face and a candidate of unim-

peachable character. A white knight appeared, none other than Theodore Roosevelt, who had led the Rough Riders up San Juan Hill and defeated the Spanish army. Moreover, Roosevelt had earned a reputation as a reformer who had fought for civil service in the assembly and had enforced the law while serving as police commissioner of New York. Platt recognized that despite his colorful rhetoric Roosevelt would play ball with party leaders.

Roosevelt won handily. He fired Payn and strengthened the civil service, but he also accepted any Platt nominees who had respectable backgrounds. Platt, however, found Roosevelt's independence hard to swallow, so he worked mightily to secure for Roosevelt the nomination for vice-president under President McKinley. He would sleep better if the unpredictable Teddy were safely ensconced on the Potomac. Roosevelt and McKinley won and Roosevelt presided over the Senate, a post that bored him. Then a madman shot McKinley in Buffalo, and Roosevelt raced down an Adirondack mountainside to await the news that President McKinley had received a mortal wound.

Roosevelt as president took control over federal patronage in New York State. Although Platt selected and elected Benjamin Odell and then Frank Higgins as governor, Platt found these men insisting on a fair amount of independence.

Meanwhile Charles Murphy emerged in 1902 as the undisputed boss of Tammany, a position that he held for more than two decades. William Randolph Hearst challenged Murphy by organizing the Municipal Ownership League and then running for mayor on a third-party ticket. Although George McClellan, Murphy's candidate, won, Hearst trailed him by fewer than 4,000 votes. In 1906 Hearst promptly decided to run for governor and eventually the presidency. He made peace with Murphy, who agreed to back him for the Democratic nomination. When

Facing page: Buffalo became a center of world interest in 1901 when the Pan American Exposition was held there. Unhappily, it gained notoriety as well when President William McKinley was assassinated at the event. Courtesy, The New York Public Library Picture Collection, The Branch Libraries

Below: Fourth of July celebrations like the one shown here in Fly Creek around 1910 have always been a part of small town American life. The brass band parading through the town's main street is usually followed by picnics and fireworks that last well into the night. Courtesy, New York State Historical Association, Cooperstown.

In the late nineteenth century, well-heeled upper and working class women united in their efforts to achieve female suffrage. Parades were a popular way to further their cause. Courtesy, National Archives

it seemed that Hearst just might win the election, President Roosevelt sent Elihu Root, his secretary of state, to Utica, where he excoriated Hearst as a demagogue, a corruptionist, a man of weak morals, and an inciter of crime. Hearst lost.

The Democrats finally captured the governor's office in 1910 after Hughes left to become a justice of the United States Supreme Court. Governor John Dix called for a direct primary, the direct election of United States senators, and income tax, all leading progressive measures. The Democratic and Republican parties, however, were deeply divided and stonewalled progress on these proposals.

Governor William Sulzer, a Tammany candidate who sometimes defied Murphy, won his post in 1912 partly because of the rebellion by Progressive Republicans against the Taft Administration. When Sulzer told Murphy that he intended to follow his conscience and be his

Above: The New York State Capitol in Albany was depicted in watercolor by Thomas W. Fuller. Courtesy, Albany Institute of History & Art

Left: The New York office of the National Association of the Women's Suffrage Association was headquartered at 505 Fifth Avenue. A monthly suffrage journal and many pamphlets advancing the suffrage cause were issued from there. Courtesy, The New York Public Library Local History and Genealogy Division

During World War I, the American Red Cross co-ordinated a heroic supply system that produced and delivered 23 million articles of clothing to soldiers at the front, four million items of hospital supplies, six million refugee garments, and 300 million surgical dressings. Courtesy, U.S. War Department Central Staff, National Archives

own man, Murphy was reported to have shouted, "Like hell you are." Soon the quarrel turned into a dog fight, with Murphy pressuring the legislature to impeach Sulzer for misrepresenting campaign expenses and committing perjury. Sulzer was found guilty of these charges, which probably a majority of the officials had violated also. Sulzer's removal from office was Murphy's means to punish him for his independence.

The outbreak of war in 1914 naturally engaged the attention of most New Yorkers, a majority of whom had close relatives on one or the other side of the conflict. The United States entered the war in 1917, and the federal government ordered all men from 18 to 45 to register for the draft. Over 500,000 New York men put on the uniform, and 14,000 lost their lives.

World War I brought many changes to the home front, not the least of which was the introduction of daylight saving time. Each county had a food administrator who encouraged farmers and householders to grow more food. New York industries led all states in producing goods for the army, navy, and merchant marine. Shipyards turned out many Liberty ships to transport men and goods to France. General Electric made searchlights, submarine detectors,

Next page: The seemingly casual atmosphere of the small town bank allowed tellers time for neighborly chats with their customers. Shown here in 1912 is Cooperstown First National Bank located on Main Street. Courtesy, New York State Historical Association, Cooperstown

and parts for radios. In Rochester, the Bausch and Lomb Optical Company made gunsights and binoculars; Eastman Kodak made dozens of items for the armed forces. The Savage Arms Company in Utica and Remington Arms of Ilion produced rifles and machine guns. New Yorkers bought more than a fourth of the bonds sold by the federal government to finance the war. Audiences in theaters, offices, and factories listened to three-minute speeches urging citizens to buy bonds. Private agencies—the Red Cross, the YMCA, the Salvation Army—enlisted volunteers and raised funds to assist servicemen and their families.

The armistice on November 11, 1918, led to statewide celebrations. When the troops returned to New York, each division received a ticker-tape welcome.

The war accelerated changes within the state. Immigration came to a halt but many farm families, including blacks from the South, moved to the cities to fill jobs. Numerous communities found the advantages of working together for local charities and established community chests, later renamed the United Way. The drafting of many immigrants and their sons speeded the process of "Americanization" and the entry of women into the work force, along with the wom-

Above: Military signaling, especially the use of radio signals, became a regular feature of twentieth century warfare. The production of signal equipment became an important part of wartime manufacture. Courtesy, U.S. War Department General Staff, National Archives

Facing page: The gentlemen of Cherry Valley, New York, proudly posed in front of the local service station during the Washington Day Celebration of 1912. Courtesy New York State Historical Association, Cooperstown

en's sùffrage amendment, marked greater participation of women in the life and work of the Empire State.

The Little Renaissance flowered in New York City between 1908 and 1917. Fundamentally it represented an artistic rebellion against genteel culture as exemplified by Henry James in literature and the classical school of art and architecture. Highly individualistic, the rebels charged about in many directions. Many were content to smash idols of the establishment, and almost all engaged in Puritan-bashing and needling the bourgeoisie. While some imported the latest artistic fashions from the Left Bank of Paris, others derided Old World standards as decadent. Like Emerson, they called for a genuine American art grounded in the regional scene and American character.

The Armory Show in 1913 stimulated popular interest in modern art, because the battle between modernists and traditionalists spilled over into the daily press and even the barbershops. Could scenes of alleys and tenements really be art? Had not art always tried to show the best

This "War is Over" parade took place in 1918. Returning veterans were welcomed with brass bands when they returned. Courtesy, New York State Historical Association, Cooperstown

and noblest concepts and examples of humankind? The battle raged from the coffee shops of Greenwich Village to the marble halls of museums. Today the modernists have become the new establishment, and the museums proudly display their paintings by John Sloan, Robert Henri, and others of that generation.

Intellectuals such as Walter Lippmann founded the *New Republic* and several little magazines with tiny circulations but big ideas that paved the way to the literary renaissance of the 1920s. Socialist ideas influenced many authors who at the same time insisted upon individualism of

the most pronounced kind. News of the Russian Revolution awakened great excitement, but when the Bolsheviks overturned democratic institutions in Russia, many intellectuals became disillusioned. A few made excuses for the brutality, fanaticism, and anti-intellectualism of the new Soviet state.

The Statue of Liberty greeted millions of European immigrants arriving in the Empire State and America. But tens of thousands of Americans came into the state by train from the South, Middle West, and Far West. Babe Ruth left Boston to join the New York Yankees, where he belted out homers from 1920 on. Jack Dempsey of Colorado came east to become heavy-weight champion in 1919 and later to operate a restaurant in New York City. William Gibbs McAdoo of Georgia left there to practice law in New York City, where he became a prominent Democrat—so prominent in fact that he challenged Alfred Smith for the presidential nomination. Hearst of San Francisco followed the example of Joseph Pulitzer, another outlander from St. Louis, to operate a newspaper in New York City. From nearby Vermont came John Dewey, who taught at Teachers' College of Columbia University, where he reshaped the educational theory and practice of the early part of this century.

Young people from the farms and villages of the Empire State also contributed a great deal of talent to its burgeoning cities. Elihu Root, Grover Cleveland, and George Eastman grew up in central New York but moved to cities, the first to New York City, the second to Buffalo,

Upstate New York's diversified economy character-ized by commercial agriculture, manufacturing, and com-merce, required modern banking services. Shown here is a 1917 bank vault in Cooperstown, which offered the latest in security facilities. Courtesy, New York State Historical Association, Cooperstown

the third to Rochester. Charles Evans Hughes grew up in Glens Falls before he attended college and made a career in New York, Albany, and Washington. From the Southern Tier came Boss Tom Platt of Owego and David Hill from Elmira.

Frank Gannett, whose birthplace was near Canandaigua, attended Cornell University and in 1907 took control of the *Elmira Gazette,* the first of his chain of newspapers.

What traits characterize most of these individuals in addition to hard work, energy, and innate ability? Imagination, competitiveness, and a willingness to take risks. Getting ahead, a trait observed by visitors to the state even before the Revolution, had become a secular religion before whose idols many New Yorkers, including adopted sons and daughters, were committing their whole life—or "body, boots, and britches," the delightful title of Harold Thompson's book on New York folkways. Was it mere coincidence that the most popular book around the turn of the century was *David Harum,* a novel about a shrewd banker in Homer near Cortland? Edward Noyes Westcott has David Harum say, "Do others or th'll do you—do 'em first." A calumny on the upstate character? Probably, but one might note that not too far from Cortland was the birthplace of John D. Rockefeller, where his father allegedly brought up his sons "sharp" by cheating them on occasion.

World War I and its aftermath marked a sharp change in the lives of New Yorkers. Immigration declined, at least from abroad. Urbanism was beginning to change into a suburban society because of trolleys and automobiles. The progressive spirit that had infiltrated both parties and brought about more social justice lost some of its momentum. Various factors—the school, the job, sports, the press, the draft, and an enlarged electorate—were Americanizing the immigrants and enlarging the middle class. The next decade would present a new challenge: the perils of prosperity.

Until midway through the twentieth century, the Bronx was known as the borough of parks. Joseph F. Hefele captured these leisure time pursuits as they were enjoyed by the common man and woman. Courtesy, New York State Library

PROSPERITY AND DEPRESSION 1920-1945

Boom, bust, and wartime recovery characterized both state and nation during this period. Immigration from Europe slowed to a trickle during the Depression and World War II. Nevertheless the Empire State remained a magnet for ambitious young people from almost every state. All the factors undergirding growth—splendid transportation, abundant capital, labor of all levels of skill, entrepreneurs, and cheap power—sustained the manufacturing, commercial, and financial supremacy of the Empire State.

After the Wilsonian crusade for the League of Nations fizzled out, Americans turned inward from Europe. Stimulated by crusaders against prohibition and a phalanx of intellectuals throwing their spears at middle-class and Puritan standards, "permissiveness" of many varieties corroded old patterns of behavior. Nevertheless a flowering of literature, music, scholarship, science, and medicine took place despite the sneers of cynics and expatriates. Coolidge prosperity, the envy of the world, burst its bubble in 1929, but New Yorkers, led by Franklin Roosevelt and Herbert H. Lehman, pioneered in promoting social legislation to combat the Depression and to regulate business. When a united nation defeated the mighty Wehrmacht and toppled the Japanese warlords, New Yorkers, like other Americans, felt renewed confidence in the American way of life.

During the 1920s the population of the state registered a gain of 21 percent, roughly the same as the national figure, but during the next decade the rate of growth slowed to 8 percent.

Several factors slackened population growth. During the 1920s Congress placed limits on immigration, banning all Asians and restricting persons from eastern and southern Europe. When the Depression set in, the government granted visas only to relatives of citizens or to those who could prove they would not become public charges. The Depression also caused many young people to postpone getting married and having children. In fact the birthrate, which had been almost 30 per 1,000 in 1900, fell to less than 13 in 1936, the lowest figure for many years to come. Meanwhile the death rate had also fallen from 18 per 1,000 in 1900 to less than 11 per thousand in 1950, the result of better medical attention and new drugs such as sulpha.

The number of foreign born dwindled after 1914, although the ranks of the second generation expanded. The census of 1950, which included data on foreign stock (foreign born plus their children), showed the Italian contingent in the lead, followed by Russians (chiefly Jews), Ger-

Page 162: Until 1927 Jones Beach was an inaccessible sand bar, on a windswept reef with sparse grasses, and a few summer shacks. The New York State park system began construction, and by 1929 was ready for use. The construction project included the building of access routes, as well as construction of various pavilions for eating, dancing, skating, and other recreations. Courtesy, The New York Public Library Picture Collection, The Branch Libraries

Facing page: Originally an outpost of the Dutch West India Company, Harlem became the twentieth century center of black cultural, political, and social life in New York City. Courtesy, The New York State Department of Economic Development

Below: Buffalo is New York's largest inland port, and became a major depot for raw materials from the west and manufactured goods from the east. Before World War II stopped civilian automobile production, many of Detroit's cars passed through the Lake Erie port. During both world wars, Buffalo's large industrial plants were of considerable value to America's war efforts, providing weapons, supplies, and food. Courtesy, The New York Public Library Picture Collection, The Branch Libraries

Immigrant Demographics

Although immigrants settled along the urban corridor of the Empire State, they did not spread out evenly. The census of 1920 shows that the three largest contingents in order of population in various cities were as follows:

New York	Russians (chiefly Jews), Italians, British (especially Irish)
Buffalo	Poles, Germans, Canadians
Rochester	Italians, Germans, British
Syracuse	Italians, British, Poles
Utica	Italians, Poles, Germans
Albany	British, Italians, Germans
Schenectady	Italians, Poles, British
Yonkers	British, Italians, Austrians
Niagara Falls	Canadians, Italians, British
Jamestown	Swedes, Italians, British
Binghamton	Czechs, British, Italians

mans, Poles, and Irish. In 1950 the Empire State had about 4.3 million residents who were born outside the country; the largest concentration was in New York City, where 42 percent were foreign born.

Meanwhile blacks, who had started to arrive in considerable numbers before 1920, kept moving to New York City. Harlem became known as the black capital of the world because of its swanky nightclubs, talented musicians, and literary luminaries.

More than 80 percent of New Yorkers in 1940 lived in urban centers, that is, places of 2,500

Buffalo was laid out by Joseph Ellicott in the same general plan as Washington, D.C. This aerial photograph shows the nine main streets that lead like spokes of a wheel from the main business area. The central avenue extends north along Main Street for two and a half miles. Courtesy, The New York Public Library Picture Collection, The Branch Libraries

or more inhabitants. The urban growth rate slackened after 1920, whereas rural population showed a small increase. This shift was caused by suburbanization and by the Depression years, when rural folk found it difficult to find jobs in the cities. The spread of hard-surfaced roads and automobile ownership, the development of centralized schools, and rural electrification stimulated city-dwellers to move to the outskirts and even into the open countryside.

The greatest growth took place in counties beyond the limits of the larger cities. For example, Nassau and Suffolk counties on Long Island and Westchester north of The Bronx grew rapidly. By contrast Manhattan itself lost 19 percent of its population during the 1920s while the other four boroughs of New York City kept growing.

Rural counties lying beyond the pull of the larger cities did not gain from suburbanization. Counties in the Catskills, Adirondacks, and Southern Tier had a declining or stagnant population growth rate. Furthermore, if one looks more closely at rural population, one finds a growing number of families who did not engage in full-time farming. In fact more than half of those living in farmhouses worked for agencies serving farmers or commuted to city jobs.

Meanwhile, almost two million New Yorkers took up residence in other states, the largest number in Connecticut and New Jersey. And more than 100,000 New Yorkers escaped the harsh winters by moving to Florida and California.

The most significant development in the economy of the state was the widespread adoption of the "horseless carriage." Vehicle registrations, 576,000 in 1920, soared fourfold in the "golden twenties," but the Depression saw the sales of new cars leveling off. The government prohibited the manufacture of new cars during World War II, but once peace returned the automobile companies could hardly meet the demand.

The automobile revolutionized the lives of farmers, workers, and city-dwellers. Farmers at first placed milk cans on a rack in the back seat of their "tin lizzies" but soon purchased trucks to carry their milk and crops to market. An increasing number of office and factory workers bought cars and also purchased houses miles away from work. The country schoolhouse gave way to centralized schools to which children rode in yellow buses. Town, county, and state officials assigned a larger chunk of their budgets to the construction and maintenance of highways. The relatively small federal grants were greatly expanded after 1933 when the New Dealers spent billions on roads in order to provide jobs for the unemployed.

The automobile had a tremendous impact upon city life. The trolleys lost riders and in many cases transit companies bought buses, which, however, had a difficult task competing with automobiles. City officials had to assign a large number of policemen to direct traffic when motorists insisted on driving to work or to shop. Factories, stores, and office buildings had to provide parking space for their employees and customers, a goal seldom achieved successfully. Wealthy families who had lived within walking distance of stores and offices deserted Victorian mansions

Above: Construction began on the Holland Tunnel, named for its chief engineer, Clifford Holland, in 1920. It was opened in 1927. It runs from lower Manhattan to Jersey City. In 1976, when this photo was taken, the tunnel handled more than nine million cars, 44,000 buses, and 1.7 million trucks eastbound into New York City. Courtesy, The New York State Department of Economic Development

Below: Between 34th and 59th streets, Fifth Avenue emerges from a wholesale clothing, textile, and bric-a-brac district to become the aristocrat of shopping thoroughfares. Aside from many large emporia, the avenue boasts hotels, clubs, and churches. Courtesy, The New York Public Library Picture Collection, The Branch Libraries

on Main Street for smaller houses on the outskirts, where golf courses, country clubs, and private schools sprang up to serve their needs. Even the shape of new houses changed because of the scarcity of domestics and the problem of snow removal. Architects incorporated the garage into the house and built a short distance from the street.

Although the main automobile factories were concentrated in Michigan, New York factories made automobile parts. Moreover, dozens of enterprises sprang up to serve buyers and owners of cars and trucks. Dealers in new and second-hand cars competed vigorously for business, as did operators of filling stations and garages. Along roadways sprang up tourist cabins, roadhouses, restaurants, and "ye olde gifte shoppes ." The country stores in small villages often had to board up their premises, because rural families drove to cities in order to secure lower prices, greater variety of goods, and better styles. Harness makers, blacksmiths, and carriage makers closed their doors or more often began to sell gasoline. Horses became less useful on the farm as well as in the city. Livery stations and horse barns around country churches disappeared. Of course, all these changes took place before World War II ended the manufacture of cars and rationed gasoline.

The motor-car industry gave a great stimulus to the business of advertising. To be sure, drug

Facing page, top: Cook's Garage in Cooperstown, New York, offered automobile accessories and served as a showroom. Even during the Depression, local enthusiasts stopped to browse. Courtesy, New York State Historical Association, Cooperstown

Facing page, bottom: Cook's Garage featured a variety of transportation modes available to modern America in 1937. Out front, of course, is the newest model automobile. Courtesy, New York State Historical Association, Cooperstown

Below: Cooking devices in the early nineteenth century were generally coal-fueled ranges, which necessitated separate appliances for stoves and ovens. The development of gas and electric-powered stoves enabled the stove to feature a side oven that cut down on space and enhanced cleanliness. From Lutes, Today's Housewife, *1921*

America's fascination with cars even extended to the quiet country gas station. This Herkimer County Oasis was a welcome sight to weary travelers in 1938. Courtesy, New York State Historical Association, Cooperstown

companies before World War I popularized Lydia Pinkham's nostrum, Dr. Sloan's Liniment, and Fletcher's Castoria. The tobacco industry used such slogans as "I'd walk a mile for a Camel" and "Blow some my way," a discreet way of cultivating the flapper market. The automobile companies emphasized appeals for individuals to outspend their neighbors by buying the latest-model car. Advertising firms opened their doors on Madison Avenue in New York City, where the writers of their copy invented slogans that changed American consumption habits. In 1922 Sinclair Lewis wrote *Babbitt,* a devastating satire on the go-getting seller of real

estate. Three years later Bruce Barton, the chairman of a leading advertising firm, depicted Jesus Christ as a hard-charging businessman in his book *The Man Nobody Knows.*

New York's pattern of manufacturing differed considerably from the national pattern. Nondurable goods outranked heavy goods such as steel and machinery. In 1950 employment in nondurable industries stood at 64 percent of all manufacturing workers, whereas the national figure was only 48 percent. The clothing industry, which enrolled one in five manufacturing employees, accounted for much of this difference. The second leading manufacture was printed and published materials, another nondurable-goods industry.

In 1900 the first voice broadcast by radio was accomplished. By 1932, as evidenced by this photo of a Cooperstown, New York, radio shop on Main Street, radios had become a common home appliance. Courtesy, New York State Historical Association, Cooperstown

Employment of women in manufacturing was slightly higher than in the nation, partly because the clothing industry has always hired a large number of women. In 1920 one in four workers was a woman, a percentage that gradually rose to one in three in 1944 at the height of World War II. A large number of women also worked in retail establishments.

After the victorious doughboys disembarked in New York Harbor and marched up Broadway, they discovered an economy marked by confusion and uncertainty. Farm prices had collapsed; factories that had made guns, ships, and uniforms laid off workers. But the economy turned around by 1922 and good times returned, at least to most of the urban states. Scientific management and technological innovations contributed to a large increase in productivity.

New York City—and to a lesser extent upstate cities—acquired a new skyline when promoters

The proliferation of consumer goods, especially for the housewife, are widely displayed in this picture of Roots Hardware store taken in Cooperstown, New York, around 1920. Courtesy, New York State Historical Association, Cooperstown

Tunes like "Rosie the Riveter" and "Minnie's in the Money" sang the praises of women working in the defense industry during World War II. After the war, "Rosie" and "Minnie" were expected to retire gracefully to their "natural" place—the home. Official Navy photo, courtesy, The Brooklyn Public Library, Brooklyn Collection, Eagle Collection

financed skyscrapers housing the headquarters of many national corporations. Sixty stories above the street workmen balanced themselves on girders, while far below other workmen operated giant cranes and poured truckloads of cement. Each year new buildings were constructed, but the race came to an end in 1929, although the Empire State Building was not completed until 1931, its 86 stories forming what was then the tallest building in the world.

The forces that stimulated and later undermined this era of prosperity are outside the scope of this book. Although most Americans enjoyed a higher standard of living, a disproportionate share of the new wealth ended up in the coffers of large corporations that basked in the warm sunshine of a friendly federal government. Surging profits and manipulation of stocks by Wall Street bulls led millions to buy stocks. A craze to get rich swept the country, enticing ordinary folk to buy stocks on margin or to purchase lots in Florida. Why not? Did not the newspapers and magazines run stories on how John Jones had quadrupled his money by buying a glamour stock? To meet the demand for securities, promoters organized holding companies and investment trusts whose assets reflected hopeful expectations more than actual values. The great bull

market kept roaring as foreign investors rushed to take a flyer, and even corporations placed their reserves into brokers' loans—loans made by brokerage houses to individuals who were buying securities on margin. Several observers warned of a coming shakeout and a few of a violent collapse, but promoters and politicians rushed to reassure the public that all was well. The Republicans, who controlled the White House and Congress, claimed credit for the new era of perpetual prosperity that would see poverty "banished from the nation," in the phrase of Herbert Hoover, the new president.

The speculative mania reached its climax in October 1929 when the bubble burst and stock prices plummeted, bankrupting many businesses, banks, and individuals. By 1932 manufacturing output had fallen to half the 1929 total, and prices, employment, and foreign trade likewise declined precipitously. Hard times marked most of the 1930s and the country did not emerge from the Depression until 1940, when America began to rearm.

Strong governors of national stature—Alfred E. Smith, Franklin D. Roosevelt, Herbert H. Lehman, Thomas E. Dewey—provided leadership in this period. During the 1920s Al Smith, the darling of the urban masses and immigrant population, set the political agenda. The red-faced, harsh-voiced smoker of big cigars and wearer of brown derbies presented a sharp contrast to the traditional governors who were drawn from upper-crust families of English-Dutch stock. City-dwellers easily identified with the uneducated and somewhat uncouth Al Smith, who grew up in the Fourth Ward, a maze of tenements at the foot of the Brooklyn Bridge. As a youth Smith swam in the East River, served as altar boy, and participated in amateur theatricals. At 13, when his father died of overwork, Smith left school to help his mother bring up the family. At first he ran errands for a trucking firm, then for four years he rolled barrels of fish in the Fulton Fish Market from four in the morning to five in the afternoon.

A young man of popularity and dependability, Smith caught the eye of Tom Foley, whose saloon was also a branch of the Tammany machine. Foley gave Smith minor assignments, which the young man completed promptly. Foley rewarded his protege by moving him up the ranks of the Democratic party. In 1903 Foley picked Smith to run for a seat in the assembly. In Albany Smith kept silent for the first year but watched every move of the party leaders. He won friends on both sides of the aisle, exercised his talents as a barroom tenor, and won a reputation as a hard worker who scrutinized every bill placed on his desk. Before long his fellow legislators recognized that this uneducated man knew more about state government than anyone else. In 1911 Smith rose to majority leader and two years later became speaker of the assembly, where he wielded the gavel with fairness and ability. Smith impressed independents and Republicans when he served on the committee investigating factory conditions and spoke as a delegate to the constitutional convention of 1915.

Smith, unquestionably a cog in the Tammany machine, followed the orders of Boss Charles Murphy. When Murphy decided to oppose the constitutional amendments in 1915, Smith went along, although he had helped frame some of the reforms. Nevertheless Murphy himself came to respect Smith's judgment and saw the advantages of supporting social legislation. Smith was rising above the narrow interests of the party machine and in a sense was pulling Murphy along with him.

In 1918 Smith received the Democratic nomination for governor and defeated Governor Charles Whitman, only to lose his office in the Harding landslide of 1920 even though Smith ran far ahead of James Cox, the Democratic candidate for president. However, Smith made a comeback in 1922 and easily won reelection in 1924 and 1926.

During his first term Smith impressed citizens with his cabinet choices, which included independents and men of high ability. He soon discovered that the governor's hands were tied by scores of independent commissions, agencies, and departments that took orders from political bosses such as chairmen of legislature-appointed committees. Smith appointed a nonpartisan

Facing page: Forty-second Street and Fifth Avenue stand at the heart of Manhattan. Until the turn of the twentieth century, the area bounded by Fifth and Sixth avenues and 40th to 42nd streets was occupied by the Croton Reservoir. The New York Public Library, shown on the right, replaced it. The library, completed in 1911, was designed by Currier and Hastings. Courtesy, The New York Public Library Picture Collection, The Branch Libraries

Robert Moses is shown here speaking from the porch of the Taylor mansion in Islip, Long Island, at the dedication ceremonies for the Hesksher State Park in June 1929. Courtesy, Long Isiand State Park Commission

committee to study reorganization of state government, but when the Republican-controlle legislature refused to approve funding, the members of the committee paid their own expense The commission recommended the consolidation of the 187 agencies, departments, and board into a dozen or so departments whose heads would be appointed by the governor with th consent of the senate. It recommended that voters should select only the governor, lieutenaı governor, and comptroller, each for a four-year term. It urged the establishment of an executiv budget that the governor would assemble with the aid of his department heads and that woul list expenditures and revenues for the next year.

The Red Scare swept New York and the nation after the Communist takeover in Russı and revolutionary unrest in Europe after World War I. In 1920 the Republican majority the assembly refused to seat five duly elected Socialists. Smith, who personally opposed socialis and detested Communists, valiantly stood for the right of voters to elect legislators of their ow choice. His defense of civil liberties was supported by Charles Evans Hughes and other promine citizens.

At first Smith made little or no progress in reshaping the structure of state government becau of the opposition of Republicans and the politicians who feared the loss of patronage and pow over the scores of agencies. Their main argument was that consolidation would grant too mu power to the governor. Smith and most academic experts of political science at that time insisted that the only way to secure efficient government was to fix responsibility. If anything went wrong, the public could demand the governor set it right. Smith learned to go over the heads of his opponents, and he had the ability to simplify the issues and to make even statistical material interesting to the voters. He achieved most of his objectives by means of constitutional amendments, a complicated procedure requiring ratification by two separately elected legislatures and then submission to the voters. Consolidation into 18 departments took place by 1926; the executive budget went into effect three years later. At last the governor had control of the bureaucracy and the budget.

The expansion of the park system was another noteworthy achievement under Governor Smith, who appointed Robert Moses to develop the system through the Council of Parks, created in 1923. Moses inherited 35 commissions managing small parks and historic sites such as battlefields. By 1928 Moses had doubled the number of parks and enlarged the acreage to 125,000 acres. He personally directed the Long Island State Park Commission, which created Jones Beach, whose beauty and management became world famous. Moses insisted that the parks should offer recreation as well as conservation to the millions of middle-class citizens who were buying their first automobile in the 1920s. He also took steps to build parkways on Long Island. Although a genius in planning and a talented administrator, Moses ran roughshod over any individual or commission blocking his centralized control of the park system.

The most controversial political issue was the question of waterpower: how it should be developed. The Republicans favored the lease of power sites to private companies, but the Democrats advocated public ownership and development through a New York State Power Authority. Neither party got its way, but the private utilities became stronger by building more dams and by combining small units into giant holding companies.

If the state Democratic party seemed highly successful in electing Smith as governor, the national organization exhibited turmoil and confusion. (Will Rogers loved to say, "I don't belong to an organized political party. I am a Democrat.") The basic cleavage was between the rural, dry, Protestant South versus the urban, wet, Catholic Northeast. In 1924 William G. McAdoo, a lawyer and son-in-law of Woodrow Wilson, had most of the Southern and Western delegates, whereas Smith had a solid quarter of the delegates. McAdoo refused to disavow the support of the Ku Klux Klan, the secret society opposed to blacks, Jews, Catholics, and immigrants. Tammany Hall packed the galleries with noisy rooters, who converted no delegates and convinced radio listeners that Smith supporters were vulgar buffoons.

Since the Democrats required a two-thirds majority of the delegates, McAdoo and Smith could block each other's candidacy. As a result the delegates sweated through 103 ballots before they gave up and approved John W. Davis, whose candidacy never got off the ground.

Four years later Smith ran a stronger race and captured the Democratic nomination. Many Democrats realized that no Democrat could defeat Herbert Hoover, who had earned a world reputation as a humanitarian and a manager. A greater handicap was Coolidge prosperity, which persuaded a majority of voters not to rock the boat. To be sure, bigotry plagued both sides, but Smith suffered more than he gained. In spite of this, Smith doubled the Democratic vote of 1924 and captured a majority of voters in many large cities formerly controlled by the Republicans.

New Yorkers were accustomed to Smith's raspy voice, mannerisms, and accent, but out-of-staters found him a provincial figure who seemed to disdain Americans west of the Mississippi or south of the Mason-Dixon line. Hoover's upbringing on an Iowa farm seemed more traditional than that of someone reared on the sidewalks of New York. Henry L. Mencken, in one of his more sagacious comments, observed that Smith's world "begins at Coney Island and ends at Buffalo."

Mohawks in High Steel

How many people know that a number of the ironworkers who performed the risky job of putting together the girders and spans of the George Washington Bridge, Rockefeller Center, and dozens of other skyscrapers were descendants of the Mohawk Indians? In fact, Mohawks are recognized from coast to coast as excellent workers in high steel.

These ironworkers hail from two reservations: the Caughnawaga, west of Montreal, and the St. Regis, along the St. Lawrence River, with some 39,000 acres which are half in Canada and half in New York surrounding Hogansburg, its trading center. Only a few hundred of the 3,000 inhabitants on the St. Regis reservation are full-blooded Indians, because other tribes and French Canadians have intermarried with the Mohawks.

Adaptability and mobility have characterized these Indians in the Mohawk Valley and the St. Lawrence Valley. The coming of the French and the Dutch, soon followed by the English, disrupted the old way of life. By 1640 the Mohawks had become part of the international fur trade, first as trappers, then as middlemen between the traders in Montreal and Albany and the western tribes. British and French explorers and traders were quick to recognize their prowess as canoemen. Mohawks for almost two centuries guided timber rafts carrying oak and pine over the Lachine Rapids on the St. Lawrence. Like the other Indian tribes the Mohawks had to contend with firearms, firewater, and disease, which reduced their numbers sharply. Mean-while, French Jesuits and English Anglicans converted many Mohawks to Christianity, a faith somewhat disruptive to old religious beliefs and tribal customs. No doubt the greatest shock resulted from the Revolutionary War, in which the Mohawks remained loyal to the king. The Mohawks retreated to Canada and lost most of their land within New York State. Chief Joseph Brant received a land grant along the Grand River in Ontario, where a settlement grew up called Brant's Town.

Another kind of shock revolutionized Mohawk life when the railroad age opened. Engineers were given the task of constructing railroad bridges across the St. Lawrence River. Braves on the Caughnawaga reservation watched with fascination as ironworkers gingerly made their way on

George Washington Bridge, which connects New York to New Jersey, was opened in 1931. Photo by Audrey Gibson

the girders. This kind of work—hard, dangerous, and seasonal—appealed to them. Furthermore, ironworkers received the highest wages on construction jobs.

Did centuries of stalking deer and following trails give Indians a special skill in high steel? One observer pointed out the Indian habit of putting one foot in front of the other whereas Europeans seemed to walk in more of a straddle. At any rate, contractors hired the fearless Mohawks, whose reputation for skill and fearlessness spread across the country.

After 1910 Mohawk ironworkers began to take jobs in the United States. During the 1920s, corporations rushed to build skyscrapers as their headquarters in Manhattan and other large cities. Mohawk crews were catching hot rivets far above the streets of New York. Some Mohawks took rooms in the North Gowanus section of Brooklyn, and before long their families joined some of them. Most of them maintained close ties with their relatives in the St. Regis and Caughnawaga reservations. Older or injured ironworkers would retreat to the reservations, where their small savings would go farther. Here they tended to slough off the ways of white society and pick up some of their old customs. During the 1950s a minority became militant defenders of Indian rights when Robert Moses took away some of their land for the St. Lawrence Seaway and power project. Some of the youth joined the old men in learning the chants used in the religion of the Long House. The cemetery on the St. Regis reservation bears mute testimony to the clash of cultures. Many graves are marked by lengths of steel bent to form crosses. Nearby, Mohawks come to the longhouse to chant and beat drums.

Smith needed the electoral votes of New York in order to win, and therefore he had to have strong candidates for state offices. Franklin D. Roosevelt seemed a splendid choice: a scion of an old Hudson Valley family, a Harvard graduate, and the Democratic nominee for vice-president in 1920. Roosevelt would appeal to many anti-Tammany Democrats and independents. True, his health remained a question mark, but his vigorous campaigning nullified that issue.

In 1928 Roosevelt carried the state for the office of governor by 25,000 votes while Smith lost his presidential bid by more than 100,000. Clearly, some New Yorkers split their tickets, partly because they had reservations about Smith's occupying the White House and Katie Dunn Smith entertaining foreign dignitaries. Herbert H. Lehman, candidate for lieutenant governor and an outstanding philanthropist, attracted many Jewish votes. Probably more decisive was the split in Republican ranks. Albert Ottinger, Republican candidate for governor, had quarreled with Hamilton Ward of Erie County, who controlled the Buffalo machine and did not throw his weight behind Ottinger.

Smith's defeat had an unfortunate effect upon his relations with Roosevelt and even the Democratic party. Devastated by his smashing defeat, the Happy Warrior sulked in his quarters and blamed it on bigots and snobs; but he consoled himself with plans to help Roosevelt in governing

Herbert Lehman was the son of German Jewish immigrants. He was part of the Progressive tradition in New York state politics—a tradition dating back to Theodore Roosevelt's term as governor and continuing through the terms of Charles Evans Hughes, Alfred E. Smith, and Franklin Delano Roosevelt. Lehman was governor from 1933 until 1942. Many of the programs put into effect during his time in office were models for Roosevelt's New Deal. Courtesy, New York State Library

Despite the Depression, Williams' Market on Main Street in Cooperstown displayed a wide variety of goods. Courtesy, New York Historical Association, Cooperstown

his beloved Empire State. After all, the handicapped and amiable country squire of Hyde Park would certainly need Smith's aid in combating the Republicans in the legislature and in managing the bureaucracy. Smith took a suite in the De Witt Clinton Hotel in Albany, where he awaited a call from the new governor. A week passed but no call. Swallowing his pride, Smith asked for an appointment, which Roosevelt graciously granted. Smith found that Roosevelt had already written his inaugural speech without consulting him.

Roosevelt had made up his mind to run his own show. Roosevelt had his eye on the White House and had to demonstrate his independence of party bosses and his leadership capacity. Therefore he had to emerge from the shadow of the great governor and scotch stories that he was weak and a lightweight, terms often bandied about in Smith's entourage. Then there was the Moses problem. Robert Moses had cut the budget of the Taconic State Park Commission which Roosevelt headed while he lavished funds on the Long Island Park Commission under Moses' jurisdiction. Roosevelt, who loved gossip, had heard the snide comments Moses had made about his leadership ability, or lack of it, when the Smith cronies were deciding whether to ask Roosevelt to run for governor.

If Moses was abrasive and Smith ultrasensitive to any affront, Roosevelt was sometimes evasive and devious, traits that infuriated his rivals and dismayed even his friends. At any rate he refused to reappoint Moses as secretary of state, although he left him in charge of state parks. Moses had cleverly arranged his term to continue to 1930, and he controlled the various boards that selected the leader of the state council on parks. Smith could hardly complain about Roosevelt's general stance. Had he not reappointed 16 out of 18 members of Smith's cabinet and declared on every occasion that he would carry out Smith's program? Indeed Roosevelt was to propose legislation that went beyond Smith, who was inching toward more conservative stands. Smith began to associate more and more with John J. Raskob and other wealthy supporters, who appointed him to a well-paying position as manager of the Empire State Building. Eventually Smith by 1934 was to join the conservative assault on the New Deal.

Smith turned over to Roosevelt a state government hailed by many experts as a model, with its reorganized departments and executive budget. Of course the Republicans still controlled the legislature and could throw roadblocks in the path of legislation aiding the urban centers. Almost immediately the legislators tested his mettle by passing lump-sum items that permitted the chairmen of the senate and assembly finance committees to determine how money was to be spent. Roosevelt vetoed these parts of the budget, only to have his veto overridden. Governor Roosevelt appealed to the courts and won a striking victory.

Roosevelt found it more difficult to secure labor and social legislation. He backed Frances Perkins, head of the department of labor, in her efforts to expand the workmen's compensation law, permit workers to choose their own doctors, and curb employers from stalling settlements on claims. He persuaded the legislature to enact a 48-hour week with a half holiday each week. He failed to get a system of unemployment insurance, but he secured a system of old-age pensions though they were crippled by limiting amendments. Nevertheless one can see the beginnings of Social Security, perhaps the most lasting legacy of the New Deal.

Roosevelt advocated programs almost always with one eye on their value in attracting national attention. He championed the cause of public regulation of utilities, a position popular not only upstate but also in the Western and Southern states, because utility companies had imposed excessive rates, watered their stock, and corrupted legislatures. In New York State they owned the Republican party and thus controlled the legislature. Roosevelt called for a strengthened public service commission and demanded that utilities earn only a reasonable return on their investment, which should not include inflated valuations. If Roosevelt failed to harness the utilities, progressives across the nation gave him credit for trying. He recommended the public development of the St. Lawrence River power potential, but such a project required federal support, which President Hoover opposed.

His four years in the governor's chair honed Roosevelt's skills as an administrator. True, he permitted too much squabbling among officials, and he often settled for half a loaf. Experts in public policy point out that public agencies should not be judged by the same standards as private companies, because these agencies necessarily have to take into account local sentiment and placate influential politicians. Roosevelt knew how to manage people, massage politicians, and manipulate the media. He had learned from Al Smith how to educate the public and not talk down to them. He also had patience. He would wait for an opening before he added another stitch in the pattern of his grand design. Unlike Moses, he avoided namecalling and seldom displayed vindictiveness. Persons who crossed him, however, found that he had a long memory when it came to rewarding allies with patronage.

The Depression and the election of 1932 gradually overshadowed all other issues, especially after 1930. More than a third of the manufacturing firms in New York City closed their doors, a proportion only slightly smaller than that for unemployment. Even the lucky ones with jobs found their wages cut to the bone. By 1932 Woolworth's was paying saleswomen seven dollars a week. If the man in the wheelchair did not see the housewives scavenging for vegetables under pushcarts or the long lines at soup kitchens, his wife, Eleanor, did and reported back. Roosevelt became one of the first governors to recognize that the state and federal governments had to assume responsibility for the care of the needy.

Private charities and local governments tried hard to handle the increasing load of welfare, but by 1931 many cities could not sell their bonds and were teetering on the brink of bankruptcy. Roosevelt called a special session of the legislators to address the problem. The Weeks Act set up the Temporary Emergency Relief Administration to supervise more state aid to localities for work and home relief. T.E.R.A. granted relief to 379,000 families with 1,500,000 individuals. New York became the first state to adopt a plan putting tens of thousands to work on public projects and to include medical care as part of the relief program. Once again one can see that Roosevelt was serving an apprenticeship for federal management of difficult problems.

Tammany spoilsmen gave him more trouble than Republican obstructionists, however. While Boss Murphy lived, he ruled his district lieutenants with iron discipline and kept blatant graft under control. Then Murphy died in 1924 and the lid was off. Perhaps the scandals of the Harding Administration and the conspicuous skullduggery on Wall Street were other manifestations of a lowering of public standards of honesty. Boss John Curry, seldom cited for his mental acuity, could not keep his greedy henchmen from lining their pockets. James J. Walker, the debonair mayor of New York City, epitomized the jazz age. When he was not attending nightclubs and squiring actresses to riotous parties, he was taking jaunts to Paris, Churchill Downs, and other fleshpots. And the public hailed their mayor as the ultimate showman of Manhattan glitz. So what if he did not tend the store!

But the metropolis could not afford this prodigal waste whereby scores of clubhouse crooks siphoned off city funds. By 1926 its annual expenditures had topped half a billion dollars and its debt equaled that of all the states combined. Scandals began to pop up. In 1928 Arnold Rothstein, a notorious gangster, was murdered. Did Tammany politicians block a thorough investigation because it might disclose their close associations with gambling and prostitution? So it seemed. The next year Congressman Fiorello La Guardia challenged Walker for mayor and brought out evidence linking a Democratic magistrate with a large loan from Rothstein. The press, Republicans and citizens in general, demanded a cleanup. The flamboyant mayor began to look more and more like a tawdry wastrel who had neither the ability nor the desire to guide the city through hard times.

Roosevelt was trapped. If he agreed to demands for an investigation, he would affront Tammany Hall chieftains who could deprive him of a solid state delegation to the Democratic national convention. If he did not investigate, his rivals could charge him with covering up scandals. Naturally he waffled and claimed that the governor did not have the authority to intervene in local affairs, but rising pressure forced him to ask the appellate division of the state supreme court to investigate magistrate courts and to convene a blue-ribbon grand jury to hear evidence. The Republicans, eager to divert attention from the economic collapse under Hoover, nominated Charles Tuttle for governor, but Tuttle's campaign was ineffective. Roosevelt won reelection by 725,000 votes, a margin that made him an obvious presidential candidate in 1932.

In 1931 the legislature created a joint legislative committee to investigate the affairs of New York City. Judge Samuel Seabury, the counsel, uncovered graft in many city departments. Walker was charged with accepting favors from business firms, granting contracts to companies operated by his friends, and refusing to explain the source of his outside income. Walker resigned on September 1, 1932, and took a voyage to Europe with a Hollywood actress.

Tammany leaders tried to sidetrack the nomination of Herbert H. Lehman for governor by sending him to Washington as United States Senator. Lehman marched up to the political conclave and declared that he would run for governor no matter whom they endorsed. They backed down. Both Smith and Roosevelt made many speeches for Lehman, who won by more than 800,000 votes despite his lack of charisma and color. But the public recognized his integrity and dedication, and they knew his reputation as a financier, administrator, and philanthropist. Furthermore Lehman would keep alive the Smith-Roosevelt tradition of gradual change and reforms that the taxpayers could afford. Lehman was to hold the office for a decade, in which he cooperated closely with President Roosevelt, Mayor La Guardia, and even Robert Moses. His last term was for four years after 1938, a change accomplished by a constitutional amendment.

La Guardia, who began his stormy career as a Republican, soon earned a reputation as one of the most capable administrators in the history of American cities. Colorful, feisty, provocative, La Guardia chased the crooks out of City Hall and imposed strict standards of honesty. He shifted his party membership to the American Labor party, which enlisted many union members, especially in the clothing industry. This third party backed Roosevelt and Lehman in 1936, but by 1938 Communists had infiltrated the Manhattan branch. When the Communist element took over, David Dubinsky, the head of the International Ladies Garment Workers' Union, walked out and organized the Liberal party, which soon secured more votes than the American Labor party.

During the 1930s all levels of government—federal, state, local—expanded their services and touched the lives of citizens in ways never before experienced. The federal government offered many new programs providing jobs on public works, subsidies to farmers, and cheap credit for home owners and home builders. Local communities constructed facilities such as roads, airports, and low-rent apartments in cities. New York, more so than most states, aided the unemployed, factory workers, the aged, and slum-dwellers.

The Little New Deal in Albany expanded several progressive programs first advanced by Charles Evans Hughes and later enlarged by Al Smith and Franklin D. Roosevelt. By comparison with his predecessors' programs, Lehman's cornucopia of social legislation was more like a breakthrough toward a welfare state in which the government underwrote a minimum standard of living. Lehman and Roosevelt raised the banner of "freedom from want" and stressed the rights of labor about which progressives felt uneasy. Interestingly, Lehman was advancing his program quite independently of Washington except for Social Security, which Governor Roosevelt had urged. Under Lehman the State instituted a minimum-wage system and granted to workers in intrastate business the same right to organize and bargain collectively that the National Recovery Administration and the Wagner Labor Relations Act did for workers in interstate commerce. Lehman also pioneered in public housing.

What accounts for Lehman's remarkable successes? First of all the Depression, the worst in U.S. history in depth and duration, provided a climate of urgency favorable to change. Upholders of the status quo found it progressively more difficult to oppose measures to help the jobless, the elderly, women, and children, especially when the federal government was moving in that direction. The main opponents in the business community had lost much of their credibility and also their political clout. In New York City and in some upstate centers, cadres of social workers, planners, and foundation experts were urging proposals such as unemployment insurance. Academic experts publicized the way England, Sweden, and Australia were meeting unemployment, housing issues, and health problems. Lehman, who had taught in the Henry Street settlement house, had contacts with these individuals and was willing to experiment. Doggedly and persistently he wore down the opposition.

To be sure, certain groups thwarted some of his proposals. The public utilities blocked public development of waterpower resources, although they had to submit to stricter regulation of rates. The medical community checked health insurance, and commercial farmers stood in the way of labor laws protecting migrant workers.

The Depression and the Little New Deal weakened the power of Old Guard Republicans, who found a growing number of Republican legislators accepting the central tenets of the Little New Deal. When Thomas Dewey won the governorship in 1942, the party platform accepted the welfare state in principle. Dewey claimed, however, that he and his associates would provide a more efficient administration.

Tom Dewey grew up in Owosso, Michigan, where he sang in the church choir, joined the Boy Scouts, and inherited a strong Republican loyalty. After graduating from the University of Michigan and Columbia Law School, he spent six years in private practice. Then he served as chief assistant to George Z. Medalie, United States Attorney for the Southern District of New York, in which capacity he attracted attention for his successful prosecution of Waxey

By 1870 Macy's boasted more than one million dollars in sales. Despite austerity during World War II, the store's sales continued to rise as evidenced by these Christmas shoppers in 1942. Courtesy, Library of Congress

Gordon, a notorious gambler. In 1935 a grand jury in Manhattan asked Lehman to institute an investigation of racketeering. Lehman offered the post to several prominent Republican lawyers who all refused but recommended Dewey. Lehman had some misgivings about Dewey's youth but agreed to the appointment. Dewey promptly began a relentless pursuit of mobsters such as Lucky Luciano, the King of Vice. His popularity led the anti-Tammany forces to choose him to run for district attorney of New York County on the same ticket as La Guardia. The victorious Dewey indicted scores of corrupt officials and jailed many loan sharks. He tracked down Dutch Schultz, who collected protection money from restaurant owners and poultry dealers.

The young lawyer with piercing dark eyes and a little black moustache won a state and national following as a crime buster. The Republicans were looking for a candidate against Lehman in 1938, so they selected Dewey, who cut the Lehman margin to only 64,000 votes.

Meanwhile the Democratic party was falling apart because of rivalries and scandals in the metropolis. Machine Democrats hated New Deal Democrats such as Lehman, Roosevelt, and Wagner, and in 1942 they nominated John J. Bennett, Jr., the state attorney general. The American Labor party regarded Bennett as antilabor and put up their own candidate, Dean Alfange, who garnered 403,000 votes. Dewey won the governorship in a landslide, an office to which he was reelected in 1946 and 1950.

Dewey formed a strong organization based on county chairmen who disciplined legislators who defied Dewey. To be sure, several chafed under Dewey's strict control, but they were grateful for patronage that they had lost under the long period of Democratic control. Furthermore they recognized Dewey's ability as a vote getter who attracted moderates in the rapidly growing suburbs. Dewey appointed dozens of public-relations officials who filled the press with his achievements and sniped at the work of his predecessors. An ardent partisan, Dewey selected an all-Republican cabinet and high officials.

World War II naturally preoccupied Dewey and the legislators. The state government tried to aid the war effort in various ways, such as setting up an Emergency Food Commission. It arranged for the transportation and housing of migrant workers and encouraged high-school students to assist farmers during vacations. Because new farm machinery was scarce, the EFC arranged for repairs to existing machines. Wartime labor shortages created many problems. Many high-school students dropped out to take high-paying factory jobs. Juvenile delinquency rose. The State set up centers where working mothers could leave their children.

A large surplus piled up because construction of roads and state buildings was postponed and because full employment increased revenues from taxes. By 1946 the Postwar Reconstruction Fund totaled $450 million.

New York shifted from war to peace more smoothly than after World War I. The State aided small businesses to get started again and to find contracts. A tremendous housing boom took place because of the low construction rates from 1929 to 1945. Hundreds of thousands of demobilized veterans decided to get married and start families. By 1947 some 30,000 veterans and dependents were living in 214 housing units.

Dewey's main achievements took place after 1945, when war needs no longer preoccupied state officials. Most constructive but also most controversial was Dewey's strong support for an antidiscrimination measure that he pushed over the opposition of reactionaries, some employers, certain labor unions, and bigots. The Ives-Quinn Act of 1945, which banned discrimination in the workplace for race or religion, set up a commission to collect data and pass judgment on claims of discrimination in hiring and promotion. Although Dewey relied primarily on educating the public and persuading violators to desist, he insisted on fines and jail sentences for persons found guilty of discriminating. This act ended discriminatory clauses in application forms, want ads, and membership in unions. Its success led Dewey and the legislature to outlaw

discrimination in education and housing. What was most remarkable was the commission's ability to persuade firms to end discriminatory practices without judicial wrangling and public coercion. Several other states copied the Ives-Quinn Act, and two decades later the federal government passed similar legislation.

New Yorkers experienced heady prosperity, hard times, and a war economy in the quarter century that began in 1920. Fortunately a series of able governors—Smith to Dewey—provided

Facing page: During their heyday, railroads provided employment opportunities for black men. Shown here is a porter outside a private car on the Delaware and Hudson line. Courtesy, New York State Historical Association, Cooperstown

Left: In the suburban boom of the 1920s and 1930s, the square model house that the Bossert firm offered had a variety of innovations in space utilization and the maximization of floor space with a minimum use of wall area. Louis Bossert and Sons offered the public this simple and inexpensive design around 1926. Courtesy, Bossert Houses, Louis Bossert & Sons, Inc.

THE Meadowbrook is a favorite Bossert design offering an amazing number of ingenious variations both in plan and design, all of which are most economical, because, the building being square, the greatest amount of floor space is enclosed with the least amount of wall area.

The front entrance can be on the side or on the gable end of the building.

Porch is of ample size and is made unusually attractive with pergola beams and flower trellises. From this porch handsome double French doors open directly into the spacious well-lighted living-

READY-CUT OR SECTIONAL FLOOR PLAN

1. Width, 24 ft.
2. Depth, 24 ft.
3. It has five rooms and bath, with a dining alcove.
4. The porch is 20 x 8 ft.
5. Living-room, 24 x 12 ft., with a dining alcove 6 x 9 ft. and space provided for fireplace.
6. A dining-room or bedroom on first floor is 9 x 10 ft.
7. The kitchen is 9 x 9 ft.
8. A china-closet is provided in the kitchen.
9. A butler's pantry and rear entrance, 5 x 9 ft., with ample space for ice-box and stores with door to kitchen and dining-room and entrance to cellar.
10. Second floor, two bedrooms, each 9 x 12 ft.
11. A bath 6 x 5 ft. 6 inches.
12. From each bedroom are two large closets for storage.
13. Each bedroom has four windows.

First Floor Plan

Second Floor Plan

BOSSERT HOUSES

strong leadership not only in the restructuring of state government but also in the erection of a safety net for the old, unemployed, and poor. Toleration of individuals, partially begun under the Dutch and British and enhanced by the Bill of Rights and the abolition of slavery within New York State, reached a new high in the Ives-Quinn Act.

In this period Franklin D. Roosevelt won four of the seven elections and guided the nation through the Depression and global war. Never before had a New Yorker exercised so much power in the White House. And probably never again will it happen. No New Yorker secured the nomination of a major party between 1952 and 1984. The star of California and other Sunbelt states rose, eclipsing the Empire State not only in political leadership but also in population growth and economic expansion.

Facing page: The Albany campus of the New York State University system draws students from all parts of the state. The campus features modern architecture with classrooms located in a rectangle and resident towers a short walk from each quadrant. Courtesy, The New York State Department of Economic Development

Below: Normal schools were early colleges whose function was to train elementary and high school teachers. From these somewhat inauspicious beginnings developed New York State's university system—now including four university centers and numerous four-year and two-year institutions. Shown here is the Buffalo Normal School. Courtesy, New York State Library

The Waning of the Postwar Boom 1945-1975

When California in 1963 elbowed New York State into second place in population, few residents felt envy or alarm. After all, did not the Empire State still lead in trade, banking, publishing, transportation, and manufacturing? A decade later, however, they were dismayed to find both metropolis and state teetering on the brink of bankruptcy, a tax burden the highest in the nation, and more than a million New Yorkers who had fled to other states. More ominous was the relative decline in the standard of living and the industrial base. Whereas in 1950 the per capita income stood a healthy 25 percent above the national level, by 1973 it had fallen to 13 percent—and the trend was downward. These indicators were offset by such achievements as the broadening opportunities for education, especially on the collegiate level.

Most shocking of all was the loss of approximately 700,000 residents in the 1970s, a loss experienced by no other large state. New York City lost more than 10 percent of its population in the 1970s but retained a higher percent than the 12 next-largest cities in the Northeast. Buffalo, for example, lost more than 23 percent between 1960 and 1975. New York City, however, fell from more than half of the state's population in 1950 to approximately 40 percent by the 1980s.

Mobility and diversity continued to characterize population during this period. New York remained overwhelmingly urban, but the suburban fringe grew at a much faster pace than the center cities. People were spilling over the boundaries of all cities and moving beyond the boundaries of counties to rural areas. After 1963, the United States Census Bureau began to rely more upon a new statistical tool, the Standard Metropolitan Statistical Area (SMSA), which took a large urban center, added the rural sections of its home county, and attached other counties within its orbit. For example, the Rochester SMSA includes not only Monroe County but also Orleans, Livingston, and Wayne. If one looks at Buffalo in 1940, one finds 576,000 people in the center city and 383,000 outside. By 1970 the figures shift to only 463,000 in the center city and 881,000 outside.

New York City is a more complicated case and, as usual, a special case, because its SMSA includes Bergen County in New Jersey as well as Westchester, Putnam, and Rockland counties, the last county lying west of the Hudson River. On the other hand the New York SMSA does

Page 190: The main entrance of the Metropolitan Museum of Art, considered the Grande Dame of art museums, is located on Fifth Avenue and 82nd Street. The Metropolitan was founded in 1870 and designed by Richard Morris Hunt. The collection inside covers 5,000 years of art from all over the world, in addition to a library of 250,000 books and related research materials. Courtesy, New York Convention & Visitor's Bureau, Inc.

Facing page: Originally founded in 1809, St. Patrick's Cathedral is the second oldest Roman Catholic church in New York. It was moved from the original site on Mott Street to the current site on Fifth Avenue and 50th Street in the middle of the nineteenth century—construction began in 1852. Once an uptown outpost, the cathedral is now the hub of New York, directly across the street from Rockefeller Center. Courtesy, New York Convention & Visitor's Bureau, Inc.

The Population by Nationality

The 1960 figures to the nearest thousand are quite interesting

Nationality	New York State	New York City
Italy	1,477	859
U.S.S.R.	739	564
Poland	684	389
Ireland	492	312
Germany	674	324
Austria	316	219
United Kingdom	433	175
Canada	326	6

not include Nassau and Suffolk counties, which showed a gain of more than a million in the 1950s alone. One must take care in making comparisons, because the census bureau has changed the boundaries of some SMSAs.

To better their conditions: that motive inspired two large groups of American citizens, blacks and Puerto Ricans, to make their homes in New York State. Other factors played a part—the adoption of the mechanical cotton picker, segregation and harassment in the South, overpopulation in Puerto Rico. These newcomers came to find work, not to seek welfare. Nevertheless, some who found work lost their jobs and subsequently had to apply for relief. The relatively generous payments in New York State—Medicaid, Aid to Dependent Children, etc.—tended to anchor these newcomers, who otherwise might have gone home or migrated to other parts of the country. In fact, when Puerto Ricans did return to their home island, the effect upon the schooling of their children was often disruptive.

Most newcomers, whether they came from abroad or from this country, were young people from a rural background and with a poor education, the latter no fault of theirs. Because they had inadequate command of the language and few marketable skills, they had to take low-paying or unpleasant jobs. Black women often worked as domestics and cleaning women, and the men took odd jobs until they found more permanent positions. Many entered the garment industry a traditional open door for the semiskilled.

Although blacks constituted the great majority of nonwhites, Asians swelled their total to 310,000 by 1980. Native Americans (Indians) had a state total of 39,582, with almost 12,000 in the metropolis. By 1980 nonwhites numbered more than 20 percent of the state population and close to 40 percent of the residents of New York City.

The Puerto Rican immigration deserves special attention because of its size, mobility, and concentration in New York City. In 1940 only 61,663 persons from the island were living in New York City, but the postwar boom and cheap air fares stimulated a vast migration to the mainland, the number climbing to 429,710 within the next two decades. Other persons of Spanish language origin such as Cubans, Central and South Americans, and Spaniards also settled in New York, and the Spanish-language contingent constituted about 9 percent of the state population and about one in five in New York City. Contrast this statewide figure, 1,659,300, with the black population of 2,402,000, three-fourths of whom in 1980 were living in the metropolis Westchester and Erie counties also had more than 100,000 blacks who settled in the large cities upstate.

Bright, beautiful paintings found on store gates along 125th Street in Harlem, between Adam Clayton Powell, Jr., Boulevard and Frederick Douglass Boulevard are an attempt to brighten up the urban grayness of Harlem's major commercial thoroughfare. The artist, Franco, is shown here with a completed work. Courtesy, New York Convention & Visitor's Bureau, Inc.

Persons of foreign stock (birth and parentage) still formed almost 48 percent of the population of New York City and about 27 percent of the state population in 1980. They were the result of the great wave of Europeans who swarmed into New York Harbor before 1929. Italians headed this list, followed by persons from the Union of Soviet Socialist Republics, who were mainly of Jewish background. A majority of the immigrating Italians, Jews, Irish, Germans, and Austrians found a home in the metropolis, as did Puerto Ricans and blacks. Roman Catholic Poles made Buffalo their main center. Most people from the United Kingdom settled upstate. Canadians of English background settled in Buffalo, Rochester, and other cities in western New York, but French Canadians spilled over to Plattsburgh, Massena, and lumber towns north of the Adirondacks.

The state, especially New York City, attracted a considerable number of whites—business people, professionals, skilled workers—who were likely to settle in the four suburban counties outside New York City proper or on Long Island. Meanwhile, close to a million and a half whites between 1950 and 1970 left New York City, some finding homes in New Jersey and Connecticut, others seeking new lives in Florida and California. During the same period a half million blacks, most of them from the Carolinas and Virginia, were moving to the city, and after 1965 a considerable number of blacks from the West Indies arrived. One can only speculate what all this churning of people was doing to neighborhoods, parishes, stores, housing, and the like. It caused turmoil in the schools and colleges, drove up social-service costs, and changed political alignments.

Because the federal government does not compile statistics on religious affiliations, one must rely upon estimates by private groups. Pollsters survey voters according to race, religion, and income level, and also use exit polls. One estimate in 1952 assigned to Roman Catholics and white Protestants the same percentage, 37, while allotting 18 percent to Jews. The religious breakdown for New York City in 1952 was almost one-half Catholic, one-quarter Jewish, and slightly less for Protestants, a majority of whom were black. Four out of five blacks were Protestants, perhaps half of those Baptists.

By 1980 the racial and ethnic composition of New York State had undergone considerable change, especially in the growth of nonwhites and Puerto Ricans. Blacks, with 2,402,000, and the Spanish-language group, with 1,659,000—about one million of Puerto Rican stock—had grown substantially. Meanwhile, persons of Italian ancestry had risen to more than a tenth of the state population, according to census figures of 1980. No wonder they became politically powerful in both parties: Governor Mario Cuomo, a Democrat, and Senator Alfonse D'Amato, a Republican. Well behind the Italian figure of 1,938,000 stood the Irish at 1,010,000, which would not include persons of third, fourth, and fifth generations. Germans and British each numbered almost 900,000; Poles 608,000.

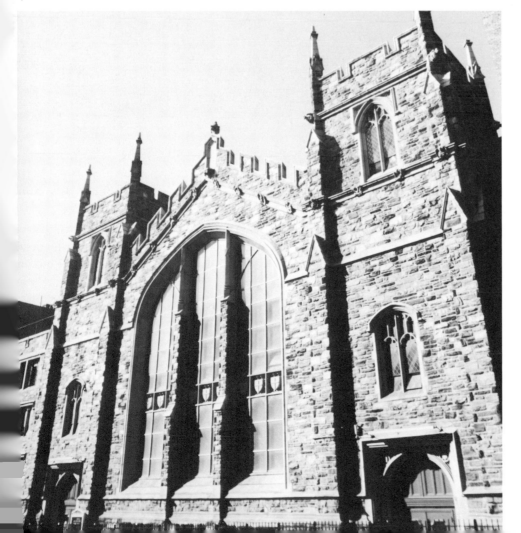

The Abyssinian Baptist Church, the oldest black church in New York City, is located in Harlem. The church became prominent under the leadership of its former pastor and New York City congressman, Adam Clayton Powell, Jr. It has been a powerful force in the black community since early in the century. Courtesy, New York Convention & Visitor's Bureau, Inc.

The Democratic party in New York State had a substantial majority of enrolled members, but the Republicans between 1945 and 1975 won all but two gubernatorial elections. What factors accounted for Republican successes? First of all, governors and state officials after 1936, as well as many mayors, were elected two years after presidential contests, and Republicans almost always turned out in greater numbers than Democrats, a higher percentage of whom were poor, black, and less likely to register. Second, the Democrats did not mobilize their massive majority in New York City, because the old Tammany machine was creaking and paralyzed by bitter personal and factional struggles. Rising groups—Jews, Italians, blacks—jockeyed for position to seize the reins of power from the faltering Irish leadership. Third, the Republicans built strong organizations (Republicans disliked the term "machine") in suburban areas. The three counties of Nassau, Suffolk, and Westchester provided a fourth of the Dewey vote in 1950 and a third of the Rockefeller vote in 1970. Finally, the Republicans fielded two dominant figures: Thomas Dewey and Nelson Rockefeller. Both knew the importance of organization and skillful staff members, and Rockefeller could and did spend lavishly in all his campaigns. Rockefeller attracted a sizable vote among blacks because of the family benefactions to black colleges and causes. When Rockefeller embarked upon his massive construction projects, he pleased many Italian Americans who had a large stake in the construction business.

During his second administration after 1946 Dewey established the State University of New York. Previously the Empire State had relied upon private colleges and universities to provide higher education for most students except those entering the fields of education, agriculture, forestry, and the like. Before World War II, New York actually ranked 47th in per capita spending for higher education. New York City had founded and financed City College of New York and its sister institution, Hunter College for women, before 1914. It added Brooklyn College in 1930 and Queens in 1937. All four colleges, whose academic standards were among the highest in the nation, had enrolled 78,000 students by 1956, twice that of the State University of New York at that time.

After World War II thousands of veterans sought admission to colleges, and the federal GI Bill of Rights provided them with funds to attend them. The existing colleges could not handle all these students, although they expanded their faculties and put up temporary buildings. In 1946 the legislature opened three emergency colleges, at Utica, Plattsburgh, and Sampson Naval Training Center near Syracuse. Dewey appointed Owen D. Young, head of General Electric Company, to head a committee to study the problem and make recommendations. Should they establish a centralized system like California's? Should the state university offer a full-blown program or merely supplement the private institutions? The commission recommended using the existing system of public institutions as the nucleus of a state university: 11 teachers' colleges, 5 experimental institutes, 6 agricultural and mechanical two-year institutes, and 5 contract colleges—4 of them at Cornell (Agriculture, Home Economics, Veterinary, Industrial and Labor Relations) and one at Alfred (Ceramics). The commission urged the establishment of a system of two-year colleges financed in part by the State, in part by local governments, plus low tuition charges. The State University soon took over the College of Medicine at Syracuse University and also the medical college at Long Island University. The Young Commission urged the establishment of university centers which would include professional schools and offer instruction for graduate students seeking doctor's degrees. The State absorbed the University of Buffalo, which became one of the university centers, and transformed the Teachers' College at Albany into a university center. New centers were founded at Stony Brook on Long Island and at Binghamton. The State University made slow progress under Dewey and did not start its explosive growth until the 1960s under Governor Nelson Rockefeller.

Dewey increased state aid for elementary and secondary education but at a slightly lower rate than the growth of the state budget. Teachers in Buffalo, who had found their salaries eroded

Facing page: Governor Nelson Rockefeller was the son of the greatest of the robber barons. He was a popular New York governor, and was elected three times—1958, 1962, and 1966. Rockefeller ran unsuccessfully for the presidency in 1964 and 1968. His pet project and proudest achievement was the Albany Mall that bears his name. Courtesy, New York State Archives

Below: Founded in 1944, the Fashion Institute of Technology, a unit of the State University of New York, is located in the Garment Center of New York on Seventh Avenue. FIT enrolls nearly 12,000 students pursuing careers in the garment and textile industries. It is also located across the street from the garment industry museum, housed in the International Ladies Garment Workers Union building. Courtesy, New York Convention & Visitor's Bureau, Inc.

*Located at Cornell University in Ithaca, the Herbert
F. Johnson Museum of Art houses a collection of European and American paintings, sculpture, prints, drawings, photographs, and art from Africa, Oceana, and
the Americas. Courtesy, The New York State Department of Economic Development*

by wartime inflation, struck for higher salaries. This enraged Dewey and shocked the public,
with the result that the legislature passed the Condin-Wadlin law prohibiting strikes by public
employees.

Dewey pursued a course of moderate change, well behind the liberal Republicans but ahead
of the conservatives. Dewey hesitated to spend money if it meant increased taxes. An ardent
partisan, he always promoted Republican programs and backed Republican candidates. He
helped to win for his party an increasing share of upstate voters even in the cities where Catholics,
immigrants, and industrial labor formed a majority. Like other upstaters he attacked Tammany
Hall, which often obliged its foes by creating scandals. Tammany Hall, in the period from 1897
to 1966, controlled the mayor's office for only 14 years, just 2 years longer than La Guardia
was mayor. Independent Democrats and "good government" forces also enjoyed more success
than Tammany Hall. The suburban ring of counties—Nassau, Suffolk, Westchester, and
Rockland—have almost always rolled up large majorities for the Republican party.

Governor Dewey worked hard but quietly to secure another Republican nomination for
president in 1948. President Truman seemed to face a hopeless task because of the defection
of the Dixiecrats and the followers of Henry Wallace. Imagine the public's and Dewey's surprise
when Truman carried many farm states and won. Having lost two races for the White House,
Dewey decided to give up further efforts. Nevertheless he did not abandon his party and in
1952 took an active and perhaps decisive role in persuading General Dwight D. Eisenhower
to enter the Republican primary. When some party members favored Taft for the nomination,

Dewey whipped these delegates into line. Dewey also suggested that Eisenhower choose Richard Nixon for vice president.

Perhaps the two most significant achievements of his third term, beginning in 1950, were the creation of the Niagara Power project and the opening of 366 miles of the New York State Thruway in 1954, the latter subsequently to bear his name. Dewey took a hand in selecting his successor for the Republican nomination for governor, Irving Ives, an able moderate. The Democrats put up Averell Harriman, a millionaire and a statesman who had distinguished himself in diplomacy. He won by the slim margin of 10,000 votes.

The Democratic leaders faced a threat of losing votes to a coalition of union labor and left-wing liberals who organized the American Labor party in 1936 to support Roosevelt for a second

Left: Crafts were often taught in public high schools in hopes that such training would equip graduates for useful productive lives. Shown here is a woodworking class at the Plattsburg Normal and High School. Courtesy, New York State Library

Left: Although mundane concerns like earning a living were evident in public high school curricula, the offerings of a library were not neglected. Shown here is the Library of the Plattsburg Normal and High School. Courtesy, New York State Library

term. Almost all the funds and most of the foot soldiers in this party were members of the International Ladies Garment Workers' Union, headed by David Dubinsky, and the Amalgamated Clothing Workers Union, led by Sidney Hillman. In 1936 the small Communist party opposed Roosevelt, but in the next year switched its policy when the Kremlin urged it to join forces with any group against fascism. The hardworking Communists gradually won control of several county units. Dubinsky, who had defeated the Reds in his own union, organized the Liberal party in 1943, which attracted 330,000 votes in 1944, just enough to enable Roosevelt to win New York State. A few years later Hillman left the ALP because he could not swallow the tactics of the Communists. His defection destroyed the ALP, which in 1954 failed to secure the 50,000 votes needed to stay on the ballot. The Liberal party continued to attract about 250,000 voters and almost always endorsed Democratic candidates for governor and president.

Meanwhile, "reformers" in New York City challenged old-line Democratic leaders by joining district clubs and by running their candidates in the primaries. These reformers were drawn from the ranks of professionals, young college graduates, and voters who had become politically awakened because of their ardent support of Adlai Stevenson in his two races for president against Eisenhower. They attacked Carmine De Sapio, who in 1949 had become the Democratic chieftain of New York County, the first person of Italian extraction to hold that post.

The administration of Averell Harriman caused few ripples of excitement. The governor, a man of patrician bearing, hesitated to enter the hurly-burly of politics, and he always seemed to be looking with one eye to Washington. Clearly, he had hopes of winning the Democratic nomination for president. Under Harriman state aid to local school districts rose more rapidly than under Dewey, if only because the booming birth rates after 1947 sent school enrollments skyrocketing. The minimum wage was increased and public housing was expanded. Harriman had to take steps to clean up the waterfront of New York City, long the private preserve of criminals.

Both Dewey and Harriman had shown caution in spending and borrowing, but Rockefeller abandoned such restraints because he wanted to solve problems in mass transit, higher education, housing, and conservation. Moreover, cutting a ribbon on a new dam or bridge gave him a thrill and a chance to win public acclaim. Such projects required lots of money, and all sections of the state wanted new buildings such as hospitals, dormitories, and dams. Was it not cheaper, Rockefeller argued, to build today rather than to wait, when construction costs were rising 10 percent a year?

When Rockefeller entered office in 1959, the state budget totaled less than $2 billion; when he left in 1973, it had risen to $13 billion. To pay for new buildings, including the Albany

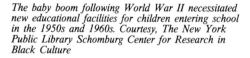

The baby boom following World War II necessitated new educational facilities for children entering school in the 1950s and 1960s. Courtesy, The New York Public Library Schomburg Center for Research in Black Culture

The Verrazano-Narrows Bridge

Let's play a game of trivia.

What is the longest suspension bridge in the United States? Answer: the Verrazano-Narrows Bridge, linking Brooklyn to

Staten Island remained a largely rural community until this century. The only way to get off the island was to take a ferry to Long Island or the one to the Battery in downtown Manhattan. To be sure, one could go to New Jersey by bridge and ferry, but relatively few wanted to go west.

ings. True, residents would receive compensation, but what would remain of the neighborhood? Most business people and homeowners hailed the project, because they could drive to work and because their property would rise in value.

Robert Moses hired Othmar H. Ammann as chief engineer. Born and educated in Switzerland, Ammann had become the world's greatest builder of bridges. He had directed the construction of the George Washington Bridge across the Hudson, the Golden Gate Bridge in San Francisco, and scores more. Ammann was 80 years old, but he could watch the workers 12 miles away through the telescope mounted in his apartment on the 32nd floor of the Hotel Carlyle. Perhaps he remembered that John A. Roebling had directed the work on the Brooklyn Bridge from his sickbed some distance away. In 1964 dignitaries cut the ribbon, opening the structure to traffic, and within a decade its two decks carried an

The Verrazano-Narrows Bridge, completed in 1964, was named in honor of Giovanni da Verrazanno, whose expedition of 1524 eventually led to the dicovery of New York Bay. Photo by Michael R. Gregory

Staten Island with a span of 4,260 feet.

How much wire is in its cables? Answer: Enough to circle the earth five times at the equator.

How tall are the towers? Answer: 680 feet high.

In 1946 Robert Moses persuaded the state legislature to authorize a bridge across the Narrows. The project ran into endless delays; however, when the "Authority" (The Triborough Bridge and Tunnel Authority) actually started work in 1959, residents in the Bay Ridge region of Staten Island organized protests. The bridge and its approaches would uproot 7,000 people and destroy 800 build-

average of 122,000 vehicles daily.

Staten Island lost much of its bucolic charm as thousands of second-generation immigrants moved there. Property values soared. Crime increased but remained well below that of Manhattan and Brooklyn. The air around the toll booths became polluted. The people of Bay Ridge took their money and scattered far and wide.

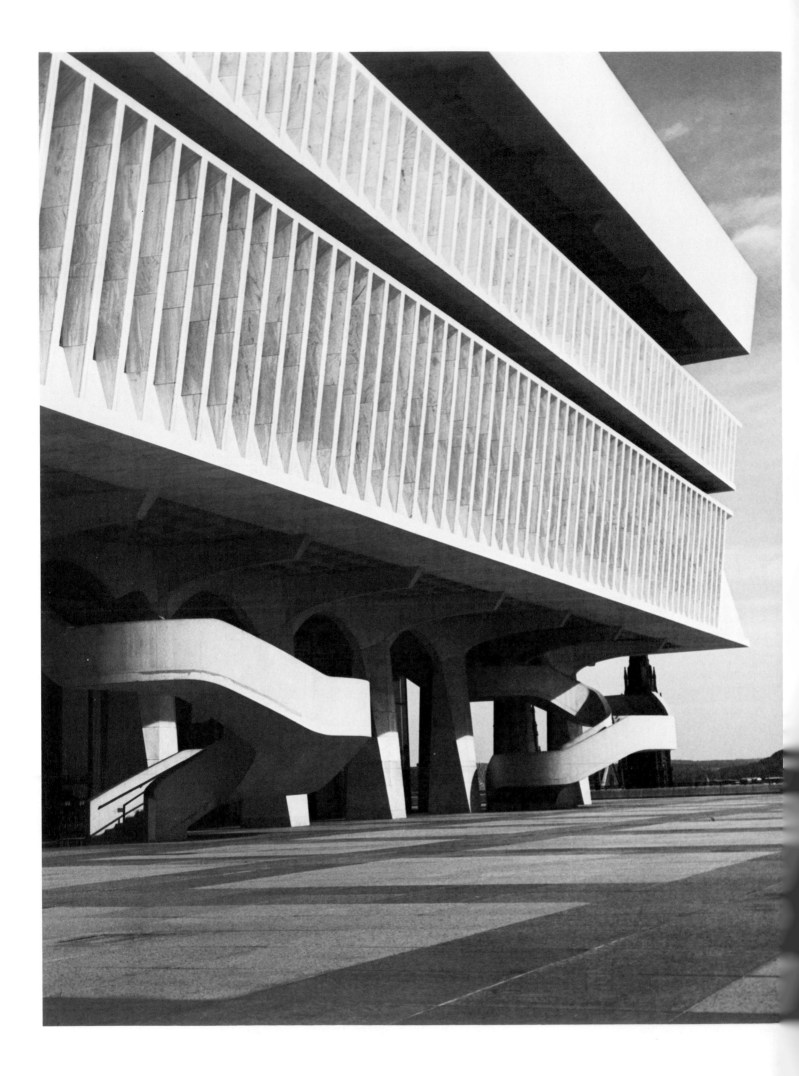

Above: The juxtaposition of the nineteenth century Albany capitol building and the late twentieth century Empire State Plaza creates an unexpectedly pleasing sight. The political controversy surrounding the older edifice was not very different from the events surrounding the construction of the more recent structures. Courtesy, The New York State Department of Economic Development

Page 202: The Empire State Museum is the cultural center of the Empire State Plaza. Collections inside include entomology, geology, mineralogy, archaeology, and New York State and local Indian artifacts. Courtesy, The New York State Department of Economic Development

Page 203: The Greek god Prometheus who stole fire from heaven and gave it to mankind presides over the lower plaza at Rockefeller Center. The fountains and gardens of the center create a welcoming panorama for visiting tourists and New Yorkers alike. Courtesy, New York Convention & Visitor's Bureau, Inc.

South Mall (now the Nelson A. Rockefeller Empire State Plaza), Rockefeller and his legislative allies raised the sales tax and increased income taxes on corporations and individuals, until New York State's taxation led all other states. Citizens had to pay a graduated income tax reaching 15 percent, a crushing burden when added to federal taxes. No wonder many executives moved their firms to other states and wealthy persons moved their place of residence to Florida, which had no income or estate tax.

When taxes failed to bring in enough revenue, Rockefeller turned to borrowing. The state constitution provides that bond issues guaranteed by the "full faith and credit" of the state must receive approval by the voters. By 1973 voters had approved various referenda for road construction and purchase of forest land amounting to $3.4 billion, triple the $1.1-billion debt he had inherited from Harriman. Alarmed by this increase, voters rejected new referenda and the legislature opposed new taxes. Faced with this situation, Rockefeller made greater use of backdoor financing, using devices already developed by Robert Moses. Why not build a bridge or housing project, charge tolls or rents, and then float bonds backed in vague terms as a "moral obligation" of the State? No need to submit any referenda to the voters.

By 1973 public authorities such as the Urban Housing Authority, the State Dormitory Authority, and scores of other agencies had borrowed $12 billion. Bankers gobbled up these bonds because they earned handsome commissions when they resold them to their clients. Purchasers believed the state's credit stood behind these bonds, and they were right because the state could not repudiate these "moral obligation" bonds without jeopardizing its credit. Excessive taxation and debt by 1975 imperiled the credit rating of New York State, and only the intervention of the federal government saved the Empire State from bankruptcy.

Although John D. Rockefeller, Jr., taught his sons the importance of frugality and industry, he did not deny them all the luxuries—swimming pools, travel, expensive hobbies—that seemed wise to him or were requested by them. Nelson was a prodigal spender as a boy, as an undergraduate at Dartmouth College, and as a government official. He was a social activist and an incurable optimist. His greatest ambition was to become president of the United States. The best route leading to the White House, he thought, passed through the governor's mansion in Albany. Unlike Harriman, another presidential aspirant, he loved crowds where he could press the flesh and bearhug politicians. Behind his charm and winning smile lurked a ruthless and scheming manipulator.

Rockefeller's first budget attracted attention from coast to coast because it called for a sharp increase in state aid for schools, housing, roads, and hospitals. When it called for higher fuel taxes, an increase in the income tax, and the withholding of taxes from wages, many taxpayers and especially conservative Republicans were infuriated. Some formed the Conservative party to defeat the governor's program and thwart his bid for the Republican nomination for president in 1960.

Rockefeller decided to expand the State University of New York by spending hundreds of millions of dollars for buildings and even new campuses. The legislature agreed to a minimum-wage law and extended workers' compensation to more employees. By the end of his first term his administration had improved more than 5,200 miles of road at a cost of more than a billion dollars. New projects included the Southern Tier Expressway, the Adirondack Northway, and Interstate Route 81 running from Pennsylvania to Watertown. Rockefeller, an avid collector of art, urged the creation of the Council on the Arts with the mandate to take music, plays, and exhibits to the public. Political scientists and experts in state government praised him for his imagination, his appointment of nationally known experts, and his courage in fighting reactionaries.

In 1962 Rockefeller endorsed an ambitious proposal for a new state center in downtown Albany to provide space for more than 30 state agencies. The state condemned the buildings on 98 acres of land between the Capitol and the Governor's Mansion. Scores of yellow cranes and earthmoving machines bulldozed these buildings, and in the area there arose 11 buildings surrounding an office tower with 44 floors. A splendid Cultural Arts Center housed new quarters for the State Museum and State Library. Originally budgeted for $250 million, the cost kept escalating until various estimates placed it at more than $2 billion. Did Rockefeller achieve his avowed goal of building "the most spectacularly beautiful seat of government in the world?" The early verdict of architects has been less than enthusiastic.

Meanwhile, Rockefeller was spending much time and more money seeking the Republican nomination for president. In 1964, however, Senator Barry Goldwater won the hearts and votes of the party delegates but lost the fall election to Lyndon Johnson in a Democratic landslide. He lost the Empire State by the amazing margin of 2,669,597 votes, enabled Robert Kennedy to win a seat in the United States Senate, and carried down to defeat many members of the senate and assembly. The Democratic leaders in the state legislature, however, fell to quarreling over who should become speaker and majority leader. When Rockefeller offered more revenues to the metropolis, the Democrats did not fight hard against his proposal for a 2 percent sales tax.

Meanwhile, politicians were thrown into turmoil by the ruling of the United States Supreme Court that provisions in the state constitution awarding greater representation to

Hospital workers, among the poorest paid in New York City, began organizing in the late 1950s. Shown here is a picket line from a 1959 strike. Courtesy, Allis Wolfe

Above: Located in Harlem at 515 Lenox Avenue at 135th Street, The Schomburg Center for Research in Black Culture houses more than 3.5 million manuscripts, photographs, paintings, films, and video tapes. The center is one of the world's leading research facilities devoted to the study of blacks. Courtesy, New York Convention & Visitor's Bureau, Inc.

Right: Shown here is a Harlem coffee shop around 1960. Courtesy, The New York Public Library Schomburg Center for Research in Black Culture

lightly populated districts upstate than to New York City and other large cities violated the principle of one man-one vote. Clearly, this ruling would hurt the Republican party and rural districts. The Republicans made many desperate maneuvers to forestall this ruling but failed. New York City won more seats, but suburban districts such as those on Long Island made the greatest gains. The principle of one man-one vote was subsequently extended to local governmental units, where suburban areas reaped the most benefits.

Rockefeller vigorously promoted conservation measures, and the voters approved several bond issues for the purchase of more forestland. He also pushed a program to construct sewage-disposal plants to check pollution. This program made considerable progress in cleaning up the Hudson and other rivers.

The federal government enacted a system of health insurance (Medicare) for persons over 65. In addition the federal government was to pay half the cost of medical benefits for "needy" persons of any age. The Rockefeller administration defined "needy" broadly and covered about 40 percent of all families. Counties and the state were each to pay a quarter of the total cost of the program (Medicaid), which shot upward, causing many counties to levy sales taxes to pay for their share. County executives complained that welfare, including Medicaid, took more than half of their budget.

Higher education was perhaps Rockefeller's favorite program. In 1970 he called for a doubling of public and private facilities within the decade, and this goal was reached. To avoid the trouble of seeking voter approval for more bonded indebtedness, he utilized public authorities such as the State Dormitory Authority, whose bonds would be backed by room charges from students. He faced a ticklish problem in the City University of New York (CUNY), which included four senior colleges (Brooklyn, City, Hunter, Queens) and six two-year community colleges plus a Graduate Center and a college of Police Science. CUNY did not charge tuition, whereas the State University of New York (SUNY) charged students $400 a year. The trustees of CUNY did not want to give up their independence to SUNY, whose standards at that time did not match those of CUNY. But city fathers and CUNY wanted more state aid for operating and construction costs. After a confrontation Rockefeller backed off and agreed to set up a construction fund for CUNY, provide 50 percent of its operating costs, and grant it continued independence.

At the end of Rockefeller's 15 years in office SUNY had become the largest system of higher education in the nation and CUNY the third largest. The state system had 246,000 students on 71 campuses at a cost of upwards of $2 billion. Rockefeller revolutionized higher education by making the public sector the dominant one, although Cornell, Columbia, and some other private institutions maintained their national prestige. His program won him warm friends in the construction industry, whose unions endorsed him despite his Republican label.

CUNY adopted the policy of "open admissions" under which virtually all high school graduates had the right to attend a unit of the system. Unfortunately the influx of poorly prepared students created many difficulties. The CUNY administration had to hire hundreds of new teachers and find classrooms for tens of thousands of additional students. A considerable number of students had to attend remedial classes, a great comedown for the senior colleges once famous for their high academic standards.

The crisis in housing kept growing worse, largely because of the deterioration of the housing stock due to poor maintenance. The city retained rent controls after World War II, and landlords complained with justification that income from rents did not permit them to make repairs. Each year thousands of apartment buildings were abandoned by their owners in order to avoid payment of taxes. New York City did not dare lift rent controls, but it asked the state to grant subsidies for middle-income housing. Rockefeller set up the Housing Finance Agency (HFA), which encouraged middle-income housing projects by subsidizing the builders. Many citizens and the state legislature thought it was the only way to secure quarters needed by newcomers and young couples who had accepted jobs in banks, insurance companies, and law firms. HFA in the 15 years after 1960 financed scores of projects and in the process ran up a debt of almost $6 billion.

Subsidies for low-income housing, however, stirred up much more opposition. Rockefeller set up the Urban Development Corporation (UDC) with power to borrow money on its own and to initiate projects wherever it saw fit. Homeowners in Queens and in the suburbs feared that poor people and blacks would invade their neighborhoods. Perhaps property values would fall? Legislators balked at Rockefeller's bill, but he rammed it down their throats only to find citizens organizing protests and appealing to the courts. Despite these obstructions the UDC built more than 30,000 housing units in 100 developments throughout the state.

Rockefeller had a greater impact upon the lives of more citizens than any other governor. A sympathetic study by Robert Connery and Gerald Benjamin pointed out his numerous achievements but ended with the judgment: "He achieved mightily, but tried to do too much too fast." Less favorable was economist Peter McClelland of Cornell, who found Rockefeller's use of public authorities blatantly undemocratic and constitutionally suspect. McClelland charged the governor with engaging in a spending spree and using the powers of the governorship "with a flair and cunning no predecessor since Al Smith had managed." Rockefeller bullied the state legislators to grant him more power, and the judges silently acquiesced in the rush for power.

His administration brought higher spending, higher taxes, and more government regulations. In the 1970s New York State had the dubious reputation of having the worst business climate of all the states. The list of burdens was long: fiscal policies leading to ever-increasing taxes, high labor costs, high energy charges, environmental controls, and state-regulated employment costs such as unemployment benefits to strikers. No wonder many business people decided not to expand and a considerable number moved their factories to other states.

Population shifts in the 1960s led to factionalism and intergroup conflicts. As late as 1965 professors Wallace S. Sayre and Herbert Kaufman, eminent political scientists at Columbia and Yale, viewed the current scene and declared that city officials had displayed

A small group of early nineteenth century buildings and historic seagoing vessels like the Peking, pictured above, were saved from oblivion by the development of the South Street Seaport Museum. The museum combines historic structures and memorabilia of old New York, with a vibrant commercial tourist attraction in present day southern Manhattan. Courtesy, The New York State Department of Economic Development

Above: Located on the Upper East Side of Manhattan, just a block off the City's "Museum Row," the Whitney Museum began in inauspicious settings in an alley in Greenwich Village. Today it houses modern art by American artists. Courtesy, New York Convention & Visitor's Bureau, Inc.

Top: In the middle of Museum Row, on Fifth Avenue across the street from Central Park at 89th Street, Frank Lloyd Wright's "giant snail" is the home of 6,000 works of contemporary art. Among the masters presented at the Guggenheim are Picasso, Kandinsky, and Chagall. Courtesy, New York Convention & Visitor's Bureau, Inc.

great ability in guiding the city. Like most other Americans they did not foresee the turbulent days ahead when rioters swept through most large cities and set whole blocks on fire. In New York few predicted the black revolt, the flight of a million whites, the loss of almost a half million jobs in manufacturing, and the explosion in welfare costs.

Robert Wagner, Jr., mayor from 1954 to 1965, had carefully and shrewdly balanced the competing claims of county bosses and reformers, the various ethnic groups, and the demands of municipal workers. John Vliet Lindsay, an Ivy League patrician, entered office with a vision of bringing blacks and Puerto Ricans into the mainstream of politics. He helped found the Urban Coalition, a group of executives of national corporations, civil-rights proponents, and members of various humanitarian organizations. Few blacks and Puerto Ricans joined the coalition.

This elitist approach met resistance among municipal employees and working-class whites who felt that concessions to new groups threatened their jobs and neighborhoods. The conflict came to a climax in the Ocean Hill-Brownville neighborhood in Brooklyn, where a new school board dominated by black partisans removed a number of teachers, mostly Jewish. Blacks and Jews, longtime allies in the civil-rights movement and in the Democratic party, clashed in a bitter quarrel, the worst example of intergroup tension since Irish Catholics faced Protestant nativists in the period from 1850 to 1875.

Middle-class whites and blue-collar workers felt that the Lindsay technocrats were shifting funds to Manhattan and favoring blacks and Puerto Ricans. The residents of Queens, the legendary territory of Archie Bunker, denounced Lindsay for failing to remove snow clogging their streets. Lindsay, who associated with the "limousine liberals" of Manhattan, believed that innovative programs for the underprivileged would attract grants from the Great Society programs of President Lyndon Johnson. Moreover, if he could demonstrate his ability to solve urban problems, he might win the Republican nomination for president.

But first Lindsay had to win reelection in 1969. To accomplish that goal, he had to appease traditional voters, party chiefs, and municipal workers. He offered the civil-service unions extraordinarily generous raises, especially in fringe benefits, which later undermined the city's solvency during his second administration. In addition the city spent a great deal of money on welfare and increased the budget for CUNY. Between 1966 and 1971 higher-education costs rose 251 percent and welfare 225 percent.

Rivalry between Lindsay and Rockefeller for public favor and the Republican nomination for president intensified, although both belonged to the camp of moderate Republicans and both advocated civil rights. Rockefeller upstaged Lindsay several times, but Lindsay organized an association of the six largest cities that demanded and got more state aid.

The economy of New York City was running into stormy weather in the 1970s. The garment industry, traditionally the avenue whereby unskilled newcomers entered the job market, was losing many thousands of jobs each year. Unable to find work, Puerto Ricans and blacks had to fall back on relief, straining city resources. The recession of 1973-1975, the most severe since the Great Depression, frightened bankers who had already lent large sums to real-estate investment trusts and to Third World countries that could not pay for skyrocketing oil prices imposed by OPEC in 1973. The number of city employees rose from 200,706 in 1961 to 294,502 in 1975, mostly in the welfare department and in CUNY.

In 1973 Abraham Beame, who followed Lindsay, presented a budget full of gimmicks, all designed to conceal an enormous deficit. Eighteen times in 1974 New York City offered short-term notes exceeding $8 billion. Banks began to ignore these offerings and to unload their holdings. In April 1975 the City could find no buyers for its notes. The metropolis and the state were facing bankruptcy together.

A cultural explosion accompanied the education expansion after World War II. Colleges and universities added more courses in art and musical appreciation, and many erected new centers devoted to the creative and performing arts. Old museums added new wings and reached out to wider audiences. New museums sprang up in every corner of the state, many of local interest but several winning regional and even national attention.

New York City retained its national preeminence in cultural matters: art, music, ballet, theater, and publishing. The Lincoln Center for the Performing Arts in 1966 provided a new home for the Metropolitan Opera Association and New York Philharmonic Symphony Orchestra. The Metropolitan and Brooklyn art museums expanded their activities and collections as did the Museum of Modern Art, founded before World War II. Two new museums—the Guggenheim and the Whitney with its new building in 1966—stressed works by contemporary artists.

Upstate saw the birth of new art centers and museums. In Lewiston, near Buffalo, and in Saratoga Springs new performing-arts centers sprang up that brought ballet, symphony concerts, and artists to large audiences. When the state government built the Albany "Mall," it moved the old State Museum of Natural History to the Cultural Arts Center. It developed new exhibits devoted to the Adirondacks, metropolitan New York, early agriculture, and Indians. A short list of new museums would include the Munson-Williams-Proctor Art Institute, in Utica, housed in a fine building designed by Philip Johnson. Syracuse acquired the Everson Museum with fine ceramics and a lively program for its members. In 1947 the George Eastman House became a museum of photography drawing

Left: The International Museum of Photography at the George Eastman House in Rochester was founded in 1947. Five hundred thousand fine art images and 25,000 books on photography along with current and older periodicals on photography are housed here. Courtesy, The New York State Department of Economic Development

Left: Located in Binghamton, New York, the Robeson Art Center includes American decorative arts, paintings, prints, and crafts. In addition, there are 3,500 mounted specimens of birds and mammals, local historical artifacts, and Indian memorabilia. Courtesy, The New York State Department of Economic Development

Right: Housed in a building from 1850 the Erie Canal Museum in Syracuse offers a collection of memorabilia and artifacts dealing with the history of the Erie Canal. Exhibits focus on the impact of the canal on the nineteenth century life. They include patent models, commemorative china, textiles, nineteenth century household items, tools, maps, and paintings. Courtesy, The New York State Department of Economic Development

Above: The Farmer's Museum in Cooperstown, New York, is composed of 12 buildings, interpreting nineteenth century rural and village life. Much of the museum is housed in a large stone barn. There are 60,000 volumes in the library, which the museum shares with the New York State Historical Association. Courtesy, The New York State Department of Economic Development

Top: Cooperstown in upstate New York's Otsego County was first settled in 1786 by William Cooper. Situated in a popular recreation area since the early nineteenth century, it has come to be known as the village of museums. Courtesy, The New York State Department of Economic Development

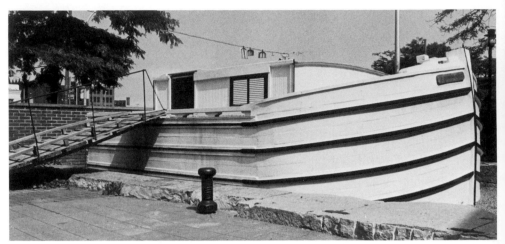

upon the matchless resources of the Eastman Kodak Company. A handsome bequest by Margaret Woodbury Strong set in motion the creation of a museum designed to tell the story of New Yorkers from rural pursuits to industrial and urban life. It also has a superlative collection of dolls from all over the world. In Buffalo the Albright-Knox Museum added new collections of art after World War II.

In the Southern Tier Corning became a museum center when the Rockwell Art Museum was added to the Corning Glass Museum. The Rockwell museum has a collection of paintings and sculpture by Frederic Remington and other artists of the West. Visitors to the North Country could visit the splendid collection of Remington art in his home city of Ogdensburg. Who would expect to find in a tiny hamlet in the depth of the Adirondacks a first-class museum? At Blue Mountain Lake Harold Hochschild founded and developed the Adirondack Museum, featuring photographs of great camps, hotels, and the logging industry as well as exhibits of boats, stoves, and furniture made from bark. The Erie Canal continued to hold its particular fascination for residents of New York State. In Syracuse a new museum was begun in the old Weighlock Building, and in Rome local initiative led to the creation of the Erie Canal Village.

The federal government has also encouraged the formation of new museums, the most recent being the one at Ellis Island. Nearby is the refurbished Statue of Liberty, whose centennial in 1986 was marked by a stupendous celebration. A decade earlier the National Park Service opened its reconstruction of Fort Stanwix in Rome, where attendants dressed in period uniforms acted and spoke like Revolutionary soldiers. The feminist movement stimulated a drive to commemorate the famous convention of 1848, when Elizabeth Cady Stanton and her associates issued their proclamation of grievances against male-dominated society. In 1982 a National Historical Park opened in Seneca Falls.

In 1945 the New York State Historical Association moved its headquarters to Cooperstown, a charming village and the beneficiary of many gifts by the Clark Foundation. The Fenimore House exhibited a fine collection of American folk art, and across the road the Farmers' Museum with a fine stone barn and a score of buildings suggested a crossroads village. In 1939 the Baseball Hall of Fame opened its doors, a shrine for the millions of baseball fans. In Mumford, near Rochester, the Genesee Country Museum offered a reconstruction of a 19th-century village with more than 50 town and farm buildings.

This listing is only a sampling of the scores of new museums that dot every region of the state.

Metropolitan New York continued as art capital of the nation and rivaled Paris and London in importance. Abstract expressionism, dominant in the latter half of the 20th century, found its center in New York and influenced photography, sculpture, pop art, playwriting, and other

Above: The outdoor exhibits of the Farmer's Museum include farm implements, technology, agricultural innovations, and transportation. Courtesy, The New York State Department of Economic Development

Above, left: The Strong Museum in Rochester was founded in 1968. Its unique collection is concerned with social and cultural development of the northeastern part of America from 1820 to 1940. Courtesy, The·New York State Department of Economic Development

Below: Lincoln Center for the Performing Arts on the west side of Manhattan houses the Metropolitan Opera, the New York City Ballet and Opera, the New York Philharmonic, Alice Tully Hall, the Julliard School of Music, two small theaters, and a museum and library of the performing arts. Courtesy, New York Convention & Visitor's Bureau, Inc.

fields. Painters, many of them reared in New England, the South, and the West, tended to gravitate to the lofts of SoHo in Manhattan, where they assimilated or rejected but continually debated the latest trends from Europe, Asia, and Africa. American artists such as Jackson Pollock became internationally known.

The commercial theater enjoyed great popularity in the period after 1950 when plays by such dramatists as Tennessee Williams, Arthur Miller, and Eugene O'Neill attracted large audiences to Broadway's 30 or more theaters. Another 30 stages sprang up "Off Broadway," where plays experimental in nature and controversial in theme provided vehicles for new writers and actors. Playwrights were also affected by abstract expressionism, and they explored the meaning of reality in such plays as O'Neill's *The Iceman Cometh.*

Popular music had its center in New York, although country music emanated from Nashville. During and after World War II Richard Rodgers wrote the music for *Oklahoma, The King and I,* and *South Pacific.* Oscar Hammerstein II wrote the memorable lyrics. No

musical comedy captivated audiences more quickly than Frank Loesser's *My Fair Lady.*

Jazz did not make New York City its headquarters until after World War II. Harlem and Greenwich Village were the first to welcome this art form, but before long its composers were accepted by academic musicians and they sought to purify the form—with the result that it became less popular. Gradually jazz became an art form attracting sophisticated specialists in Carnegie Hall, and the Beatles swept New York State and the nation.

The metropolitan area remained the center of the communications and information industry. The three most important radio networks—American, Columbia, National—had their headquarters in New York City. Television captured the public's fancy after 1945, and within the next two decades almost every household had one or more sets. Its impact was staggering on entertainment, the family, Hollywood, advertising, elections, and sports. Who will forget the shooting of Lee Harvey Oswald after the assassination of President John F. Kennedy, the drama of Watergate, the Boston Pops concert at the Bicentennial, and the celebration of the restoration of the Statue of Liberty in 1986?

Publishing has its capital in Manhattan, although the printing of most books has been done elsewhere. The *New York Times* has kept its lead over the *Washington Post,* the *Los Angeles Times,* and Gannett's *U.S.A. Today* and is read by opinion makers and high officials in government and business throughout the nation. Equally influential in its more narrow confines is the *Wall Street Journal.* After World War II the trend toward consolidation of newspapers continued, indeed accelerated. Although some famous newspapers died, suburban papers sprang

Above: The world famous Apollo theater in Harlem was a starting point for the careers of many black artists including Ella Fitzgerald, Nat King Cole, James Brown, and Michael Jackson. It has recently been renovated and is again a popular showcase for musicians and singers. Courtesy, New York Convention & Visitor's Bureau, Inc.

Top: Harlem's Cotton Club where Lena Horne got her start is legendary. The best in blues, bebop, jazz, and pop all played at the Club. Courtesy, New York Convention & Visitor's Bureau, Inc.

up. Among them is *Newsday* on Long Island, which has a booming constituency. The two main newsweeklies—*Time* and *Newsweek*—are edited in New York, as are most other national magazines and journals. The *Reader's Digest,* boasting the largest circulation in the world, has its art-filled offices in Pleasantville. *Forbes, Business Week,* and *Fortune* are edited close to the heartbeat of the financial community.

Philanthropic institutions are numerous throughout the state, although Manhattan has attracted the largest agencies. For example, the Ford Foundation, with assets of more than $3 billion, is the largest. The National Council of Churches has its headquarters in New York, as do many of such mainline denominations as the Presbyterian and Episcopal churches.

The cultural hegemony of New York alternately repels and fascinates outlanders, who do not conceal their distaste for what they see as the arrogance of New Yorkers. Interestingly, most of the individuals at the top of the corporate and cultural worlds were born and reared outside metropolitan New York. The decline of New York City was thought in certain quarters to be just retribution for the city's flagrant waste in city government. Governor Rockefeller's candidacy for president, especially against Senator Goldwater, infuriated the real-estate promoters and small-business people in the Sunbelt who distrusted the moguls of Wall Street and the mavens of the media. "Pride goeth before destruction, and a haughty spirit before a fall." No doubt many in the Bible Belt applied those words of wisdom to the imperial city at the foot of the Hudson.

Above: Built as the home of the New York Oratorio Society, Carnegie Hall was opened on May 5, 1891. It subsequently became a New York City landmark and stage for such immortals of the music world as Mischa Elman, Efrem Zimbalist, Toscanini, and Caruso. Mid-twentieth century programs have included popular and folk music as well. It was thoroughly remodeled and reopened in 1987. Courtesy, The New York State Department of Economic Development

Top: Shea Stadium in Flushing, Queens, is the home of the "miracle" Mets. For some reason, every time they win a pennant or a World Series, it is called a miracle. Courtesy, New York Convention & Visitor's Bureau, Inc.

Left: Frederick Law Olmsted and Calvert Vaux created Central Park in the Romantic tradition. While it may appear as if man has done little to alter these 840 acres, every detail was carefully planned. Courtesy, New York Convention & Visitor's Bureau, Inc.

Financial Crisis and Recovery After 1975

ord to City: Drop Dead. That headline in the New York *Daily News* in November 1975 greeted residents of the Big Apple after President Gerald Ford rejected appeals by State and City for aid to avoid bankruptcy. This rejection dismayed New Yorkers, who had been watching storm warnings since January when Governor Hugh Carey bluntly warned that the days of wine and roses were over.

A decade later New Yorkers, still chastened by events, had some reason to feel better about their progress from the brink of insolvency. The state and New York City had won back a good credit rating. The economy had recovered, with the unemployment rate below 6 percent in July 1987, slightly below the national rate. Perhaps most heartening of all was the glorious centennial celebration of the Statue of Liberty with all the hoopla of the traditional harbor and Broadway greetings to Lindbergh in 1927 and to the returning soldiers in 1945.

In the 1970s more than a million persons left the state, but after 1980 population figures turned upward. In August 1987 the Public Policy Institute reported that the population rose by 225,000 to 17.8 million from 1980 to 1984.

In February 1975 the Urban Development Corporation (UDC) found bankers refusing to buy its new series of one-year notes. Bankruptcy threatened. The next month New York City found no takers for its bonds. Would police and fire fighters continue to work if their paychecks stopped? Would the schools close their doors? Would the collapse of New York's credit set in motion a national panic?

Governor Rockefeller had sponsored the UDC in order to meet the need for moderate-cost housing. This agency borrowed money for mortgage loans on housing developments it constructed. Construction workers, tenants, politicians, and bankers loved this program because it meant jobs, low rents, patronage, and handsome fees. Officials, however, set rents at levels below operating costs and set aside nothing for repayments on original costs. Tax exemptions and federal grants concealed the shortfall, but the charade would not last forever.

How did the metropolis get into its mess? Put simply, rent controls, the addition of tens of thousands of new employees to the payroll, and lavish fringe benefits to city workers, especially police, fire, and sanitation employees contributed to the problem. To complicate matters, the City had not recovered from the downturn of 1969-1970 and the sharp recession in 1973, which added to welfare rolls and cut revenues.

Population of New York State and New York City, 1950-1980

Population statistics provide useful information even though they conceal as much as they reveal.

Year	New York State	New York City
1950	14,830,200	7,892,200
1960	16,782,300	7,782,000
1970	18,241,400	7,895,600
1980	17,558,100	7,071,600

Preliminary figures for the 1980s indicate a reversal in the downward trend. It is estimated that the state's population in 1986 had risen to 17,800,000

Right: Governor Hugh Carey was in office from 1974 until 1982. He set the pattern for his successor by earning both his bachelor's and law degree from St. John's University. Carey was a World War II hero and the father of 13 children. Courtesy, New York State Archives

Page 214: A synonym for financial power for two centuries, Wall Street is home to some of New York's oldest and most powerful banks and financial securities firms. Courtesy, New York Convention & Visitor's Bureau, Inc.

Governor Mario Cuomo was elected to his second term in 1986 with the highest winning margin in New York State's history. He is shown here with New York State Attorney General Robert Abrams and Robert Morgenthau, District Attorney for New York County. Photo by Joan Libby

Despite his congressional record as a liberal Democrat, Governor Hugh Carey resolutely and courageously faced up to the crisis. He set up the Municipal Assistance Corporation (MAC) to stretch out the City's debt and also to dole out enough money to cover essential services. Felix Rohatyn, an investment banker, was appointed to guide the city administration through the minefields, and to coerce or cajole city workers, bankers, and citizens to accept austerity. The bankers, themselves guilty of tolerating slipshod practices from officials, demanded sharp cuts in city employees and a three-year freeze on wage increases. At first workers protested, and some policemen handed out leaflets in terminals warning visitors of increased crime. Some sanitation men declared they would make New York "Stink City."

MAC bonds received the backing of the sales tax and stock-transfer fees collected in the city. Investors still looked askance at these bonds, forcing Carey to set up the Emergency Financial Control Board (EFCB). Its mission was to require a balancing of the budget in three years and the adoption of strict accounting procedures. EFCB could even fire officials who obstructed its work. These measures, however, did not attract enough money, so city and state officials appealed to the federal government. Many congressmen from the South and the West, previously the butt of jokes and sarcasm by metropolitan writers and spokesmen, opposed any aid to a city sunk in corruption and committed to extravagance. Swallowing his initial reluctance because he feared a national financial crisis, President Ford agreed to lend $2.3 billion but only on strict conditions that the secretary of the treasury would monitor it.

Painfully New York City had to go through the wringer. Gone were cheap subway fares and free tuition at CUNY, two sacred cows that no politicians had dared to touch. Mayor Abraham Beame had to declare a five-year moratorium on the construction of subsidized middle-income housing. Beame had to pare the capital budget to the bone, which meant no repairs and hardly any construction of schools, bridges, subways, and sewers. Fun City became Pothole City.

The ax fell heavily upon city workers. The workforce dropped from 273,474 to 229,192 by 1981, mostly by attrition, which led to a deterioration in city services. Employees at first received no wage increases and had to contribute more money to their pension fund. In fact the union pension funds became critical in restoring the credit of the city, because 40 percent

Above: This view of the New York Stock Exchange, located on Wall Street between Broad Street and Exchange Place, is the hub of financial activity of the city. It was designed in 1903 by George B. Post. Courtesy, The New York State Department of Economic Development

Facing page: Park Avenue is the home of many famous corporations, hotels, churches, and clubs. Looking north from Grand Central Station, it changes from a business district to one of the most renowned residential areas of the nation. Courtesy, New York Convention & Visitor's Bureau, Inc.

of their funds were used to purchase City bonds. Because Puerto Ricans and blacks had less seniority than most city employees, they took the brunt of dismissals. During the first years employees suffered a decline in real wages, but after 1980 they gradually recaptured most of their losses.

By 1984 operating expenditures, adjusted for inflation, had fallen 16 percent. Capital expenditures dropped drastically and in 1984 were 56 percent lower than in 1975. The results were more leaky water mains, late subway trains, seedy schools, and rundown apartment buildings. The poor suffered most of all—a drop of 40 percent in the real value of income they had received in 1974.

The state government also suffered the pangs of withdrawal from its addiction to deficit spending. It fell to a liberal Democrat, Hugh Carey, to demand retrenchment and frugality, a basic tenet of the Democratic party throughout the 19th century. In Carey's first year as governor he demonstrated courage and leadership of the highest caliber, although he subsequently earned a reputation for aloofness and morose behavior. Carey saw that state and local taxation had soared to 60 percent above the national average and was driving business out of the state. He took the lead in cutting personal income taxes, increasing personal exemptions, and eliminating some business taxes. When he left office, the rate for earned income had fallen from 15 percent to 10 percent. His successor, Mario Cuomo, who defeated Republican Lewis Lehrman, millionaire businessman and exponent of supply-side economics, continued the policy of reducing New York's taxes in order to check economic decay. All political leaders subscribed to the belief that New York State must encourage economic growth by reducing taxes.

New York's recovery astounded many pessimists who feared the downward decline of the 1970s would become a collapse in the next decade. Finance, insurance, and real estate led the parade toward recovery, but manufacturing continued to lose jobs in line with the national trend away from manufacturing to services. During the 1970s the manufacturing sector lost 370,000 jobs, the largest decline taking place in iron and steel, clothing, shoes, furniture, and leather. Upstate centers such as Syracuse, Buffalo, Elmira, and the Capital District were especially hard hit. Whereas employment in manufacturing in 1987 was about 1,220,000 jobs, in 1972 it had been 1,679,300. The flight of firms from New York City left hundreds of thousands of workers high and dry.

What was most significant was the transformation of the state's economy from one based on the processing of materials to one centered on the processing of information.

The headquarters of Fortune 500 companies in New York City fell from 125 in 1969 to 61 in August of 1986, a drop of more than half. These figures do not take into account some mergers and moves to the suburbs such as that of International Paper Company to a site in Westchester County. Furthermore, corporations that moved to Stamford, Connecticut, or to New Jersey continued to rely upon Manhattan advertising, public relations, legal, and banking services.

New York City remains a world center of finance and information as well as culture. Six of the nation's 10 largest banks list their headquarters in Manhattan, and three of the five largest insurance companies are located in the city. Most shares are traded on the stock exchanges in the city. Commodity exchanges are concentrated here, among them cotton, produce (wheat and other grains), coffee and sugar, and commodities such as hides, silk, rubber, and metals.

Kennedy International Airport handles about a third of the nation's overseas travel and about half of the freight by air. New York continues its role as the most important distribution center in the country, and the largest shopping center in the world. Buyers come to the metropolis to inspect and purchase the latest in clothing, furs, leather goods, and household articles. The convention center, named in honor of former Senator Jacob Javits, will enable New York City to compete with Chicago for large conventions and trade shows.

New York remains the world center for collecting and disseminating information. The *New York Times* provides the agenda and often the outlook for the three television networks, and

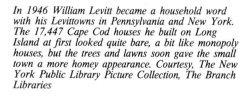

In 1946 William Levitt became a household word with his Levittowns in Pennsylvania and New York. The 17,447 Cape Cod houses he built on Long Island at first looked quite bare, a bit like monopoly houses, but the trees and lawns soon gave the small town a more homey appearance. Courtesy, The New York Public Library Picture Collection, The Branch Libraries

the *Wall Street Journal* reflects the views of the financial and corporate world throughout the country. Almost every national magazine from the weekly news journals to specialized periodicals emanates from New York. Most journals of opinion, ranging from the extreme left to the extreme right, have found New York their stomping ground.

Dominant in the art world, New York has had to share some of its preeminence in music and drama with other centers, although Broadway has no real competitors as the center of commercial theater (except of course for London).

But the congested way of life in New York and the spread of crime, incivility, and high cost of living have tarnished the image of the Big Apple. Moreover the loneliness of life, the pressure on young people to "make partner" in the big law firms or to rise to the top in the banking world have offset the glitter and culture of the metropolis. Although many executives try to escape to the suburbs after five o'clock, they find that the hectic pressures have taken a great toll on health and family life. Nevertheless there is always a new cohort of graduates with Masters of Business Administration and young lawyers eager to climb the greasy pole of success. In addition New York City has attracted entrepreneurs from around the world. Canadians own a great deal of the real estate of Manhattan. The scion of the Rothschild family, whose banking house in Paris was nationalized by Mitterand, moved to New York. Having outgrown Australia and established a strong foothold in London, Rupert Murdoch has sought to conquer the world of communications in America, starting with the *New York Post.*

A distinctive political culture has generally characterized the Empire State, largely because of the diversity of its population, economic interests, and regions. The New Deal coalition begun by Al Smith and cemented by Franklin D. Roosevelt enrolled most ethnics, workers, Catholics, Jews, and blacks, including some intellectuals. Opposing this coalition were the dwellers in the countryside, most persons of the old native stock, and the middle class in the cities and suburbs.

Since World War II the suburban dwellers have become increasingly important in numbers and political power. By 1980 the most powerful boss in the state was Joseph M. Margiotta, chairman of the Nassau County Republican party. In contrast the old Tammany machine had become paralyzed by factional feuds, ethnic rivalries, and ideological conflicts. Although the great majority of voters in New York City remained Democratic by enrollment, they ignored or defied precinct leaders. Only the blacks, Puerto Ricans, and Jews remained loyal to the Democratic party. The party has lost a large number of its German and Italian supporters, as well as a considerable number of Irish, who have moved to the suburbs, acquired more affluence, and resisted high taxes and extensive favors to minorities. Who would have predicted a century ago that the Republican state ticket of 1986 would be headed almost entirely by Irish Catholics and Senator Alfonse D'Amato! Unlike the situation in California, Pennsylvania, and Illinois, blacks in New York State have lost ground in winning high office in both the metropolis and state government.

The fissure between New York City and the rest of the state remains the main faultline in state politics. In 1982 Mayor Edward Koch created an uproar with his disparaging remarks about rural life, restaurants—or rather their scarcity—in Albany, and the "sterile" life in the suburbs. Upstaters who had been belaboring the metropolis for decades as a cesspool of corruption, crime, and chicanery, unlimbered their heavy artillery once again. Whether upstaters live in cities or countryside, they have often joined forces against New York City.

The rising dominance of suburbanites has become the most significant development on both the state and local levels. Suburbs, however, differ markedly one from the other. Some zone their land in order to attract wealthy professionals and upper management; others have thousands of modest houses catering to blue-collar workers and white-collar employees. Some suburbs around New York City are heavily Italian in population, some Jewish, others black.

The countryside has a wide variety of interests: dairying in dozens of counties, vineyards

Above: Recently, Asian immigrants have achieved success by opening and running small groceries in New York City. Photo by Sarah Lewis, courtesy, Allis Wolfe

Above: Flags of all 157 member states of the United Nations fly in the front of the organization's headquarters on 42-47 streets on First Avenue in Manhattan. The Secretariat building, shown here, is 39 stories high and 72 feet wide. Courtesy, New York Convention & Visitor's Bureau, Inc.

in the Finger Lakes region, and resorts in the Adirondacks, Catskills, and around the lakes. Likewise the metropolis has a myriad of disparate neighborhoods whose composition varies as to race, roots, and religion. Harlem, Chinatown, and the Hasidic community beneath the Brooklyn Bridge are three that come easily to mind. The homeowners on Staten Island and in Queens view with some disdain mixed with envy the "beautiful people" who live in the luxury condominiums of Manhattan.

Few citizens since World War I have questioned the system of private enterprise and democratic government as expressed in the two-party system. Hundreds of thousands of immigrants who arrived as believers in Marxist doctrines have abandoned these beliefs, supported traditional parties—especially the Democratic party—and sought to "make it" into the ranks of the middle class. A considerable number of each group have climbed the ladder from grinding poverty to comfortable middle-class status. An even greater number have seen their children acquire education and move still farther up the ladder. Although blacks and Hispanics of the past half century have moved upward as rapidly as the Irish in the mid-19th century and the Italians early in the 20th century, they have acquired higher education much more rapidly. Of course the proliferation of community colleges and much public aid were not available to newcomers prior to World War II. The City of New York, however, did set up free college education to the ablest students as early as 1880.

New York State has witnessed the formation of more political third parties than other states. No doubt this development arose from the great diversity of people and occupations, as well as from the superior numbers. In 1986 three of the dozen minor parties organized since the 1930s retained a slot on the state ballot. The Liberal party was an offshoot of the American Labor party, which by 1943 had become too cozy with Communist policies. The Liberals have normally supported Democratic candidates, but the party has occasionally run its own slate if ignored by Democratic chieftains. The Conservative party was formed by Republicans who opposed Governor Nelson Rockefeller's high spending and high taxes. The Conservatives have tried and succeeded in pushing the Republican party to the right and in defeating moderate Republicans such as the late Senator Javits.

The Right to Life party began when a group of Long Island homemakers, mainly of Roman Catholic background, protested efforts to liberalize the state's law against abortion. Victorious in Albany in 1970, they soon attacked the U.S. Supreme Court decision that women had the right to a safe legal abortion. This party had several predecessors as a single-issue organization, such as the Anti-Masonic party of the 1820s and the Prohibition party of the late 19th century.

Third parties have a difficult time getting their name on the ballot, because leaders of the two main parties have thrown obstacles in their path. For example, they have to secure 50,000 votes for governor in a general election. Once on the ballot, the leaders of the third parties can use to advantage another provision in the state electoral regulations. The law says that parties may nominate candidates already endorsed by other parties, which means that voters do not feel that voting for the third-party line will waste their ballot. Politicians therefore seek one or more cross-endorsements in order to fatten their final tally. In 1978 two out of three candidates for the state legislature ran on more than one ticket.

To maximize their leverage, minor parties sometimes nominate their candidates before the convention of the Republican or the Democratic party in the hope of pushing one of these parties to the right or the left. Thus in 1980 the Conservatives picked Alfonse D'Amato, an obscure town supervisor on Long Island who was challenging Senator Javits, a Republican moderate of national stature. D'Amato secured enough conservative Republicans to win the primary and subsequently the election.

Leaders of third parties have little hope of supplanting a major party. What they want is support for their ideological position plus a certain amount of patronage. Once the two majo parties have selected their nominees, their candidates generally soft-pedal extremist positions and move toward the center, where most of the New Yorkers who call themselves "independents" are located. This group, roughly a third of the total electorate, can often decide the outcome.

Once elected, officials work hard to stay in office. They are always trying to impress their constituents with their efforts to bring home the bacon in the form of grants, jobs, and lower taxes. Officials sometimes supplement their fairly modest salaries with extravagant perks such as pension benefits and "lulus," payments in lieu of salaries. Enterprising reporters and political foes, however, have challenged officials who violated the law or splurged in riotous living at public expense. In 1986 the administration of Mayor Edward Koch was clouded by revelations of corruption in areas such as parking violations. Joseph M. Margiotta, Republican party chairman of Nassau County, who had the most powerful political machine in the state, was convicted of fraud and extortion in 1981 after a long trial. Six years later juries convicted several Democratic chieftains of taking bribes.

Above: Mayor of New York City since 1977, the flamboyant, outspoken Ed Koch has been one of the most popular and visible mayors since Fiorello LaGuardia. Courtesy, Joan Vitale Strong

Left: This view of lower Manhattan from the Brooklyn Bridge taken in 1979 shows the mix of old and new architecture that still characterizes the oldest part of the city. Just south of the Brooklyn Bridge, which is to the right in this shot, is Schermerhorn Row, a vestige of the bustling early seaport. Nestled between two glass and steel edifices is the former home of the first police precinct, built in 1909. Courtesy, The New York Public Library Picture Collection, The Branch Libraries

Political leaders look to Albany and Washington for pork-barrel projects and patronage. One can make a case for patronage as the cement to maintain party discipline. It has been suggested also that the spoils system has some advantages over the system whereby rich men literally buy nominations and elections by flooding the media with their commercials and hiring expensive public relations firms. Citizens are partly to blame for ineffective government when they demand more services but call for lower taxes.

In the towns and villages one can still find a lingering allegiance to the New England tradition of public service with citizens scrutinizing every item in the budget. Woe to the highway commissioner who does not clear away the snow in time for the milk trucks and school buses to roll. In short, citizens demand a certain level of performance even if they tolerate some inefficiency and waste.

Since the near bankruptcy of metropolis and state in 1975, New York's political leaders have shown more caution in offering grandiose schemes. For its part, the electorate seems to be more skeptical of promises and less committed to party loyalty. The percentage of persons listing themselves as independents has risen steadily. Other polls indicate that the great majority of citizens oppose the dismantling of the welfare state created by Al Smith and Franklin D. Roosevelt and greatly enlarged by Nelson Rockefeller. Rather they want the current makeshift system slimmed down and put into workable shape.

The Empire State has led the nation in melding together an astonishing number of diverse groups recruited from every corner of the globe. On the eve of the Revolution the French observer Crevecoeur noted that in the Hudson Valley "a new man" was emerging, a blend of a half dozen people. Subsequent observers, both foreign and native, marveled at the fusion through immigration of a mixture of people. Charles Darwin and other scientists speculated that the process of natural selection had deposited on our shores the most vigorous European stock and that the new environment and opportunities stimulated them and modified their characteristics. During the past generation New York has received thousands of refugees, some fleeing from Castro's tyranny and the stifling oppression of Eastern Europe, others escaping from blood feuds

New York's skyline is punctuated by some of the most distinguished architecture in the world. The two giants of this panorama are the Empire State Building at Fifth Avenue and 34th Street and the World Trade Center Twin Towers guarding the southwestern edge of the city. Courtesy, New York Convention & Visitor's Bureau, Inc.

in the Middle East, and still others taking flight from the poverty of the Caribbean Islands.

In 1986 the United States celebrated the centennial of the statue titled "Liberty Enlightening the World." Citizens whether by birth or adoption have made this Statue of Liberty the personification of the hopes of millions—themselves, their parents, and the throngs of new immigrants passing through the Narrows into New York Harbor.

Emma Lazarus, who wrote her famous poem to raise funds for the original statue, expressed the feeling of millions:

> *Give me your tired, your poor,*
> *Your huddled masses yearning to breathe free,*
> *The wretched refuse of your teeming shore,*
> *Send these, the homeless, tempest-tost to me,*
> *I light my lamp beside the golden door.*

"The seat of empire," George Washington's happy phrase, still aptly describes New York State as it enters the service economy and informational society. The collapse of the bull market on Wall Street in October 1987 sent shock waves through the state, nation, and world. Financiers, politicians, and citizens could not help wondering whether October 1987 would rival that of October 1929 in losses and precipitate another catastrophic depression.

New Yorkers thus approach the next century in a mixture of apprehension and confidence. A combination of factors—huge deficits in the national budget and trade balances, hostilities in the Persian Gulf and Central America, and uncertainties about political leadership in Washington—have made citizens jittery about the future. On the other hand, New Yorkers have usually shown great resilience and flexibility in facing uncertainty and courage in overcoming hard times. They have had to stand on the cutting edge of change. Was it not Yogi Berra, the dugout philosopher of the New York Yankees who reputedly observed: "It is deja vu all over again"?

Page 226: In this painting, Thomas Cole illustrated a scene from James Fenimore Cooper's novel The Last of the Mohicans. *Set against the backdrop of the rugged American wilderness, the painting depicts the life of the Mohican Indians of the Hudson Valley. Courtesy, New York State Historical Association, Cooperstown*

Below: The recent structural restoration of the Statue of Liberty enables access to areas of its interior considered unsafe for many years. The funds to restore her were contributed in part by schoolchildren from across the country—just as in the nineteenth century, schoolchildren in France were among the benefactors of the original project. Courtesy, New York Convention & Visitor's Bureau, Inc.

Right: Currier and Ives, successful purveyors of popular culture in the nineteenth century, produced the Great Bartholdi Statue. Liberty Enlightening the World around 1884. This lithograph enabled Americans across the country to view the great colossus. Courtesy, The New York Public Library

Facing page, top: The establishment of New York State's canal and railroad system brought growth and vitality to many upstate communities in the first half of the nineteenth century. Here artist Lewis Bradley captures the vitality of Utica, New York, in this cityscape done around 1850. Courtesy, New York State Historical Association, Cooperstown

Facing page, bottom: Completed in 1750, the Hasbrouck House near Newburgh served as George Washington's headquarters from August 1782 through August 1783. Recognizing its importance as an early historic site, the house was purchased by New York State in 1850. Courtesy, New York State Historical Association, Cooperstown

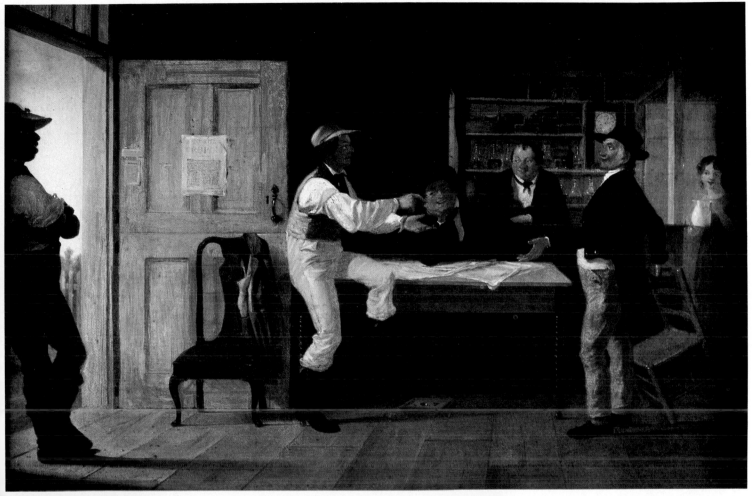

Above: This painting, originally titled A Political Argument, *was painted by James Goodwyn Clonney in 1873. The scene, showing two antagonists voicing their views across a table as amused bystanders look on, was probably a common sight in country taverns. Courtesy, New York State Historical Association, Cooperstown*

Left: Villa on the Hudson, Near Weehawken, *has been attributed to Thomas Chambers, an Englishman who came to America in 1832. Chambers' sweeping and rhythmic compositions were often inspired by published prints. He based this painting of the Stevens mansion on a print by William Henry Bartlett. Courtesy, New York State Historical Association, Cooperstown*

Facing page: The killing and scalping of Jane McCrea of Fort Edward as she awaited her fiance, a British officer, caused many frontiersmen to rally to the support of General Gates. Courtesy, New York State Historical Association, Cooperstown

Above: The Village Post Office, *painted by Thomas Waterman Wood in 1873, captures the flavor of nineteenth-century village life. The sleeping newborn, the farm family, the solicitous clerk, and the smartly dressed woman of fashion are all represented. Courtesy, New York State Historical Association, Cooperstown*

Right: This watercolor and pastel drawing depicts the heroic exploits of Commander Oliver Hazard Perry during the Battle of Lake Erie on September 10, 1813. After the battle, which Perry won, he declared, "We have met the enemy and they are ours—two Ships, two Brigs, one schooner and one sloop." Courtesy, New York State Historical Association, Cooperstown

Page 232-233: In this detailed oil study, genre painter William M. Davis depicts the process of cider making as it was practiced on Long Island in the 1870s. Cider was a popular farm product. Apples were not as subject to insect or weather damage, they stored well, and were easy to pick. Courtesy, New York State Historical Association, Cooperstown

Above: George Washington has been a favorite subject for artists. Here, Henry Hintermeister captures Washington taking the oath of office at Federal Hall on April 30, 1789. The painting was done in 1928. *Courtesy, Fraunces Tavern Museum, New York City*

Left: La Destruction De La Statue Royale a Nouvelle Yorck *presents a fictitious view of the destruction of the statue of George III in 1776. The statue stood in Bowling Green at the foot of Broadway. Courtesy, The New-York Historical Society, New York City*

Above: Kite flying brings a rainbow of colors beneath the New York City skyline. Photo by Mark Ferri

Left: St Patrick's Cathedral rises into the sky, a sharp contrast to the modern buildings surrounding its Gothic spires. Photo by William Waldron

Facing page: The Statue of Liberty is illuminated by a sky filled with spectacular fireworks, as Lady Liberty celebrates 1987. Photo by Cheryl Klauss

Above: This unnamed stream north of Piseco Lake is located in Hamilton County. Photo by Daniel E. Wray

Right: This farm in Salem is reminiscent of days gone by. Photo by Daniel E. Wray

Facing page: Buffalo's City Hall is pictured in this photo by Mark E. Gibson.

Left: Congress Park in Saratoga Springs, New York, brings quiet relaxation to visitors. Photo by Mark E. Gibson

Left, below: Niagara Falls, the most massive falls in the nation, are a powerful, unforgettable sight. Photo by Mark E. Gibson

Facing page, top: The location of the United Nations and one of the busiest centers of commerce in the world, Manhattan bristles with buildings and businesses. Photo by Mark E. Gibson

Facing page, bottom: A brilliant orange sky silhouettes the lighthouse at Fire Island National Seashore. Photo by Audrey Gibson

Above: Always exciting, horseracing is a popular—and sometimes profitable—sport at Saratoga Race Track. Photo by Daniel E. Wray

Left: Fort Ticonderoga is a fascinating historic site that offers visitors a glimpse into the days of the American Revolution. Photo by Mark E. Gibson

Facing page: Battery Park is commonly called "the Battery" after all the harbor defenses it has been home to. Photo by Audrey Gibson

The Statue of Liberty greets visitors from around the world, as well as this ferry that brings throngs of visitors close up to this historic site. Photo by Mark E. Gibson

Above: This view of the Hudson River was taken at Hadley in Saratoga County. Photo by Daniel E. Wray

Right: These hikers not only enjoy the beauty of Mt. Hadley in Saratoga County, but also receive some healthy exercise. Photo by Daniel E. Wray

Facing page: Loon Lake displays its dazzling autumnal colors in this quiet, year-end scene. Photo by Daniel E. Wray

PARTNERS IN PROGRESS

The companies featured in this section are as varied in size, activity, and style as New York itself, a state whose harbor in New York City welcomes the world, and whose mountains, hills, and plains stretch to the borders of the Midwest. Many of the Partners in Progress profiled in these pages are world-renowned corporate giants that helped New York become the business capital of the world. Many others are the small and medium-size companies whose entrepreneurial spirit fuels the tradition of ingenuity and industriousness in this state. All of these organizations, large and small, have played a vital role in making New York one of the strongest states in the union.

Each year New York is consistently ranked one of the nation's top states in terms of industrial output. New York's leading industries—banking and finance, publishing, insurance, machinery, apparel, and electrical equipment, to name just a few—are testament to the state's industrial might.

As well, New York, with its tremendous network of state universities, community colleges, and private institutions of higher learning, is an educational powerhouse that is able to provide the state's employers with an educated work force.

And even with all that brain and brawn of man-made industry, New York still has plenty of room, across the state's vast plateau, for agriculture. New York is a rich agricultural state, leading the nation in the output of apples, and is ranked among the top producers of dairy cows and dairy products. New York's farmers also produce greenhouse products, hay, corn, and potatoes, as well as grapes for New York State's burgeoning wine industry.

In addition to all these good works that New York has to offer, the state is also one of the nation's major purveyors of fun, enjoyment, and relaxation. New York is, in fact, a premier tourist state, with New York City, the Adirondacks, the Catskills, the Finger Lakes, and Niagara Falls, as well as the sandy beaches of Long Island.

The employees of the organizations featured in this section, whether their families have been in New York State since the 1600s, or whether they are the first generation to live on American soil, are all part of that continuing legacy of business strength in New York State.

The first colonial families in New York were Dutch: settlers arrived to live on Manhattan Island, and soon thereafter they established farms, villages, and towns along the banks of the Hudson, all the way up to Albany. Later that area witnessed the building of the huge Hudson

River Valley estates, and the Hudson River Highland region was made legendary by writers like James Fenimore Cooper and Washington Irving. New York City, meanwhile, with its unsurpassed port facilities, had by then already become an economic stronghold.

With the opening of the Erie Canal in 1825, settlers of various ethnic European strains—Irish, Scotch, German, French, and others—began moving westward in huge numbers. Villages sprouted up along the Erie Canal, and the new Chewango Canal was then built, linking other areas to the Erie. And as the immigrants of New York City moved westward, they settled in Buffalo, Rochester, Binghamton, Schenectady, and elsewhere. Soon railroad tracks were laid and the trains began to roll westward, running parallel to the Erie Canal's route, giving even more strength to the westward surge through New York State.

The Erie Canal firmly established New York State as the backbone of America's early industrial might. The great Erie waterway, and subsequent rail routes, opened up commerce to the western frontier, vastly increasing the scope of New York's—and America's—commercial reach.

As the Erie route got rolling, during the 1840s New York began receiving some of the most significant imports in its history: its people. Huge waves of European immigration began during

Page 248: The Tontine Coffee House was painted by Francis Guy, an Englishman, in about 1798. Built in 1792, it became the main meeting place for business leaders in New York City. Courtesy, The New York Historical Society

Right: New York harbor as seen from Brooklyn Heights was filled with a variety of ships in the 1880s. Ferry lines and steamboats competed with the still prevalent packets. Courtesy, New York State Library

the 1840s and continued into the twentieth century. Many of the "huddled masses" described by poet Emma Lazarus passed by the Statue of Liberty by ship, on their way to becoming citizens of this country. Those people went on to build this state, settling in New York City and beyond, out to the westernmost borders of the state.

As part and parcel of its industrial vibrance, New York has also produced many important political figures, such as Theodore and Franklin Roosevelt, Al Smith, Thomas E. Dewey, and Nelson Rockefeller. Those statesmen helped enrich New York's heritage and also establish its importance as a business center.

New York, so grandly titled "The Empire State" and with its giant metropolis of New York City, is often considered a monolithic place. But in profiling the companies that chose to support this important literary and civic project, the authors have witnessed and described an aspect of New York that differs from that reputation. While New York's legacy does at times seem awesome, amidst that prowess there is also a humbleness and warmth of its people. In New York the entrepreneur and the employee, whether they be large-scale or small-scale, have a genuine sense of gratitude for their good fortune in having settled in a place that abounds in so much opportunity.

THE BUSINESS COUNCIL OF NEW YORK STATE

The Empire State developed from the classic conditions for a complex economy: revolutions in transportation and industrialization, the presence of a substantial skilled work force, capital, and management. New York State was foremost an empire of prosperity—prosperity in agriculture, commerce, and industry; New York was, and is, an empire built on business.

In the 1970s, as was the case in the smokestack states of the northern regions of the nation, there was an exodus of business from New York, with 437,000 private-sector jobs lost between 1970 and 1975. With the loss of business and of jobs was a draining away of population as well. Government was growing faster than the private-sector economy, and New York had one of the heaviest tax burdens in the United States. Coupled with all this was the nation's highest corporate tax rate and no real investment incentives in place. Existing business organizations seemed pessimistic, and it looked as if New York State's economy was draining irreversibly away to the Sun Belt.

Current president Daniel B. Walsh. Photography by Timothy H. Raab

Formally established in 1980, The Business Council of New York State was formed with the purpose of business helping business. Pictured here is Raymond T. Schuler, founding president. Photography by Donna Joy Abbott

Growing out of these conditions, with a vision of the positive that could be done for New York with enough persistence and creativity, was The Business Council of New York State. Formally established in 1980, it was a coalition of interests with roots in initiatives of the late 1970s; the concept of the organization was business helping business. The Business Council from the beginning had an ambitious agenda: the improvement of New York's economic environment through the enhanced well-being of the business community, its workers, and the families of its work force.

The council is a statewide business advocacy group, a coalition of small and large companies from every part of the Empire State, together with other private-sector organizations working in unison for New York's future. Two-thirds of the council's 3,500 member firms employ 50 or fewer workers; others are among the world's largest corporations. Local chambers of commerce, small business councils, eco-

nomic development councils, and trade associations comprise the rest of the membership. By the 1970s the business community lost much of its voice in New York's decision making; The Business Council has regained that voice.

Efforts of The Business Council are geared toward improving economic potential for New York's businesses, in turn offering greater potential for New York's people and an expanded tax base for its governments. Government affairs efforts are pointed at opening up the state's business potential, while direct services to members help members save money—business helping business.

The Business Council, led by founding president Raymond T. Schuler and now by his successor, Daniel B. Walsh, helped New York turn the corner. In the past decade more than one million private-sector jobs were created in New York, and the state matches or exceeds the national growth rate. The council wants New York State to be the most desired headquarters state for business, also seeking internationalism, to make New York integral to the global economy. To improve education and thereby provide a more competitive work force, to forge public- and private-sector bonds, to reform taxes and corporation law and product liability, and to establish a coordinated economic development policy are goals for the future, a future The Business Council of New York State plans to be a great one.

The headquarters building of The Business Council of New York State.

NEW YORK STATE MUSEUM

In 1986 one of the nation's oldest and largest museums celebrated its sesquicentennial. Housing 4.5 million artifacts and natural specimens, the New York State Museum is the only museum devoted to researching and teaching the natural and human history of the state. In a sense, the New York State Museum is the dynamic memory of the Empire State. Anchoring one end of the international-style Governor Nelson A. Rockefeller Empire State Plaza in Albany, the museum hosts more than 600,000 visitors in an average year, 75,000 of them children in school groups, another quarter-million tourists.

Since its founding in 1836 the museum has housed nationally recognized collections assembled and interpreted by important scholars such as James Hall, progenitor of American paleobotany; famous botanist John Torrey; ethnologist Lewis Henry Morgan, considered the founder of American anthropology; and mycologist Charles Peck. Today 45 historians, scientists, and curators extend the museum's tradition of encyclopedic, critical study.

The New York State Museum's present building, opened during the bicentennial of the American Revolution in 1976, houses three permanent exhibit halls and a dozen changing exhi-

Life among the upper class in New York City in the 1890s is recreated by these Fifth Avenue cafe diners on view in the New York Metropolis Hall at the New York State Museum in Empire State Plaza, Albany.

bitions annually that fill 160,000 square feet of space, supported by impressive, state-of-the-art exhibit preparation facilities. Interdisciplinary exhibitions on the natural and human history of New York employ thousands of artifacts in realistic settings, holistically illustrating the state's past.

Objects on exhibit are drawn from study collections filling 25,000 square feet of floor space and including, among their millions of items, more than 3,000 rare specimens of North American fungi, one of the world's finest collections of invertebrate fossils,

The most accurate and realistic reconstruction ever made of life in northeastern North America at the end of the Ice Age depicts the first people to inhabit New York State in a new permanent exhibit at the New York State Museum.

Within a stunning marble facade, the New York State Museum houses 4.5 acres of exhibits that blend science and artistry to recreate "living" moments in time.

and the most extensive and complete collection of New York's minerals. The first and best documented collection of Shaker furniture is at the New York State Museum, as are examples of New York-made furniture spanning two centuries, an extensive collection of transportation-related vehicles, and the foremost collection of Eastern Woodland Native American artifacts in the United States. Building these collections and others, the New York State Museum staff has salvaged and restored the diverse treasures of New York's heritage, natural and human.

The museum is long established as a leading research institution. Part of extensive national and international scientific and cultural networks, landmark research efforts such as the Colonial Albany Social History Project and ecological and geological studies plumb the past and explore the future. As the interaction of people with the environment and people with people has shaped New York, and always will do so, the New York State Museum will continue to be the state's vital record, the repository of its past, and the harbinger of its future, indeed showing past to be but prologue.

METROPOLITAN LIFE INSURANCE COMPANY

Dynamic change and New York have long been synonymous. In the middle of the nineteenth century, as America transformed itself from an agrarian society into an industrial power, New York's chief city emerged as the nation's leading "Metropolis"—and the hub of financial activity.

How appropriate that during this period a company was created in New York with "Metropolitan" in its name—a company that has become a financial giant. The growth of Metropolitan Life Insurance Company is as remarkable and dynamic as New York's, and each has contributed to the other's success.

With the powerful magnet of a booming economy, New York attracted millions of people who left farms here

In 1911 Met Life agents made their rounds on bicycles. Today Met Life sales representatives carry lap-top computers and have access to SONIC, a companywide computer network.

and abroad to find a new livelihood in the state's growing commercial centers. Detached from the security of life in small villages, families faced many financial perils through the ups and downs of business cycles.

Met Life recognized the need in this changing society for new sources of stability—and the company has grown tremendously for over a century by helping achieve financial growth and security.

In addition to providing insurance, Met Life helps individuals and organizations manage retirement and investment assets—from multibillion-dollar pension funds for thousands of employees to a single person's annuity or mutual fund. In insurance, the company offers several types of coverage, including life, health, auto, homeowners, and disability. Many coverages are provided through employers' group plans, as well as directly to individuals.

While expanding the range of its financial products and services, Met Life has also extended its geographical scope. To its operations throughout the United States, the firm has added of-

Met Life built, and continues to own and manage, Stuyvesant Town and Peter Cooper Village in New York City—home to some 11,000 families.

fices in Canada, Europe, and Japan.

Today Met Life and its affiliated companies have more than $115 billion of assets under management. More than 43 million people are covered under Metropolitan insurance policies. Committed to the welfare of those it serves, Met Life has been a leader in developing programs responsive to community needs, including the nation's largest private health information effort.

The company traces its origins to a dramatic period of political as well as economic upheaval—the Civil War. In 1863 Simeon Draper, a prominent New York entrepreneur, began a business to help provide insurance for soldiers of the Union Army.

This initial enterprise did not meet the success expected and by early 1868 the company had been rechartered as the Metropolitan Life Insurance Company. In the expanding postwar econ-

Met Life headquarters—including its landmark tower—consists of these three buildings on Madison Avenue in New York City.

omy, Met Life established itself quickly, but was fairly small among the many competing insurance companies.

Then, in 1879, Met Life took a giant step by pioneering a new product called "industrial" insurance. Aimed at protecting the average worker, this coverage could be purchased in small amounts—costing as little as five cents a week. To make payment convenient, a Met Life agent collected the premiums at the insured's home.

As one of the first U.S. companies to offer industrial insurance, Met Life had the right product to meet the needs of the time—and the firm was catapulted into unprecedented growth.

An interesting footnote here is that to launch its industrial operation, Met Life had to recruit field men in England, where the product had been developed. In all, Met brought some 600 English field men to the United States.

By 1893 a prospering Met Life moved to the site of its present headquarters at One Madison Avenue. There, in 1909, it erected the Metropolitan Life Tower—the world's tallest building at the time. Modeled after the renowned bell tower of St. Mark's Basilica in Venice, Met Life's graceful spire remains one of New York's great landmarks, and is now beautifully lit at night.

In the 1920s—another period of tremendous economic expansion for the nation—Met Life cemented its position as the leader in providing financial security to American workers by pioneering in the field of group insurance and pensions. Today about half of the *Fortune* 100 companies protect their employees with Met group policies, and Met Life, together with its affiliates, has more than $60 billion of asts under management in its pension business.

Today the company is also a leading force in helping employers and other organizations manage health care costs. In fact, in 1985 the State of New York selected Met Life to administer the Empire Plan, the health care program for state and local government employees, both active and retired, and their dependents.

The firm's innovative role in health care management reflects its leadership in another area: office technology. In the 1950s Met Life became the first insurance company to use electronic

Established in 1909, Met Life's visiting nurse service for policyholders was a pioneering effort.

data-processing equipment. It continues today on the cutting edge of electronics and telecommunications.

The company's products and services have also evolved to meet the changing needs of the American economy. During the 1970s, for example, under the direction of Richard R. Shinn, president and chief executive officer, Met Life entered multiline marketing with the sale of auto and home owners insurance through a subsidiary, Metropolitan Property and Liability Insurance Company.

In the 1980s the pace of dynamic change quickened under Met Life's current president and chief executive officer, John J. Creedon. In a period of unprecedented diversification, the firm has built on its strengths through strategic acquisitions in many areas.

The two most prominent examples are Century 21, the world's largest real estate franchise sales organization, and State Street Research & Management Company, manager of pensions and investment funds. This period also witnessed major international thrusts with operations started in Great Britain, Japan, and Spain.

Throughout the company's his-

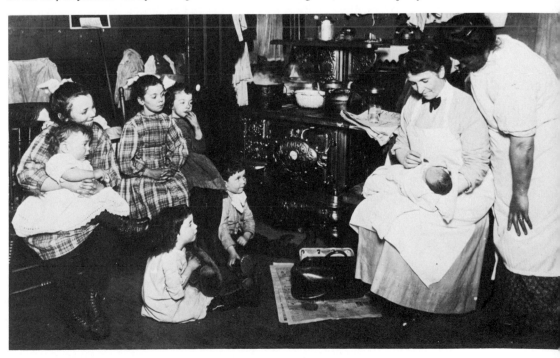

Metropolitan has offices throughout New York State, including major facilities in Utica (top) and Hauppauge (above).

tory, as the manager of billions of dollars in assets for its customers, Met Life has played an important role in investing for the expansion of the nation's economy. In addition to financial investments such as government securities and corporate stocks and bonds, the firm has been a leader in real estate development.

In 1922 Met Life broke ground in Long Island City, New York, for the country's first privately financed, large-scale housing project. Interestingly, Mr. Creedon was born in that project. To ease the housing crunch in the 1940s, the company built many communities throughout the nation. In New York City alone, Met Life created such major apartment projects as Peter Cooper Village, Stuyvesant Town,

Parkchester, and Riverton.

The company has also played a prominent role in commercial real estate development. In New York, for example, Met Life loans helped finance construction of the Empire State Building and the Rockefeller Center complex. More recently, Met Life purchased the Pan Am and Goldman Sachs buildings in New York City.

Today more than 6 million New Yorkers are protected by Metropolitan insurance. Met Life has $3.1 billion invested in the securities of New York companies, helping businesses in the state finance new facilities and create jobs. Met Life itself employs 14,000 people at 185 facilities throughout the state.

Met Life is also an innovator and leader in demonstrating good corporate citizenship. The company and its Metropolitan Life Foundation provide millions of dollars each year for a wide range of programs to improve the edu-

cational, social, and cultural fabric of society. But Met Life's most distinctive contribution has been programs aimed at improving health.

In the early part of this century Met Life focused on combating health problems such as tuberculosis, diphtheria, and infant mortality. In 1909 the company enlisted nurses from New York City's famous Henry Street Settlement to visit the homes of ill policyholders. This revolutionary program was then extended to other cities.

By the time Met Life ended its nursing service in 1953, more than 100 million visits had been made to more than 20 million policyholders. The firm continues reaching into millions of homes with messages about health through publications, films, radio, and TV. Subjects range from nutrition and safety to substance abuse and Alzheimer's disease.

Carrying this tradition of health education into the next century, Met Life has joined with The Walt Disney Company in creating a major pavilion devoted to human life and health at EPCOT Center in Florida.

The breadth of Met Life's interest in enhancing the communities it serves is illustrated by some of its recent activities in New York State: scholarships to develop future teachers, health education grants to several school districts, a major research grant to the Albert Einstein College of Medicine, programs to revitalize urban neighborhoods throughout the state, and cultural grants to many institutions ranging from Lincoln Center in New York City to the Burchfield Art Center in Buffalo.

As a source of financial security and jobs for New Yorkers, as a source of investment for New York businesses, and as a leader in supporting programs to improve New York communities, Metropolitan Life Insurance Company has made a unique contribution to New York State—a partnership in dynamic growth that is stronger than ever.

EMJ/McFARLAND-JOHNSON ENGINEERS, INC.

Behind the facade of a restored mid-nineteenth-century villa in Binghamton, New York, EMJ/McFarland-Johnson Engineers, Inc., operates a nationally prominent consulting engineering business that contrasts with the quiet old-world charm of its corporate headquarters.

The Tuscan-style villa gives EMJ/McFarland-Johnson Engineers a link to early American history as well as being part of the growth of New York State. It was built in 1854 by Charles Samuel Parsons Hall, a great-grandson of Samuel Holden Parsons who was a major general in George Washington's Northern Provincial Army. Hall, a successful attorney himself, was one of the early authors of the Binghamton City Charter, and in 1867 was village counsel when he finalized the charter papers for presentation to the state legislature.

The restoration of the Hall residence was completed in 1976 and coincided with the local celebration of the bicentennial. The building was designated as a local historic site worthy of preservation and continues to be the national headquarters for the four offices of the firm in New York State and for seven other offices nationwide.

The company was founded in 1946 by William H. McFarland and became McFarland-Johnson Engineers in 1959 with the association of John W. Johnson. During that period McFarland-Johnson began growth from a relatively small consulting firm into a major engineering design company that specialized in transportation systems, water- and sewage-treatment plants, airport and building design, flood-control systems, and environmental studies.

In New York, the firm designed sections of the New York State Thruway, the Genesee Expressway, the Southern Tier Expressway, the Adirondack Northway, and Interstate 88. Major projects included the redesigning of the complex, high-traffic intersection of Routes I-490 and I-590 southeast of Rochester and the I-88 connector with I-81 in the Binghamton area. The company also works closely with large and small municipalities across the state on water- and sewage-treatment facilities, highway projects, and airports.

Expansion of the firm's capabilities brought about design work on

EMJ/McFarland-Johnson Engineers, Inc., completely restored this 1854 Tuscan-style villa that serves as the firm's headquarters in Binghamton, New York. Photo courtesy of Helen Cardamone, Canal Country, 1982

important projects in other states, including the Atlantic City Expressway; Indiana Toll Road; the Ohio, Connecticut, and New Jersey turnpikes; and highway and railroad bridges in 15 states.

To handle increased volume and expand its capabilities, the company installed and continually upgrades one of the industry's most productive computer-aided design and drafting (CADD) systems. The CADD system enables an engineer to advance a project quickly through the various phases of conceptual design, budget estimates, construction drawing preparation, quantity development, and interdiscipline design reviews. It enables clients to view three-dimensional models of proposed facilities and to visualize how their projects will be developed in stages to fit into new sites or alignments.

In 1982 McFarland-Johnson was acquired by the internationally prominent design/construct firm, Balfour Beatty of the United Kingdom, and its name was changed to EMJ/McFarland-Johnson Engineers, Inc.

One of many dual-screened Intergraph CADD workstations EMJ/McFarland-Johnson Engineers, Inc., uses to advance a project through the various phases of project development. In this photo, one of the firm's technicians is utilizing a standard design detail for engineering analysis and input to construction drawings for a proposed new bridge abutment.

ULSTER COUNTY COMMUNITY COLLEGE

In the late 1950s and early 1960s many concerned citizens of Ulster County felt a need for the development of a community college to provide higher education opportunities in the area. With overwhelming public support expressed in a November 1961 referendum, Ulster County Community College became a legal entity.

What began as a dream in the minds of many Ulster County citizens has become, in reality, a highly respected, comprehensive community college, a unit of the State University of New York. It has recently received a 10-year reaffirmation of accreditation by the Middle States Association of Colleges and Schools, verifying the excellence of its instruction and the quality of its graduates. In the 25 years since its creation it has become a vital, integral part of the community.

The first president of the college was Dr. Dale B. Lake, appointed in September 1962 by the prominent area citizens who became the founding trustees. Lake began planning for the first entering class to be admitted in the fall of 1963. Housed in the former Ulster Academy building on West Chestnut Street in Kingston until its permanent campus could be built, the college

The college trustees and Ulster County Community College's first president at ground-breaking ceremonies on July 21, 1965, for the permanent campus in Stone Ridge, New York.

moved to the Stone Ridge site in 1967, when the first four of its buildings were ready for occupancy.

The new campus was constructed on donated land in the geographical center of Ulster County. The site, on a ridge between the Catskill Mountains on the west and the Schwangunks on the east, provides a striking background for the buildings, the names of which were selected to reflect the rich cultural heritage of the Ulster County area.

The John Burroughs Science Building was named for one of America's great naturalists, who lived for many years at his famous retreat, Slabsides, located nearby in West Park.

The George Clinton Administra-

tion Building honors the memory of New York's first constitutional and seven-term governor, who later served two terms as vice-president of the United States. He is buried in the Old Dutch Church cemetery in Kingston.

The Jacob Hasbrouck Building was named for one of the original settlers of Stone Ridge, and for his family, which figures prominently in the history of Ulster County. Hasbrouck was a well-to-do farmer who served in the American Revolution and held several public offices. His descendants included a state senator, a United States congressman, and a prominent New Paltz merchant who served as treasurer of the county.

John Vanderlyn Hall, which houses the Muroff Kotler Art Gallery and the John Quimby Theatre, among other facilities, commemorates this nineteenth-century Kingston painter, who was a protégé of Aaron Burr. Vanderlyn was well known for both his historical portraits and his neoclassical work.

The Jacob Hardenburgh Building honors a well-known resident of Ulster County, born in Rosendale, who became the first president of what was to become Rutgers University. He was the grandson of Major Johannes Hardenburgh, recipient of the Hardenburgh patent in 1708.

The Macdonald DeWitt Library is dedicated to the prominent Kingston attorney, a founding member of the board of trustees who made substantial philanthropic gifts for the construction of the library, the purchase of the residence of the president of the college, and for moneys earmarked for scholarship funds.

The Algonquin classroom building honors the native Americans who were the inhabitants of the Mid-Hudson area at the time the Dutch, French, and English came to the new world, and the Senate Gymnasium reflects the historical significance of Kingston, where the first constitutional senate in New York State met in 1777.

By 1972 the campus had grown to eight buildings and expanded its original size from 90 to 165 acres. Since that time the Kelder Conference Center, a greenhouse, and a child care center have been added.

Lake served as college president from 1962 to 1967. He was followed by Dr. George Erbstein, from 1967 to 1974. Robert T. Brown became its third and current president.

Since 1963 Ulster has developed a number of curricular offerings that are reflective of the needs and interests of the people and employers of Ulster County. More than 35,000 people have enrolled in a variety of programs that range from one-year diploma courses to two-year career and/or technical programs designed for specific employment opportunities. The college also has many excellent liberal arts programs that are designed either to stand alone or to articulate with various university programs for those students who wish to continue their education.

Areas of study include criminal justice, nursing, business administration, computer information systems, communications and media arts, engineering technologies, and the traditional first two years of a liberal arts degree. The college uses community advisory councils to maintain liaisons with the changing needs of local industries and employers.

Moreover, through its Development Center for Business, Small Business Development Center, and a campus-located chapter of Service Corps of Retired Executives (SCORE), the college offers specialized courses tailored to the needs of local businesses.

In addition to the traditional classroom learning process, the college also

Ulster County Community College's seal proclaims "truth from learning" and "wisdom from truth."

attempts to serve the citizens of Ulster County who look to it for leadership in the areas of the arts, sciences, and community services. The college is constantly working to make the Stone Ridge campus a cultural and social center for all people. Each year more than 70,000 local residents attend a variety of events or make use of college facilities that range from access to materials in the Macdonald DeWitt Library, the College Skills Center, theatrical and musical presentations, athletic events, and other special programs. Ulster makes its facilities available for events of community interest that range from senior citizens meetings, forums of political candidates, countywide athletic or musical con-

tests, to an annual meeting of the Ulster County Legislature.

A wide variety of credit courses are scheduled off campus in satellite centers in Kingston, Ellenville, Saugerties, and at the nearby correctional facilities. In addition, an array of credit-free courses further enhances the services that the college provides for the residents of the area.

In all these ways as well as others Ulster County Community College attempts to be reflective of the community it serves. The college pays homage to the rich historical and cultural traditions of the area; it attempts to meet the educational requirements of a varying student body; and it looks forward with the county to the growth and development of all of the natural resources of the Mid-Hudson area.

CHASE MANHATTAN CORPORATION

The Chase Manhattan Corporation is a global financial institution with more than 300 branches worldwide, more than 40 major subsidiaries, and some 6,000 correspondent banks. Interestingly enough, this world-famous organization began nearly 200 years ago as a local water company.

In 1799 New York City was threatened by yellow fever, and its untreated water supply was seen as the cause. A group of civic leaders that included Aaron Burr and Alexander Hamilton proposed the creation of a private water company, and the city council agreed. That same year the state legislature approved the creation of The Manhattan Company, mandated to supply "pure and wholesome" water to city residents. But Aaron Burr had a plan for The Manhattan Company to supply more than water.

Burr sought to establish a rival to the New York City office of Hamilton's Bank of the United States. Thus, he maneuvered a provision that allowed The Manhattan Company to use any capital stock not required in the water business "in the purchase of public stock or in any other monied transactions or operations not inconsistent with the constitution and laws of the United States." This provision paved the way for The Chase Manhattan Bank.

Supplying water, in fact, did not require all of The Manhattan Com-

In 1799 an outbreak of yellow fever threatened New York City, and the untreated water supply was cited as the cause. In response, The Manhattan Company was created to supply "pure and wholesome" water to city residents. Later that year, in September, The Manhattan Company also became a bank, Bank of The Manhattan Company, seen here at its original home at 40 Wall Street.

pany's capital, and the directors established an "office of discount and deposit." On September 1, 1799, the Bank of The Manhattan Company opened at 40 Wall Street. In 1842 The Manhattan Company sold its waterworks to the city and employed its entire capital in banking.

Later in the nineteenth century another bank, The Chase National Bank, was formed. Its founder was 75-year-

The Chase Manhattan Corporation is a global financial institution with more than 300 branches worldwide, more than 40 major subsidiaries, and some 6,000 correspondent banks.

old John Thompson, a former school-teacher and a specialist in currency values who in 1877 opened The Chase National Bank in a small office at 117 Broadway in New York City. The bank was named after Salmon P. Chase, the Treasury Secretary who led the fight for passage of the National Banking Acts of 1863 and 1864.

Chase National prospered under a succession of distinguished leaders, and as it entered the twentieth century it adjusted to a major expansion in the banking industry. In this new environment The Chase National Bank launched an aggressive effort to acquire other banks, and in doing so it became the nation's leading lender to commerce and industry. By 1927 it passed the billion-dollar mark in total resources, and a year later it became

The Chase National Bank was founded in 1877 and had its first permanent home here at 104 Broadway. The bank was named after Salmon P. Chase, the Treasury Secretary who led the fight for passage of the National Banking Acts of 1863 and 1864.

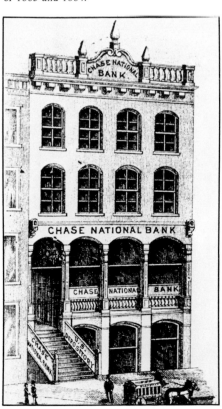

the nation's second-largest bank. Meanwhile, by that same year of 1927, the Bank of The Manhattan Company had established itself as a leader in the commercial banking community.

By 1951 Chase National had become a leading corporate, correspondent, and international bank. All that remained was to enhance its retail capabilities, and it would do this by merging with the Bank of The Manhattan Company.

Chase National was by then the nation's third-largest bank, and the Bank of The Manhattan Company was the nation's 15th largest. In 1955 the Bank of The Manhattan Company acquired The Chase National Bank, and The Chase Manhattan Bank was born. As one national magazine put it, "Jonah swallowed the whale."

The retail banking network of the Bank of The Manhattan Company complemented The Chase National Bank's traditional strengths in supporting industry, international trade, and correspondent banking. The Chase Manhattan Bank constituted a well-rounded domestic banking operation.

The institution's international profile evolved throughout the 1950s, 1960s, and 1970s as a young banker named David Rockefeller came to the fore in the bank's Foreign Department—today's International Banking Sector. This changing world view created a need for a broader global perspective to encompass political and economic developments at home and abroad. To serve this purpose, the Chase International Advisory Committee was formed in 1965. The committee consists of the bank's senior management and world financial and industrial leaders.

In 1961 the bank built a new corporate headquarters—a single tower surrounded by a plaza—in New York's financial district. The modern building, One Chase Manhattan Plaza, gave the ailing financial district a new image and sparked a downtown renaissance.

During the 1960s Chase Manhat-

In 1955 the Bank of the Manhattan Company acquired The Chase National Bank, and together they became the institution known today as The Chase Manhattan Bank. A piece of contemporary art stands outside the bank's headquarters at One Chase Manhattan Plaza.

tan became a leading proponent of corporate social responsibility. In the two decades since its inception, the bank's Corporate Responsibility Committee has contributed millions of dollars to charitable, scientific, cultural, and educational organizations, as well as establishing vehicles to provide financial counsel and loans for community economic development, small business, and minority groups.

Growth and expanding business opportunities led the bank to secure a national charter in 1965, and The Chase Manhattan Bank, N.A., was born. Four years later The Chase Manhattan Corporation was formed as a one-bank holding company, allowing Chase to expand to the financial services industry.

With the retirement of David Rockefeller as chairman of the corporation in 1981, Willard Butcher was named as his successor, and Thomas G. Labrecque was appointed president and chief operating officer. Under their leadership The Chase Manhattan Corporation continues to achieve solid growth in its target areas: global, institutional, and individual banking.

IBM CORPORATION

As the world's largest maker of computers, IBM is a legendary international corporation, and its story began in New York State. With its information-handling systems, equipment and servicers, ranging from large processors to personal computers, telecommunications systems, and office equipment, IBM serves countless areas of human activity.

IBM began in 1911 as the Computing-Tabulating-Recording (C-T-R) Co., an organization originally composed of three companies: the Tabulating Machine Co., founded in 1896 by engineer Herman Hollerith, who devised electrical machines that processed data stored on punched cards;

the Computing Scale Co., a computing scale manufacturer formed in 1891 by Edward Canby and Orange O. Ozias of Dayton, Ohio; and the International Time Recording Co. of Endicott, New York, formed in 1889 and maker of a mechanical time recorder devised by Willard Bundy.

These three companies merged, incorporating in New York State in 1911 as the Computing-Tabulating-Recording Co., maker of tabulating machines, scales, time recorders, and punched cards, with plants in Endicott, New York; Dayton, Ohio; and Washington, D.C. In 1914 Thomas J. Watson, Sr., joined C-T-R as general manager, and the following year he be-

came president. At that time the growing company had 1,346 employees and its computing skills were being used by such clients as railroads, chemical companies, utilities, and life insurance companies. Through the years until his death in 1956, Thomas J. Watson, Sr., guided the firm to global expansion and prosperity, becoming a legendary figure in American business history.

In 1924 C-T-R adopted the name International Business Machines. The newly christened IBM was employing more than 3,000 people and had opened offices in Canada, Brazil, other countries in South America, as well as in the Far East. Soon after, it opened

IBM corporate headquarters in Armonk, New York.

John F. Akers, current chairman of the board of IBM Corporation.

offices in the Philippines. By the early 1930s IBM was marketing machines for calculating, sorting, tabulating, and performing full-scale accounting operations. It also entered the electric typewriter business. In 1936 the company began providing the machines and services for what has been called the biggest accounting operation ever—the Social Security Program. By 1937 IBM had in excess of 10,000 employees.

When World War II began all IBM facilities were placed at the disposal of the U.S. government, and more than 5,000 IBM accounting machines were used in Washington to handle wartime paperwork. IBM also supplied equipment and products to the armed forces, and accounting machines in mobile units even followed U.S. troops in battle. Meanwhile the company continued to expand, building a new plant in Poughkeepsie, New York, in 1942 and enlarging its Endicott, New York, plant. Both plants won Army-Navy "E" awards during the war.

In 1944 the first machine that could execute long computations automatically, the ASCC (Automatic Sequence Controlled Calculator), was completed by IBM after six years of development in cooperation with Harvard University. As well, the Mark I—an electromechanical machine that used relays and tape-controlled programming devices—was built by IBM and presented to Harvard.

Electromechanical machines to punch, tabulate, and sort cards at high speed had been the heart of IBM's business since its founding. Faster machines had been developed, but even the fastest punched-card machines were to be bypassed by technological change. In 1946 vacuum tubes permitted machines to calculate several thousand times faster than the earlier electromechanical relays. IBM's first calculators and computers to use vacuum tubes were the IBM 603 and 604, the IBM SSEC (Selective Sequence Electronic Calculator), and the IBM 701, all introduced between 1946 and 1952. The IBM 603 Multiplier was the first small commercial electronic calculator, and the IBM SSEC became the first computer to combine electronic computation with stored instructions. The IBM 701 was the company's first large vacuum computer—the first of its 700 series—and could execute 17,000 instructions per second.

These machines possessed a greatly expanded ability to do complex work at high speed. Initially designed for scientific problems, the vacuum tube computers quickly moved into commercial work in the 1950s—in billing, payroll, accounts receivable, inventory control, and many other applications.

In 1956 IBM's chairman of the board, Thomas J. Watson, Sr., died at age 82. Watson had been the firm's guiding light for more than 40 years. Thomas J. Watson, Jr., subsequently became chief executive officer of IBM, and the company continued to grow and innovate, building new plants and introducing new technology. IBM's Kingston, New York, plant was completed in 1956, and the firm continued production of a large-scale computer known as SAGE for the nation's air

Thomas J. Watson, Sr., served as president of C-T-R Co., the forerunner of IBM, and guided the firm into global expansion and prosperity.

warning system. In 1957 IBM made the FORTRAN scientific programming language available to customers.

In 1960 the Solid State 7000 series computers replaced the 700 series of vacuum tube machines. Other innovations included the 1410 computer and STRETCH computing system—then the world's most powerful. IBM computers scored the 1960 Winter Olympics, tallied votes at both political conventions, and processed the United States presidential election returns. Meanwhile the company continued to expand overseas, with new plants and laboratories launched in Europe and South America. New products such as the Selectric typewriter were soon introduced. In 1962 IBM began work on

IBM engineers have designed a computer memory chip (pictured here) that can store more than 4 million bits of data—four times the capacity of any memory chip in use today. The chip can store the equivalent of about 400 pages of double-spaced typewritten text and read the data in all of its 4,194,304 memory cells in only one-fourth of a second.

a computer to help guide the two-man Gemini capsule, one of many IBM contributions to the U.S. space program.

In 1964 the IBM System/360, incorporating solid-state technology, replaced the firm's existing computer product lines. It represented the first family of computers—ranging from small to large—that were both upward and downward compatible, using the same programming instructions. Also that year IBM moved its corporate headquarters from New York City to Armonk, New York. As the 1960s progressed computer storage grew in capacity and speed, and the focus shifted to software systems designed to make the most efficient and productive use of the computer. And in 1969 IBM computers helped NASA put the first men on the moon.

The early 1970s saw the advent of monolithic, integrated-circuit technology—which places many circuits on single, tiny silicon chips. The industry's first computer with an entire main memory of monolithic technology was the IBM System/370 Model 145, introduced in 1970. This development brought major gains in speed, capacity, reliability, and data storage. Millions or billions of characters of information became available, and programming was tailored ever closer to meet the user's needs. IBM entered the photocopy business with the IBM Copier, and in 1973 it introduced the IBM diskette, a new storage medium.

During the 1980s IBM has continued its rapid rate of technological growth. In 1981 it produced the smallest, lowest-priced IBM computer system to date—the IBM Personal Computer. That same year IBM scientists fabricated a 288,000-bit memory chip that holds four times as much data in only twice the area. In 1983 the IBM Personal Computer XT, with larger memory, dual-sided diskette drive, and high-performance fixed disk drive, was introduced, and the following year IBM announced the fabrication of experimental one-million-bit memory chips.

Today IBM scientists are working on a host of projects for computers. Silicon memory and logic circuits are being further miniaturized; storage capacity and speed are being increased; new communication, display, and printing technologies are expanding the computer's usefulness; and programming advances are making the computer still easier to use and more adaptable to specific needs. The need for connectivity among many different products is growing, and today's computer networks are only the beginning. If the past is the prologue, IBM's technological future looks bright: The firm's technological innovations and the development of its many significant machines, devices, and software have garnered the company more than 10,000 patents and two Nobel prizes in physics throughout its history.

Today, with about 390,000 employees in 130 countries, IBM is a global corporation. And today, as throughout its history, New York State and its people play an integral part in the organization's activity, while IBM breathes life into New York's economy by being such a major employer in the state. The company is also a good corporate citizen. IBM has a long-standing tradition of supporting educational, cultural, and social programs in communities where it conducts business. This support includes job training for the economically disadvantaged and the physically disabled, and a broad program of grants for education, hospitals, and the arts. Through its Scientific Centers, IBM is involved with universities, research institutes, and government agencies worldwide in projects oriented toward national priorities, such as advanced technical education, agricultural research, and public health. As a memorial to IBM's founder, Thomas J. Watson, Sr., the firm annually provides more than 200 four-year college scholarships to children of employees. In addition, IBM does much to develop inner-city neighborhoods, and to support the elderly, handicapped, and others in need. In New York City, IBM Corporation invites the public to view art and science exhibitions held regularly in a gallery at its new office building at 590 Madison Avenue.

SECURITY MUTUAL LIFE INSURANCE COMPANY OF NEW YORK

For Security Mutual Life Insurance Company of New York, founded in 1886, its theme "Building on a century of service" is, like a photo, worth a thousand words. It explains concisely how the Binghamton-based firm with modest beginnings developed into one of America's leading companies in the insurance industry.

Security Mutual is ranked among the nation's top 50 mutual life insurance companies based on assets and insurance in force. The firm's $13.1 billion of life insurance in force in 1987 represented a sixteenfold increase over the 1972 amount.

The key word in the firm's theme phrase is "service"—service to its policyholders, to its field representatives, to its community, and to its industry.

Security Mutual has demonstrated a unique ability to provide basic, affordable life insurance service to its clients, while creating innovative services completely new in their day, such as preferred policies for policyholders who abstain from drinking intoxicating liquors (1900) and nonsmoker discounts (1975).

The company and its personnel have also maintained a high profile in the area of service to the community

The 10-floor Security Mutual Building was completed in 1905. The firm added on a much-needed three-story addition in 1981.

Security Mutual's chairman of the board, Robert M. Best (left), and president and chief executive officer, Paul H. Pearson (right), serve the company as leading figures in the life insurance industry. Through their involvement in major civic and cultural activities in Broome County and New York State, they have established an example for company employees to follow.

and to the life insurance industry. The organization's board chairman, Robert M. Best, and his successor as president and chief executive officer, Paul H. Pearson, are leading figures in the life insurance industry. They also are deeply involved in major civic and cultural activities in Broome County and New York State, establishing a pattern emulated by many company employees.

This background of service is behind the firm's dramatic growth, particularly remarkable in the past 10 years. From its founding in 1886 until 1975 Security Mutual sold its first billion dollars worth of ordinary life insurance. In five years, from 1975 to 1980, it sold its second billion.

Then in 1980 alone it sold another billion. Sales at year-end 1986 topped $13 billion, a 21-percent increase over the previous year. Today the company is a national leader in personal and corporate life and disability insurance, and has sales offices in major communities in 40 states.

That is a long way from the beginning, when the first asset was a premium of $18.90 on a policy that promised if a local industrialist, Charles E. Titchener, died within a year, his widow would be paid $1,000.

By 1903 life insurance in force reached $11 million, and Security Mutual constructed its home office building that still dominates the view down Court Street in Binghamton. In 1981 the company dedicated a three-story, 95,000-square-foot addition that cost in excess of $10 million.

Today Security Mutual Life Insurance Company is positioned for continued stability and growth through its organization of subsidiary and affiliate companies and its expansion of insurance services.

EMPIRE SOILS INVESTIGATIONS, INC.

Empire Soils Investigations, Inc., headquartered in the village of Groton in Tompkins County, is one of the major engineering specialty contractors in the Northeast.

Since its founding in 1953 Empire's main activity has been exploratory drilling and testing of subsurface conditions at construction sites to determine the earth's compatibility with specific building projects.

The company's expertise has been applied to scores of major construction projects such as arterial highways, airport runways, hospitals, shopping malls, industrial buildings, and transportation networks that include Buffalo's modernistic light rail rapid transit system and the Washington, D.C., subway system.

Empire now analyzes more than 1,000 sites annually throughout the Northeast, and offers capabilities that include exploratory drilling and sampling in soil and rock to depths of 1,200 feet. In testing of subsurface conditions, such factors as the strength of soil and rock formations, and a site's potential load-carrying capacity are determined to establish sound bases for

accurate engineering and building decisions.

And in recent years, because of mankind's growing concern with the potential dangers of hazardous waste (exemplified by the Love Canal tragedy), Empire has become a front runner in environmental site testing. Drilling, exploration, and groundwater monitoring at hazardous waste sites now form a significant portion of the company's business volume.

From its headquarters in Groton, Empire's management staff, headed by Bent L. Thomsen, president since 1971, oversees a busy network of six offices and four testing laboratories located in Groton, Hamburg, Rochester, and Latham in New York State, and in Highland Park, New Jersey.

In 1964 Thomsen, a civil engineer with an M.Sc. in soil mechanics, established a consulting geotechnical and materials engineering affiliate, to enable the group to provide a full range of technical and scientific services. This specialty group provides the significant talents of geologists, hydrologists, and specialized professional engineers. Its formation was a natural evolution in a growth pattern that began immediately after the company's founding.

Those most directly involved with the founding in Ithaca were B.K. Hough, professor of soil mechanics at Cornell University; R.B. Anderson, a member of the Army Corps of Engineers; and Gustave Young, a former corps member then teaching soils lab at Cornell. Anderson, who became the first president, and Young stayed with Empire until their retirements. Hough later left to establish his own geotechnical consulting firm.

Empire's first drilling equipment was not fancy: a power auger mounted on a Jeep. But it was the forerunner of a modern fleet of some 30 diversified

Company crewmen wear extensive safety gear when test drilling at hazardous waste sites.

drill rigs and appurtenant equipment, including several track-mounted rigs that can reach swamplands and steep hills.

The first drilling crew was the team of Joseph J. Aleba and W. Dean Anderson, both of whom are still with the company—Aleba as vice-president and Anderson as executive vice-president. Other current officers are Elizabeth A. Ryan, secretary, and Karl F. Stamm, treasurer.

Empire has four geotechnical and material laboratories in New York State for determining engineering and physical properties of soil and construction materials.

Two years after its founding, Empire received its first major contract, from New York State to explore the subsurface conditions for the Niagara extension of the New York State Thruway—a major arterial roadway traversing Buffalo. The firm's first branch office was opened the next year in the Buffalo area, and a testing laboratory was established there.

By the time W. Dean Anderson became president in 1959, the company had six drilling rigs in use, and headquarters had been moved first to Dryden, then to Groton.

In 1959 Empire expanded into construction quality assurance and materials testing, a service that analyzes construction materials such as concrete, steel, and roofing components. Testing and observation take place on construction sites, as well as in Empire's laboratories and at processing plants where the materials originate. That service was part of an overall ex-

Empire's first drilling equipment when the company was founded in 1953 was this power auger mounted on a Jeep.

One of Empire's latest truck-mounted drill rigs doing exploratory drilling in connection with Buffalo's light rail rapid transit system.

pansion of the workload that made the 1960s growth years for the firm. During that period significant work was performed for the New York State University Construction Fund in a vast building program aimed at increasing educational opportunities in the state.

By 1967 the drill rig fleet had been expanded to 17 units, and a new office was opened in Washington, D.C., to oversee Empire's extensive involvement in exploration programs for the subway system in the nation's capital.

The 1970s brought further growth. Quality-assurance services were further diversified, and drilling capabilities expanded into soil and rock instrumentation to monitor ground movement from tunnel construction. Offices were opened in that decade in Rochester, Syracuse, and Albany, and the drill rig fleet grew to 24 units. Additional technical and engineering staff were hired, and billings continued their upward movement.

The specialty group concept of Empire, integrating technical and scientific services, enabled the firm to undertake increasingly larger projects in the 1970s. A major new assignment was quality-assurance monitoring during construction of Buffalo's rapid transit system.

In the 1980s the company's major

new direction has been in environmental testing. Hydrogeologists have joined the staff, and Empire has installed thousands of groundwater monitoring wells at hazardous waste sites, as well as at sanitary and industrial disposal sites.

Developing expertise in this critical environmental area has meant the addition of sophisticated new technological and laboratory equipment, as well as a variety of new safety and decontamination gear—enabling Empire to maintain compliance with the requirements of the Environmental Protection Agency.

As the company prepares for its 35th year, it can look back on a history of accomplishment. In the past four years business volume has increased by more than 60 percent, to the current annual level of more than $12 million.

Total employment has grown from the first two-man drilling crew to reach 180 people. Empire Soils Investigations, Inc., is an experienced, veteran corporation in a relatively young industry—a company that has added impressive chapters to its own history with each passing year.

THE HILLIARD CORPORATION

The Hilliard Corporation of Elmira, New York, is a special applications engineering company that manufactures a broad line of motion-control products, oil-filtration and reclaiming equipment, starters for gas and diesel engines and gas turbines, and, through its subsidiary, Star Systems, plate and frame filter presses for the food and beverage industry. Founded in 1905 as The Hilliard Clutch and Machinery Company with the invention by William J. Hilliard of a friction clutch, the firm survived its early difficult years as it slowly expanded its product line. Today Hilliard sales exceed $12 million annually. The corporation operates through a wide network of manufacturers' sales representatives and manufacturing licensees in Canada, Japan, France, and England.

In 1925 Hilliard became a corporation and was licensed by General Electric to manufacture its newly developed oil reclaimer, the firm's second

important product line. Edward A. Mooers started work at Hilliard in 1928 as general manager and was the driving force and guiding spirit of the company for 54 years. In 1933 Mooers and Theodore LaBrecque worked together to design Hilliard's own oil reclaimer, the Hilco oil reclaimer. During the Depression Hilliard's few employees had to play many roles as they developed other new products and struggled to keep their small company going. The wisdom and loyal support of the firm's board of directors was vital during that crucial period.

During World War II Hilliard became a war plant and manufactured a variety of essential products. A transmission-like device was designed to protect sailors from injury by absorbing the recoil when the gun turrets on Navy cruisers were fired. The 152 Model GM-1 oil reclaimers made for the Manhattan Project at Oak Ridge were used in producing U-235 for the atomic bomb.

Today Hilliard continues to build on its 80-year reputation for problem solving. It stands ready to develop and

The late Edward A. Mooers was the key executive of The Hilliard Corporation for 54 years.

build special engineered products. Its past performance is demonstrated by the bidirectional overrunning clutches for four-wheel-drive, all-terrain vehicles and electric brakes for robots, elevators, and escalators. Hilco oil reclaimers process insulating oil for utility customers, while Hilco filter cartridges and housings serve the needs of oil and gas pipeline customers, as well as the needs of many industrial customers. Hilliard air, gas, or steam engine starters go on gas pipeline compressors, generator packages, and cogeneration units. Through its subsidiary, Star Systems, Hilliard offers an equally long history of proven products for the food and beverage filtration industry. In January 1988 Hilliard acquired Delta Filter Corporation, a manufacturer of air-filtration products, which will further enhance the company's plans for future growth.

In order to compete successfully in today's markets, Hilliard depends on its strong Engineering Department, its energetic salespeople, and its skilled work force. The firm has steadily up-

The Hilliard Corporation work force in 1907. William J. Hilliard, inventor of the company's first friction clutch, is at center.

Above: *A modern Hilliard oil reclaimer, which is used for processing insulating oil for a utility customer.*

Right: *One of several computer-controlled machines that supports Hilliard's standard and special engineered, quality products.*

dated its factory, which is equipped with the latest computer-controlled, vertical machining centers, shape-cutting machines and lathes, as well as state-of-the-art welding equipment. Hilliard's facilities have grown to cover 250,000 square feet.

In 1982 Edward A. Mooers retired as chairman of the board of The Hilliard Corporation after spending his life building the company. Mooers not only was the central figure in Hilliard's development, but he also contributed greatly to his community, including serving as Elmira's mayor for six years. When Edward Mooers retired, with the affection and admiration of his organization, he was succeeded by his daughter, Nelson Mooers van den Blink, who became chairman and chief executive officer. Hilliard's president and chief operating officer is Gerald F. Schichtel, who joined the company in 1970 and became factory manager three years later. As The Hilliard Corporation moves ahead, it remains committed to designing and manufacturing quality products, ready to meet the challenges of a changing environment.

NEW YORK STATE ELECTRIC & GAS CORPORATION

In 1852 eight businessmen invested $75,000 to sell gas light in Ithaca. Today New York State Electric & Gas Corporation is one of seven large electric and gas utilities in New York State, and among the nation's top 500 corporations, according to *Forbes* and *Business Week* magazines.

NYSEG serves one-third of the state's land area and one-tenth of its population, and has 719,000 electric and 134,000 gas customers. It has assets of $4.2 billion, annual sales exceeding one billion dollars, 4,500 employees, and 72,000 common stockholders. NYSEG's service area is predominantly rural and suburban. The largest of 13 small cities it supplies is Binghamton, where it has its corporate headquarters.

Gas lighting was still in its infancy when the Ithaca Gas Light Company was organized on October 28, 1852. That company, which built its first plant for making gas from coal the following year, was the forerunner of NYSEG. The firm grew quickly through the end of the century, when

The Clinton House in Ithaca, where a small group of citizens formed NYSEG's predecessor, the Ithaca Gas Light Company, in 1852.

The largest of NYSEG's hydro facilities, the Upper Mechanicville Hydroelectric Station on the Hudson River, is controlled by an on-site computer.

it began competing with electric light. Although Ithaca Gas responded aggressively, the popularity of electricity climbed, and, after Ithaca Gas Light was acquired by Associated Gas & Electric Company in 1910, Associated bought the rival Ithaca Electric Light and Power Company. In 1915 Ithaca Gas Light became Ithaca Gas and Electric Corporation.

Under Associated, the Ithaca company expanded to a regional utility. Its name was changed to New York State Gas and Electric in 1918, New York State Electric Corporation in 1928, and New York State Electric & Gas Corporation in 1929. By 1924 the firm had acquired 12 new companies, and in 1928 it added Eastern New York Electric & Gas Corporation with 42 companies.

Early this century more than 240 local companies or interests were combined to form the present corporation. By 1937, still a subsidiary of Associated, NYSEG's service area had reached its present size.

This fast growth eventually spelled financial disaster for Associated, which was dissolved by a U.S. bankruptcy court in 1949. NYSEG was sold, and it became a major, independently owned, utility. The first offering of NYSEG's stock lasted three months, resulted in the sale of 880,000 shares, and brought in NYSEG's first 13,500 shareholders. Today NYSEG has 78,000 stockholders and more than 54 million shares of common stock outstanding.

Most of the company's electricity is generated by burning coal at six plants in New York and one at Homer City, Pennsylvania, which NYSEG co-owns with Pennsylvania Electric Company.

Somerset Station on Lake Ontario

Today's lineman operates much more efficiently and safely than his counterpart did in the horse-drawn bucket truck of 1900 (inset).

in Niagara County was completed in 1984 for one billion dollars and is New York State's most modern coal-fired plant. Somerset's 662 megawatts and the company's 946-megawatt share of Homer City account for nearly two-thirds of the generating capacity NYSEG owns. Its other coal-burning plants, built during the 1940s and 1950s, are being renovated to extend their lives another 15 to 20 years for about one-eighth of the cost of new facilities. NYSEG is first in the state and 11th among the nation's largest utilities in generating efficiency.

The company's nine hydroelectric plants can generate 72 megawatts. The largest, the 16.8-megawatt Upper Mechanicville Hydro Station on the Hudson River north of Albany, began service in the fall of 1983.

NYSEG owns 18 percent of the $6.3-billion Nine Mile Point 2 nuclear plant near Oswego on Lake Ontario that is due to start operating in 1988. It will supply NYSEG with 196 megawatts. The plant has been built and will be operated by Niagara Mohawk Power Corporation.

NYSEG has helped more than 1,000 businesses successfully locate or expand in Upstate New York. It main-tains a computerized list of commercial and industrial sites and buildings in its service area, and tries to match them with expanding businesses' needs. No-cost assistance NYSEG provides industry includes identifying communities that meet a business' requirements, proving the availability of the work force required, arranging site visits, handling all necessary paperwork, and providing information on financing, tax incentives, and training.

NYSEG is a utility leader in environmental protection, thanks to its success in building and maintaining facilities that meet federal and state environmental, safety, and health standards. One-third of the cost of building the Somerset plant, more than $300 million, was spent on environmental controls, including equipment to control air pollution and protect migratory birds and Lake Ontario's aquatic life. The Electric Power Research Institute recently completed a High Sulfur Test Center at Somerset that will seek better and cheaper ways to control sulfur dioxide emissions from coal burning plants.

Each of NYSEG's 13 operating districts has a consumer representative who helps customers take advantage of such company services as deferred bill payments, notification of a friend or relative before a customer's electric or gas service can be shut off, budget bill-ing, conservation assistance, senior citizen roundtables, information booklets, and a mobile mini-office.

Project SHARE, started by NYSEG in late 1982 and administered by the American Red Cross, helps needy elderly or disabled customers overcome energy emergencies. By the end of 1987 SHARE had distributed nearly one million dollars to 4,700 families.

NYSEG conducted more than 23,000 home energy surveys free of charge during 1987 to help home owners reduce energy consumption and costs.

To help today's students become energy-wise consumers tomorrow, NYSEG offers personnel and a full range of educational materials that are monitored by an advisory panel of local teachers. Mini-grants support innovative energy education projects.

New York State Electric & Gas Corporation spends more than $12 million a year on research to make electric and gas service more efficient and cheaper, and to reduce its impact on the environment. About one-half of these research funds go to state and national research and one-half to company projects. Recent efforts have centered on determining how conservation will affect future energy consumption.

Modern Somerset Station in Niagara County helps make NYSEG's generating system among the most efficient in the United States.

SPENCE ENGINEERING COMPANY, INC.

Paulsen Spence began his career as a salesman for a company that made pressure regulating and reducing valves. Before long he designed an improved pressure regulating valve, and in October 1925 he filed a patent application.

The following year Spence and several associates formed Spence Engineering Company, Inc., to produce this newly patented regulator. One problem still remained: The new business did not have proper manufacturing facilities.

At that time Paulsen Spence met Leon Dexter—head of Rider-Ericsson Engine Company, located in Walden. The firm had been founded in 1874 by Captain John Ericsson, famous for building *The Monitor,* a ship that made history in the Civil War in the first clash of ironclad warships.

Dexter was seeking a new product to supplement Rider-Ericsson's faltering pump sales. Recognizing the market potential of Spence's innovative regulator, he agreed to a deal

Spence's patent led to his own engineering firm, Spence Engineering Company, Inc., which today is a recognized leader in the regulator field—selling throughout America as well as abroad.

whereby the young enterprise could use Rider-Ericsson's production facilities in downtown Walden.

Slowly but steadily Spence Engineering grew, and its sales eventually eclipsed those of Rider-Ericsson. By 1939 the thriving venture had purchased its host firm's plant and manufacturing equipment. It was soon holding more than 30 patents and producing a full product line.

Spence Engineering's equipment is vital to most industrial operations in times of war and peace, and during World War II the firm earned the coveted Army-Navy "E" Award for production efficiency. After the war Spence distribution and production continued to expand to include new regulators and fluid-control items.

In 1961 Paulsen Spence died unexpectedly. Leon Dexter then directed the company until 1965, when Joseph Ahern was appointed president. Two years later Spence Engineering left the old Rider-Ericsson factory in downtown Walden (known affectionately as "The Foundry") and moved to a 50,000-square-foot modern complex on the city's outskirts. That facility was expanded by 6,000 square feet in 1978 and 20,000 square feet in 1985.

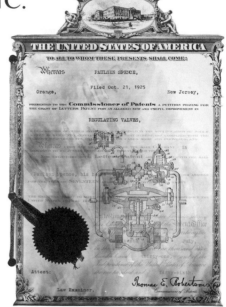

Pictured here is the patent Paulsen Spence received for his design of an improved pressure regulating valve.

Spence Engineering was purchased in 1984 by the Watts Regulator Company of Lawrence, Massachusetts. Watts, founded in 1874, produces valves for the water safety and flow control, water quality, industrial, and steam markets.

Joseph Ahern remained as Spence's president until his retirement in 1985; Stephen Banyacski, a 24-year company veteran, then assumed the position.

Today Spence Engineering Company, Inc., is a recognized leader in the regulator field, selling throughout America as well as abroad. Its equipment is used throughout the plants of Ford Motor Company, General Motors, General Electric, Westinghouse, Du Pont, and many other major companies.

Spence regulators are also used widely in hospitals, public buildings, schools, public utilities, textile mills, dairy farms, nuclear submarines, and skyscrapers such as the Sears Tower, the World Trade Center, and Rockefeller Center.

LOVELL SAFETY MANAGEMENT CO., INC.

During the 1920s and 1930s the rate of U.S. worksite accidents began to skyrocket, and the high costs of workers' compensation threatened many companies with bankruptcy. In 1936 Jac M. Lovell, a young labor attorney, decided to respond to this problem. He founded Lovell Safety Management Co. in an attempt to control, and ultimately reduce, the expense of workers' compensation to businesses.

Jac Lovell first originated the safety group concept while working on a project with the Cleaners & Dryers Board of Trade to help control that organization's workers' compensation costs. Today the original cleaners group—still managed by Lovell—is the oldest existing safety group in New York.

Lovell made history in the workers' compensation field by devising the concept of compensation management by a "safety group"—a group of employers who are part of a common industry and share similar insurance exposures. Safety groups focus primarily on claims control and safety promotion. Targeting various industries, Lovell developed specific safety groups for hospitals, municipalities, contractors, manufacturers, and others. Today Lovell is New York State's leading manager of safety groups.

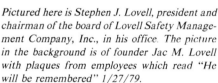

Now, more than 50 years later, Lovell Safety Management serves 1,200 client companies—and their approximately 120,000 employees who rely on Lovell expertise in workers' compensation cost control. Lovell safety group members have realized workers' compensation insurance savings in excess of $123 million since 1936.

Lovell safety groups develop safety and claim-control plans with help from a Lovell safety specialist, who visits the workplace and prepares a report that outlines those areas where safety procedures need improvement. Lovell also provides management training programs on general safety, handling of hazardous materials, health management, and accident investigation for supervisory personnel. Among the company's many services is a communication system that keeps members up to date on the latest techniques in safety management and OSHA developments.

Pictured here is Stephen J. Lovell, president and chairman of the board of Lovell Safety Management Company, Inc., in his office. The picture in the background is of founder Jac M. Lovell with plaques from employees which read "He will be remembered" 1/27/79.

Today the Lovell Group is subdivided into many different areas. Lovell Safety Management Co., Inc., is the Lovell Group's parent company; it manages workers' compensation safety groups, administers self-funded workers' compensation plans, and provides unemployment insurance claims services with cost controls. Lovell & Lovell, P.C., a law firm, is a representative and manager for self-insurers of workers' compensation and disability benefits. Safety & Health Management Consultants, Inc., provides technical expertise on a wide variety of occupational safety and health issues and safety training.

In all of these areas, the Lovell Group's goal is to provide the lowest-possible cost to its clients for their workers' compensation insurance. In the past 50 years Lovell has developed safety group management into an effective tool to help many industries prevent accidents, promote safety, and reduce costs. It has proven that Safety Pays Dividends.

Lovell's top executives are pictured here in the firm's conference room. They are (from left) Richard F. Andree, vice-president/director of safety and health; Stephen J. Lovell, president and chairman of the board; Martin R. Vulpis, vice-president/director of sales and underwriting; and Frank Roccanova, vice-president/director of claims.

THE CROSBY COMPANY

The Crosby Company started as a small concern before the turn of the century—with one man's dream about a simpler and cheaper way to make parts for the growing bicycle industry. When World War I and World War II turned Buffalo and industrial cities like it into boom towns, the little bicycle parts manufacturer started producing military supplies, reaching new peaks of employment and production. When inflation rocked the Northeast in the 1970s and early 1980s, the firm took a nosedive and flirted with death. But with the help of a Chapter 11 bankruptcy, it carried on the fight for survival. Today The Crosby Company is a small company again, a metal-stamping plant looking toward the next century with a scaled-down operation and dreams of better days.

The firm's history closely parallels the up-and-down tale of the city it calls home. "We almost took the knockout punch," says Henry W. Crosby, Jr., president of the company and the

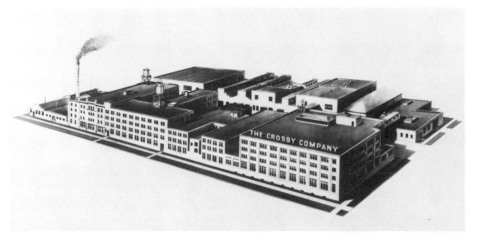

The Crosby Company has operated in a Pratt Street industrial facility since 1910. At one time 20 buildings were used by the firm.

grandson of founder William H. Crosby. "We went into Chapter 11 in 1983, came out of it in 1985, and hopefully we're a better company for it. We're a leaner, more aggressive operation. That's what the 1980s and 1990s demand." Crosby is proud of his company and the family tradition that forged it.

He says his grandfather was a "no-nonsense" Canadian who came to Buffalo to work as a sales manager for another metal-stamping plant shortly before he hatched his idea for a better way of making bike parts. At the time most bicycles weighed 50 or 60 pounds because they were made of heavy cast and drop-forged parts. The heavy bikes were expensive and difficult to operate. Crosby made a simple observation: Bicycle parts had to be lighter, more durable, and less expensive. And he decided he would do it.

In the spring of 1896 he set up machinery in a rented building in Buffalo and began making parts for the growing bicycle industry. Numerous bicycle manufacturers went to The Crosby Company and were pleasantly surprised to find that some of their parts could be made lighter through metal stamping. With Crosby at the fore-

front, the industry made major strides over the next few years, and it was not long before 20-pound bicycles were hitting the streets with new biking enthusiasts aboard them. As the bicycle industry took off, the innovative Crosby firm pedaled with it.

"We are ready," the firm stated in a 1900 advertisement, "to furnish samples of our new 'V' clusters with oval rear lugs. You can't afford to miss them. They are perfection. It's up to you." Buoyed by its success, Crosby applied its technology toward more and more diverse types of manufacturing: lawnmowers, automobiles, railroad equipment, and more than 70 others.

Between 1900 and 1910 the company began to play an important role in revolutionizing the automobile industry. Among the Crosby parts that helped make the American automobile lighter and more efficient were rear-axle housings, flanges, hub caps, step hangers, motor parts, running boards, oil pans, carburetor parts, clutch parts, roller bearing cages, steering wheels, and brake drums.

The rented space became inadequate, and the company purchased a new complex at 183 Pratt Street on Buffalo's east side. Crosby was making use of 20 buildings there by 1910. By the time World War I broke out the firm was 20 times its original size and concentrating heavily on the railroad

Canadian-born William H. Crosby founded The Crosby Company in 1896. He began the business with the idea of fabricating lighter, stronger, and less expensive bicycle fittings. His son and grandson have succeeded him as company presidents.

Crosby now uses metal stamping presses like this 24-foot-tall Bliss model, which is capable of applying 800 tons of pressure.

industry. Because its size and versatility were considerable, the plant became a key Buffalo supplier for the wartime effort. The firm not only made helmets but taught other companies how to make them. The Army's canvas machine gun belts were replaced by metallic clips made by Crosby. Parts were made for Army trucks and, although it was kept secret until years after the war, thousands of bomb fins were stamped by Crosby workmen.

Later the use of metal stampings increased and broadened in the United States, again to Crosby's benefit. Some products, including one brand of household incinerator, were made entirely by Crosby. The manufacture of auto parts continued to flourish, and companies found themselves using Crosby parts for dozens of household devices ranging from refrigerators to washers to sewing machines.

After the stock market crash of 1929 Crosby greatly reduced the volume of its operation, but managed to survive the Depression, concentrating much of its efforts on the production of parts for bathroom scales.

During World War II Crosby again came to the aid of the military. The company made magazines for Thompson machine guns and numerous other devices for the American war machine, including what the firm called "specialties" for the Manhattan Project. The company was, and still is, proud of its wartime efforts. "The minds, equipment, and experience of this organization will serve Uncle Sam and our allies for the duration. We know no other course," the company states in a brochure from the era.

Since World War II the operation has seen fluctuations in its business, and in recent years has fallen on hard times. The work force hit its peak at 1,500 during the latter days of World War I, declined after the stock market crash, and leveled off at about 800 in

the 1940s. Today's version of The Crosby Company has about 60 workers, the lowest number since the early days of the founder, who died in 1944. But Henry Crosby, Jr.—who followed his grandfather and father into the operation—is optimistic about the organization's future. Like the city of Buffalo, The Crosby Company has seen its worst days and is on the rise again, he contends. He has been president since 1959.

The firm's present product line includes numerous machine and motor parts, including parts for pay telephones and bowling pinsetters. Henry Crosby hopes the versatility of his company will bring new customers over the next few years. He is also hoping that the shrinking overseas value of the American dollar will prompt more U.S. businesses to buy American-made parts again.

"We're working hard on broadening our customer base over the next few years, especially in the eastern United States," he says, "We've been in this business for 90 years now, and we plan on being in business for at least 90 more."

The Crosby Company's present product line includes parts for bowling pinsetters and pay telephones.

AUBURN STEEL COMPANY, INC.

Quality products plus fast, personal service add up to growing demand and expanding markets for the Auburn Steel Company, the first Japanese-owned steel mini-mill in the United States.

Higher production and sales have resulted in a larger work force and increased economic benefits for Auburn and New York State, fulfilling the hopes of Paul Lattimore, the late mayor of Auburn whose vision and efforts brought the firm to his city.

More than 300,000 tons of steel pour annually from Austeel's modern, 70-ton electric arc furnace into continuous casting and rolling mills in a 200,000-square-foot, horseshoe-shape facility designed for efficient and fast production of special quality steel items. Austeel's reputation for quality products and rapid, personal service has brought orders from its output of reinforcing bars; square, round, and flat bars; and angle and channel steel from a widening circle of customers—the metal-fabricating and forging industries, steel centers, and reinforcing bar fabricators throughout the northeast quadrant of the United States.

Hideshi Numaguchi, president, and William Humes, executive vice-president, of Auburn Steel Company, Inc.

The present annual output is more than double the 150,000 tons projected in a 1971 Batelle Memorial Institute feasibility study made at the request of the mayor and city council. The study indicated that 150,000 tons could be sold within a 150-mile radius—Upstate New York and northern Pennsylvania. "But," explains William

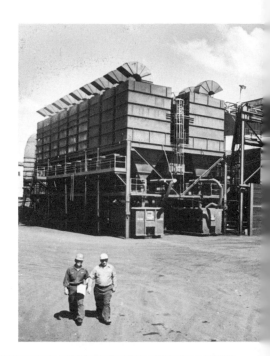

A view of the outside of the scrap metal melting building.

Auburn Steel produces special quality steel items from scrap metal that comes from wrecked and abandoned vehicles, farm equipment, home appliances, and other objects that have outlived their usefulness. In this view an employee taps the melted steel.

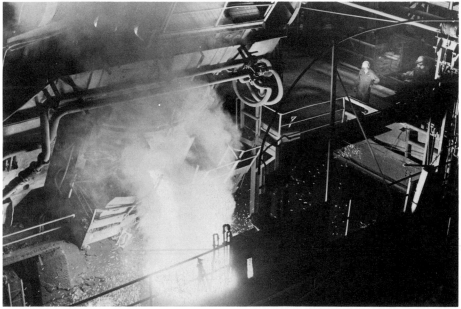

Humes, executive vice-president, "we found the market in that area would not take all 150,000 tons. So we had to expand our marketing area, first to 300 miles, then to a 500-mile radius." The expanded region stretches from the Atlantic west through Ohio, Indiana, and Michigan, south through Pennsylvania, New Jersey, Maryland, and West Virginia. An occasional order comes from as far away as Florida, North Carolina, and Kansas.

Austeel employs more than 320 men and women. Sales totaled about $85 million in 1987. The company returned about $65 million of that amount to the local and state economy in wages and salaries, taxes, and the purchase of raw materials, other goods, and services. Multiplied by a factor of four to six, the number of times economists say money usually rolls over, the economic impact of that $65 million swells to between $260 million and

$400 million.

The firm's principal raw material is scrap metal from wrecked and abandoned vehicles, farm equipment, home appliances, and other objects that have outlived their usefulness. Most of this scrap comes from dealers in the central New York area, which also fulfills another goal of Paul Lattimore for a minimill: Help rid the area's environment of unsightly scrap through recycling. Using scrap metal to make new steel also has economic benefits for Austeel. Recycling the old metal requires one-third the energy needed to make steel from iron ore.

Auburn Steel Company employs more than 320 men and women at its Auburn plant. Here an employee cuts a billet at the caster.

The firm has invested more than $2 million through "the most elaborate, sophisticated, and effective pollution control systems known to man," according to Humes. "We've eliminated gas emissions and smoke, and installed effective dust-filtering systems." Another half-million dollars was spent to control voltage fluctuations so plant operations will not affect the lights, televisions, and other electric equipment of its residential and business neighbors.

The idea for Austeel began with a news article about a successful South Carolina minimill that Mayor Lattimore read in 1971. "Why not one in Auburn?" he asked himself.

The mill offered a potential for the return to Auburn of high-paying production jobs, with their economic benefits. After convincing the city council to provide funds for a feasibility study, he contacted the respected Batelle Institute for a study to determine if the city had available the skilled or trainable workers, raw materials, low-cost electric power and natural gas, and potential sales, customers, and marketing area. Auburn already had excellent industrial sites, and state and local governments offered tax abatement and financial help programs.

Batelle's positive findings paved the way for the next and most difficult step—finding a firm willing to locate such a mill in Auburn. Armed with the Batelle study results, Lattimore first approached several U.S. steel companies, but found no takers. He then went to Washington and left the Batelle report with the embassies of a number of foreign nations with steel industries.

The Japanese embassy's staff forwarded the report to Tokyo, where officials passed out Batelle's findings to several companies. Executives of Kyoei Steel Ltd. showed almost immediate interest. After talks with Lattimore and others, Kyoei and Sumitomo Corp., a trading company, formed the Auburn Steel Company. Today Sumitomo owns 90 percent of Austeel and Kyoei, 10 percent.

The Auburn Steel Company, being Japanese owned and American managed, has over the decade developed a highly successful synthesis of American and Japanese management styles. This very personalized approach emphasizes team building, cooperation, extensive two-way communication, and a genuine interest and concern for all employees' needs. The major thrust is fair treatment for all employees with no class hierarchy. All employees are paid on a salaried basis. There are no time clocks, and all employees receive the same benefits such as hospitalization, vacation, and payment for sick time or personal leave. Despite the fact that all employees are paid for absences, the absenteeism rate is approximately one-half of one percent.

By recycling old metal Auburn Steel helps clear the area's environment of inoperative scrap and saves the company energy costs. Pictured here is a section of the rolling mill.

In addition, the company has never laid off employees for lack of work. There were some very slow times, and when they occurred, surplus employees were assigned other responsibilities without any change in salary.

Today the employees of Auburn Steel Company display a high esprit de corps, and morale is excellent as exemplified by an annual turnover rate of 3 to 5 percent.

The combination of these elements has made Auburn Steel Company, Inc., one of the most efficient and productive mills in the world.

CHICAGO PNEUMATIC TOOL COMPANY

Hand chipping cement from bricks for reuse is time consuming and costly. In the late 1800s Joseph Boyer, a recycler of building materials, invented the first practical air-powered chipping hammer. Recognizing the potential for speeding up the cleaning of rough castings, J.W. Duntley, a foundry foreman of little education but lots of energy and imagination, founded his own sales organization and introduced the Boyer hammer to foundries in America and the United Kingdom. This partnership between inventor and salesman resulted in the founding of Chicago Pneumatic Tool Company in 1894. Backed by Charles M. Schwab, president of U.S. Steel, the firm was incorporated in 1901, combining several small companies.

The first acquisition was the Boyer Machine Company, specializing in the Boyer Riveting Hammer. This tool received national attention in Norman Rockwell's "Rosie the Riveter" (a good symbol for a company that has received awards for a commitment to equal opportunity). Except for improved materials and production methods, the useful tool is still produced today in Utica.

Another unusual, colorful acquisition was the Grant Tool Company, a steam engine manufacturing company—a forerunner of today's air compressors—in which Turkish rugs and stained-glass windows graced the offices, and polished brass cuspidors stood by each machine in the spotlessly clean shop.

Chicago Pneumatic air tools were used to remove rust and corrosion from the Statue of Liberty and reinforce the basic structure.

To meet demands for industrial air tools, acquisitions continued between 1901 and 1910, and Chicago Pneumatic was listed on the New York Stock Exchange in 1918. J.W. and W.O. Duntley joined their father in the business, and each was at one time president. The Duntleys' initiative and salesmanship produced phenomenal growth as the number of patents and products expanded rapidly. Although some have been discontinued owing to changing demand, all are of historical interest.

The railway speed recorder, another Boyer invention, is still in use, providing a visual and printed record of speed and performance to the diesel engineer and traffic control. As American railroads grew, so did Chicago Pneumatic products, from rivet busters and the "Little Giant" iron fireman to roundhouse turntables, from engineer's valves and bell ringers to the Rockford Rail Service Motor Car, which transported workers to their jobs on the tracks.

Storage batteries for electric vehicles were manufactured, as were portable air drills, Duntley vacuum cleaners, and the gasoline "Little Giant" truck. One of the earliest and largest customers for these vehicles was the Coca-Cola Company; by 1914 Chicago Pneumatic was the fourth-largest manufacturer of commercial cars in the world.

During both world wars Chicago Pneumatic produced tools to manufacture and maintain military equipment, including jeeps, tanks, planes, warships, tankers, and Liberty merchant vessels, and to construct domestic and overseas military bases. In 1949 a new plant meeting the requirements of expanded business was built in Utica, and the facilities from Detroit and Cleveland moved there. This structure is the largest in the world built specifically to produce air tools.

Chicago Pneumatic air tools help build and maintain subway systems, commercial buildings, and bridges such as the Golden Gate Bridge in San Francisco.

Chicago Pneumatic is the world's best-known supplier of air-powered auto service tools. Here CP nutrunners are used to drive large nuts on passenger cars.

Norman Rockwell's "Rosie the Riveter" was shown with a Chicago Pneumatic Boyer riveting hammer in The Saturday Evening Post, *circa 1940.*

In 1954 Chicago Pneumatic announced the first torque-controlled screwdriver and developed torque-controlled impact wrenches and nut-runners for the automobile, appliance, and electronics industries. For the first time unskilled operators could swiftly drive threaded fasteners to correct tightness in one operation. The company is the world's best-known supplier of air-powered auto service tools to gas stations, car dealers, collision repair shops, pit crews for racing cars, and such major chains as Sears, Roebuck and Co. The organization has also played a leading role in air tool noise reduction, introducing the first "silenced" demolition tools in 1964. The Hushed Power lines include grinders, screwdrivers, and drills, all improving the work area by reducing noise levels.

Wherever skyscrapers, bridges, roads, factories, or railways are constructed or maintained, Chicago Pneumatic is there. Its tools refurbished the Statue of Liberty and constructed New York City subway tunnels, the World Trade Center, and the Albany Plaza. The firm's portable air compressors appear on construction sites; paving breakers mend New York State highways; and riveters and nibblers repair 747 jumbo jets and the space shuttle. On every bridge in New York City, including the George Washington Bridge, the Chicago Pneumatic logo may be seen. Wherever coal and metal is mined, Boyer riveting hammers, compressors, and rock drills are used.

After a major role in both world wars and the postwar boom of the 1950s and 1960s, Chicago Pneumatic stood alone without competition, a pioneer in high-quality hand tools. Then patents began to expire—in the 1970s Asians and Europeans began to compete with higher productivity and huge volumes at low cost. Customers increasingly demanded cheap throwaway tools. To meet this competition, a process of reorganization and change was begun.

As it was for much of corporate America, 1986 was a year of significant change for Chicago Pneumatic. New ownership continued the consolidation and restructuring, including a streamlined, competitive manufacturing cycle time, improved delivery time, and new product introduction. Today Chicago Pneumatic Tool Company is positioned for the future, a vital and dynamic world-class competitor strengthening the number of products that use air to speed processes in manufacturing, mining, and construction, a company with a rich, proud heritage of ingenuity, invention, and quality.

Chicago Pneumatic's main plant in Utica is the largest facility in the world built specifically for the production of air tools.

PRICE WATERHOUSE

Price Waterhouse is a full-service business advisory firm of tax advisers, management consultants, and independent accountants. PW professionals provide a wide range of services to businesses, individuals, nonprofit organizations, and government entities.

When Lewis D. Jones came to New York from London in September 1890 as the agent of Price, Waterhouse & Co., America's public accounting sector was still in the pioneer stage. British investors were pouring money into the United States, and they looked to accountants to ensure that their finances were handled prudently.

At the time New York City had a population just exceeding 2.5 million and a mere 15,000 telephones. Jones arrived 15 years before the first subway train (the East Side I.R.T.) ran to Wall Street and 18 years before the first skyscraper (the 47-story Singer Building) was completed.

The second Price, Waterhouse & Co. agent, William J. Caesar, arrived in New York in June 1891 and soon moved west to open an office in Chicago. Three years later Jones and Caesar exchanged offices, and Caesar established himself in New York. With the consent of Price, Waterhouse partners in London, these two United States agents and a Chicago associate formed the firm of Jones, Caesar & Co. on January 1, 1895, and were able to issue reports and accounts signed in that name.

On July 1, 1899, came the official transformation of Jones, Caesar & Co. to the United States firm of Price, Waterhouse & Co. With this development the list of clients began to include many important companies. The territory allotted to the firm included the United States, Canada, Mexico, and South America, and staff from the New York office traveled far and wide to complete client work.

Today the United States firm of Price Waterhouse has a total staff of more than 12,000 and 112 offices in cities across the country. The headquarters office of Price Waterhouse is located in New York City's Exxon Building, and the firm's New York City office is in the Citicorp Center. Other offices in the state are located in Buffalo, Rochester, Syracuse, and Long Island. The U.S. firm is part of a worldwide network of firms that has more than 33,000 staff members in approximately 400 offices in 100 countries and territories.

Clients of Price Waterhouse have based their confidence in the firm on its in-depth capabilities, tradition of professional integrity, and commitment to the highest ethical standards. Today Price Waterhouse is meeting its clients' needs with a full range of busi-

Price Waterhouse analyzes the issues and opportunities of emerging computer technology and develops practical applications to meet highly specialized and complex business needs.

ness services that can be counted upon in the boardroom, before stockholders and regulatory bodies, and for day-to-day management decisions.

Significantly the Price Waterhouse clientele includes more *Fortune* 500 companies than any other accounting firm, more of the *Forbes* 100 U.S. multinational companies, and more companies in the Dow Jones averages than any other firm—and almost half of the industrials on the Dow Jones list.

In addition to industrial giants, consulting services, Price Waterhouse has formed specific industry groups to meet the special needs of industries such as high technology, financial services, manufacturing, real estate, health care, insurance, retailing, entertainment, petroleum, public utilities, law firms, and government contractors. As well, Price Waterhouse has developed innovative services to meet client needs in the areas of strategic management consulting, telecommunications, acquisitions and mergers, employee benefits, personal financial planning,

Price Waterhouse professionals provide valuable business advice to clients in a broad range of industries.

Samuel Lowell Price (1821-1887) (above) and Edwin Waterhouse (1841-1917) (above right), founders of Price Waterhouse.

Price Waterhouse clients include growth companies and start-up ventures. The firm's clients represent a cross section of American enterprise— industrial, commercial, governmental, scientific, medical, charitable, educational, financial, and professional. Price Waterhouse's depth and diversity of experience are applied to the specific needs of each client. Since its founding, the firm has built its reputation on a businesslike orientation and approach to client work, and dedication to the concept that each client is entitled to distinguished service.

In addition to providing accounting and auditing, tax, and management

reorganization and bankruptcy, litigation consulting, government matters, actuarial consulting, inventory management, customs matters, international trade issues, and valuations.

Price Waterhouse is organized so that decisions affecting clients are made by partners who have full professional authority. Clients deal directly with these decision makers, not with off-site personnel in a central office. Each client has one Price Waterhouse partner who is directly responsible for coordinating all work performed for the client both nationwide and worldwide.

A long history of service has earned Price Waterhouse a role as one of the leaders in the profession. The firm takes seriously the responsibilities of leadership, playing an active role in public and private-sector organizations

that address public policy issues and taking aggressive stances on those issues. For example, Price Waterhouse professionals frequently testify before congressional committees on business concerns, consult with the IRS and Treasury Department on tax issues, and work with industry associations to develop professional standards. This has allowed the firm to offer constructive proposals regarding matters that affect its clients and its profession.

Price Waterhouse professionals are also concerned members of their communities, actively involved in civic organizations concentrating on a variety of local issues. They are dedicated to helping their communities as well as their clients.

While a century of providing distinctive client service has contributed to the Price Waterhouse reputation, it is the firm's people who have always been the most important element in sustaining and enhancing that image. The firm invests in professionals who can master advanced business techniques and sophisticated technologies, and it continues to monitor the quality of service to ensure that it meets high firm standards.

H. KOHNSTAMM & CO., INC.

Founded in 1851, H. Kohnstamm & Co., Inc., is a renowned international manufacturer of pigments and colors for the food, drug, and cosmetics industries, as well as a producer of industrial colors, flavors, and cleaning supplies. But the firm also boasts a family saga: Currently in the fourth generation of Kohnstamm family leadership, it is considered to be America's oldest family-owned and family-managed chemical company.

The story of H. Kohnstamm & Co. began in Switzerland in the early nineteenth century, when members of the Kohnstamm family became dealers in ultramarine blue, a newly discovered synthetic color. Seeking new markets, family member Joseph Kohnstamm traveled to New York City. In 1851 he opened a business in Lower Manhattan, where, despite moves to several different buildings, the firm's headquarters has remained ever since.

In 1852 Joseph was joined by his brother Hesslein. As importers the Kohnstamms supplied colors to the paint industry, the patent leather industry, the ostrich feather and artificial flower trades, and the printing ink industry. They also supplied the laundry business: By this time the use of bluing as a means of whitening laundry was recognized, and ultramarine blue was an essential ingredient in bluing.

In 1865 Joseph Kohnstamm went back to Switzerland, where he died soon afterward. Brother Hesslein induced a cousin, Heiman, to join him in New York. When Hesslein died in 1876, Heiman, along with nephews Emanuel and Emil, revitalized the reorganized partnership as the business of H. Kohnstamm & Co.

By 1880 the firm had grown from importer to full-fledged manufacturer, making geranium lake, a coal tar synthetic color, at factory quarters in Brooklyn. Kohnstamm was also making laundry soap, and by the 1890s it was producing food colors and bleaches

as well. The company opened offices in Chicago and Boston, starting what would later become a national warehouse and office network.

When Heiman Kohnstamm died in 1898, the family's second generation—Emil, Emanuel, Edward, and Joseph Kohnstamm in New York, and Max Kohnstamm in Chicago—assumed command. After Congress passed the first National Pure Food and Drug Act in 1906, Kohnstamm became the nation's first company to produce the food colors with the purity specified by the act. Within a year the firm had a large plant in Brooklyn and was producing a broad range of colors. Seven years later it decided to begin manufacturing true fruit flavors for the food and beverage industries.

Prior to World War I Germany had a world monopoly in making aniline dyestuffs. When war brought a submarine blockage of German exports, H. Kohnstamm worked to develop aniline dyes. Soon it was producing them on its own, helping America break the German color monopoly. The war also helped Kohnstamm's Laundry Division, as the modern "institutional" laundry came into being.

In 1922 company leader Emil V. Kohnstamm died, having served the firm for 55 years. Edward G. Kohn-

Paul L. Kohnstamm, the fourth generation to represent this family-owned business, is the firm's chairman and treasurer.

Warren Malik is H. Kohnstamm & Co., Inc.'s, current president.

stamm became president; Joseph Kohnstamm, vice-president; Lothair S. Kohnstamm, secretary; and William Longfelder, vice-president in charge of the Laundry Division.

In 1925 the firm took out the first group life policy from the Prudential Insurance Company, thus becoming one of only a few American corporations to offer this protection to its employees. Kohnstamm has long held a strong record in employee relations: Many of its employees have had careers at the company lasting 40 to 50 years. And despite the hardships of the Great Depression, Kohnstamm kept every employee on the payroll.

When Edward G. Kohnstamm died in 1938, Lothair Kohnstamm, son of Emanuel Kohnstamm, became company president. The following year the firm became the nation's first color maker to obtain government certification under the new laws of the Food and Drug Committee Act of 1938, this time for colors, drugs, and cosmetics. Kohnstamm thus became the only U.S. company producing a complete line of colors for three industries: foods, drugs, and cosmetics.

During World War II Kohnstamm provided America's military with important dyes and colors, and the Laundry Division supplied military hospitals and other installations. After the war the Laundry Division continued to make important contributions such as

the creation of Diasan, a laundering additive that has helped reduce staphylococcus infection in hospitals.

Meanwhile, Kohnstamm's Color Division began serving the plastics industry. By 1953 demand for Kohnstamm colors had grown so much that the corporation acquired General Color Company, a cadmium pigments maker. Kohnstamm also developed "certified" food lake colors—insoluble pigments that are odorless, tasteless, and do not bleed. The Flavor Division (an outgrowth of the Color Division) also grew with advances in the processing of fruit juices.

In 1950, with the death of Lothair Kohnstamm, the presidency passed to Louis J. Woolf, son-in-law of Joseph Kohnstamm. Seven years later he became chairman of the board, a post that he held until his death in 1961. Succeeding him as president was Paul L. Kohnstamm, son of Lothair Kohnstamm and grandson of Emanuel Kohnstamm. Paul Kohnstamm is the firm's chairman and treasurer.

During the 1960s the company launched manufacturing ventures in India, Mexico, Canada, and Colombia, bolstering previous manufacturing acquisitions of laundry supply and color manufacturers in Great Britain. Today the firm has a solid international presence, with five overseas manufacturing affiliates and sales representatives worldwide.

But H. Kohnstamm & Co.'s strongest commitment throughout its long history has always been to New York, having never left the city of its birth. Today H. Kohnstamm & Co. is considered to be the fourth-oldest U.S. chemical firm, and the only surviving one still privately owned and owner-family managed. Company chairman Paul Kohnstamm's position as the fourth-generation family leader is remarkable, considering the average life span of family-owned businesses. Today Paul's son and daughter are company directors: The fifth generation—and even the sixth—waits in the wings.

DORSEY MILLWORK, INC.

Already lifelong partners, they became partners in the business community of New York State as well when in 1960 brothers Arthur and Edward W. Dorsey bought Robbin's Door and Sash Company of Albany, located on North Ferry Street in industrial North Albany. Edward Dorsey had been a salesman for Andersen Company—the Andersen line remains a staple of the business—when the Dorsey brothers came from Boston to open Dorsey Millwork. From beginnings that included the small site, the two brothers, secretary Marion McMartin who remained with the company for the next three decades, three other employees, and a truck, Dorsey Millwork grew steadily, selling to retail lumber dealers and millwork distributors, and keeping abreast of changes in the mainstream of the construction industry.

The 2,000 square feet in the North Albany facility was outgrown within a year; Dorsey Millwork moved to a larger site slightly west of Albany. Another move followed in 1970 to yet larger quarters, and finally, in 1985, the Dorsey brothers built an office and warehouse complex to house their inventory on steel racks, some 50 employees, and a fleet of 11 trucks. There the inventory is tracked by computer, as are all financial transactions from accounts receivable to payroll. From this 84,000 square feet of work space, Dorsey Millwork serves an area with a

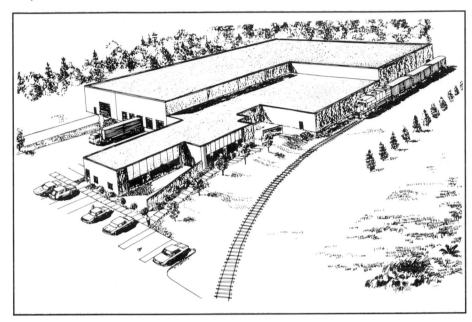

The new Dorsey Millwork 84,000-square-foot warehouse at 36 Railroad Avenue in Albany, New York.

radius of approximately 150 miles, from the Canadian borders to Westchester County, and from Rome and Utica to Vermont, western Connecticut, and western Massachusetts.

From the earliest days of the business through its present complexity, the company's service philosophy has been a personal one—customers always have access to Edward or Arthur Dorsey, hands-on managers who still will deliver a product personally or handle a problem. Personal service is a cornerstone of Dorsey Millwork.

Technology in the construction industry has been carefully followed by the principals of Dorsey Millwork. Three decades ago products were

mainly wooden, shipped in parts; windows were single-strength glass; and energy efficiency was just a vague concept. Products mainly were shipped by rail, and shipping itself was more time consuming in an industry then largely composed of small lumberyards. Products had to be assembled before installation and tended to be heterogeneous in size and style. The past three decades witnessed the rationalization and standardization of building materials, the advent of the large-chain lumberyards, the rise of energy-efficient technologies, and the shipment of preassembled units, particularly windows and doors, handily installed and maintenance-free. Products now cross the country in three days on trucks driven over superhighways.

Edward and Arthur Dorsey kept pace with these changes, developed successfully by specializing in doors, windows, and moldings for residences; producing some special millwork or fabrication; and paying close attention to the needs of their customers. After nearly three decades Dorsey Millwork remains integral to the building of the Capital District and the construction industry of the Empire State.

The Dorsey brothers, Edward W. and Arthur, founders of Dorsey Millwork, Inc.

NEW YORK STATE CREDIT UNION LEAGUE

It was an idea for the times, the outgrowth of progressivism and a response to consumerism in the prosperous era following World War I. Rooted in European experience, it had no apostle of its own, instead stemming from widespread need at that point in New York's history. That idea, long since in the mainstream but novel for the times, was the credit union.

Beginning with a 1909 Albany visit by Canadian credit union advocate Alphonse Desjardins, the Russell Sage Foundation consulted with Leonard Robinson, organizer of credit unions among New York State's Jewish farmers. Their purpose was to draft credit union legislation for New York. Their most effective ally in passage of the state's 1913 credit union bill—the second such law in the nation—was then-State Senator Franklin Roosevelt. By 1915 there were 17 credit unions in the state; by 1919, 49; and by 1921, 82.

Steady growth was reflected in the need for a central organization to publicize the credit union movement, study and prepare legislation, provide a network among the state's credit unions,

standardize procedures, and generally work to benefit credit unions. From this need the New York State Association of Credit Unions was formed in 1917, and reorganized in 1921. At a time when the nation's women were obtaining the vote, women were among the association's first officers and directors.

During the Depression New York's credit unions pioneered group life insurance for their borrowers. It was during the 1930s, too, that 170 credit unions, now organized as the New York State Credit Union League, were regionalized in eight chapters and began to operate a credit information exchange and support credit union legislation. Franklin Roosevelt, now president of the United States, signed the Federal Credit Union Act in 1934. Always interested in a national organization, the league was among the first supporters of the Credit Union Na-

The 1948 annual meeting of the New York State Credit Union League was photographed at a time when postwar inflation and consumerism made credit unions more important than ever. Photo circa 1948.

tional Association. The league and CUNA both continued to advocate improvements in legislation and in credit union practices.

In 1961 an affiliate of the league was created to provide league members with technical assistance. After the league's 1974 move from New York to Albany, this affiliate, known as League Marketing Group, began to assist credit unions preparing for yearly audits, subsequently adding services in data processing, new-car loan promotion, financial planning, insurance, and a statewide automated teller system. The 1977 establishment of the Empire Corporate Federal Credit Union offered member credit unions a source of credit during peak borrowing seasons. In a decade Empire's assets passed the billion-dollar point, and the league had moved to larger quarters in Albany, housing nearly 100 staff members. By 1987 the New York State Credit Union League offered a broad spectrum of services to members, New York's credit unions realizing the bright promise offered nearly three-quarters of a century before.

GRAHAM CORPORATION

When the Graham Corporation cele-brated its 50th anniversary in 1986, employees of Graham's flagship opera-tion in Batavia took out an advertise-ment covering nearly two pages of *The Batavia Daily News*. The ad took the form of a letter to Frederick D. Berkeley III, the company's president, chairman of the board, and chief exec-utive officer. In part, it thanked him for the "innovation and leadership" he has shown to his workers since taking the helm in 1962. The letter was signed by every single one of the 349 employees of the Batavia plant. "No celebration of Graham's 50th anniversary would be complete without a special thanks to the one person most responsible for the success of our company," the em-ployees wrote.

"We meant it," says Betty O'Brien, a 31-year employee and Berkeley's secretary for 25 of those years. The Graham Corporation is that kind of company. The firm has subsidiaries on both sides of the Atlantic Ocean, but those who work in the corporate head-quarters view it as a people-oriented,

friendly operation that is an important part of Batavia life.

Graham, one of the world's fore-most manufacturers of vacuum and heat-transfer equipment, is the only publicly held corporation that is based in this small city of 16,000 people lo-cated roughly midway between Buffalo and Rochester. Graham is Batavia's largest employer, and its 40-acre site is the city's largest manufacturing fa-cility.

The company has gained an inter-national reputation as a designer and builder of equipment for chemical plants, oil refineries, nuclear and fossil power plants, food-processing plants, steel mills, aircraft and rocket test fa-cilities, paper mills, marine vessels, and other industrial facilities from Buffalo to Rumania to Saudi Arabia.

Berkeley—forever proud of the firm's good name—says he appreciates his workers as much as they appreciate him. He contends that the company's "all for one, one for all" spirit has held Graham together, even during a recent "period of retrenchment" in which the business fell on hard times and shut down unprofitable subsidiaries in Fort Erie, Ontario, and Tulsa, Oklahoma, in 1986. "If it were not for the people of western New York, their strong work ethic, and their loyalty to this company, I think we may have gone out of exis-

This massive multistage vacuum pump is typical of the modular type of systems Graham builds for power plants and oil refineries.

tence," Berkeley says.

But that hasn't happened. Berke-ley sees better days ahead for the com-pany founded by his father, Frederick D. Berkeley, and a fellow engineer, Harold M. Graham. Although incorpo-rated by Graham in 1936, the business was founded in its present form by the two men in late June 1941. Graham, a native of Nova Scotia, and Berkeley, from New York City, met in the mid-1920s, when Berkeley convinced Graham to join the old Ross Heater Manufacturing Co. in Buffalo, now known as ITT Standard. The two ex-perts in the field of heat transfer and steam jet ejector equipment became fast friends and stockholders of the Ross firm.

The twosome sold their stock in 1935 and eventually ended up together again as fellow engineers in the Lum-mus Co., located in New York City, where Berkeley was a sales engineer for oil refineries, chemical plants, and heat-transfer equipment and Graham

Frederick D. Berkeley (1901-1962) (left) and Harold M. Graham (1889-1956) (right) became friends while working as engineers for a Buffalo firm in the 1920s. They founded the Graham Manufacturing Co., Inc., predecessor to Graham Corporation, in 1936.

was chief engineer of steam jet ejectors and surface condensers. The Graham-Berkeley team decided to start their own company and incorporated in 1941. The first contract landed by the firm was a large order of tank suction heaters for the U.S. Navy, manufactured in a leased plant in Oswego. The fledgling company quickly outgrew that facility and in 1942 purchased the Batavia plant that is still the Graham flagship.

During World War II the company earned honors from the U.S. Maritime Commission for outstanding production achievement in the design and manufacture of heat-transfer equipment that was used to help power the American fleet. Peacetime brought the end of all government contracts, but Berkeley and Graham were determined to manufacture their products for commercial applications that would make the organization a viable peacetime business.

They did it, gearing the product line to process plants and other industries with a need for the kind of massive equipment that they could design and build. A Harold Graham invention from the war years, called the Heliflow heat exchanger, was patented and found numerous commercial applications that resulted in a broad line of heat exchangers that are still manufactured by the company.

The company has benefited from the steady leadership of three presidents: Graham, from the inception until his death in 1956; Berkeley, from 1956 until 1962; and Berkeley's son, Frederick Berkeley III, from 1962 to the present. "My father and Harold Graham were, first of all, good engineers," says Berkeley, who worked his way through the organization after beginning as a summer helper on the

---

Graham manufactures surface condensers like this one, which is used in a power plant for a food company. This unit condenses exhaust steam from a turbine, which, in conjunction with a gas turbine, produces 120 megawatts of electric power.

shop floor in 1946. "They got along extremely well, they trusted each other, they didn't compete. Each had talents that complemented the other. They were great believers in knowing their products and how the products could be utilized. They built pilot models and tested them. They made it their business to investigate and become knowledgeable about what they were selling."

When the younger Berkeley took over the business, he moved the corporate headquarters from the New York City area to Batavia. In 1968 the company made its first public stock offering. Graham grew and subsidiaries were opened in Canada, England, and Wales, as the company continued to broaden its image and product lines in world markets. Today Graham Corporation employs 852 people—down from a record high of 1,062 in 1984—and recorded sales of $59 million in 1986. Its stock is traded on the American Stock Exchange.

While the firm's technology has grown since the early days of Graham and Berkeley, the approach to business remains the same. A project engineer's work is checked by a second engineer. After the equipment is installed, a full complement of engineers is available to take care of any customer operating problems. Berkeley states Graham Corporation does its engineering in house and does not sublet design work.

"There are companies that could fabricate some of our equipment for us, but we design it, build it, and accept total responsibility for its success," Berkeley asserts. "That's how we operate."

NORTON COMPANY/COATED ABRASIVE DIVISION

In 1872 Herman Behr, not long arrived in the United States from Germany, had a one-man business in a rented loft above a Brooklyn bakery. He produced pouncing paper, used to manufacture felt hats, selling it to local firms from his only suitcase, and soon he was confident enough to incorporate as Herman Behr and Company. At the same time, in Troy, John A. Manning was operating Manning Paper Company, founded by his father in 1846, producing manila fiber rope paper used to wrap electrical cable and to make flour bags.

Manning believed his paper would make a superior backing for sandpaper but was unsuccessful in so marketing it, even to Herman Behr and Company. In 1912 Manning's firm itself began to produce sandpaper and that year constructed a factory in Watervliet on the present site of Norton Company's Coated Abrasive Division, its ultimate successor and beneficiary. Seven years later, acknowledging the source of prosperity gained during World War I, this firm became Manning Abrasive Company.

During the 1920s both firms, Herman Behr and Manning Abrasive, grew to importance in the national marketplace. This period ushered in the true automobile age, and with it a need for new, more, and better coated abrasives used in metalworking production of all sorts—the market for such coated abrasives tripling between

"Good Workmen Know the Difference" was a Behr-Manning slogan in the late 1920s, when the testing laboratory and its "automatic machines" were photographed at Watervliet.

1909 and 1919 and then nearly doubling again in the following decade. In 1928, as industry leaders and innovators, the two companies merged, becoming Behr-Manning and centralizing their operations in Watervliet, creating the largest sandpaper-manufacturing firm in the United States. Three years later Norton Company of Worcester, Massachusetts, a leading manufacturer of grinding wheels, electric furnace abrasives, and

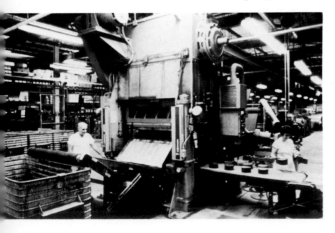

With this new high-speed machine, carbide dies punch through the press to produce the same product as the older machine in the lower photo (opposite page), but now with negligible waste and tripling of the production rate.

similar products, consolidated with Behr-Manning, the two concerns already long acquainted through business. In 1932 Pike Manufacturing Company, maker of sharpening stones, was added; Norton Company's three divisions formed the world's largest abrasive producer, although Behr-Manning would retain its name until 1968.

Behr and Manning, Behr-Manning, and Norton Company represent the three stages of development of the U.S. abrasives industry as a whole. Herman Behr and John Manning were entrepreneurs producing essentially handmade, labor-intensive, nonstandardized products used chiefly in woodworking, leather, and hat-making industries. Few firms, perhaps no firms, had high-production mechanized capabilities for manufacturing,

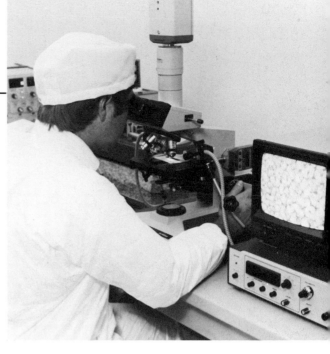

while user industries largely employed abrasives in finishing or polishing applications via muscle power or rudimentary machines. This situation remained the status quo in both producer and user industries until World War I.

After World War I rapid growth and accelerating technological development created new industries, given impetus by new consumer demands. Coated abrasives and sandpapers increasingly were employed in high-production standardized metalworking. In turn, the output of coated abrasives became more mechanized and technical in nature, thereby helping to guarantee a more universal and long-lasting product for end users such as the automotive industry. This consumer need further drove technical innovation in the abrasives field, expansion into international markets, intra-industry cooperation in standardizing production, and new combinations of leadership as the abrasive industry was rationalized. It was then that Behr and Manning became Behr-Manning, major producer, and was assimilated by Norton Company to lead the field.

Finally, after 1939, the coated abrasives industry entered its most recognizably modern and technologically intense period, as new machinery and the introduction of automation both further demanded and made possible standardized, high-volume production.

At the same time the same factors greatly increased the use of coated abrasives in the metal-, leather-, and woodworking industries, and in one of the most pervasive industries of the twentieth century, plastics. The coated abrasives industry's gross sales grew more than 500 percent between 1929 and 1959, and again Norton Company was a leader.

Norton's Watervliet plant was evolving into the firm's research center

Pictured here is an old, labor-intensive Norton Company mechanical press used to convert coated abrasive fiber-backed products.

for coated abrasives. Eventually employing a work force of some 500 people, Watervliet produces more than 100 varieties of sandpaper used in wood- and metalworking, automotive manufacturing and refinishing, and individual consumer applications. When the Norton product line was introduced in 1972, Watervliet's Coated Abrasive Division had applied new technology to create a long-lasting industrial product, the first of numerous modern commercial successes that incorporated synthetics in Norton's high-performance answers to the needs of the optical and electronics industries. The Coated Abrasive Division, part of the original structure of Norton Company, exercises an expertise based on more than a century of experience, keeping Norton a leader in the field. In all, more than 40,000 product varieties are made by the Coated Abrasive Division, from home consumer items to disks, belts, rolls, and products tailored for specific industrial needs.

Norton Company now has 113 plants in 27 countries employing 23,000 people. A diversified, vertically integrated firm exceeding 100 years in age, Norton is a world leader in the de-

Norton Company's Watervliet testing laboratories today are highly technical, electronic facilities of great sophistication.

velopment and production of industrial ceramics, plastics, sealants, chemical process materials, scientific and medical tubing, and industrial safety equipment, as well as coated abrasives.

While Norton Company has diversified into numerous product areas, the Watervliet Coated Abrasive Division is an integral part of a worldwide firm with operations in Canada, India, Asia and the Pacific, Japan, Europe, Africa, Latin America, and the Middle East. Norton today is truly international, with its Coated Abrasive Division maintaining Norton's position as the world's largest manufacturer of abrasive products.

JARDINE EMETT & CHANDLER

Jardine Emett & Chandler has its roots in China, in Scotland, in San Francisco, in Hong Kong, or in Schenectady, New York, and was founded in 1832, 1906, 1929, or 1986. Based upon a complex series of acquisitions and mergers built ever upward from solid businesses grounded in solid performance, Jardine Emett & Chandler emerged in 1986 as a modern, worldwide company. Today the firm is among the 10 largest insurance brokers in the United States and is the largest operating company of the international Jardine Insurance Brokers Group. With 32 offices nationwide, a professional staff of 1,200, and annual revenues of $94 million, Jardine Emett &

R.J.O. Barton, president and chief executive officer of Jardine Emett & Chandler, Inc., is also group chief executive of Jardine Emett & Chandler's parent company, Jardine Insurance Brokers Group, which is headquartered in London.

Chandler has established itself as a rapidly rising star in the U.S. insurance brokerage market.

Historically, its story opens in Canton, China, in 1832. Two Scots businessmen, James Matheson and William Jardine, established a small trading company dealing in cotton and opium. Four years later the firm entered the insurance business through an arrangement between its own underwriting account—Jardine Matheson and Friends—and the First Canton Insurance office. By acquiring insurance companies and vertically integrating them according to conventional nineteenth-century financial wisdom, Jardine Matheson was able to collect premiums and commissions.

Despite long-term resistance by Far Eastern merchants, Jardine Matheson emerged during the next 150 years as one of the world's largest international trading companies. While commerce grew ever more complex so, too, did the insurance requirements of the mercantile community. Eventually, the expertise of insurance brokers became a vital necessity, and Jardine Matheson became a respected presence in Hong Kong, the Asiatic-Pacific Basin, and in London. By 1982 Jardine Matheson began direct investment in the continental United States.

Jardine Matheson's entry into the United States came with the acquisition of Bache Insurance Services Inc., a group of affiliated companies whose strongest firms were Albert M. Bender & Co., founded in 1881 in San Francisco, and Ter Bush & Powell, started in 1906 in Schenectady, New York. The two businesses were consolidated into a national brokerage organization known as Jardine Insurance Brokers Inc., and was structured with divisions on both the East and West coasts. The Eastern Division, centered in Schenectady, employs 240 people in a modern office space created in a landmark downtown building.

The Eastern Division is built upon the solid foundation of its Ter Bush & Powell predecessor, which enjoyed a long-standing and well-earned reputation for excellence in commercial insurance and servicing of insurance needs

In 1832 two Scot businessmen formed the partnership of Jardine Matheson & Co. in Canton, a city of Imperial China. Today Jardine Emett & Chandler, the largest operating company of the international Jardine Insurance Brokers Group, is one of the 10 largest insurance brokers in the United States.

for other groups. On this underpinning was created Jardine Emett & Chandler's Mainstreet USA approach that characterizes much of its Upstate New York business.

Ter Bush & Powell gained the majority of its expertise through a long association with the Civil Service Employee Association of New York State. In 1936 CSEA named Ter Bush & Powell as its broker, and subsequently, its insurance claims administrator. This major account, which served in the evolution of the firm's skill in handling risk services for large corporate accounts, was of great significance in the development of the Schenectady company. Eventually this strength contributed much to the success of Jardine

Emett & Chandler's Eastern Division.

While the Eastern Division is buttressed by several out-of-state offices, Schenectady remains the company's largest facility, overseeing divisional and corporate functions, mass marketing, and internal accounting. Expansion of a second office at the Avenue of the Americas in Manhattan took place in 1987. There 140 employees service *Fortune* 500 client companies. In Syracuse, 20 employees service Mainstreet USA business, and in Cedarhurst, Long Island, 14 employees handle personal insurance lines and small business accounts.

Ter Bush & Powell, a longtime Schenectady business, was acquired in 1980 by Bache Group, which merged with San Francisco's Albert M. Bender & Co. to form Bache Insurance Services Inc. A year later the holding company merged with Prudential Company of America. This latest merger made it legally necessary for divestiture of the insurance brokerage

firm. It was soon acquired by Jardine Matheson, which had been searching for a U.S. component for its international brokerage network. In 1982 Bache Insurance Services Inc. became Jardine Insurance Brokers Inc.

The final chapter in the history of Jardine Emett & Chandler spotlights Emett & Chandler Companies Inc., which got its start in 1929 in Southern California and developed into a highly successful regional brokerage com-

pany. In the 1960s the firm evolved into a full-service insurance broker and provider of complete insurance-related services for corporate clients, pioneering unique insurance/self-insurance programs for large corporate accounts. The next decade brought expansion into Arizona and New York City. By the time Emett & Chandler merged with JIBI in 1986, it was a major national brokerage with annual revenues exceeding $47 million.

The establishment of Jardine Emett & Chandler in May 1986 brought together two strong firms with strong traditions. In turn, it has become the largest operating company of the international Jardine Insurance Brokers Group, which ranks among the world's 10 largest brokers. Jardine Emett & Chandler offers a complete range of insurance-related services to middle-market, *Fortune* 500, and group/association clients, with worldwide access to international markets.

As New York State emerges ever more fully into the global economy, firms such as Jardine Emett & Chandler help to assure, and insure, its successes.

Clients such as the New York Authority look to Jardine Emett & Chandler to assist them in managing their various insurance programs. With an annual outlay of more than $8 million for a variety of benefit plans, the Power Authority works closely with JE&C to make its programs as responsive and cost effective as possible, both in design and funding.

READER'S DIGEST

The tranquil, campus-like setting in Pleasantville, New York, that is home to Reader's Digest might mask the publishing company's worldwide scope. Known best for its flagship magazine, the firm today ranks as a business leader in the world of international publishing and direct-mail marketing.

Reader's Digest magazine has a monthly U.S. readership of 50 million and 100 million worldwide. Its 39 editions are published in 15 languages and circulate in nearly 200 countries around the globe. Statistics alone place the company atop any ranking of international publishers. But as George V. Grune, chairman and chief executive officer, is fond of saying, "Our magazine may be the most visible part of our business, but it's only part of what we do."

Reader's Digest is one of the world's largest book publishers and marketers of recorded music. It also sells home videos and travel and financial services through the mail, and helps raise millions of dollars for schools and youth organizations. Reader's Digest is a major supporter of pro-

Reader's Digest headquarters, Pleasantville, New York.

grams for youth, education, the arts, and humanities, both directly and through Reader's Digest Foundation.

Started in 1922, *Reader's Digest* was the brainchild of DeWitt Wallace. Failing to interest other publishers in his idea for a magazine that would "digest" articles from other sources, Wallace borrowed $5,000 to publish it himself.

The magazine's success was imme-

diate. Circulation topped one million in the 1930s; the company soon began expanding overseas with the launch of an edition in Great Britain in 1938, followed by a Spanish-language edition for Central and South America, and then Portuguese and Swedish editions. In 1939, with circulation surging at more than 3 million copies, the company moved to its Pleasantville headquarters.

The popularity of condensed book sections, which had been appearing in *Reader's Digest* since 1934, prompted the firm to launch a separate division in 1950. Now more than 20 million copies of *Reader's Digest Condensed Books,* published in 10 languages, are sold around the world annually. U.S. sales account for half of that volume. Each *Condensed Book* features three to four selections, often best-selling works of contemporary authors.

The ability to package quality products and find vast markets led Reader's Digest into the recorded music business in 1959. Working with leading record companies as well as making its own recordings, Reader's Digest produces music collections that range from popular to jazz, classical to country, and rock to the big bands.

Here Reader's Digest employees sort through the daily orders, payments, and other correspondence from customers.

More than 100 million people read Reader's Digest, making it the world's most widely read magazine. The company also ranks among the world's leading book publishers, recorded music and home entertainment producers, and direct mail marketers. Photo by Glenn Pawlak

Many of the music packages, which are available as records, tapes, and compact disks, have sold more than one million copies and gone platinum.

The growth-minded company then turned its sights to publishing general books—how-to, home repair, self-help, travel, nature, cooking, and many other reference titles. Sales average 300,000 to 500,000 copies per volume, and some top one million.

Success propelled Reader's Digest to become a publishing force that exceeded the original dreams of DeWitt Wallace and his wife and partner, Lila Acheson Wallace. With worldwide circulation of the magazine at 30 million and its book and music divisions performing equally well, the Wallaces retired in 1973 from day-to-day management of the corporation.

A new management team took the helm of Reader's Digest. Under the leadership of Grune, the company continues the heritage of care and respect for employees, encouraging creativity and innovation, and a commitment to philanthropic causes.

Reader's Digest is stronger than ever. It achieved record domestic and international profits in 1986 and 1987.

The firm is making significant investments in its business operations. In 1985 it opened a new $15-million data center in its Pleasantville headquarters, featuring state-of-the-art computer technology. A year later the company bought *Travel-Holiday*, marking the first domestic magazine acquisition in Reader's Digest history. The company subsequently purchased *The Family Handyman, 50 Plus,* and a 50 percent stake in Dorling Kindersley, a London-based book publisher and packager.

As for the future, Grune says, "Our growth will come from other magazines, expansion of current businesses, and development of products and services to be marketed by mail. We will build on our strengths and focus on our objective: to ensure Reader's Digest remains an international business leader in the publishing world."

Only recently—as part of management's belief that open communications is good for business—Reader's Digest opened its doors to provide others a glimpse inside this company that takes great pride in "making a difference" in people's lives around the world.

Making a difference extends beyond the firm's publishing and business ventures. Throughout its history, Reader's Digest has followed a philanthropic tradition begun by its founders. Until recently their philanthropic activities were largely unknown because they refused any public credit for their generosity. From 1965 to 1985 their foundations donated more than $200 million to organizations in New York City alone.

The institutions and programs are in keeping with the ideals Reader's Digest has always promoted. The belief that people could better themselves prompted DeWitt to fund such groups as Outward Bound, Boys Club, and the New York Public Library.

Lila, who believed that people were at their best when surrounded by beauty, gave to the arts, conservation projects, and historic restorations. In recognition of her considerable support for The Metropolitan Museum of Art, a vast new wing housing the museum's collection of twentieth-century art was named after her in 1987.

Today's management continues to expand that generous tradition. Through donations that are double matched by the Reader's Digest Foundation and many hours of volunteer activities, employees support hundreds of worthwhile community organizations.

From book and magazine publishing to support of philanthropic causes, Reader's Digest is in the business of serving people and enriching their lives.

In late 1985 Reader's Digest opened a new state-of-the-art data center at its Pleasantville headquarters.

CENTRAL HUDSON
GAS & ELECTRIC CORPORATION

Central Hudson Gas & Electric Corporation is a private utility in the public service, serving its customers, investors, employees, and communities. Throughout its long history Central Hudson has played a major role as a developer of the Mid-Hudson Valley region.

Central Hudson's origins stretch as far back as 1850, when small gas lighting companies began sprouting up in places like Poughkeepsie, Kingston,

and Catskill. Electricity arrived in 1883 in Newburgh—to the amazement and delight of its residents—with a generator built by Thomas Edison himself, and other Mid-Hudson Valley communities soon followed suit. By the turn of the century there were about 60 gas and electric companies throughout the region.

The Central Hudson System had its official beginning on November 12, 1900, when Newburgh's two gas and electric companies merged to become the Newburgh Light, Heat & Power Company. The new firm's leaders included William R. Beal; his son, Thaddeus R.; and John L. Wilkie.

The following year Beal, Wilkie, and their associates founded the

Poughkeepsie Light, Heat and Power Company, and launched a string of new consolidations throughout the region. By 1911 these partners had formed the Central Hudson Gas and Electric Company, linking their Poughkeepsie, Newburgh, and Cornwall properties. In 1912 Central Hudson became the first utility in the nation to establish a policy of customer ownership, with 2,714 shares of common stock sold. Thaddeus Beal would serve as presi-

The Montgomery Street station at the turn of the century. Located in Newburgh, it was one of Thomas Edison's earliest power stations and, although built in 1884 (by Edison himself), the facility still exists and is an active Central Hudson substation.

dent of Central Hudson from 1912 until his death in 1932.

In 1919 Central Hudson founded the United Hudson Electric Company, which had as its first goal the construction of the valley's largest generating projects, the Dashville and Sturgeon Pool Hydroelectric plants. Soon it expanded into Saugerties, Kingston, Catskill, and other communities in Ulster

and Greene counties. By the end of 1926 there were 75 companies operating under the Central Hudson System, and the growing organization became the Central Hudson Gas & Electric Corporation.

By 1950, the firm's Golden Jubilee year, Central Hudson was undertaking three of the largest projects in its history: construction of the first unit at Danskammer, development of the Neversink Hydroelectric Plant, and conversion of the gas system from manufactured to natural gas. From then on throughout the post-World War II period and up to the present day, the company has continued to advance and diversify in its energy sources, its clientele, and its service to the community.

Since its early days Central Hudson Gas & Electric has grown by leaps and bounds. In 1900 the combined load of all Mid-Hudson Valley electric plants was probably no more than 3,000 kilowatts. Today the area's peak load is nearly 770,000 kilowatts, for which the firm has a system capability of nearly one million kilowatts. In 1900 the Newburgh Light, Heat and Power

The Roseton Plant, located on the Hudson River near Newburgh, is owned by Central Hudson (35 percent), Niagara Mohawk (25 percent), and Consolidated Edison (40 percent).

Reciprocating steam engines powered the generators at the Montgomery Street station during the early days of electricity.

Company had only 5,000 customers. Central Hudson has approximately 232,000 electric customers, as well as 50,000 natural gas customers in the Mid-Hudson Valley. The employee ranks have grown as well; at the turn of the century only a handful of employees were needed to operate the Newburgh system; today the company has 1,320 employees doing jobs that weren't even dreamed of in the old days. The firm now has 2,600 square miles of franchise territory, a far cry from its earliest days in Newburgh.

Today the Mid-Hudson Valley is a growth area. The population of the region has increased by more than 43 percent since 1960 and is expected to double again during the next 25 years. To meet this challenge Central Hudson

developed an energy strategy in the early 1980s, the cornerstone of which is diversification of fuels used to produce energy and growth in capacity to supply new customers. Central Hudson's fuel diversification strategies include conversion to coal and development of nuclear, hydroelectric, wind, and solar power to cut fuel costs and reduce dependence upon oil. In addition to handling those energy initiatives, Central Hudson is also working

to promote the expansion of natural gas use and to improve service to customers by using computer and electronic technology.

Meanwhile, Central Hudson continues to pursue economic development for the Mid-Hudson region, with the primary goal of creating jobs and improving the quality of life.

As a regional energy company with a regional perspective, Central Hudson provides leadership in planning and promoting the economic development of the Mid-Hudson Valley both through its own resources, through the Mid-Hudson Regional Economic Development Council, and through other organizations. The firm also supports the efforts of the Hudson

River Valley Association, a group dedicated to promoting tourism in the Hudson River Valley.

Central Hudson believes in contributing to the communities it serves and, as an investor-owned utility, has a strong sense of commitment to private-sector economic development and the well-being of its public. Central Hudson's involvement in community affairs has always been a paramount consideration in company activities. The firm's president and chief executive officer, John E. Mack III, served as chairman of the City of Poughkeepsie Tricentennial, which was celebrated in 1987. Company chairman Theodore J. Carlson served as chairman of the Mid-Hudson Regional Economic Development Council, an organization that studies important economic issues fac-

The Danskammer Plant, located on the Hudson River, is being reconverted to produce coal-powered energy and is a key element in Central Hudson's fuel diversification program.

ing the region and provides leadership to other groups in the area in cultivating the idea that the development of the quality of life is a competitive asset that will help stimulate economic development. Carlson is also the author of "A Design for Freedom," a book that offers a social analysis of the utility process.

In these ways Central Hudson Gas & Electric Corporation goes beyond its initial important purpose of providing gas and electric power to the community.

V BAND CORPORATION

V Band Corporation is a worldwide designer, manufacturer, and distributor of electronic key telephone (EKT) equipment specially designed for high-density phone systems that have many more lines than telephone sets. With this product V Band serves the financial industry, where multiple phone lines are used by traders and dealers. V Band also provides this equipment to government and the military, 911 systems, utilities, airlines, tenant services, answering services, and dispatching centers.

Since introducing its first EKT equipment in 1981 V Band has become a worldwide corporation, providing telecommunications equipment for the burgeoning worldwide financial services industry and its other client markets. Today V Band Corporation employs more than 275 people in the United States and the United Kingdom. The firm's corporate headquarters and manufacturing plant are located in Yonkers, New York.

V Band's high-density EKT is a telephone with direct push-button access, typically from 30 to 300 telephone

V Band executives are shown here with a 300-button ViAX key console. They are (from left) Ronald E. Halvorsen, vice-president/marketing; Thomas E. Feil, chairman; and John R. Coutts, president.

lines. These high-density EKT systems are generally preferred by users who need many telephone lines in order to communicate in rapid succession with callers, using only one telephone set. In addition, at most EKT installations many of the telephone lines provide direct point-to-point contact to remote telephones without the need for dialing.

In the financial services industry the EKT is referred to as a "trader turret." And owing to its reduced size and greater reliability, the EKT has emerged as the business telephone console on security, commodity, and currency trading floors in banks, brokerage firms, and other financial institutions worldwide.

In the financial markets, trading room floors may contain as many as several hundred telephone stations and in excess of 1,000 telephone lines in the system. Traders use this equipment to obtain price quotation and market information and to carry out buy and sell orders. This rapid-fire use of the telephone stations requires great reliability. Traders often relocate from one telephone station to another, need access to additional direct telephone lines, and cease to need other lines. These additions and relocations must be effected quickly, and with as little interruption as possible.

V Band markets its products primarily through distributors, who provide equipment as well as installation and maintenance service to the customers. And those distributors are very distinguished companies indeed. They include AT&T, the Rolm Corporation, and Telecom Plus International, Inc.

In September 1987 the firm introduced the ViAX® Series, which is currently its principal product. The ViAX Series is a microprocessor-controlled electronic key telephone in an expandable aluminum frame that allows the user to add from one to 10, 30-button modules, plus various functional modules such as line monitors

A view of V Band electronic key telephone consoles on the trading floor at Citibank in Singapore.

and dual dynamic monitors. V Band ViAX instant-access telecommunications systems enable traders throughout the world to communicate with each other at the touch of a button. Each ViAX turret is backed by its own control/switch equipment that makes it less susceptible to systemwide failure and also requires less space than other models. As well, the ViAX system is totally modular. System components can be replaced in a matter of minutes.

V Band's expansion into foreign markets has reached major proportions in recent years. Major trading floors featuring V Band instant-access telecommunications systems have recently been installed in London, Tokyo, Singapore, Hong Kong, New Zealand, and Australia by V Band distributors. And back in 1986 a major distribution agreement was completed with Mit-

A new generation of voice data communication systems named ViAX was introduced at a three-day premier presentation in New York City in September 1987.

subishi Electric Company for the sale, installation, and service of V Band products in Japan. By the end of 1986 V Band's growing foreign sales volume amounted to 56 percent of the firm's total revenue.

The world markets that V Band serves are intensely technology driven, and to keep pace the company has maintained an aggressive new product design and development program. The ever-increasing availability of global communications facilities, by satellite, optic fiber, and other means, continues to challenge the corporation to develop ever more sophisticated terminal systems. Strong evidence of V Band's willingness to forge ahead was shown in 1986, when the company's development expenditure reached 5.3 percent of sales. That emphasis on product development has since continued and promises to become even stronger in the future.

V Band continues to grow with the world's financial services industry, the major market for its telecommunica-

tions systems. But the company is also placing increased emphasis on other markets, such as major airlines, 911 emergency services, utilities, and government applications. For example, American Airlines system operations controllers now keep in constant touch with aircraft and ground facilities

The new V Band product line includes all the new ViAX intelligent key consoles, screen consoles, and desk phones, and a new ViAX information distribution system.

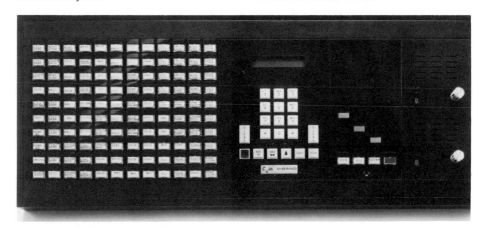

worldwide using a V Band system, and V Band turret systems are the choice for 911 applications where close coordination and reduced response time between various emergency agencies are critical.

This market diversity, along with aggressive product development, has helped to assure continued growth at V Band. To keep pace with this growth the company has expanded and added many new employees at all levels. In 1986 the firm expanded its Yonkers, New York, manufacturing plant to 34,000 square feet. That same year the V Band work force grew from 120 to 220 full-time employees, which included 53 at V Band/plc, the company's subsidiary in the United Kingdom. V Band/plc has enjoyed strong sales over the past two years, due in part to deregulation in the financial industry in the United Kingdom.

V Band's founder, chairman, and chief executive officer is Thomas E. Feil, who has served in that post since 1985 and has been a director of the firm since its inception. The company president is John R. Coutts, who has been a director since 1985.

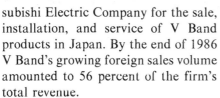

THE LAWRENCE GROUP, INC.

Founded by Albert W. Lawrence in 1954, A.W. Lawrence, Inc., was located in the historic Stockade Section of Schenectady, New York. Since that time the company has expanded to do business coast to coast, maintaining an annual growth rate of 25 percent for the past 30 years. Now with more than 600 employees, The Lawrence Group continues to keep its corporate headquarters in Schenectady, and has made its mark on both the local and national insurance industry.

In 1986 a reorganization of the firm's structure produced the parent company, The Lawrence Group, Inc., a vertically integrated company consisting of three main divisions. They are the Lawrence Insurance Group, listed on the American Stock Exchange, an insurance underwriting operation providing property and casualty insurance, health and accident in-

The Lawrence Group is headquartered in a restored early nineteenth-century Greek revival courthouse in Schenectady.

surance, reinsurance, and credit life insurance; the Lawrence General Corporation, involved in such non-insurance areas as computer software, management services, and real estate; and the Lawrence Agency Corporation, ranked 28th largest in a field of more than 100,000 brokerages, offering program administration, loss control, loss prevention, and brokerage services through blue chip carriers such as Hartford, Kemper, and Aetna.

The Lawrence Group's history boasts many firsts in the insurance industry. In 1958 Lawrence initiated the first private-carrier casualty safety group plan in New York State. The development of the Retail Merchants' Group Life program was the first in the nation. The Lawrence Group pioneered the development of the first School Dental Insurance program in New York State, one of the first group-sponsored auto and home owners' plans, the first School Workers' Compensation Safety Group in the United States, and many of the first self-insurance plans.

Albert W. Lawrence built a small insurance business into a diverse corporation, offering insurance and services to a wide variety of customers coast to coast.

A.W. Lawrence, Inc., served as a major insurer of the 1980 Winter Olympics at Lake Placid, New York, and continues to insure the Olympic Regional Development Authority there. Lawrence is the largest insurer of public school districts in the Northeast and is rapidly gaining national prominence.

The Lawrence Group's dedication to charitable, civic, and educational causes is evident. The Lawrence Loppet, held every year at Mount Van Hoevenberg in Lake Placid, is the largest cross-country ski competition in the Northeast. The annual Safety Seminar, sponsored by The Lawrence Group, is designed to educate teachers and administrators in methods to minimize school accidents and subsequent liability. The company also supports an ongoing interest in the physically disabled.

The Lawrence Group is a diverse corporation offering insurance and services to private, institutional, and commercial accounts. Its continued success makes a significant contribution to the colorful history of New York State.

TAM CERAMICS INC.

Tam Ceramics Inc. has been a mainstay of the Niagara Falls economy since 1906. "We haven't hit our peak yet!" enthuses company spokesman Robert J. Size. That is the spirit among workers at this 225-employee manufacturing center for specialty ceramic products. Unlike many other firms within view of the mist of the mighty falls, Tam is in the midst of a major expansion and anticipates a bright future.

Officials of the firm—since 1979 a subsidiary of Cookson Group PLC—are happy to be on the cutting edge of new technologies for the manufacture of materials for the ceramics and electronics industries. "We're in a changeover from mundane commodities to products for high technology," says Robert A. Rieger, president, "We're introducing four new product lines, we're completing a $6-million expan-

sion, and planning $15 million more in expansion over the next few years."

Tam makes high-purity ceramic powders that are then used in the manufacture of a wide variety of products—tile, refractories, brick colorants, weld rods, investment castings, steel, advanced ceramics, semiconductors, and electronic capacitors.

The company's product line has broadened considerably since the days it all began with a French inventor, two American entrepreneurs, and a desire to start business near Niagara Falls and its inexpensive hydroelectric power. Andrew Thompson of Albany, William F. Meredith of Princeton, New Jersey, and Dr. Auguste J.S. Rossi of Paris, France, are credited as the turn-of-the-century founders of what was then known as the Titanium Alloy Manufacturing Company.

The colorful Dr. Rossi, considered a pioneer of the titanium industry, was fascinated with engines and railroads. He studied chemistry, surveying, and mechanical drafting before graduating from the University of France as a civil

Tam uses both chemical and electronic testing to ensure the quality and consistency of its chemical formulations. This analytical laboratory is part of the company's quality-control program.

engineer and moving to New York City to practice his trade at age 20. With financial assistance from mining executive James MacNaughton, Rossi developed applications involving titanium as an additive to molten steel to increase strength. By 1900 a small pilot plant was operating, and in 1906 the manufacturing of titanium alloy was born in an arc furnace at the full-scale Tam plant in Niagara Falls.

Tam's first product was the alloy known as ferro-carbon-titanium, used to treat and strengthen steel, with the railroad industry the company's first big customer. Through the decades Tam has expanded its product line to include a wide range of titanium-oriented and zirconium-based materials. Today's product lines do not include a single material originally manufactured in 1906.

Rieger is especially proud of Tam's ceramics and electronics technical staff, responsible for the ever-changing nature of the product applications. The Tam Ceramics Inc. laboratory is the scene of research that keeps step with technological changes that bring new customers with new needs. "We have managed to maneuver ourselves into a very exciting series of niches in the ceramic industry," Rieger says. "We're a dynamic company, and we intend to continue to strengthen our position at the cutting edge of new developments in specialty chemicals, ceramics, and electronics."

At Tam's Niagara Falls plant, zirconium silicate is calcined in giant rotary kilns as part of the process to make zirconia, a ceramic powder used in refractory applications.

PHELPS MEMORIAL HOSPITAL CENTER

In October 1954 the cornerstone was laid for Phelps Memorial Hospital Center in North Tarrytown, New York, and in January 1956 the hospital's first patients were admitted.

Since then Phelps Memorial Hospital Center has provided health services to its community throughout an era of increasing sophistication in medical technology and a virtual explosion of medical knowledge. A 225-bed, not-for-profit community hospital, Phelps Memorial currently is available to serve the needs of the Westchester County villages of Ardsley, Briarcliff Manor, Croton, Elmsford, Hawthorne, Irvington, Millwood, North Tarrytown, Pleasantville, Scarborough, Tarrytown, and Thornwood—an area with a total population of approximately 80,000 people.

This community hospital overlooking the Hudson River was the result of a merger of two older, smaller institutions: Tarrytown Hospital, built in 1911, and Ossining Hospital, built in 1907. But more important, it was the result of a gift of land and building funds from the James Foundation, and

Phelps Memorial Hospital Center provides quality medical and mental health care to the surrounding Westchester County villages—an area of approximately 80,000 people.

of the further generosity of a community whose heritage embraced a generation of "philanthropists who saw need of a place where aid must be given to the injured and relief to the sick."

Phelps Memorial Hospital Center can actually trace some of its roots back to the early nineteenth century, when an enterprising Englishman, Anson Green Phelps, established a metal import business in New York. In later partnership with his son and sons-in-law (one of whom was William E. Dodge) the firm, renamed the Phelps Dodge Company, thrived under the leadership of Dodge.

Part of the Phelps Dodge Company's amassed fortune came into the hands of one grandson, Anson G. Phelps II, who, with his wife, purchased land along the Hudson River in Westchester County and built a riverside summer house there in 1851. After the death of the Phelpses, the North Tarrytown home became the property of the Presbyterian Mission Board until a great-grandson, Arthur Curtiss James, repurchased the Phelps home. He and his family lived there until 1941.

The James House is now the home of the Phelps Memorial Hospital Auxiliary. This house, plus 66 acres of land, was contributed by the James Foundation for the construction of Phelps

Memorial Hospital Center. A large donation from the Rockefeller family and a successful fund-raising campaign resulted in the necessary funds to build the hospital.

The James House Interior. The James House is now the home of the Phelps Memorial Hospital Auxiliary.

Today the Phelps Memorial Hospital Center maintains its proud tradition as a not-for-profit, acute care hospital committed to providing quality medical and mental health care, responding to the ever-changing demands of its patients by providing new and expanding services.

Phelps is governed by a board of directors elected by the Phelps Memorial Hospital Association. Membership in the association is open to all, and, as a result, the hospital is very responsive to community needs, offering programs designed to meet those needs.

NEW ROCHELLE PRECISION GRINDING CORPORATION

New Rochelle Precision Grinding Corporation's employees are (kneeling in front) W. Sooknanan and (from left in the front row) C. Fraioli, R. Osterer, M. Shabanaj, K. Hunter, I. Calabro, A. Bienvenido, and A. Heron. In the second row (left to right) are A. Santo, R. Pellegrino, M. Buzzeo, C. Leone, P. Wicha, F. Camarda, R. Kaprius, T. Rea, W. Blagmon, and M. Vigna.

In 1946 a small grinding shop opened for business on Center Street in New Rochelle, New York. Starting with three machines, New Rochelle Precision Grinding Corporation ground components to various precision sizes and tolerances.

Just one year earlier company founder David G. Osterer had been a young attorney, practicing law. But one day, in lieu of payment from a client firm with a precision grinding department, Osterer agreed to accept a small percentage of that company. Shortly thereafter he parted ways with his new partners, who offered him three centerless grinding machines as a settlement. Osterer accepted, and New Rochelle Precision Grinding Corporation was born.

Over the years the business grew, thanks to the founder's keen business sense, a willingness to work hard, and plenty of enthusiasm around the shop. Once when the company purchased a new grinder called the Cincinnati Centerless, the machine was actually christened with champagne.

In 1969 New Rochelle Precision Grinding Corporation opened a second factory in Clifton, New Jersey, at 4 Wellington Street. Four years later the firm again increased its capacity by moving its main factory to 945 Spring Road in Pelham Manor, New York.

In its 40-year history NRPGC has ground precision components for the U.S. Air Force, the U.S. Navy, and NASA. Its private-sector client list includes such corporate giants as RCA, IBM, Bulova, and Western Electric, as well as numerous machine shops, aircraft companies, steel companies, and others.

Today, with a combined space of approximately 25,000 square feet and with 30 centerless grinders, cylindrical grinders, and other ancillary equipment, New Rochelle Precision Grinding Corporation is probably one of the largest grinding facilities on the East Coast.

NRPGC is continually investing in new equipment in order to produce quality parts at competitive prices. The firm specializes in in-feed, thru-feed, cylindrical, centerless, and crush grinding of various types of material, including ceramic and carbide. Over the past few years the NRPGC has also invested substantial sums in modern bar grinding equipment. Its capacities in this area go up to 5-inch-diameter solids and 12-inch-diameter tubes of up to 20-foot lengths. This equipment makes the company highly competitive in mill run type orders.

NRPGC has not forgotten its role as a corporate citizen. Perhaps its most striking contribution is the David G. Osterer Center named after the firm's founder. The facility is located at the headquarters of United Cerebral Palsy of Westchester in Rye Brook, New York. This center can service some 300 handicapped persons with its workshop, day treatment center, camp, and other facilities.

Through the years NRPGC has been asked to purchase or to merge with other businesses. In considering these offers management has always remembered the words of its late founder, David G. Osterer, who said "Don't go into another guy's business—stay with what you know." Under current president Richard Osterer, son of the founder, New Rochelle Precision Grinding Corporation has followed that advice and remains truly a grinding specialist.

The officers of New Rochelle Precision Grinding Corporation are (from left) Robert Pellegrino, vice-president; Richard Osterer, president; and Pete Wicha, executive vice-president.

HERTLEIN SPECIAL TOOL COMPANY, INC.

The Hertlein Special Tool Company was founded in 1945 by the late Carl J. Hertlein in Mount Vernon, New York, where it is still located today. Starting from a small storefront, Carl Hertlein developed his company into a world leader in the manufacture of machine tools that set new production standards for small tool manufacturers worldwide.

Hertlein machines are used for the production of a wide range of cutting tools, such as twist drills, taps, center drills, end mills, saw blades, reamers, and special tools. Without these tools, metalworking would be impossible. They are the tools that make the world's most vital products—from airplanes, automobiles, and heavy equipment to household appliances such as refrigerators and washing machines. Today more than 90 percent of the leading tool manufacturers in the world use Hertlein machines, and the company's machines are operating on every continent.

More than 5,000 Hertlein Production Grinding Machines have been

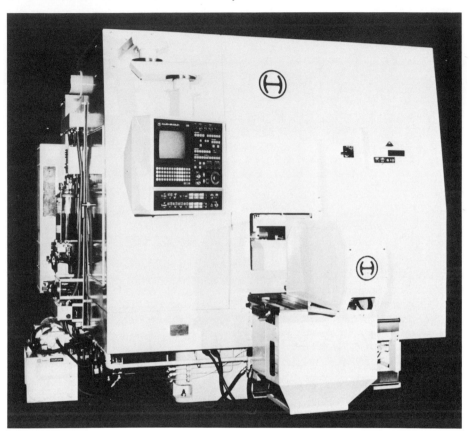

Model FG-100 Hertlein Flute Grinder was produced from 1948 until 1964. It was the first hopper loaded fully automatic machine for grinding spiral flutes from solid, hardened blanks.

built since the firm's inception, and today the company operates from a modern, 60,000-square-foot factory building with a state-of-the-art machine tool installation.

Company founder Carl J. Hertlein was originally an engineer by trade. As a young man in the early 1940s, he was employed by several important tool manufacturers, including America's then-largest toolmaker, Chicago-based Republic Drill and Tool. But in 1944 Hertlein, a New York City native, returned to his home state to launch his own tool venture.

Hertlein Special Tool Company opened for business from a small storefront on Fourth Avenue in Mount Vernon, and he was the only employee. Initially he performed contract engineering for various clients, and subsequently he purchased the stores on his storefront's adjoining sides. Soon he added even more space when he ac-

The latest Hertlein Grinding Center with a robotic loader is a rigid machine of 20,000 pounds yet can hold accuracies of two ten-thousandths of an inch with its computer numerical control.

quired buildings behind those three stores, and his work area grew.

In 1950 Carl Hertlein, seeing his company grow steadily, purchased another building on Seventh Street in Mount Vernon. By that time the firm's employee ranks had grown to 150. The company had also become a manufacturer of twist drills—or drill bits, as they are called in the hardware store.

Meanwhile Carl Hertlein was busy working on the development of the flute grinder—a machine that would make the flutes in drills. This resulted in a new device that became a major commercial development. The invention enabled drill manufacturers to grind the flutes into the drill after it was hardened instead of milling them while the material was still soft. This process of "grinding out of the solid" not only made the hardening process much easier, more important, it made drill production four to five times faster than it had previously been. At the same time it caused the industry standards for twist drills to be tightened considerably because the process substantially improved the accuracy and consistency of the product.

Needless to say the innovation resulted in major new growth for the company. Hertlein now not only manufactured drills, but also manufactured the machines to produce them. At first the machines could only grind the smaller sizes—up to one-quarter inch in diameter—but developments continued, and soon Hertlein developed a machine that could grind up to a half-inch diameter. This range covered approximately 80 percent of all drills produced.

Thus Hertlein began producing his own machinery to make the drills while still a drill manufacturer. But in 1953 Hertlein, whose first love was machine design, decided to concentrate solely on machine building and stop manufacturing drills. One year later he sold the drill-manufacturing portion of the business and went exclusively into manufacturing machines to produce drills.

At the same time Hertlein returned to doing contract engineering work for some prestige clients. One of the company's more important customers was Grumman Aircraft, for whom Hertlein made the hinges for the Navy carrier planes during the 1950s. In addition, Hertlein did work for the chain saw-manufacturing firm Homelite during this period.

The company continued to develop its own new machines, primarily machines that produced cutting tools—tools that included not only drills but also taps (tools for putting threads in a hole), end mills, center drills, and all types of small tools. The firm made machines for them all, and it continued to

Carl J. Hertlein, founder of Hertlein Special Tool Company.

grow. In 1964 Hertlein built a new factory in Mount Vernon on Franklin Avenue, the site of the company's current location. Today Hertlein Special Tool Company's building occupies four times the space of the prior buildings where it had been headquartered in the 1950s.

Carl J. Hertlein guided the company through continued prosperity, constantly upgrading production and product technology until he passed away in 1973. At that time his son, William E. Hertlein, assumed leadership of the firm, and he is currently the president of Hertlein Special Tool Company. The prosperous family-owned corporation also includes Julia Hertlein, wife of the founder, who has been an officer in the company since its inception.

During the high-technology era of the 1980s, Hertlein has maintained its prestige position in the industry, developing a line of CNC (Computer Numerical Control) machines. These user-friendly machines, the latest, state-of-the-art equipment available, represent an important step in the company's technological development—much of the expertise that previously was dependent upon the operator can

now be programmed into the machine. Hertlein has also built much of its own robotics.

Unlike most American machine tool builders—some of which are mired in slumps—Hertlein has always been a major exporter and continues as one today. The company started exporting its first machines as far back as 1956, and over the past 10 years it has been exporting some 50 percent of its production. The first machines were exported to England and Germany in 1956, and the company now has machines in every Western European country and nearly every Eastern European country. Hertlein machines are running at the Kama River truck plant in the Soviet Union, a major international joint venture. And in 1984 the company shipped its first machines to China, where it has found what has become a very successful market.

Today Hertlein Special Tool Company's machines continue to be updated, and the firm continues to be one of the New York metropolitan area's major manufacturing employers—and one of its major success stories.

Current Model FG-650 Hertlein Drill Flute Grinder with state-of-the-art solid-state microprocessor electronics and enclosed grinding area that is environmentally sealed for noise and oil mist.

THE HACKLEY SCHOOL

Hackley School was founded in 1899 by Mrs. Caleb Brewster Hackley as a small liberal arts boarding school for boys. Today, with a student body of more than 780 boys and girls and 70 faculty, Hackley is a bustling private college preparatory school. Its 113-acre campus, located in Tarrytown, rests on a wooded hill overlooking the Hudson River and the Tappan Zee Bridge, about 25 miles north of New York City.

Hackley first opened in the autumn of 1899, with an enrollment of just two boys, on Hackley's donated Tarrytown estate, Castle Heights. The school's first headmaster was Theodore Chickering Williams, a scholar renowned for his translation of the *Aeneid*.

The Hackley School today, located on 113 acres overlooking the Hudson River in Tarrytown.

An early photo of the Goodhue Memorial Building.

In 1900 Hackley purchased an 80-acre neighboring estate as the site of the Upper School, and a Tudor Renaissance-style complex was built there. By 1903 enrollment had reached 50 boys, and new halls, dorms, and athletic facilities were in place.

When Mrs. Hackley passed away in 1913 and Mrs. Goodhue died some four year later, the school lost its two great benefactresses. By the 1930s Hackley needed funding, and in 1940 it became aligned with the American Unitarian Association, assuring its financial security. Dr. Mitchell Gratwick became headmaster, replacing Walter Gage, who retired after serving more than 30 years.

Under Gratwick Hackley grew by leaps and bounds. Enrollment increased dramatically, and a new faculty house and other buildings were constructed, thanks to the generous donations of Herbert Allen, whose munificence would greatly strengthen the school over the years. Meanwhile, the students were introduced to Hackley's five-point system stressing intellectual training, health, extracurricular activity, community service, and spiritual development.

Hackley had remained a boarding school until the 1940s, when it began admitting day students. Since the 1970s day enrollment has been predominant. Girls were first admitted, as day students, in 1970, and today girls are almost as numerous as boys on campus.

The year 1970 also saw yet another gift from Herbert Allen establish the Kathleen Allen Lower School, built to accommodate students from kindergarten to fifth grade, and, as a result, Hackley recently graduated its first 13-year veteran. Meanwhile, coeducation attracted more students, and enrollment grew steadily. Classroom space was expanded, and many other changes were made in the school's layout. During the 1970s the student body increased by 200 day students, 20 new faculty members were added, admission standards were toughened, enrollment of girls was increased, and many new courses for the Upper School were introduced.

Today the Hackley School continues to offer a rigorous and personalized college-preparatory education, stressing classic texts and traditional disciplines. The school is highly personalized, offering small classes, special help, frequent communication with parents, student-teacher interaction outside the classroom, a largely residential faculty, and a high level of participation in team sports.

Hackley School's King Chapel was used for religious ceremonies until the early 1970s. Today it remains a vital part of the campus.

GARDEN WAY, INCORPORATED

Garden Way, Incorporated, was in part the brainchild of a pre-World War I Swiss inventor who created a compact, robust, self-propelled machine to till small areas of soil. In European production the machine, progenitor of the modern rototiller, proved popular. One of these tillers found its way into the hands of Cadwallader Washburn Kelsey, would-be American automobile manufacturer and promoter. Kelsey and his partner, Troy industrialist G.B. Cluett II, took over a former cordage factory in Troy, today national headquarters of Garden Way, Incorporated, the first U.S. manufacturer of this sort of equipment.

Originally built one at a time, Troy-Bilt rototillers entered the national vernacular as a generic name. Today raw castings for major components are produced elsewhere; precision machining and finishing are completed in the Troy plant, where "Quality is everyone's business"; and some subassemblies are produced across the Hudson River, in Waterford, New York. Each day the Troy facility manufactures and ships hundreds of rear-tine rotary tillers, supplying America's single-largest pastime, gar-

Jairo A. Estrada, chairman of the board and president of Garden Way, Incorporated, stands at the doorway of Garden Way's historic headquarters building.

dening, as well as small farmers, nurserymen, and horticulturists. Direct marketing, a regional distribution system, and a dealer network serve the U.S. market (including U.S. Factory Stores), Europe, Australia, and Canada.

A great deal has changed in the half-century leading to Garden Way's present position as producer of America's highest-quality, best-selling tiller. Acquisitions of other out-of-state firms expanded Garden Way's offerings to include chipper-shredders, walk behind and riding lawn mowers, garden carts, power sprayers, and garden tractors. This diversified product line and the energy of chief executive officer Jairo A. Estrada earned the corporation 1985 honors from President Ronald Reagan for its service to the community.

Garden Way's family approach to customers and its durable product are its stocks in trade. Customers always come first, with technical service representatives readily available toll free and correspondence efficiently processed.

Company growth was spurred by America's flight to the suburbs after World War II, when the G.I. Bill and G.I. mortgages created homes that needed gardening. Gardens were a way as well to feed their children, the demographic bulge now known as the Baby Boom, and Troy-Bilt rototillers helped feed America's largest, healthiest generation. A Little Land—a Lot of Living was a slogan of the 1940s. That direct-marketing scheme became so successful that another subsidiary of Garden Way, Precision Marketing Associates, grew out of an in-house advertising operation to become one of America's top 20 direct-response advertising agencies.

Garden Way's future is built on a tripod of the company's established strengths—quality production of hallmark yard and garden power equip-

In July 1955 a delegation from the Future Farmers of America presented a Model 2 rototiller to President Dwight D. Eisenhower.

ment, sophisticated direct-marketing expertise with carefully nurtured local sales representation, and a skilled and loyal work force. Tried and proven in the crucible of a half-century's U.S. economy, Garden Way, Incorporated, will be guided by a commitment to its customers and reliance on, and care for, its employees.

THE SEAMEN'S BANK FOR SAVINGS, FSB

When The Seamen's Bank for Savings opened its doors in 1829, New York had already swept ahead of its great rivals, Boston and Philadelphia, as the foremost seaport in the United States. At the time New York had its commercial banks attending to the city's shippers and merchants, but there was really no banking facility in which the common man—including seamen—could place his savings for safekeeping. Many seamen hid their money in a sock or under a loose floorboard. Or, worse yet, after months at sea they would receive their accumulated pay, then lose all or most of it in the local pubs.

Recognizing this problem, a group of prominent members of the maritime trade petitioned the New York State Legislature for a charter of a bank to serve the seafaring community. On January 31, 1829, a charter was obtained for the formation of The Seamen's Bank for Savings, a mutual institution, philanthropic in purpose, to be operated solely for the benefit of its depositors.

An early public statement described the bank's purpose and policy as "intended to furnish a safe and advantageous depository for the earnings

The Seamen's Bank for Savings opened in 1829 to serve the seafaring community, and for all but three years of its history Seamen's Bank for Savings has been located on Wall Street. Pictured here is the bank's current headquarters at 30 Wall Street, at the historic site of the old United States Assay Office.

of seamen and seafaring people, and those connected with the Navy and merchant service."

While Seamen's is now a major publicly owned savings institution with a broad consumer audience, the bank continues its original commitment to provide the finest in banking services for the benefit of current and future depositors.

With Najah Taylor, merchant and importer, as president, the bank opened on May 11, 1829, on the second floor of 149 Maiden Lane at the corner of Front Street in Lower Manhattan. The bank's trustees included many maritime leaders who had first sought its charter.

On its opening day the bank recorded its first depositor, James

Much of the bank's nautical history can be seen in the decor of its offices. This watercolor was done by Gordon Grant, titled Black Baller Passing the Battery—1829, *and is part of The Seamen's Bank for Savings art collection.*

Chappel, a stevedore for the famous Swallowtail line of ocean packets, who deposited a total of $233. His passbook, number one, is a prized possession of the bank.

In those early days bank employees would often row out to the tall ships moored at their anchor in New York Harbor to collect the deposits of seamen who were on board. However, recognizing limitations to future growth, the bank extended its service in 1833 to people of every calling. Soon the savings accounts of railroad workers and others began to appear next to those of seamen.

The period of the 1860s to 1880s witnessed major changes in the American way of life. The acceleration of the industrial age brought an influx of people into the country's industrial centers. The advent of steel used in shipbuilding, along with the steam- and coal-powered engine, brought the demise of the marvelous age of the wooden-hulled sailing ship. By the early twentieth century the wooden merchant ships had all but disappeared from service.

While the tide turned for the age of the clipper ships, The Seamen's Bank for Savings surged forward and continued its growth. The institution

Today the bank has 13 modern and conveniently located offices in New York City and suburban New York. Pictured here is the Sayville/Bohemia office of the Seamen's Bank for Savings.

An early public statement described the bank's purpose and policy as "intended to furnish a safe and advantageous depository for the earnings of seamen and seafaring people, and those connected with the Navy and merchant service." In 1833 the bank extended its services to people of every calling. This is a painting by Frank Vining Smith of one of those early merchant vessels, the Sea Witch, a clipper ship.

entered the twentieth century in full stride, with some $64 million on deposit by 1905.

As the twentieth century progressed, the city's commerce expanded northward throughout Manhattan. In response to that expansion, Seamen's established its first branch in midtown New York in 1943.

After adding more offices in Manhattan, Seamen's opened its first suburban office in East Meadow, Nassau County, Long Island, in 1972. Today the bank has 13 modern and conveniently located offices in Manhattan, Westchester County, Nassau County and Suffolk County, servicing more than $2.4 billion in retail deposits. For all but three years of its history, The Seamen's Bank for Savings has been located on Wall Street. Its first facility

on Wall Street was burned out in the great fire of 1835, and the bank took up temporary quarters on Pine Street. Seamen's has been headquartered at its current address of 30 Wall Street, on the historic site of the old United States Assay Office, since 1955.

The bank's service package has undergone major changes over the years. While the institution continues to offer passbook savings accounts as in 1829, the depositor of the 1980s can select from a range of deposit and loan accounts, including pension and retirement accounts, checking with interest, money market accounts, certificates of deposit, mortgages, life insurance products, and direct deposit services. In its commitment to provide the most beneficial services available, Seamen's continually evaluates new services that may fit the changing needs of its customers.

The Seamen's Bank for Savings is proud of its 158 years of service to New York area depositors. From its initial deposit of $233, the bank now serves more than 100,000 depositors and has total assets exceeding $4 billion. Although the bank customer of the 1980s is drawn from all walks of life, Seamen's has retained its historic interest in the seafaring way of life and displays that piece of its history in the nautical decor found in its banking offices. The institution's collection of marine art and memorabilia, including paintings, scrimshaw, ship sailing cards, ship models, and nautical instruments, preserves a segment of maritime heritage for future generations. The Seamen's Bank for Savings is proud of its past and is creating an exciting future for its continued role as a major New York area retail financial institution.

GRAMCO, INC.

How many cows, hogs, chickens, ducks, horses, and rabbits have been fed by Western New York's Gramco feed mills over the past 76 years? "I couldn't tell you exactly," company president Virginia C. Mattison says with a smile. "But it's in the millions for sure." Farmers have been depending on Gramco feeds to fatten their livestock since 1911.

It may come as a surprise to out-of-staters whose image of New York State is the glitter of Times Square and the magnificence of the Manhattan skyline, but not Mattison and her son Robert, who will succeed her as president at the end of 1987, that agriculture, and dairy farming in particular, play an important role in the state.

The company, headquartered in the Village of Cattaraugus in Cattaraugus County, has long prided itself on its willingness to buck national competition and to go the extra mile to satisfy the farmers who use Gramco feeds. Employing 32 people at its three mills and one farm supply store, Gramco has managed to slowly but steadily increase its business despite the recent difficulties that have afflicted farmers in New York State and elsewhere. Custom mixing its feeds to meet the needs of individual farmers has enabled Gramco to retain many of its customers for decades, Mattison says. "They keep coming back to us and that's what keeps us going."

Gramco's original mill in Springville was modernized in 1973 and again in 1986.

Donald E. Mattison headed Gramco from 1958 until his death in 1971.

The Gramco story began with James H. Gray, the son of Bryon Gray who operated nine mills in New York and Pennsylvania. James came to Springville, south of Buffalo, to run one of his father's mills in 1907. He decided to strike out on his own, establishing what was then known as James H. Gray Milling Co., Inc., with the first wholesaling operation in nearby Salamanca. Edwin Scott, a Springville lawyer who invested money in Gray's company and whose daughter married Gray, became the organization's first president. The firm quickly expanded, establishing mills at Glenwood, Colden, and Collins in southern Erie County and Cattaraugus, East Otto, and Little Valley in Cattaraugus County.

When Gray died in 1946, Lionel True took over as chief executive of the company. He was succeeded in 1958 by Donald E. Mattison—an employee since 1944 who took out a large loan to purchase the company. In 1962 Mattison changed the corporate name to Gramco—the brand name of Gray's feeds since the 1920s. He tightened credit policies and instituted a program

that allowed farmers to save money by paying cash. The company saw its major growth under Mattison, who died in 1971 and was succeeded by his wife.

Today's Gramco has mills in Little Valley, Franklinville, and Springville; a farm supply store and small corn-cracking operation in Collins; and offices in Cattaraugus. Gramco sells 25,000 tons of feed a year, approximately 85 percent of that total to dairy farmers. Soybean oil meal, wheat middlings, and corn are purchased by the hundreds of tons and moved to the mills by railroad.

Hard times for farmers have meant hard competition for feed millers, and the daily commodity prices on the Chicago Corn Exchange are more

Robert Mattison will become company president at the end of 1987.

important than ever before. Although the business is agricultural in nature, Mrs. Mattison admits "It's like playing the stock exchange and you get nervous. You buy ahead by the carload, and soybean oil meal can jump by $10 a ton one day and go down $5 a ton the next. It's big business.

"The farmer can make it today, but he has to tend to his animals seven days a week, every day of the year."

POWER LINE CONSTRUCTORS, INC.

Whenever you pass barricade lighting on a construction site in New York State; whenever you ski or play tennis, buy gas or shop in the local mall; whenever you watch your favorite team play outdoors or see an airplane land on an airstrip, chances are that Power Line Constructors, Inc., installed the lighting. This company, founded in 1963 by Delores Y. Critelli and Elmer Wahl, also specializes in the construction and maintenance of high-voltage electrical systems for municipalities, utilities, and private concerns throughout the state.

Incorporated in 1963, Power Line Constructors came under the sole leadership of Critelli in 1976 when Wahl retired. From an original payroll of four, the firm now employs as many as 50 people seasonally, and includes five full-time lighting engineers. The first office was rented space in the Jay Street bus garage. Now, from its modern headquarters building on Robinson Road in Clinton, Power Line Constructors sends site superintendents all over the state to perform the high-quality

Power Line Constructors specializes in the construction and maintenance of high-voltage electrical systems for municipalities, utilities, and private concerns. Here Power Line installs emergency lighting for a temporary thruway detour over the Schoharie Creek when the original bridge collapsed.

work for which the company is known.

While much of its work is performed in New York State, Power Line Constructors is prequalified to work in Massachusetts, Connecticut, Pennsylvania, and Maryland. Contracts read like a who's who of business and include Hancock Airport, Fort Drum, Niagara Mohawk, New York State Electric & Gas, lighting and security alarms at Marcy Correctional facility, and Griffiss Air Force Base, where the firm provides lighting and electric distribution. Villages from Lake Placid to Tupper Lake and from Boonville to Hamilton are the sites of Power Line Constructors' activities. National industries for which it has maintained power needs include General Electric, Bendix, Westinghouse, and Revere Copper and Brass. Power Line Constructors erected the steel towers for the 765-kilovolt substation at Massena, New York, for PASNY, and joined with Lord-BEC in construction of the 765-kilovolt transmission line stretching for 81 miles in St. Lawrence, Lewis, and Oneida counties. Recently this versatile firm provided all the lighting for the detour around the collapsed New York State Thruway bridge.

Power Line Constructors is unique in having been founded by a woman at a time when women did not often enter the construction industry. Critelli, a first-generation American, was raised

Delores Y. Critelli, founder and president of Power Line Constructors, Inc.

by her grandmother, "a magnificent businesswoman" who managed a store, dealt in real estate, and raised a family. Her example inspired Critelli to found and head this highly respected Women's Business Enterprise, raise three children, care for this same grandmother, and return to college for a degree. The community, too, has benefited from Critelli's efforts, for she holds many volunteer leadership roles, including the Hospital Trustees' Council, Children's Hospital, St. Joseph's Home, the Arthritis Foundation, the YWCA, and the Mohawk Valley Workshop for the Handicapped.

The newest venture for Power Line Constructors, Inc., is the fabrication of barricade lighting for use on construction sites nationwide. The future appears bright for this forward-looking company, whose line of business and leadership continue to be on the cutting edge.

CHEMICAL BANK

Chemical Bank has a long tradition of service to the consumers and to the business community of New York State, from its earliest years in the first part of the nineteenth century to the present.

Today Chemical is a global financial services organization with more than 200 branches in New York State and representative offices, subsidiaries, and affiliates across the nation and around the world.

Chemical Bank is, in fact, one of the oldest financial institutions in the United States: The bank was originally chartered in 1824, and at the time it served as a subsidiary of the New York Chemical Manufacturing Company, which had been founded the previous year by a group of leading New York merchants. By 1865 Chemical Bank had become a nationally chartered banking institution, and from that

The Chambers Street side of Chemical's head office at 270 Broadway in Lower Manhattan, circa 1919. The bank's current headquarters is on Park Avenue in midtown Manhattan.

Chemical's $35-million, state-of-the-art trading room in New York City. On an average day, the bank trades more than $44 billion in securities and currencies at its 16 dealing rooms worldwide.

point onward it continued to grow. By the twentieth century the institution had evolved from a small commercial bank designed to serve New York's mercantile community into one of the largest banks in the United States, with a strong correspondent business.

The modern Chemical Bank serves two main customer segments of the nation's—and the world's—banking market. Chemical's first customer segment consists of consumers, small businesses, and middle-market companies served on a regional basis. The second segment is comprised of corporate and institutional customers around the world.

As a worldwide financial services institution Chemical has shown a strong knowledge of international currency markets, and its reputation has grown accordingly. Recently a Euromoney survey of corporate treasurers around the world found that Chemical was rated number one in foreign exchange forecasting and foreign exchange dealing.

In addition, the modern-day Chemical is widely recognized as being at the forefront of electronic financial services. One of the institution's most important recent developments in that area is BankLink, a sophisticated corporate cash-management system that has subsequently become the world's most widely used system of its kind. Another major Chemical Bank innovation has been the Pronto home-banking and information system. At present

Pronto has the nation's largest customer base for such a product.

Chemical is also one of the largest issuers of bank credit cards in the United States. Recently the bank introduced ChemPlus, an innovative consumer banking system that automatically links a customer's checking, savings, and credit accounts.

Chemical New York Corporation, the bank holding company of Chemical Bank, was formed in 1968. The establishment of Chemical New York Corporation allowed Chemical Bank to set up additional subsidiaries in a number of diversified areas, such as consumer loans, mortgage banking, and leasing. This diversification has clearly shown major benefits to the consumer: Chemical was described as New York's "best large bank" in a recent *New York Magazine* cover story that surveyed the consumer products and services of the 10 largest commercial banks headquartered in New York City.

In one of the more significant expansions in its modern history, Chemical New York Corporation recently announced that it had reached an agreement on a merger with Horizon Bancorp, a major banking institution in neighboring New Jersey. This merger has given Chemical the ability to extend its natural marketing reach into a thriving and well-populated area that is one of the nation's major economic centers. In New Jersey the bank will thus have the opportunity to serve a host of new individual and commercial customers.

An even more important development for Chemical New York Corporation was its recent merger with Texas Commerce Bancshares, a major banking institution in the Southwest. Texas

Commerce Bancshares has affiliates in the major metropolitan areas throughout the state of Texas.

The merger with Texas Commerce Bancshares was at the time the largest merger in the banking history of the United States. With that agreement Chemical Bank became one of America's most active participants in the current trend toward consolidation of the nation's banking industry.

Over the years Chemical has been no stranger to important acquisition and merger agreements. Previous major consolidations by Chemical included mergers with the Corn Exchange Bank Trust Company in 1954, the New York Trust Company in 1959, and Security National Bank in 1975. Today Chemical continues to grow both through mergers and from within, and has a strategy that encourages selective expansion into attractive markets.

Chemical Bank has had a long tradition of being an active participant in the communities it serves, and the bank continues that tradition to the present day. Chemical's leadership still holds firm to the credo that the most appropriate role for a major bank is that of an actively concerned corporate citizen, balancing the needs of customers, shareholders, employees, and communities so that all are equally well served. The bank is actively involved in sponsoring special events, supporting community programs, and making major philanthropic contributions.

Meanwhile, the bank's financial growth continues unabated. By March 31, 1987, the primary capital of Chemical New York Corporation had reached a total of more than $6 billion. At that time assets totaled $79.4 billion and deposits, $52.1 billion.

The Chemical-Horizon Bancorp agreement, announced in May 1986, will be the largest merger between a New York and a New Jersey bank. Celebrating at the signing (from left) are Horizon president William J. Shepherd, Chemical chairman Walter V. Shipley, and Horizon chairman Robert B. Etherington.

Chemical's traditional preeminence in serving the New York Region's small and mid-size businesses was the subject of this recent feature article in The New York Times.

GOLUB CORPORATION

The first and founding generation of Golub Corporation, Bernard (right) and William (far right) Golub.

If pioneers are defined as persons breaking trails for the future, then the Depression of the 1930s bred pioneers William and Bernard Golub. By 1932 the Golub brothers, sons of wholesale grocer Lewis Golub, had been in the grocery business all their lives, originally delivering orders to grocery stores with a horse-drawn open wagon. That year the young brothers, having studied a Long Island supermarket business, opened their first such market in Green Island, New York, an Albany County community on the Hudson River. The Troy *Record* described it:

... This market is unique in merchandising circles in northern New York in the totally unrelated lines of merchandising gathered under one roof and on one floor. The different lines represented in the various departments cover meat, groceries, fuel, men's furnishings, vegetables, baking goods, hardware, candy, paint and wallpaper, cosmetics, and modern home appliances. The central idea behind the market is to provide a selling mart for all kinds of retail items, reducing overhead and trouble for the shopper. The principle has been used successfully in some parts of the country, but in this section it is entirely new.

Lewis Golub, a second-generation manager of the family firm, is chief executive officer of Golub Corporation.

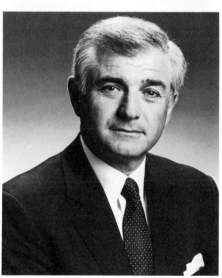

Neil Golub, president of Golub Corporation, has been involved all of his life with a dynamic and growing business.

It was the birth of Central Markets, some 40 years later transformed into the well-known Price Chopper group of supermarkets. In that first Green Island store, the Public Service Market, merchandise was piled on tables in grocery, meat, and produce departments—departments side by side with barber, jeweler's, and shoe repair shops; an antique dealer; and a cafeteria. It was a no-frills operation well suited to the hard times of the Great

Depression, bargain-priced merchandise in a one-stop-shopping location. It was a concept to be refined, expanded, and ambitiously and carefully developed throughout Golub Corporation's history—new then, practical, in step with its era. Considered good, the volume of the Green Island store and the Golub wholesale business together was one-half that of a single Price Chopper market of the 1980s.

Upon success of the Public Service Market, the Golubs opened a second store, converting an automobile dealership's large Schenectady garage into a supermarket, the first bearing the Central Market name. Other stores soon opened in Watervliet, Troy, and Glens Falls, and the Golubs phased out their wholesale grocery business, long run in association with Golub partner Joseph E. Grosberg. When Grosberg ultimately retired in 1943, the firm became Golub Corporation.

Golub Corporation was innovative. It was among the first companies to stock nonfood items in its supermarkets. In the early 1950s it introduced Green Stamps to its customers, and William Golub developed creative programs to help local farmers adopt modern business methods while gaining Central Market outlets for their first-quality produce.

By the late 1950s Golub Corporation operated 25 stores in New York State plus one in Massachusetts. Seven new stores opened in 1963 and four in 1965—a remarkable growth rate accompanied by dramatic sales increases.

In 1972, on the verge of Golub Corporation's next major transformation, Bernard Golub, chairman of the board, died, leaving behind a family firm including some 35 busy and prosperous stores. The next concept, developed by Bernard and William Golub, was the Open 24 Hours policy, nurturing community confidence and providing around-the-clock service. At the same time Golub Corporation created its Consumer Service Department, one of only a few in national retail merchandising.

Bigger changes were to come, accompanied by even greater sales increases and expansion. In 1973 a fully involved conversion effort culminated in a new identity for the entire chain: Price Chopper Discount Foods. Price Chopper disdained sales gimmicks in favor of everyday low prices, becoming well known for community involvement via charitable contributions and participation in community events. In 1975 a 30,000-square-foot, ultramodern Plattsburgh Price Chopper opened, the first store with an in-house bakery. Seven more stores in New York, Vermont, and Massachusetts were acquired by buying the assets of another chain. That year Utica's 40,000-square-foot Hypermarket opened, "the trend of the 1970s." The year 1975 saw the opening of the first Mini-Chopper, Golub Corporation's entry into the convenience store field. The 1970s and 1980s were marked by steady remodeling and expansion, including the opening of a first Pennsylvania Price Chopper. In 1983 the first Super Center—containing 50,000 square feet—opened in Loudonville, introducing the bulk foods concept now in use in many Price Choppers. By 1987 Golub Corporation operated a network of 59 supermarkets in four states, 15 service station and Mini-Chopper outlets, and a drugstore, employing nearly 9,000 persons. Under the leadership of chairman and chief executive officer Lewis Golub and president and chief operating officer Neil Golub, Price Chopper projects opening five new stores per year, ever expanding what it offers the consumers of New York.

In 1986 the opening of "the Store of the Future" near Glens Falls was Price Chopper's prototype for its tomorrow in New York, a huge, varied, and sophisticated market offering the most possible goods and services, from food items to banking and insurance, to the people of New York—the ultimate refinement of the well-named little Public Service Market of a half-century ago.

A Central Markets store, the forerunner of the Price Chopper line of supermarkets.

The fifth generation of Price Chopper stores, the Super Centers are Golub Corporation's most sophisticated and modern facilities—the firm's stores of the future.

PHILIP MORRIS COMPANIES INC.

Philip Morris Companies Inc., with its hundreds of brand names in tobacco, beer, and food products, is arguably the world's largest and most successful consumer goods company. In addition to its tobacco companies, Philip Morris U.S.A. and Philip Morris International, it also owns General Foods Corporation and Miller Brewing Company, both of which are featured separately in these pages.

Philip Morris is one of the world's largest producers of cigarettes, with brands including Marlboro, Benson & Hedges 100s, Merit, Virginia Slims, Parliament Lights, Players, Cambridge, Saratoga, English Ovals, and many other brands that are well known overseas. Philip Morris U.S.A. leads this country's cigarette industry, while Philip Morris International markets cigarettes in more than 170 countries and territories. The company's Marlboro trademark alone is one of the most profitable and well known in the world.

Philip Morris' cigarette business represents the cornerstone of the giant corporation's history. Its roots go back to mid-nineteenth-century London where Philip Morris, Esq., owned a tobacco shop on Bond Street. Having first operated as an American offshoot of that English company, Philip Morris

An early Philip Morris storefront.

was incorporated in Virginia in 1919, with headquarters in New York City. Philip Morris U.S.A. and Philip Morris International, along with holding company Philip Morris Companies Inc., today are managed from the Philip Morris World Headquarters at 120 Park Avenue.

In addition to serving as a corporate headquarters location for decades, New York has also contributed a colorful piece of Philip Morris history. During the early 1930s company executives visiting the Hotel New Yorker noticed a bellhop's distinctive voice when he paged hotel guests. They asked him to announce a "call for Philip Morris," and were so impressed with his delivery that they lured him on the spot, and starting with his first in 1933, Little Johnny was famous in Philip Morris commercials for some 30 years.

Today Philip Morris Companies Inc. is one of New York State's largest employers, providing jobs for more than 10,000 people. It is also one of the state's most distinguished corporate citizens, funding museums, schools, social welfare programs, public policy centers, and New York's Lincoln Center for the Performing Arts. Recognized as a leading patron of the arts, Philip Morris was dubbed "One of America's corporate Medicis" by *Newsweek* magazine.

The majority of the corporation's philanthropy is nonetheless centered on social causes, such as health and welfare, education, support for women and minorities, and civic activities. The company has funded and managed the New York City Partnership summer jobs program for inner-city youth, and it has aided many other similar programs and projects. In short, Philip Morris has been a key contributor to the social well-being of its home state.

In addition to its cigarette operations, General Foods, and Miller Brewing Company, other important Philip Morris units include Philip Morris

New York has served as the corporate headquarters location for Philip Morris Companies Inc. for decades, and the firm is one of New York State's largest employers, providing jobs for more than 10,000 people.

Credit Corporation, which provides financing for Philip Morris customers and engages in other financial services, and Mission Viejo Realty Group Inc., a community development company in Southern California and Colorado.

MILLER BREWING CO.

In April 1974, while the national recession still gripped New York State, Miller Brewing Co. executives made an announcement that started a series of economic ripples that continue to shower benefits on the state and particularly central New York.

After considering more than 350 locations in several states, Miller, the world's second-largest brewer, selected a 440-acre site near Fulton, 25 miles northwest of Syracuse, for its new Northeast brewery. The $120-million brewery would create hundreds of permanent jobs, plus those needed for construction.

Miller first planned a brewery that would produce 2 million barrels of beer annually; but in May 1975, shortly after construction began, the Milwaukee-based company announced two more economic boosts for the area: The brewery's capacity would be doubled to 4 million barrels, and a plant to produce 550 million aluminum cans per year would be located next to the beer-making facility. Both meant more employment for central New York.

Still more was to come. In mid-1976, shortly after the Fulton brewery began shipping beer and the can plant started production, Miller said it would invest another $81 million to double the brewery's capacity again—to 8 million barrels per year.

Miller's parent company, Philip Morris Companies Inc., gave the area still another economic lift in June 1977: A glass container plant would be built near Auburn, 25 miles west of Fulton, creating more jobs. That plant began making containers in November 1978, and produces a yearly volume in excess of one billion 12-ounce and 7-ounce clear and amber glass bottles.

The brewery marked a major milestone on April 6, 1987, when it shipped containers holding its 75-millionth barrel of beer. "That 11-year output of the brewery is enough to fill more than 25 billion 12-ounce bottles of beer," ex-

plained Gerrald E. Church, the brewery's resident manager.

Miller's 1986 spending in New York totaled $311 million—demonstrating the continuing economic impact of its three production facilities. That total—an increase of $48 million over the 1985 figures—included $78.9 million in wages, salaries, and benefits to 1,839 employees, 1,388 in the brewery, 163 in the can plant, and 388 in the bottle factory; $198.1 million on energy from utilities, and on goods and services from New York suppliers; $21.5 million for local and state taxes; and $12.5 million to expand and improve the brewery and container plants.

When the usual multiplier of four to six is applied for money put into circulation by a business, Miller's expenditures gave the state an economic wallop of more than one billion dollars in each of those years, and the 1987 impact is expected to be in the same range.

A major factor in Miller's selection of the site for its New York brewery was the limitless supply of good water from Lake Ontario that travels through a 35-mile pipeline, which passes near the brewery, from the lake to Syracuse. Syracuse and Onondaga County voters approved spending $45 million to tap the lake in 1962. Miller Brewing Co. has proven to be a great asset to the community and plans to participate in its future prosperity.

Colorful hot air balloons rise over the Syracuse area in the annual Balloon Festival sponsored by Miller Brewing Co.

This control panel allows Miller personnel to see the status of operations and equipment, and spot problems immediately.

GENERAL FOODS

Headquartered in Rye Brook, New York, General Foods Corporation is the largest food company based in this country, with some 50,000 employees in the United States and in 22 other countries in North and South America, Europe, and the Asia-Pacific area.

General Foods has the broadest product line of any food company in the world. Its products include Maxwell House, Sanka, Brim, and Yuban coffees; Oscar Mayer and Louis Rich meats; Entenmann's, Freihofer, and Oroweat baked goods; Post cereals; Birds Eye frozen foods; Jell-O; Minute rice; Kool-Aid; Ronzoni pasta; Shake 'n Bake; and Tang, among others. In all, General Foods sells its products under more than 60 major brand names.

This corporation was formed from a number of companies, most of which were established during the nineteenth century. From the beginning the fortunes of General Foods were linked closely to New York State. In 1845 New York inventor Peter Cooper patented a gelatin dessert. By 1897 Pearl B. Wait of Le Roy, New York, had developed a variation of Cooper's invention, and began producing it under a brand name his wife had coined—

Entenmann's cakes and pastries roll by an inspector at the company's plant in Bay Shore, New York. Beginning as a small bakery in Brooklyn, Entenmann's now sells its products throughout most of the United States.

The General Foods corporate offices building in Rye Brook, New York, opened in 1983, providing office space for about 1,800 employees. Its distinctive architecture has won critical praise worldwide.

Jell-O. The venture was soon purchased by a neighbor, Orator F. Woodward, for $450. By 1906 sales of Jell-O reached nearly one million dollars, as homemakers rushed to buy what was soon called "America's Most Famous Dessert."

In 1896 William Entenmann, an immigrant from Germany, opened a bakery in Brooklyn, New York, and began delivering his baked goods from house to house. The bakery soon moved to Bay Shore, Long Island, and expanded delivery routes as Entenmann's baked products launched a major business.

The Freihofer baking business, which had been founded in 1884 in Philadelphia, moved to Troy, New York, in 1913. Today it is a thriving baked goods business covering major portions of the Northeast.

In 1915 Emanuele Ronzoni, who had come to the United States in the early 1880s and worked as a helper in a macaroni factory, established his own pasta business in Long Island City, New York. It soon flourished.

Today General Foods has important operations throughout New York State, with a total of 4,600 employees there. Corporate and divisional headquarters are at Rye Brook and White Plains. Technical Research is head-

quartered at Tarrytown. Entenmann's headquarters and main plant is in Bay Shore, Ronzoni in Long Island City, and Freihofer in Albany. Avon is host to a major frozen food-processing plant. Other plants, distribution centers, and offices are located at DeWitt, Fulton, Hawthorne, Manhattan, and Saratoga Springs.

General Foods is not only a major contributor to the state's economy, it also participates fully in New York's cultural and social life. In the 1950s the chairman of General Foods, Clarence Francis, spearheaded the fund-raising effort to build New York City's Lincoln Center for the Performing Arts. In 1986 General Foods donated $2.4 million, the largest grant in its history, to help found the Biotechnology Center at Cornell University in Ithaca, New York. Among other things, the center will conduct research on improving nutrition and the world food supply.

Despite its heavy involvement in New York State, General Foods can trace its roots back to many areas of the United States, and to many other countries as well. Its earliest antecedents date to before the American Revolution. In 1765 Dr. James Baker, a Massachusetts physician, opened the first chocolate mill in the New World. Thus began Baker's chocolate. By the late 1830s packages of Baker's cocoa could be found on the shelves of Abe Lincoln's store in Springfield, Illinois.

General Foods is the direct descendant of the Postum Cereal Company, begun by C.W. Post. Working at the

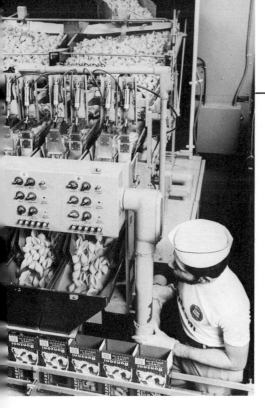

Jumbo shells of pasta tumble through the automatic packaging machinery at the Ronzoni plant in Long Island City, New York. Long New York's favorite pasta, Ronzoni now is pleasing consumers in other areas of the country, too.

kitchen stove in his little white barn in Battle Creek, Michigan, Post developed Postum, a hot, grain-based beverage that is still sold today. In 1895 he went into business on a capital investment of $68.76.

Meanwhile, other innovators and entrepreneurs also were developing new packaged foods for a rapidly developing nationwide consumer marketplace:

—In 1882 businessman Joel Cheek quit a successful wholesale grocery partnership to develop a new coffee, which met success when it was tried out on diners at Nashville, Tennessee's, most prestigious hotel, the Maxwell House. Several years later Teddy Roosevelt visited the hotel and pronounced the coffee "good to the last drop!"

—In 1883 a Bavarian immigrant named Oscar Mayer opened a meat market in Chicago with his brother, a venture that would eventually grow into a nationwide company, with Oscar Mayer and Louis Rich becoming household names.

—In 1903 a shipload of coffee beans was soaked with sea water during a storm. Their owner, European coffee importer Ludwig Roselius, experimented on the brine-soaked beans, and this led to development of a decaf-feinated coffee method and the introduction of Sanka-brand coffee a few years later.

—In 1914 Clarence Birdseye was with the U.S. Fish and Wildlife Service in Labrador, where he observed that fish caught through the ice by Eskimos would freeze stiff the moment they were exposed to the frigid air. They still tasted fresh when defrosted and cooked weeks later. Realizing the secret was in the quick freezing, Birdseye saw commercial possibilities but lacked the resources needed to make his venture grow until it became a part of General Foods in 1929.

The companies founded by these innovators began to be acquired by Post's Postum Cereal Company soon after World War I. Between 1925 and 1929 Post acquired 10 firms, adding Jell-O gelatin, Maxwell House coffee, Franklin Baker coconut, Walter Baker chocolate, and Log Cabin syrup, among others. After acquiring the rights to Clarence Birdseye's quick-freezing process, General Foods founded the frozen foods industry in 1930.

Still other businesses became part of the General Foods family: Sanka decaffeinated coffee in the 1930s, Yuban coffee in the 1940s, Kool-Aid soft drink mixes in the 1950s, and Oscar Mayer, Entenmann's, Oroweat bread and rolls, Ronzoni, and Freihofer in the 1980s.

Outside the United States, General Foods' Canadian business grew up with its U.S. parent, partly because many of the corporation's predecessor companies already had Canadian operations. In 1947 General Foods began expanding operations beyond North America and acquired the British Alfred Bird & Sons desserts firm. Since then General Foods has acquired a number of businesses in Europe (including Hollywood chewing gum in France, Gevalia coffee in Sweden, and the German-based HAG AG coffee business) and in Latin America (including Kibon ice cream in Brazil and Rosa Blanca soups in Mexico). It has also acquired interests in overseas com-panies (such as majority interest in the Simmenthal processed meat and fish business in Italy) and formed joint ventures (with Ajinomoto in Japan, for example, where coffee is a principal General Foods product). Today GF products are sold in more than 100 countries.

Throughout its history General Foods has developed new products and new businesses internally. Many were innovations at the time, from the first all-coffee instant coffee in 1950 (Instant Maxwell House) up through the present. GF Technical Research has developed such original food concepts as quick-cooking Minute rice, Tang powdered breakfast drink, Cool Whip non dairy topping, Maxim freeze-dried coffee, Shake 'n Bake coating mix, Stove Top stuffing mix, and Crystal Light drink mix.

In 1954 General Foods began selling food to restaurants and other institutional feeders. Today its food service business supplies coffee and other food products to restaurants, hospitals, company cafeterias, and other institutions from coast to coast.

General Foods Corporation was acquired by Philip Morris Companies Inc. in 1985. It is an important part of the Philip Morris family, and continues to be a major innovator in the food industry and an important corporate citizen of New York State.

Two big hits with American consumers at the turn of the century were the horseless carriage and Jell-O gelatin, which originated in upstate New York. Before long, motorized trucks were delivering "America's Most Famous Dessert" to markets around the country.

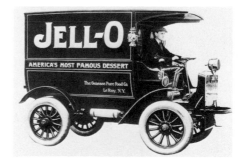

ARCATA GRAPHICS/BUFFALO DIVISION

One thing that *Reader's Digest*, the *National Enquirer*, *Golf* magazine, and the Harlequin Romance series of paperback books have in common is their popularity with American readers. Another is that all of them are printed at the Buffalo Division of Arcata Graphics.

There are those who say that Americans just do not read as much as they used to in this age of multichannel cable television and videocassette recorders. But don't try to tell that to the 1,500 employees at Arcata Buffalo. Located on a 60-acre site in the village of Depew, close to a mile south of the Greater Buffalo International Airport, Arcata Buffalo continues to churn out books and magazines by the hundreds of millions every year.

Even some Buffalonians are surprised to learn that workers in the Depew plant print some of the world's most popular periodicals and books by some of America's best-loved authors. On a given day samples from the publishing cycle may range from a novel by Sidney Sheldon to a union magazine for operating engineers to a guitar handbook to a fashion knitting magazine and to another on travel in the Caribbean Sea islands.

Today's version of Arcata Buffalo is a high-technology operation utiliz-

Rotogravure cylinders are etched with images and become the equivalent of printing plates in the production of periodicals such as Reader's Digest *and the* National Enquirer.

ing satellite receivers, state-of-the-art color-plating techniques, and sophisticated folding and labeling equipment. The advanced gravure facility that prints the weekly copies of the *National Enquirer,* for example, can turn a roll of paper on the press into bundles of finished product in 2.2 minutes. Arcata Buffalo can print and tabloid fold 1.2 million *Enquirers* in 24 hours.

Other numbers tell the Arcata Buffalo story: The plant is capable of printing 2 million books in a day; its combined operations print some 24 magazines per second; *Reader's Digest* alone counts for 17 million monthly copies. Arcata Buffalo is the largest mailer in the eastern region of the U.S. Postal Service, mailing 300 million

Here a worker feeds magazine sections into a binder in the plant's publishing area.

pieces per year at an annual cost of close to $30 million. The plant even has its own post office branch that is a bigger revenue producer than the main post office of the city of Seattle. The Buffalo operation uses 400 million pounds of paper each year and hundreds of tons of ink.

"Ours is the largest and most diversified printing plant under one roof in the United States," says John D. Netsel, vice-president/marketing at Arcata Buffalo.

But all the jaw-dropping numbers had humble beginnings. It all began with a man named James Watson Clement, whose establishment of a printing shop in Buffalo was at least indirectly related to the illness of his mother back in 1878. The story relates that Clement was operating a printing plant in nearby Batavia that year when he received word that his mother was seriously ill in Chicago. The dutiful son rushed to his mother's bedside and then headed back to Batavia after she made a marked improvement. On the way

back home Clement stopped off in Buffalo for shop talk with some fellow printers. Clement was impressed with what he saw in Buffalo and decided to take a chance at expanding into the fast-growing city.

Clement forged a strong local reputation, and after his death in 1907 the J.W. Clement Co. continued to build its following on a national scale, gaining recognition as a printer of almanacs, catalogs, and company publications. J.W. Clement was one of the nation's largest printing firms when it was acquired in 1965 by Arcata National Corp. of California. Renamed

Arcata's Buffalo Division is headquartered in suburban Depew, near the Greater Buffalo International Airport.

Arcata's Buffalo Division, the former Clement plant is now part of Arcata Graphics, headquartered in Baltimore with more than 6,000 employees nationwide.

The national corporation has a proud story of its own, also with humble beginnings. Started by a group of investors who bought some redwood timber tracts in Arcata, California, for a lumbering operation in 1905, Arcata has grown into one of the nation's three largest printing firms.

Arcata Graphics is actually a subsidiary of Arcata Corp., still headquartered near the original timberland in California. The graphics operation recorded $500 million in sales in 1986. In addition to Arcata Buffalo, Arcata Graphics runs the nation's largest printing plant dedicated to book printing in Kingsport, Tennessee, according to staff services manager Margaret R. Wilmot. On a national scale, Arcata Graphics prints approximately one-third of America's paperbacks—some 400 million books per year—with customers including such publishers as Simon & Schuster, Warner, and the popular Harlequin romance series. This output makes Arcata Graphics the largest printer of rack-size books in the competitive U.S. market.

"Printing is the ninth-largest business in the United States. The gross national product for printing operations is $120 billion a year," Wilmot says. "It's also a changing business. We serve every major publisher in the United States. The biggest change in the marketplace has been the consolidation of publishers into larger and larger operations. The technology is changing so fast and is so expensive, product efficiency is more important than ever. The equipment is costing millions and millions of dollars and constantly has to be updated. When something breaks down, you don't just go out and buy another automatic copy machine."

Arcata Buffalo is recognized as a national pacesetter in the printing of both books and magazines. Most of the work is done in the 800,000-square-foot main plant, but the process begins in the 30,000-square-foot A.G. Colorplate building across the street; there plates and bromides are made to ensure that customers' artwork can be accurately transformed to paper. Included at A.G. Colorplate is a satellite dish that receives information for copy changes just before deadline, testing and screening equipment to check resolution, and a separation previewer that gauges the effect that changes in paper, ink, and retouching will have on reproduction. The latest in retouching techniques are used to make sure artwork will reproduce well on the big Arcata presses.

The printing of the *National Enquirer* and *Reader's Digest* are such major operations that each has its own pressroom in the sprawling plant. Eight high-speed letterpress units in the Buffalo plant can print, slit, fold, and deliver 128 pages from one piece of paper. In addition to printing books, Arcata Buffalo creates soft-cover designs for promotions and book covers.

Netsel believes the computer revolution has had major impact on the printing industry and will have even more impact over the next decade. "We expect to see even faster turnaround times because of the use of the computer in all areas of graphic arts," he says.

STEBBINS ENGINEERING AND MANUFACTURING CO.

The Stebbins Engineering and Manufacturing Co., a pioneer in chemical-resistant linings and mortars, was born in 1884, when H.W. Stebbins joined with Howard Friend to form a partnership in West Carrollton, Ohio, to provide consulting services and to make apparatus, including complete mills, for the then-infant U.S. pulp and paper industry. Stebbins' family had long been involved in papermaking in England. Friend was a papermaker.

A key industry problem of the day was blocking corrosion of the metallic digester shells in which wood chips are cooked with bisulphite liquors in the first stages of papermaking. The partners solved the problem by developing and engineering special chemical-resistant brick and mortar linings. In 1889 the company installed the first brick and cement linings in a paper mill in North America.

Providing consulting services, materials, equipment, and installation crews to the paper industry still is an important part of the business. In 1898 the firm moved to Watertown, New York, where Stebbins and Augustus F. Richter formed a new partnership of-

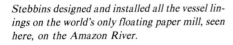

Stebbins designed and installed all the vessel linings on the world's only floating paper mill, seen here, on the Amazon River.

Tile tankage under construction for a southern chemical plant. Experienced Stebbins field crews work on many sites throughout the United States and Canada.

fering the same services and materials. A major reason for the move to Watertown was to be nearer to clients in the pulp and paper industry, which was then concentrated in the Northeast, especially in the Adirondacks, New En-

gland, and Eastern Canada.

As the industry matured, so did Stebbins and Richter, improving and developing new lining materials and installation techniques to remain in the forefront of the industry. Over the past 100-plus years Stebbins' research staff has developed many types of chemical-resistant brick, tile, membranes, and mortars that the company manufactures in its own plants and supplies on an installed basis for its clients.

A measure of its success is that today nearly all brick linings in sulphite digesters in North America are installed with Stebbins materials and/or are maintained by the firm's crews, according to Alfred E. Calligaris, president, chairman, and chief executive.

Company executives attribute much of the firm's growth to its continuing research in the chemical-resistant linings field—research that has often found that many of the lining materials available have not been able to meet Stebbins' specifications.

As a result, the company has developed its own proprietary line of chemical-resistant brick in a wide range of sizes, shapes, and thicknesses; an extremely dense tile developed in the mid-1930s that has been classified as "chemical stoneware" because of its performance in government testing; the jointing of mortars for bricks and tile; and membranes used under the tile or brick linings. Stebbins today "remains deeply committed to the development of improved lining materials and techniques," Calligaris emphasizes.

More than 95 percent of the firm's proprietary materials are installed by Stebbins field crews, Calligaris notes. The company has a cadre of 150 experienced, top bricklayers who serve as lead men or specialists. Members of this group direct installations as foremen or superintendents.

Many members of these crews exceed 15 years of experience with the company. Stebbins constantly keeps its field personnel up to date on improvements in materials and construction, and once each year all field personnel attend a field crew meeting where the entire field operation is reviewed.

On larger projects Stebbins sends management teams from its Watertown headquarters to direct operations with the field crews. The firm provides support functions for the projects through its Watertown staff, more than 100 men and women in the research, engineering-estimating-drafting, contract administration, corporate financing and accounting, and other departments.

The firm was incorporated in 1903 by the partners as Stebbins Engineering and Manufacturing Co. (SEMCO), with Stebbins as president and Richter as treasurer. Its headquarters have remained in Watertown since its founding.

Since 1903 Stebbins has evolved into an international specialty contractor, serving a wide spectrum of clients not only in papermaking, but also in the chemical, food-processing, mining and metallurgical, water-treatment, and electric power-generating industries

A structural tile, high-density storage tank for the pulp and paper industry. Stebbins has designed and constructed more than 1,500 of these large storage tanks throughout the United States and Canada.

throughout the United States and Canada and in many other countries.

Clients are located in countries on all continents, including Mexico, Argentina, Brazil, and Venezuela in South America; Great Britain, France, Germany, and Spain in Europe; India, Japan, and South Korea in Asia; Egypt, South Africa, and Nigeria in Africa; Saudia Arabia, Iran, Iraq, and Israel in the Middle East; and Australia and New Zealand.

Stebbins provides its clients with technical services, materials, equipment, and field crews to combat corrosion through the use of all types of chemical-resistant brick, tile, mortars, and membranes.

Canadian Stebbins Engineering and Manufacturing Co., its Canadian division based in Ottawa, was established in 1927 to direct the company's operations in that country. The division now directs operations in Eastern Canada, and a Canada West division, based in Vancouver, directs projects in that region.

Other major divisions are based in Seattle, Washington (the West and Alaska); Port Allen, Louisiana (the South); and Greenville, South Carolina (the Southeast). Divisional offices in Watertown handle work in the northeastern region. Projects in other countries are handled through international divisions based in Watertown and Ottawa.

As it enters its second century, Stebbins is contemplating new operations to expand the company's endeavors. One is managing construction. "We asked ourselves, 'What are our strengths,'" explains Calligaris. "We're really good at managing our work. So we're thinking of going into large commercial projects that involve masonry work."

One reason for this direction is the nearly one-billion-dollar rehabilitation and expansion of Fort Drum, the military base just outside Watertown, which is being made over to house the U.S. Army's new 10th Mountain Division.

Consideration also is being given to seeking commercial masonry contracts "anywhere in North America," and some general contracting work, Calligaris says.

An interior view of an oxidation tank constructed for a fossil fuel power plant.

NEW YORK CASUALTY INSURANCE COMPANY

In 1976, when two key executives of an old and respected Watertown-based insurance company decided to leave their secure positions and form their own firm, they believed they were making a move that was both a challenge and an opportunity.

Today New York Casualty Insurance Company, started in 1976 by Rose Frattali and Ervin J. Dickey, Jr., is a well-established and growing firm. Since 1982 New York Casualty has been a wholly owned subsidiary of the Phoenix Mutual Life Insurance Co. of Hartford, Connecticut, the 15th-largest U.S. life insurance company.

Mrs. Frattali was elected president in 1984 and chief executive officer the following year. She is believed to be the only female chief executive of an insurance company in New York State, and one of only two or three in the nation.

The company's growth, plus a solid reputation for service, has put New York Casualty well on its way to the goals set for the new enterprise.

Finding the capital necessary for a new insurance company was more difficult than had been anticipated. Under New York State law in 1976, a new company needed start-up capital of $2.2 million. Today that figure is $5 million. Numerous meetings with local businesspersons and bankers brought, first, encouragement, and then, needed financial commitments.

Among a myriad of other things to do, the two executives had to obtain a license from the New York State Insurance Department, select a name, and find a home for the company.

It was not until after the license had been granted by the State Insurance Department that the executives discovered it was the first property and casualty license granted by the department in 22 years to an independent, New York-domiciled company. It was also very exciting when the name "New York Casualty" was approved (the first choice from a list of 10 possi-

Rose Frattali, co-founder, president, and chief executive of New York Casualty Insurance Company.

bilities), since it had the sound of an old and established company. The certificate of authority was finally granted on December 15, 1976.

As for a home, the firm is still domiciled in its original place of business, the Marine Midland Bank Building.

In order to sell insurance an insurance company must be represented by agents. These agents must sign contracts with the firm and be licensed to represent it by the New York State Insurance Department. None of this can take place until after the company's certificate of authority has been issued. Although New York Casualty had been seeking support and commitment from independent agents for months, a mountain of paperwork remained before these agents could sell the firm's policies. Since the individual signature of each agent was required, and the agencies were scattered all over Upstate New York, a logistical problem of some proportion had to be resolved if New York Casualty was to be able to commence writing insurance on January 1, 1977.

With only two weeks remaining in the year, and with the Christmas holidays falling within the period, it was obvious that any attempt to complete these transactions by mail would be fruitless. Thus, the executives decided that each potential agency would be visited in person during the remaining days, and the paperwork would be completed on the spot. While one group kept busy typing contract forms, license applications, and appointment papers for each potential agency, another set about planning itineraries and making dates for visits to these agencies. The routes were established to enable each traveler to leave the city on one major artery and return by another, stopping at agents' offices all along the route.

Early on a bleak December morning, on the heels of a sleet storm, five executives departed the office, each toward a different point of the compass.

Ervin J. Dickey, Jr., co-founder of New York Casualty Insurance Company, retired in 1987.

Two days later the weary travelers returned to the office—mission accomplished! In 48 hours an agency force had been mobilized, and the fledgling company was now prepared to write its first policy.

On January 1, 1977, the new firm opened for business with a staff of 14 heavily experienced people, all of whom had been associated with the Agricultural Insurance Company—a firm that had been a part of the Watertown community for 128 years. This small staff included all of the same elements found in larger insurance companies. There was an Underwriting Department, Marketing Department, Claims Department, Financial and Accounting Department, and an Office Services Department to support these. EDP services were purchased from a service company and, at that time, supported the firm's financial and management reporting and accounting requirements. As it progressed, the company developed its own EDP facilities and expanded support to include policy writing, statistical computing, and customer billing operations.

On January 1, 1977, a Watertown agency wrote the first policy—a homeowner's contract covering a dwelling in Burrville, New York. From that small beginning the firm has grown steadily to its current stature.

In 1987 premiums are expected to exceed $21 million, nearly 15 times the first year's total. The bulk of that income comes from policyholders in New York State. New York Casualty is now represented by 240 independent agents—200 in New York State and 40 in Pennsylvania. The staff has grown

to a total of 74 people.

At this point in time New York Casualty has reached an enviable level of achievement within its operating territory. However, even in its home state, New York, there are unexplored regions, and the company has realized its potential market share only in an area immediately surrounding its home office. There is ample opportunity for further growth and prosperity in the balance of New York State, and the Pennsylvania marketplace has hardly begun to be developed. It is obvious that there is every reason to expect New York Casualty to continue, and to expand upon its already successful course.

Other than the founders, key people involved in forming the company were Victor D. Lincoln, executive vice-president, who heads the Underwriting Department; Roy J. Sauter, vice-president, and head of Marketing; Richard H. Kelsey, secretary/treasurer; Richard J. Lake, vice-president, who heads the Office Services Department; and Thomas F. Coughlin (deceased), vice-president in charge of the Claims Department. Dickey, who headed the new company during its start-up years, retired in 1987.

Roy J. Sauter, vice-president of New York Casualty Insurance Company.

Victor D. Lincoln, executive vice-president of New York Casualty Insurance Company.

PEOPLES WESTCHESTER SAVINGS BANK

On August 2, 1853, 14 of Westchester County's leading citizens met at the Franklin House in Tarrytown to discuss the establishment of the county's first savings bank. The undertaking was a bold one, the first mutual savings bank in America had been chartered only 37 years before, in Boston. Although New York State had 32 savings banks by 1853, none of them was in a small village like Tarrytown.

After careful planning, the Westchester County Savings Bank, today known as Peoples Westchester Savings Bank, became a reality. On the evening of September 10, 1853, the Bank opened for business in the front of a small hat shop in Tarrytown, New York. The line that formed in Elias Mann's hat shop in the Bank's first hours included "seamstresses, clergymen, sash makers, masons, blacksmiths"—77 people in all, most of them of humble means. That first evening the bank accepted $814 in deposits.

At the time the institution opened, Franklin Pierce had just become presi-

The present corporate headquarters of Peoples Westchester Savings Bank at 3 Skyline Drive in Hawthorne. Today, with a network of 26 offices, the Bank holds assets of $1.5 billion.

The cover of an old bank book from Westchester County Savings Bank.

dent of the United States, and an Illinois lawyer named Abraham Lincoln had just served one term in Congress. The lower Hudson Valley had been connected with New York City by railroad in 1849: Tarrytown was at the end of the line, which opened up all kinds of opportunities for trade. Before that time trade had been largely dependent on horses and river steamers. America was in the midst of a new era of expansion and prosperity, and the leaders of Westchester County were not about to be left behind. They had resolved that a savings bank was needed to meet the growing needs of the community.

The Bank had a total of 23 original founders, among whom were some very distinguished members. Many belonged to families that had lived in Westchester County for years, and several were New York City businessmen who made their homes in Tarrytown. Perhaps the most well-known founder was celebrated writer Washington

Irving, who was living at Sunnyside, his beautiful home on the Hudson River in Tarrytown. Irving was working on his five-volume biography of George Washington when the Bank was founded, and he served as a trustee from 1853 until his death in 1859. Other founders included George D. Morgan, brother of J.P. Morgan and son of one of the first of America's great bankers, J.S. Morgan, and General James Watson Webb, the editor of the *New York Courier and Inquirer,* who had an estate in Mount Pleasant. Nathaniel B. Holmes, who became the Bank's first president, was a businessman and one of the founders and officers of Christ Church.

While the founders of the Bank were intent upon providing the area with a means for growth, they were equally concerned with helping people of modest means who had no place to safeguard their funds. Many of the first depositors were immigrants whose assets were too meager to merit the notice of commercial banks. The founders expressed their reasons for forming the institution by inscribing this statement in the first bankbooks that were printed: "To provide a safe and advantageous deposit for the surplus earnings of the farmer, mechanic, laborer, domestic, and others who may find a serious delay and inconvenience and even great risk in making investments of small sums in the usual manner."

By the end of its first year, the Bank reported deposits of $25,558. Encouraged by this healthy growth, the trustees rented two "banking rooms" adjacent to the hat store. Growth continued in spite of the Civil War, and in 1864 Westchester County Savings Bank settled into new offices in Tarrytown, at the corner of Turnpike Road (now Route 9) and Main Street. Today that site houses Peoples Westchester's Tarrytown office.

Gradually the towns and villages of Westchester County grew. More and more wealthy New Yorkers built homes there, and by the 1890s it was said jokingly in Tarrytown that "one couldn't throw a stone without hitting a millionaire." John D. Rockefeller, Sr., purchased land at Pocantico Hills in 1893 and built a magnificent estate. General Howard Carroll built a magnificent replica of a medieval Norman castle atop a hill at Benedict Avenue in Tarrytown. Other millionaires arrived as well, and some of them commuted to New York by their own yachts.

This influx brought increased local trade and helped increase accounts at the Westchester County Savings Bank. Meanwhile, industry also came into the area. In 1899 John Brisben Walker and Amzi Barber began making steam automobiles at a small factory on Kingsland Point in North Tarrytown. After

being acquired by the Maxwell-Briscoe Company in 1903, the factory was later purchased by General Motors, and today it is one of GM's most important plants.

At the turn of the century the Bank had outgrown its frame house, and in 1898 it built a new building. Settled there as the twentieth century opened, on January 1, 1900, the Bank reported deposits of more than $2 million, in more than 4,500 accounts. The vast majority contained modest savings from $5 to $500.

Real estate loans granted by the Bank in the early 1900s became instrumental in the development of Westchester County as it exists today. Westchester County Savings Bank participated in many local lending programs for public works, enhancing the development of the county's various communities.

By World War I the Bank's total resources were approaching $5 million. Deposits began to reflect the trend of American families toward mutual savings banks for safeguarding funds. The stock market crash of 1929 and the ensuing Depression gave proof that market speculation was undependable and that savings were safe in a bank paying a reasonable return. In fact, between 1929 and 1933, when more than 9,000 banks failed, Westchester County Savings Bank had the largest surplus in relation to deposits of any bank in New York State. It shared its good fortune with its depositors, paying them an extra dividend of 8 percent. Moreover, throughout its entire history the bank has never failed to pay its depositors a semiannual dividend.

When the United States entered World War I, the Bank helped raise funds by buying liberty bonds. During

Growth continued even throughout the Civil War, and Westchester County Savings Bank settled into new offices in Tarrytown at the corner of Turnpike Road (now Route 9) and Main Street. The old frame house pictured here served as the Bank headquarters from 1864 until 1898. Today the site houses Peoples Westchester's Tarrytown office.

Westchester County Savings Bank, the predecessor of Peoples Westchester Savings Bank, opened for business in 1853 in front of a small hat shop in Tarrytown. Shown here are the original bylaws of the Bank, printed in 1853. Among the 23 founders were Washington Irving, author of the well-known story The Legend of Sleepy Hollow, and George D. Morgan, a member of the prominent Morgan banking family.

World War II the Bank urged depositors to use their savings to buy war bonds. The Tarrytown *Daily News* editorialized on April 30, 1943: "The Westchester County Savings Bank, that old Rock of Gibraltar of banking institutions, made a handsome contribution to our war bond drive. It invested $1.7 million in war bonds. The Bank's purchase put Tarrytown over the top by more than 100 percent."

During its first 100 years the Bank had seven presidents. Succeeding

Nathaniel B. Holmes was Nathaniel Bayles, a leading citizen of Tarrytown whose cooperation was sought for the Village's most important developments. Frank Vincent, who became the third president in 1864, had served as a trustee since 1860. Benson Ferris, Jr., president for 20 years beginning in 1879, was prominent in community activities and, in his will, left a substantial sum to create the Young Men's Lyceum Library. Under the long presidency of Isaac Requa, from 1899 to 1933, deposits tripled, and the surplus of the bank increased nearly tenfold. His son, Isaac Requa, Jr., was president from 1833 to 1939. The Bank then came under the presidency of Arthur I. Davidson. Today Peoples Westchester is headed by William F. Olson, the Bank's Chairman, President, and Chief Executive Officer.

In 1939 Savings Bank Life Insurance was authorized in New York State. Since then SBLI has grown to more than $11 billion in sales of policies, making it a major producer of individual policies in the state. The Peoples Westchester Savings Bank's Life Insurance Department, established in 1975, and its offices are staffed by specialists who have passed the same licensing examination required of all other life insurance salespeople in New York State.

The Bank continued to grow through the 1950s and 1960s as Americans continued to choose mutual savings banks to safeguard their funds. But it was during the 1970s that the institution took the steps that led to its enormous growth and to its becoming the Peoples Westchester Savings Bank.

This growth largely was achieved through mergers with a number of local thrift institutions. In 1971 The Bank for Savings of Ossining, chartered in 1854 as the Sing Sing Savings Bank, was merged into Westchester County Savings Bank. In 1975 came the merger with the Tuckahoe Savings and Loan Association, a bank that had been incorporated in 1890. In 1977 Peoples

Tarrytown, the bank's home base, is exquisitely interpreted by Benson J. Loosing in 1860. This woodcut of a view of Tarrytown and the picturesque Hudson River is entitled, "Distant View of Tarrytown."

Savings Bank of Yonkers merged into the institution, expanding the market area in the southwestern portion of Westchester. It was after this acquisition that Westchester County Savings Bank became known as Peoples Westchester Savings Bank.

Still more mergers and acquisitions were in store. In 1979 Westchester County Savings and Loan Association, chartered in 1920, merged into Peoples Westchester, adding three new branches in Croton, Ossining, and Thornwood. That same year a decision was made to move the Bank's executive headquarters to the Mid-Westchester Executive Park in Hawthorne, New York, and consolidate all operational and staff functions at that location. By 1979, after four mergers, the Bank's assets reached more than $860 million, and it had expanded to 17 branches throughout Westchester County.

As the Bank entered the 1980s still another acquisition was in store. January 1, 1982, was the consummation date of the triple merger with Peekskill and Greenburgh Savings Banks, whose original incorporation dates were 1859 and 1869, respectively.

During this period many savings banks in the United States were facing trying times. Savings rates were the lowest in history, money market funds (which preceded Money Market Accounts) were causing a massive outflow of funds from savings banks, and there was increased inflation in rates paid on deposits. With the rise in interest rates caused by deregulation, savings banks had to pay more on deposits than they were taking in on mortgages and bonds.

In the early 1980s, through deregulation and changes in state and federal laws, Peoples Westchester was given new powers to diversify and expand. The Bank began offering expanded services such as VISA Debit Cards, Auto Loans, Commercial Loans, Personal Loans, and Corporate Checking Accounts, enabling it to compete more effectively with other financial institutions. However, in order to fully exploit these new opportunities in a meaningful way, the Bank needed capital.

Peoples Westchester had been a mutual institution—a bank owned by the depositors—though depositors had no voting rights and could not receive income from their ownership except in the form of interest on their savings. As a mutual institution, the only way a savings bank could add to capital was through retained earnings—the amount left after expenses are subtracted from revenues. In a stock form of ownership, the Bank can raise capital through retained earnings and by selling stock.

So, in order to raise needed capital and compete effectively, on December 17, 1985, the trustees voted unanimously to convert the bank to a stock form of ownership. On June 13, 1986, following a highly successful subscription and community offering, the Bank's conversion to a publicly traded thrift took place.

Conversion to a publicly held bank

The Tarrytown office of Peoples Westchester Savings Bank as it exists today. The edifice was built in 1898 and has been designated as a historical landmark.

was the most significant step in the institution's long history. The increased capital substantially enabled Peoples Westchester to further expand its real estate, consumer, and commercial lending services, as well as retail services.

Today Peoples Westchester Savings Bank has evolved into a competitive regional bank with headquarters based in Westchester County. It is a dominant financial institution in the county, and continues the tradition of being closely allied with the community. With a current network of 26 offices, the Bank holds assets of $1.5 billion. From its traditional base of mortgages and saving accounts, the Bank's expanded services now include Individual Checking, Business Checking and Money Market Accounts, 19 Automated Teller Machines, Pension Services, Savings Bank Life Insurance, Education Loans, Consumer Loans, and Commercial Loans. Peoples Westchester Savings Bank is also a member of the NYCE 24-Hour Banking Network of 24-hour banking machines.

LAWLER, MATUSKY & SKELLY ENGINEERS

Based in New York State since its founding in 1965, Lawler, Matusky & Skelly Engineers (LMS) provides environmental science and engineering consulting services, from the original concept through project construction.

The firm was founded in New York City by partners Thomas P. Quirk, John P. Lawler, and Felix E. Matusky, and its offices were located first at 50 Church Street and later at 505 Fifth Avenue. In 1971 LMS moved to Rockland County, where it has since remained, with offices in Pearl River and a laboratory in Nyack. The company has used the name Lawler, Matusky & Skelly Engineers since 1974.

Since its early days in 1965 the operation has seen its staff grow from five to more than 165. Its revenues have also skyrocketed, from $150,000 to approximately $10 million. In 1970, only five years after its founding, LMS was already ranked within *Engineering News-Record's* top 500 engineering firms. The organization has retained this distinction every year since.

LMS has helped government and industry to protect the quality of New York State's environment. In addition, it has provided ample, safe water supplies from ground and surface sources

Lawler, Matusky & Skelly Engineers take samples of the Hudson River. The firm has completed many varied ecological projects concerning the Hudson River; it has evaluated the movement and levels of contaminants in the Hudson, designed and tested devices to protect the fishery, and designed facilities to reduce or eliminate pollutant discharge to the river.

The City of Glens Falls water-pollution-control plant.

to meet the state's growing water needs. The company has conducted more than 500 environmental investigations involving measurement and analysis of the chemical, physical, and biological quality of New York State's major water bodies and tributaries, including the Hudson River, Lake Erie, Lake Ontario, Lake George, Lake Champlain, the Finger Lakes, Long Island Sound, and New York Harbor.

On the Hudson River, for example, LMS has completed a variety of important projects. The firm has evaluated the movement and levels of contaminants in the Hudson by using mathematical and physical modeling techniques, has designed and tested devices to protect the fishery, and has designed facilities to reduce or eliminate pollutant discharge to the river.

Combating the hazardous waste problem, LMS conducts investigations throughout New York State to determine the source and extent of the problem, and designs measures to correct it. LMS has also designed wastewater-

treatment facilities for private and municipal clients throughout New York, the most recent being a secondary wastewater-treatment plant for the City of Glens Falls.

Since its inception LMS has also helped the electric power industry to study the environmental effects of electric generating facilities—fossil, hydro, and nuclear. LMS also develops alternatives to mitigate negative environmental impacts found in those studies. The firm has been retained by all of the major electric utilities in New York State, and it has conducted studies at more than 25 generating plants in New York.

Over the years LMS has become a company whose environmental engineering expertise is depended upon both by government and by New York State's corporate giants. The many major clients that LMS serves in New York include IBM, General Electric Co., General Motors, Consolidated Edison, and Harris Corporation, as well as government groups such as the state's Department of Environmental Conservation, the City of Glens Falls, and the City of New York.

BANKERS TRUST COMPANY

Bankers Trust Company, with headquarters in New York City, was founded in 1903 as a trust company and became a commercial bank in 1917. The institution continued to grow and prosper through the years, and in the early 1980s it launched a radical departure from its traditional commercial banking activities. At that time Bankers Trust sold off its retail banking network of 100 branches and redirected its resources toward merchant

Today Bankers Trust has become universally recognized as a major force in the domestic and international marketplace.

trepreneurial spirit of an investment bank.

As part of its merchant banking strategy, Bankers Trust has been organized into two principal units. Financial Services brings together the institution's principal credit and financing arms: commercial lending, investment banking, and money and securities markets activities. PROFITCo comprises the bank's trust, investment management, securities processing, cash management, and private banking businesses.

The success of Bankers Trust's move into merchant banking has been

Charles S. Sanford, Jr., chairman of Bankers Trust Company.

banking, focusing its businesses on major corporations, financial institutions, and governments.

Today Bankers Trust has become universally recognized as a major force in the domestic and international marketplace as a worldwide merchant bank—an institution combining the lending capability and noncredit services of a commercial bank with the intermediary skills, flexibility, and en-

demonstrated by the bank's strong earnings performance over the past several years. When the Bankers Trust merchant banking strategy began to take form in 1979, net income stood at $114 million. By 1986 net income had nearly quadrupled, reaching $428 million. As well, the institution is one of the most profitable major banks in the nation, based on return on equity of 16.30 and return on assets of .79.

In its relatively new role as a worldwide merchant bank, Bankers Trust has gained a good reputation for analyzing deals quickly and for committing a large amount of its own financing, while also assuming the job of enlisting others to complete the financing package. In this way in a very short period of time the institution has become a leading banker for many of the world's top national and multinational companies. And the bank's chairman, Charles S. Sanford, Jr., has become one of the leading figures in the world banking industry.

With the sale of its retail branch network, Bankers Trust now has six private banking centers in the New York metropolitan area, in addition to its headquarters and operations center. With its current facilities the bank continues to be a vital employer in New York City and New York State, with a statewide staff of about 8,000. Bankers Trust also maintains representative offices and subsidiaries in major cities throughout the United States. Overseas Bankers Trust, which has become an active participant in the Eurodollar markets, has an international network of branches, representative offices, and subsidiaries in more than 35 countries.

PFIZER, INC.

In 1849 two young emigrants from Germany—Charles Pfizer, a chemist, and Charles Ehrhart, a confectioner—formed a partnership in Brooklyn, New York, to make fine chemicals. This was the start of Pfizer, Inc., today a worldwide corporation active in health care, agriculture, specialty chemicals, materials sciences, and consumer products, employing some 40,000 people.

For most of its first 100 years Pfizer moved at a modest pace, manufacturing and selling fine chemicals in bulk to processors and packagers whose labels went on the final products. During World War II the U.S. government enlisted Pfizer in a program to develop penicillin. The company's expertise in using large-scale fermentation technology, which it had pioneered for the production of citric acid, was the key factor in Pfizer's breakthrough in penicillin production. Pfizer penicillin ac-

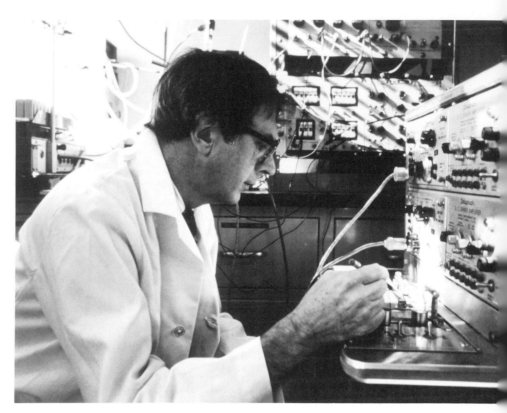

A medicinal research pilot plant at Pfizer's central research facilities in Groton, Connecticut.

companied Allied troops onto the beaches of Normandy in 1944, and when penicillin was released for civilian use in 1946, Pfizer was producing 85 percent of the nation's supply.

As the firm entered its second century in 1949, three decisions dramatically reshaped its future. The decision to market its new science-based discoveries under its own label created a worldwide manufacturing and marketing organization, and it began applying its expertise in antibiotics to improve animal health, thus inceasing food productivity for a hungry world.

In 1949, following a worldwide soil-screening program, Pfizer scientists discovered a new antibiotic trademarked Terramycin that was able to successfully treat more than 100 diseases. In 1950 the company established an Antibiotics Division—the forerunner of Pfizer Laboratories—to introduce this new discovery under its own label. Pfizer had thus paved its entry into pharmaceutical marketing.

Next Pfizer moved abroad, establishing foreign trade subsidiaries (now

Dr. Jay Constantine analyzed pharmacological data as part of a study of presynaptic alpha-adrenoceptors. Dr. Constantine was one of the principal researchers in the discovery programs that led to prazosin and, currently, trimazosin.

Pfizer International) in 1951. Within a few years Pfizer had higher sales abroad than any other American-based pharmaceutical company. In 1952 it moved full scale into the animal health field by establishing the Agricultural Division.

Thus, in the three years after its 100th anniversary, Pfizer launched a new era. By the end of the 1950s the firm had developed a broad line of antibiotics and other drugs to treat a wide range of illnesses. During the 1960s it broadened its bases through a number of acquisitions. By the end of the decade Pfizer had grown tremendously in the pharmaceutical, agricultural, and specialty chemicals fields and had boosted its interest in consumer and materials science products.

In the 1970s Pfizer greatly increased its outlays, spending nearly $2

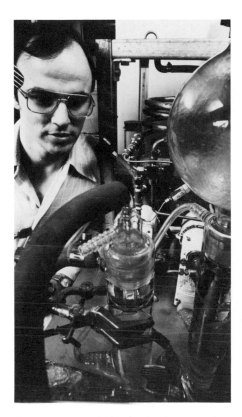

Progress was made in the development of an antiscalant agent, Flocon, for application in desalination plants. Extensive field trials were conducted in the Caribbean and Middle East with favorable results. Research on Flocon is under way at Pfizer's Central Research campus in Groton, Connecticut.

billion on research and development and new facilities. This helped produce such major new pharmaceuticals as the antihypertensive Minipress and the antiarthritic agent Feldene, as well as antibiotics Geopen and Geocillin. Numerous new animal health and nutrition products were also introduced, and Pfizer entered new fields such as recombinant DNA, plant genetics, and magnetic particle technology. As Pfizer entered the 1980s its expanded capabilities spawned many new licensed products, such as Procardia, an agent for the treatment of angina; Cefobid, a third-generation injectable cephalosporin antibiotic; and Spectrobid/Bacacil, a broad spectrum semisynthetic penicillin.

Today Pfizer has a diversified line of products serving health care professionals, farmers, consumers, and industrial organizations worldwide. Its products are present in more than 140 countries, from developing nations to highly industrialized ones. The company's businesses are grouped into the five categories of health care, agriculture, specialty chemicals, materials science, and consumer products.

In health care Pfizer makes five major categories of pharmaceuticals: antibiotics, anti-inflammatories, central nervous system agents, cardiovascular medicine, and antidiabetic agents. Pfizer Hospital Products is a leader in artificial joint implants and surgical equipment, while the company's Shiley operation makes implantable heart valves and blood oxygenators used in coronary bypass surgery.

In agriculture Pfizer provides animal health products, antibiotic and vitamin feed supplements, and agricultural genetics products including hybrids of corn.

In specialty chemicals Pfizer makes bulk chemicals—such as vitamins, food bulking agents, acidulants, and preservatives—for the food, beverage, pharmaceutical, and chemical industries.

The firm's materials science operations help production in the steel, coatings, plastics, chemicals, and electronics industries, among others.

In the consumer sector Pfizer boasts the Leeming/Pacquin line—with such products as Visine eye drops, Desitin skin care lotions, Ben-Gay pain relief ointment, and Unisom sleep aid—and the Coty line of fragrances and cosmetics. Other consumer products include dietary foods, nonprescription drug products, and household items and beauty aids.

From its headquarters in New York City, Pfizer oversees a worldwide network of research and production facilities. The company has production facilities at 116 locations in 42 countries, along with major pharmaceutical research centers in the United States, the United Kingdom, Germany, France, and Japan.

Today Pfizer is a global company, but its roots in New York City—and therefore, New York State—run deep. During the 1970s, when other corporations were relocating, Pfizer chose to keep its headquarters in Manhattan. The firm's plant in the East Williamsburg section of Brooklyn is where Pfizer was born in 1849. Not many multinational corporations based in New York City can boast such a direct local link to their past. At its height the Brooklyn plant employed some 2,000 workers, and it was the only Pfizer plant until the end of World War II, when the company began expanding. The plant still employs 700 people in pharmaceutical production, and there are third-generation Pfizer employees working there. Pfizer recently announced plans to join with the City of New York and other groups to help revitalize the neighborhood surrounding the plant.

Conducting cardiovascular research, these doctors are employing computer models of the complex kidney enzyme renin in the search for inhibitors as potential antihypertensive agents.

NORTH AMERICAN INSTRUMENT CORPORATION

Phillip H. Morse, a 1964 graduate of the University of Maine, was an energetic young salesman for the United States Catheter and Instrument Corporation. During his time with that firm, Morse developed his intimate, hands-on knowledge of the emergent special procedures market, his curiosity and creativity aroused by the particular problems of communicating with key members of the medical community in a sales territory that included seven midwestern states. By observation of, and occasional participation in, procedures, Morse rapidly increased his knowledge of angiographic techniques.

One thing he noted was that contemporary valve systems then employed in angiography were composed of reusable metal manifolds and stopcocks. Morse realized that this metal fluid-control system prohibited observation of the system at work, blocking possible sighting of air bubbles or foreign matter. Morse knew that physicians could not be totally certain that potentially lethal air bubbles were not in the system before injection.

Morse began development of a new system he envisioned as safer in that it would be totally transparent. This feature would reduce the possibility of injecting air bubbles into patients, since it permitted the doctor to fully see if bubbles were in fact present. Fifteen months after providing his employer with drawings and a prototype of his device, Morse was officially notified that the company was not interested in developing his idea of a transparent system. Morse, completely convinced of the worth of his idea, resigned his position and founded North American Instrument Corporation (NAMIC®) in May 1969.

Renting an uncomfortable, drafty, 300-square-foot office space on the second floor of the Colvin Building in downtown Glens Falls, Morse began to develop his transparent manifold system. His persistence and dedication overcame myriad obstacles, and by the autumn of 1970 the Morse Manifold® system was being evaluated at Albany Medical Center by Dr. Julio A. Sosa. The evaluations were unilaterally successful, and North American Instrument Corporation soon had to move into a space more than five times larger in Hudson Falls, New York.

Between 1972 and 1975 the progress of the new corporation was noteworthy; continued improvements of the Morse Manifold System were suggested by physicians and integrated into the design. Outside firms were contracted to add the improvements, with the company conducting final assembly and quality control. In order to streamline production of the system, North American Instrument Corporation acquired its subcontractor, Glens Falls Precision Machine, ensuring

Phillip H. Morse, inventor and developer of the Morse Manifold System, built a one-man company into a firm employing more than 325 persons in three facilities totaling 90,000 square feet. Photo by Chase Photography

North American Instrument Corporation's corporate headquarters is on Pruyn's Island on the Hudson River in Glens Falls, New York. Constructed in 1984, it is a 60,000-square-foot facility. Photo by Richard K. Dean

complete, closely monitored quality control.

After his first year of operation, Morse remained his firm's sole associate, a one-man operation rationing his time among sales, assembly, shipping, and bookkeeping. By 1975 North American Instrument Corporation included seven full-time associates, two of them salesmen. The company purchased the building it had been renting and expanded to 11,000 square feet. All the while Morse's firm continued to refine and enhance the Morse Manifold System. The organization increased its direct sales force to five, so that by 1979 it was estimated that the

reusable Morse Manifold was employed in 8 out of every 10 cardiac catheterizations performed in the United States.

When sales exceeded the million-dollar mark, Morse's corporation was in a stable position and was able to undertake a new round of product development. Morse began to evolve a system he had conceived as early as 1971, a disposable version of his highly successful reusable Morse Manifold System. This new project necessitated acquisition of new technologies, and during development of the disposable system countless obstacles were overcome. In 1981 North American Instrument Corporation introduced the disposable Morse Manifold, which was an instant success due to its quality, convenience, and ease of use. Morse's firm increased its number of associates to more than 70, and NAMIC began

to rent additional space in the Glens Falls/Hudson Falls area to house its increased work force.

A sales force of 10 introduced a second-generation disposable Morse Manifold System in 1984. The total success of NAMIC's various product lines forced the firm to commence an ambitious program of expansion. By the autumn of 1983 NAMIC was moved into a new, 16,000-square-foot molding plant. A year later NAMIC's assembly plant and corporate headquarters were relocated into an impressive, new 60,000-square-foot facility on Pruyn's Island on the Hudson River in Glens Falls. By the middle of 1987 Phillip H. Morse's good idea and initiative had produced a corporation with a domestic sales force of 23, more than 325 associates, and three facilities totaling more than 90,000 square feet—an Upstate New York success story.

MERRILL LYNCH & CO., INC.

In 1907 Charles Edward Merrill, the 22-year-old son of a small-town Florida doctor, arrived in New York City to work in the financial office of a textile firm. Merrill soon met Edmund Calvert Lynch, a Johns Hopkins graduate then selling soda fountain equipment. The two men formed a lifelong friendship that would lead to the foundation of Merrill Lynch & Co., Inc.

In 1909 Charles Merrill moved over to George H. Burr & Co., a commercial paper house, and he persuaded Lynch to work for him there. In

Current chairman and chief executive officer William A. Schreyer (left) and president and chief operating officer Daniel P. Tully of Merrill Lynch & Co., Inc.

1914 Merrill set out on his own as Charles E. Merrill & Co., and he soon talked Lynch into joining him there as well. In 1915 the firm's name became Merrill, Lynch & Co. Legend has it that the printer forgot the comma between Merrill and Lynch on an early stationery order, and the cost-conscious company briefly used Merrill Lynch as a title. In 1938, after Eddie Lynch's death, the now-famous commaless name became permanent.

The new firm sought to attract investors beyond the social and economic elite served by old-line houses. This focus on the average investor became the core of the Merrill Lynch philosophy. The company specialized in underwriting new securities for growing businesses. It raised funds for the newly emerging chain store industry, and through the 1920s it presented the investing public with a long catalog of budding retail enterprises, along with companies in other new growth areas such as automotive, movies, and oil.

Charles Merrill was one of the few financiers to warn of the coming storm. Thanks to his prescience, the company trimmed its sails sufficiently to absorb the 1929 buffeting. But Merrill still foresaw a prolonged bleak period for Wall Street, and he withdrew from the retail business to concentrate on investment banking. In early 1930 he arranged for the sale of the firm's retail business to E.A. Pierce & Company. Most Merrill Lynch employees and partners were transferred to Pierce.

E.A. Pierce, which started in 1885 as the Stock Exchange firm of Burrill & Housman, thus became Merrill Lynch's other main root. By 1930 managing partner Edward Allen Pierce had built it into the country's largest "wire house"—a securities broker with nationwide branches connected by private wire.

In the 1930s Pierce was a leader in the movement to reform the securities industry. His company survived the

Charles E. Merrill (left), directing partner, and Winthrop H. Smith (right), managing partner, are seen in this early 1950s photo working on the balcony of Merrill's Manhattan apartment (the Queensboro Bridge is in the background). It was Smith who persuaded Charles Merrill to come back to "the Street" in the 1940s, founding the modern firm and, in effect, the modern version of the securities business.

troubled decade, but there was growing doubt that enough partners would agree to renew the partnership agreement when it expired at the end of 1939.

At that point, Winthrop Hiram Smith—who had come to Pierce with the transfer of the Merrill Lynch retail business and was then managing Pierce's Chicago office—persuaded Charles Merrill to return to the securities business. Merrill decided to make a go of creating a "department store of finance," one that would "bring Wall Street to Main Street." On April 1, 1940, the new firm was ready for busi-

ness as Merrill Lynch, E.A. Pierce & Cassatt. The Cassatt name represented an old-line Philadelphia firm whose business had been absorbed by Pierce and Merrill during the 1930s.

Merrill Lynch's pitch to the average investor quickly drew nationwide attention, and by the end of 1940 more than 12,000 new accounts were opened, boosting total customers to 50,000. In 1941 the firm became Merrill Lynch, Pierce, Fenner & Beane. Charles E. Fenner had founded Fenner & Solari in New Orleans in 1905 and was later joined by Alpheus C. Beane, Sr. Originally a cotton house, Fenner & Beane had developed into the nation's second-largest wire house, after Pierce, and was first in commodities trading. The merger strengthened Merrill Lynch in

---

Chairman Donald T. Regan (later Secretary of the Treasury and Chief of Staff to President Ronald Reagan) and president Ned B. Ball watch the opening announcement of the listing of Merrill Lynch stock on the New York Stock Exchange in July 1971.

the important commodities area.

In 1943 Charles Merrill had a severe heart attack and thereafter returned to his office only on a few occasions. However, he remained actively involved in the company right up to his death in 1956, keeping an eye on details through memorandums, telephone calls, and conferences. Meanwhile Winthrop Smith, who had helped coax Merrill back into the retail securities business, took over day-to-day operations as managing partner.

In early 1958 Alpheus C. Beane, Jr., son of the late co-founder of Fenner & Beane, withdrew from the firm. The partners then decided to honor Winthrop Smith's enormous contributions to the firm by changing the company name to Merrill Lynch, Pierce, Fenner & Smith in early 1958.

Merrill Lynch had started with 31 general partners in 1940, and by 1958 it had 71. With the Stock Exchange now allowing member firms to incorporate, the company added an "Inc." to its name in 1959. By 1970 it had 1,400 employee stockholders. Then, in 1971, it was able to invite the general public in as stockholders, providing a welcome source of expansion capital, and Merrill Lynch became the first Big Board member firm to have its stock listed on the Exchange. A holding company, Merrill Lynch & Co., Inc., was established in 1973, permitting greater organizational flexibility.

Maintaining its leadership in serving individual investors through its network of some 500 branch offices and with such innovative products as its

The Teleport, the world's first satellite communications center and "intelligent" commercial park, is located on Staten Island. Merrill Lynch is a major sponsor of this facility in its determination to develop the finest telecommunications and information-processing facilities in the financial services industry.

Cash Management Account® (CMA®) financial service, Merrill Lynch has also developed into a top tier capital markets firm and a pioneer in the globalization of the financial markets. It has also moved into insurance services and, through an affiliate, currently provides various real estate services.

With nearly 5 million individual, business, institutional, and governmental clients in 30 countries, Merrill Lynch is prominent in all areas of investment banking, including mergers and acquisitions; as a market maker in corporate, U.S. government, and municipal securities; and as a manager of mutual funds with assets totaling some $80 billion.

Long the leader in municipal financings, Merrill Lynch has been especially active in its home state. It has been senior manager for New York State and numerous transportation, housing, health, urban development, and energy agencies and projects. It worked with New York City during its mid-1970s financial crisis and managed its initial market reentry in 1979. All told, Merrill Lynch & Co., Inc., has raised $78 billion through nearly 1,000 issues for New York State, its counties, cities, agencies, and authorities over the past three decades.

FERREE PLASTICS, INC.

When Charles M. Ferree, still in his late teens, found himself a job running a machine in a plastic molding factory in Erie, Pennsylvania, he didn't quite realize what he was getting into. Like the other jobs he had worked—pumping gas and other traditional tasks—Ferree just viewed the work as a means to a paycheck. Five decades later the Ferree name is synonymous with plastics to folks in Lockport, located some 20 miles northeast of Buffalo in Niagara County.

That's because Ferree Plastics, Inc., the company founded by Ferree, who died in 1977, and now run by his two sons, is one of the community's biggest employers. The firm records annual gross sales of more than $10 million and is still expanding, something of a departure in a county that has hit upon hard economic times in recent years. Founded as a small family operation for the "minting" of plastic bingo chips, today's version of the company has about 275 employees and manufactures plastic parts for a wide spectrum of industries, ranging from medical to automotive to computers.

With the use of molded plastic parts continuing to boom in American industry, Ferree president Charles M. Ferree, Jr., sees only better times ahead. "My father had a vision. He could see plastics was the coming thing. But I don't think he ever realized how big it was going to get," says Ferree with a smile. He and his brother, vice-president William H. Ferree, recently announced plans for expansion of the firm's new facility in Newfane that will add another 60,000-square-foot manufacturing building and hopefully increase employment by 100 percent over the next two years.

The good times are a far cry from the days when the Ferrees lost almost everything they had in a devastating 1960 fire. "We lost almost all our machinery and didn't have enough insurance to cover our debts," Ferree recalls.

Charles Ferree, Sr., founder of Ferree Plastics, at his desk in 1947.

"But we started from the ground up, worked 12, sometimes 18 hours a day. I like to say that we rose up like a phoenix from the wreckage."

Ferree credits his father as the man most responsible for the success of the company. Born in Erie, Pennsylvania, Charles Ferree, Sr., was remembered by his family as an intelligent man who had read and seen enough to know that plastics was an industry of the future. Invented in 1869 by American printer John Wesley Hyatt, plastics did not really come into widespread use until World War II. When Ferree took his job at the Erie plant, the plastics boom was just beginning in America. Their use was still largely a curiosity.

After taking the factory job in Erie, Ferree's interest in the field grew. He worked his way through the ranks in the company and then came to Buffalo, accepting a job as a foreman for the old Sterling Molders Inc. plant. Fascinated by the possibilities of plastics, he worked his way through the ranks of that organization and bought into it as a partner. "Sterling Molders was a pioneer in the plastic injection molding field," claims Charles Ferree, Jr. "My father was proud to be in on the ground floor. He was instrumental in getting the company involved in the manufacturing of plastic steering wheels, plastic spoons and forks, plastic dishes, plastic parts for Wurlitzer music boxes, and plastic piano keys. They were innovators in making electronic resisters, cases for electrical parts, boat parts, cups. The field was beginning to expand."

Sterling moved all of its operations from Buffalo to Lockport in 1952. The company grew to a 150-worker operation with 22 molding machines by the late 1950s. The times were prosperous enough that the Ferree family began its own offshoot company, making only bingo chips, in 1959. But then disaster struck. The November 1960 fire razed the Sterling plant, leaving only four workable machines. Ferree and his sons pooled their money to buy the machines and the property from the other partners, and began operating as Ferree Plastics, Inc., two months after the fire.

"We had about a dozen employees, so we took our shifts at the machines with everyone else," Charles Ferree, Jr., recalls. "We got greasy and grimy like the rest of the workers. I never wore a suit to work until 10 years ago." After "about five very bad years," the business began to take off, Ferree says. At first specializing in the simplest manufacturing—making such items as combs, brushes, and shrink packaging—Ferree Plastics began to branch out with products that were more varied and precise. Today the company serves about 100 customers, making parts for a myriad of industries. The line of Ferree products ranges in size from a tiny guard for a hypodermic needle to the liner for a walk-in business safe. The firm manufactures many automotive parts for the Lockport Har-

rison Radiator Division plant, as well as parts for computers, toys, electrical appliances, cash registers, gardening equipment, and farm equipment.

The phrase "custom injection molding" best describes what Ferree Plastics does today, says Charles Ferree, Jr. "We sell a service," he explains. "The customer tells me what part he wants and gives me a blueprint. We make the part to his specifications. It's a long way from the days when we made combs. Now we make precision gears that have to fit just exactly right. We're also making assemblies—several parts that fit together—for more and more of our customers." The firm's engineering expertise allows it not only to follow customer blueprints but also to assist customers in solving problems

Charles M. Ferree, Jr., current president of Ferree Plastics, Inc.

and improving product design.

Ferree is excited about the future of the plastics industry and what that holds for his firm. Already ingrained in almost every fabric of American life, the versatile, man-made material is being used in more and more products. The plastic soft drink can has recently been designed and test marketed. Several cars with plastic bodies are already being sold in the United States. Plastic engine parts are being designed, and one chemical company, Du Pont, is expecting the need for plastic auto parts to increase by 400 percent by the year 2000.

"When my father first got into the business, maybe one percent of the automobile parts were plastic. Now 60 percent of the parts on some cars are plastic," Ferree points out.

He adds that Charles Ferree, Sr., would probably have been pleasantly surprised.

The Indian Point 2 nuclear power plant, in Buchanan, New York, is Consolidated Edison's most economical source of electricity. It has been serving the utility's customers since 1974.

CONSOLIDATED EDISON COMPANY OF NEW YORK, INC.

Today's Con Edison is the product of acquisitions, dissolutions, and mergers of more than 170 electric, gas, and steam companies that once served New York City and Westchester County.

The Con Edison electric system dates back to the birth of electric service in America on September 4, 1882, when the Edison Electric Illuminating Company of New York began supplying electricity to a square-mile district in Lower Manhattan. All of the equipment that made this momentous event possible, from the dynamos to the underground conductors to the incandescent lamps, was invented by Thomas Alva Edison, built and installed under his close supervision.

Con Edison's steam system also traces its roots to a historic day,

March 3, 1882, when another corporate ancestor, New York Steam Company, began supplying its first customer, the United Bank at Broadway and Wall Street. The bank used steam to operate two elevators. By the end of 1882 New York Steam had 62 customers and had shown the world that district steam services were indeed practical.

But Con Edison's history goes back even further—to 1823, when its first corporate ancestor, the New York Gas Light Company, was chartered. Gas was used for both indoor and street lighting in those days, until the cleaner and safer electric lighting came into common use. In 1884 six gas companies, including New York Gas Light Company, were combined to form the Consolidated Gas Company of New York (Con Gas).

Over the years Con Gas acquired a controlling interest in the New York Steam Company, as well as a number of gas and electric firms. In 1936 the corporate name was changed to Con-

solidated Edison Company of New York, Inc., to reflect the fact that electricity had become the dominant part of the business.

Today Con Edison is the fourth-largest electricity company in the United States in terms of the number of customers served, providing electrical power to New York City and Westchester County. Its 660-square-mile service territory contains the most concentrated urban area in the nation.

As a natural gas distribution company, Con Edison is the 12th largest, as measured by the number of customers, serving more than one million. Con Edison's gas territory, smaller than its electric territory, includes most of Westchester County and the New York City boroughs of the Bronx, Manhattan, and part of Queens. As with electricity, one gas customer does not necessarily mean just one person. A customer could be a large family or a business or an apartment building with many families.

As a steam company, measured by sales volumes, Con Edison has the largest district steam system in the free world. The firm produces and sells the steam that heats and cools more than 2,000 commercial and apartment buildings in Manhattan south of 96th Street. More than 1.5 million people work or live in these buildings.

As an electricity company, gas company, and steam company, Consolidated Edison Company of New York, Inc., has evolved from its earliest days of innovation and experiment to today's vital supplier of energy for America's most populated urban area.

The dynamo room of Thomas A. Edison's electric generating station at 257 Pearl Street in Manhattan. This first successful electric generating station began serving customers on September 4, 1882, and was considered an engineering wonder in its day.

RELIABLE AUTOMATIC SPRINKLER CO., INC.

Reliable Automatic Sprinkler Co., Inc., is one of the world's largest producers of automatic fire sprinklers and sprinkler system control equipment.

Reliable is based in Mount Vernon, New York, where its major manufacturing and warehouse space is located. It also maintains sales and regional distribution centers in Dallas, Los Angeles, Atlanta, Chicago, and Philadelphia. Reliable ships products to more than 40 countries worldwide, with international sales conducted from its offices in London, England. The company employs a total work force of 400, with 375 employees located in Mount Vernon.

Reliable was founded in 1920 by Frank J. Fee, a mechanical contractor who began manufacturing sprinklers when he had trouble securing them for his own jobs. Frank J. Fee, Jr., succeeded his father as company president in 1945, and his son, Frank J. Fee III, became president in 1976. This puts Reliable today in its third generation of Fee family leadership. Also in the business with Frank Fee III are his two brothers: Kevin, who is executive vice-president, and Michael, vice-president/sales operations. The family-run company also has many employees who have served in excess of 25 years, enhancing its team-family tradition.

Today, with sales approaching $40 million, Reliable is an industry leader. The firm has two major product groups: automatic fire sprinklers and ancillary sprinkler system components. In the sprinkler area Reliable produces both of the industry's two basic types—the solder type and the frangible bulb—for virtually every type of building. Reliable also produces a broad range of valves that control water for sprinkler systems and actuate alarms.

Reliable's sales have tripled since 1980, and the company is planning to expand its facilities in the Westchester area. Reliable exports some 15 percent

Frank J. Fee, (left) president of The Reliable Automatic Sprinkler Company from 1920 to 1945, and Frank J. Fee, Jr., (right) president from 1945 to 1976.

of its annual sales, with exports going primarily to Canada, Western Europe, Australia, and Pacific Basin countries. The firm ships some products to Soviet Bloc countries—for example, it provided the sprinklers in Moscow's World Trade Center.

Until a few years ago only a small percentage of Reliable's sprinkler products were related to residential occupancies such as hotels and apartment buildings, with most products installed in shopping centers, high-rise buildings, industrial plants, hospitals, nursing homes, and other nonresidential sites. In recent years, however, fire safety awareness and new technology have opened up the residential market.

Reliable has always been an industry-minded company. Past president Frank Fee, Jr., attained many notable positions in the fire protection community, including chairman of the National Fire Protection Association. Frank J. Fee III is a member of the board of directors of the National Fire Protection Association and past chairman of the board of the National Fire Sprinkler Association. Kevin T. Fee is currently serving on the board of directors of the National Fire Sprinkler Association as vice-chairman.

The present executive management of Reliable Automatic Sprinkler Co., Inc., (from left) Kevin T. Fee, executive vice-president; Michael R. Fee, vice-president of sales and operations; and Frank J. Fee III, president.

JOHNSON & HIGGINS

Johnson & Higgins dates back to 1845, when its office at 90 Wall Street looked out upon the lofty sailing ships of New York's bustling, colorful South Street waterfront.

With its world headquarters currently at 125 Broad Street in New York, Johnson & Higgins has strayed only a few blocks from its first location. In every other aspect, however, the company has come a very long way indeed.

Johnson & Higgins has a tremendous share in New York City's rich maritime heritage, starting from the earliest days when its partners, Henry W. Johnson and A. Foster Higgins, conducted their insurance business along the New York waterfront.

The youthful partners—both then in their early twenties—quickly became recognized for their expertise in average adjusting, an aspect of insurance almost as old as the maritime trade itself. In a marine disaster if cargo has to be jettisoned in order to save a ship, the loss is "averaged" or shared by all those who hold interests in the cargo and the ship. The average adjuster's special skills and impartiality are used to determine the extent of the loss and apportion it fairly.

In the first years of their partnership, entrepreneurs Johnson and Higgins earned a reputation that encouraged shippers to call upon the firm to purchase marine insurance as well. By the time of the Civil War J&H was established enough to become commissioned by the Secretary of the Navy to survey the wreck of the Union gunboat *Varuna* off New Orleans.

Two decades later, in 1883, the firm opened its first branch office in San Francisco, followed in 1885 by an office in Philadelphia. By 1899, when the partnership was restructured as a corporation, Johnson & Higgins had established branch offices in seven U.S. cities, including Baltimore, Boston, Buffalo, Chicago, and New Orleans.

Meanwhile the J&H brokerage business was expanding to include fire, casualty, and other kinds of insurance.

The Johnson & Higgins reputation for professionalism was enormously enhanced early in the twentieth century by the efficiency with which it settled claims resulting from two world-famous disasters: the San Francisco

Johnson & Higgins expanded to include all kinds of insurance and employee benefits. The firm gained a formidable reputation in settling claims in such major disasters as the San Francisco Earthquake of 1906 and the sinking of the Titanic in 1912. Since then it has created a network of offices nationally and internationally but keeps its headquarters in New York at 125 Broad Street, only a few blocks from the company's original location.

Henry W. Johnson (left) and A. Foster Higgins (right) founded Johnson & Higgins, the oldest firm of insurance brokers in America.

Earthquake and fire of 1906, and the sinking of the *Titanic* in 1912. When World War I imperiled the nation's shipping, a senior J&H executive was named to the three-man advisory board of the Federal Bureau of War Risk Insurance.

Perhaps the company's harshest test occurred during the Great Depression of the 1930s, when insurance activity was severely curtailed by business stagnation. Johnson & Higgins weathered the crisis by stressing ingenuity and creativity in finding and providing insurance services. Equally remarkable, J&H kept its entire staff intact at a time when countless Americans were thrown out of work.

During World War II, when the federal government began to import strategic raw materials, leading marine insurance brokers were appointed to an insurance committee to provide the necessary coverages. Out of this group Johnson & Higgins was selected to act as the servicing broker. The firm's business expanded further during this pe-

Today Robert V. Hatcher, Jr., is chairman and chief executive officer of Johnson & Higgins.

riod as group insurance and pensions—previously a very small percentage of the nation's business payroll—took hold in the work place and developed quickly into the elaborate employee benefits programs that we know today.

The post-World War II business climate of acquisitions, conglomerates, and multinationals led to a period of unprecedented growth for Johnson & Higgins. During the 1950s and 1960s J&H opened a number of offices in North and South America, and created a network of offices and exclusive correspondent firms throughout the world. J&H soon became identified as a preeminent international insurance broker, a reputation that continues to grow.

Johnson & Higgins and its worldwide UNISON network currently employ some 13,000 people based in nearly 200 cities in more than 50 countries. J&H acts as insurance broker or employee benefit consultant for 75 of the 100 largest U.S. multinational corporations.

Today Johnson & Higgins serves companies worldwide, and it continues to expand its overseas operations. In the Pacific Rim, for example, the firm has set up offices in Japan, Taiwan, Hong Kong, Indonesia, Malaysia, Singapore, and the Philippines in the past two decades. With European direct investment in the United States up

30 percent in the past two years and direct investment from the Pacific Rim up almost 200 percent, Johnson & Higgins is increasingly working with foreign companies with operations in the United States.

For more than 140 years J&H has remained an independent, privately held organization. Its working directors—the firm's sole owners—continue to be actively involved and vitally concerned with serving a distinguished list of clients.

Although the clipper ships that plied the China trade in 1845 have long since given way to the space ships of the 1980s, J&H is still thriving. This fact

David A. Olsen (left) serves as president and chief operating officer and Kenneth A. Hecken (right), as vice-chairman of the board of Johnson & Higgins.

is a tribute not only to its traditions of private ownership, but also to the dedication of its worldwide staff.

And even as Johnson & Higgins moves forward into the future, the firm has not turned its back on the past. From its modern world headquarters at Broad and South streets, sweeping views of the East River and New York Harbor call forth images of the clipper ships, cargoes, and coffee houses of the company's early days in old New York.

KO-REC-TYPE

In April 1955 four men got together to form a company making typewriter ribbons, carbon paper, and Spirit hectograph masters. The four, Oscar Eaton, Jack Eaton, Robert Glenn, and Victor Barouh, capitalized the firm with 20,000 shares of stock. They rented a 5,000-square-foot loft in Brooklyn, New York, and within two months they were selling the products they manufactured. Within one year the company had racked up sales of more than $500,000 and was employing 40 people.

While the firm was beginning to show real promise, tragedy struck the ownership. Oscar Eaton was forced to resign owing to ill health, and Jack Eaton died. The burden of management fell on the remaining partners, Barouh and Glenn. Perhaps it was fate, or the ability to innovate an old concept of correcting typing errors, that led to a discovery that is still a mainstay of

A cross section of employees from Barouh-Eaton's Ko-Rec-Type worldwide operations (from left) Albert Stallings, machine operator; Victor Barouh, chief executive officer; Lydia Vasquez, supervisor/fabric ribbon department; Ricardo Rodrigo, maintenance manager; Seth Dinsky, vice-president and managing director of Brooklyn operations; Zoila Moreira, supervisor/film ribbon department; George Rottman, managing director of Long Island operations; Gunn Gunardi, art director; Barbara Glover, executive vice-president/sales; and Richard Barouh, vice-president and comptroller.

the corporation. It might even be accurate to say that the firm profited from another's mistake.

Barouh and Glenn happened to be watching a typist correcting a typing mistake. They noticed that she kept a piece of white chalk by her machine. She would erase the mistake and then rub over it with the chalk. Her efforts gave Barouh and Glenn an idea. They borrowed the chalk, rubbed it on a piece of paper, and put the sheet of paper between the error and the typewriter key and struck the key, thereby transferring the chalk over the error. Thus was born the company's best-known product: Ko-Rec-Type.

Barouh, whose fiery manner and unorthodox management style have earned him the designation of "entrepreneur," has kept Barouh-Eaton usually one step ahead of the competition. For example, the firm has been located in the industrial sector of Brooklyn for many years. During that time many area businesses closed their doors, leaving the surrounding waterfront to deteriorate and stagnate under a high crime rate.

Barouh refused to join the flight from the area. Instead, his business was instrumental in forming the Metropolitan Industrial Development Corporation (MIDC). To combat violent street crime, MIDC, together with other neighborhood business leaders, started the Street Crimebusters. Operating out of Ko-Rec-Type offices, the group, supported by the firm's donations of

Victor Barouh, chairman and chief executive officer of Barouh-Eaton Corporation.

facilities, staff, supplies, and printing services, began street patrols and other high-visibility programs to protect employees and property against crime. From those beginnings the organization has since incorporated as a nonprofit corporation, increased its membership, and broadened its constituency to include residents' groups. MIDC is now a local development corporation with more than 60 business

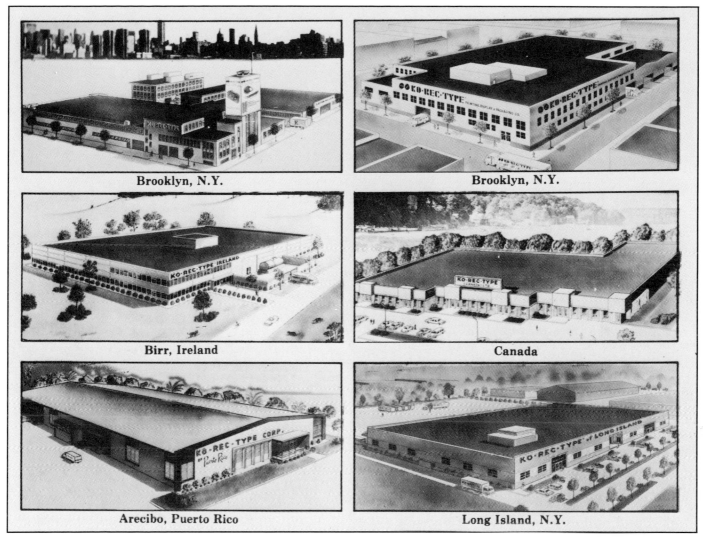

Brooklyn, N.Y.

Brooklyn, N.Y.

Birr, Ireland

Canada

Arecibo, Puerto Rico

Long Island, N.Y.

Ko-Rec-Type has facilities in New York and throughout the world.

members supported in part by development grants from several local banks. The original goal of fighting crime has been attained through the establishment of a cooperative security patrol that monitors the area during evening hours and weekends. Companies that subscribe to the patrol pay a fee based on the size of the business.

In swimming against the tide of fleeing business, Barouh not only improved his company's location, but also retained a foothold in what is today one of New York's business renaissance zones.

The firm continued to grow during the 1960s and into 1973. That year the company faced its most critical challenge. IBM began production of a new typewriter known as the Correcting Selectric II. The machine employed a special film ribbon enclosed in a cassette and containing an adhesive tape that formed a built-in correction system. Correction was only the push of a button away and lifted errors cleanly and completely. More important, it was more convenient than Ko-Rec-Type since it was a feature of the typewriter itself. Barouh-Eaton, which derived most of its revenues from conventional correction products and fabric ribbons, faced a shrinking market and an uncertain future.

A crash program headed by George Rottman, a company employee with a chemical and engineering degree, was put into effect. Out of the combined efforts and total dedication of Ko-Rec-Type employees came a system of coating film ribbon, injection molding cassettes, and assembling them into a ribbon system.

This accomplishment was no small matter at the time. The Ko-Rec-Type group had to formulate inks, design and build coaters and slitters, build plastic injection molds, and learn the molding business, all without prior experience in these fields.

It should be noted that Ko-Rec-Type accomplished this feat within six months of the introduction of the Selectric II, becoming the only independent ribbon manufacturer to produce this product.

Being the primary source of supply for the much-in-demand correction ribbons and correction tapes produced revenues and profits to fuel rapid expansion. By 1977 the company's sales had exceeded $35 million, and new manufacturing plants were established in Canada, Europe, Puerto Rico, and Long Island.

Experience has shown that technology is never static. Ko-Rec-Type, determined to be self-sufficient, maintains a full staff of designers, engineers (electrical, industrial, chemical, and mechanical), draftsmen, machinists, and toolmakers. These people not only

Leopold Ulloa, managing director of the Puerto Rican division of Ko-Rec-Type.

Richard Barouh, son of Victor Barouh, serves as vice-president and comptroller.

design and build new equipment, but also redesign, rebuild, and maintain existing equipment necessary for smooth production. More important, the firm maintains a chemistry research and development capability second to none. Chemistry is the lifeblood of the business. Ko-Rec-Type has an experienced staff of chemists responsible for research and development of the ink and coating formulations needed to make new products. Ko-Rec-Type also maintains the most modern laboratory and testing equipment available.

Achievements have been most gratifying: In fewer than 30 years its technical staff has been awarded 35 U.S. patents.

As the design of office machinery

became more sophisticated, the old-style reel-to-reel typewriter ribbon was displaced by plastic cartridges, which house the ribbons. This innovation greatly complicated the ribbon industry, as each typewriter manufacturer designs its cartridge with a unique configuration compatible only with that manufacturer's machines. As a manufacturer of inked ribbons, Ko-Rec-Type had to learn the technology of injection molding if it expected to grow and offer a comparable product to the consumer.

Ko-Rec-Type met this challenge head on with the decision to produce its

Seth Dinsky, vice-president and managing director of Brooklyn operations.

tained the willingness to work that had impressed Barouh. More important, Ulloa found ways to solve problems on his own, thus sparing the need for constant management attention. The end result is that this employee, with a minimum of education and almost no training, through his drive and determination now runs the Puerto Rico Division.

Steve Chester, managing director of the Canadian Division; George Rottman, managing director of the Long Island Division; Paul Hunton, managing director of the Ireland Division; and Seth Dinsky, managing director of the Brooklyn Division, all shared one common denominator. They joined the company as employees and worked their way through the ranks to lead their divisions. According to Barouh, it is this type of employee attitude and effort that leads to developing successful managers.

The middle management team and the individual factory and office staff of the 700-member Ko-Rec-Type family of employees witness the growth opportunities open to them as being part of an organization that promotes from within. Barouh believes a company that practices growth from within will bring out the best in its people.

own plastic spools, spindles, and cartridges. In fewer than three months it molded the first cartridge. Today it has 40 injection-molding machines in the United States, four in Canada, five in Ireland, and two in Puerto Rico. To date Ko-Rec-Type manufactures replacement ribbons for the thousands of different printers requiring special cartridges and ink formulations. No other independent replacement ribbon manufacturer in the world has a comparable complete line of ribbons. Plans call for even further expansion in this area over the next five years.

While the far-flung growth and expansion of the firm was being maintained, a different problem had to be faced. Ko-Rec-Type was presented with a major management and supervisory developmental problem. Barouh, who is noted for his disdain of classic business practices, has encouraged employees to grow into the management jobs. There is a well-known case inside the firm that demonstrates how management development takes place. Barouh needed help with moving some crates into the plant. He hired a neighborhood youth, Leopold Ulloa, to give him a hand. The boy's willingness to work, even during lunch hours and breaks, impressed Barouh. He offered the young man a full-time job. In each assignment the new employee main-

George Rottman, managing director of Long Island operations.

BRENNER PAPER PRODUCTS CO., INC.

Louis Brenner, an uneducated immigrant from Eastern Europe, arrived in America just before World War I. His first job was as a pressman in a print shop in Atlantic City, New Jersey. Several years later he decided to form his own company and opened a print shop in the Williamsburgh section of Brooklyn. He was realizing the American Dream, the one he had heard about back in Russia where his father had been a blacksmith. He worked 18 hours at his press by day, making deliveries to his customers at night.

Perhaps the thought of starting a three-generation family business crossed his mind on the morning of October 13, 1933, when Louis incorporated his little business in Brooklyn into Brenner Paper Products. He was a man of vision and imagination, and he wanted to plant roots in his new country for himself, his young family, and the generations to follow.

In his workshop he designed and printed original wedding and birth announcements. Soon he outgrew that location and moved to 26 West 17th Street in Manhattan, occupying his own building.

Through the next 20 years the company grew and prospered. During World War II the firm began to print airmail stationery for the armed services, and so began to explore the manufacture of envelopes for the announcements and stationery lines. The

Brenner Paper Products today is located at Otto Road in Glendale, Queens.

first envelope plunger machine was soon purchased. Thus started the envelope-manufacturing segment of Brenner Paper.

In December 1951 Louis Brenner died. The company passed to the direction of his son-in-law, Eugene Levenson. Levenson decided to focus on envelope manufacturing exclusively, and all other items were dropped from the production line. Levenson also opened a branch in Tampa, Florida, but some years later that division was sold off. Levenson continued to build on Brenner's achievements and increased the firm's market share in commercial envelopes. In 1969 he moved the company to its current headquar-

Louis Brenner, founder, started his company by designing and printing original wedding and birth announcements.

ters on Otto Road in Glendale, Queens. By 1983 Eugene Levenson was considering a move to sell off Brenner Paper Products. His wife, with no business background or management experience, entered the picture.

"My father started and built this firm with close employee relations," recalls Rhoda Brenner Levenson, the

This equipment was purchased by Louis Brenner and existed in his plant until the early 1950s.

founder's daughter and current president. "Over the years we had become too interested in numbers and statistics and less with employees. I decided that this company was not to be taken out of the family. The name on the door was Brenner and it was going to stay." To get input Rhoda Brenner Levenson called employees together and asked for their help. "Many of the employees still remembered my father. They knew me growing up and felt they had a stake in where our company was going."

It worked. In the next few years Brenner Paper Products operated on the premise that attention to detail, quality materials, and personal service to customers would solidify a market niche and allow the firm to compete with larger envelope manufacturers.

Brenner Paper had been concentrating on commercial envelope pro-

High-technology equipment means high-technology training. Brenner Paper has invested heavily in employee cross-training. The result has been a 25-percent increase in productivity.

duction only. A decision was reached to attack a new market; direct-mail advertising had become a major industry and was heavily dependent on "special" manufacturing with deadline delivery dates. This became the new focus.

"The employees again were the key. We found that over 40 percent of our employees had more than 20 years of employment. Their experience with us was invaluable in developing the new product mix. We decided that the first step was to show them management's commitment to them. We tried to make those changes where employees could feel the most impact. We improved work areas; lunchrooms and lounges were made more attractive. We sponsored group events such as picnics, baseball games, Christmas dances, etc. Not new ideas, but certainly ones that fit with the vision Louis Brenner had," explains Rhoda Levenson. The company began an earnest effort to develop its employee resource. It developed an in-house program to assist substance abusers, as well as incentive programs for new ideas and greater cost efficiency.

The efforts have paid major dividends. Sales have increased, production has increased, new equipment has been put on the floor, and old equipment has been updated. A machine shop was established, a parts department reorganized, and a new computer system introduced along with state-of-the-art high-speed equipment. The original company policy of servicing trade accounts only has prevailed, and Brenner Paper prides itself on its integrity in protecting its customers. In the past five years the firm has grown from 180 employees to 240 in 1987. With an annual payroll exceeding $6 million, the employees now benefit from paid holidays; medical, dental, and pension plans; and many other fringe benefits.

"We are now a family business in the best sense of that word, and our employees are part of that family. Sons of employees now work alongside their fathers. Three third-generation family members hold key positions in the company. That makes us very proud. I feel it is the realization of my father's vision," says the current president and chief executive officer of Brenner Paper Products Co., Inc.

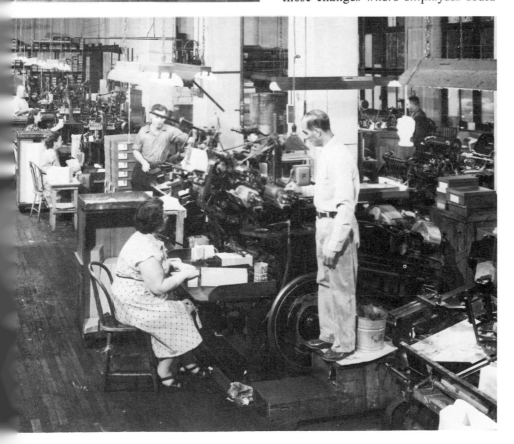

Early production methods entailed hands-on quality-control methods.

VOLLMER ASSOCIATES

For three decades Vollmer Associates has been a consultant in civil and structural engineering, transportation and infrastructure planning and design, landscape architecture, recreational planning, environmental analysis, and construction management. The New York City-based firm's clients include many government agencies, as well as private companies such as IBM, Loews Corporation, Olympia & York, and 'Rockefeller Center Development Corp., to name just a few.

Vollmer Associates was launched in 1956 by Arnold Vollmer, a civil engineer and landscape architect. At first the company was a civil engineering and landscape architecture specialist, primarily designing parks and park-

Proposed subway station improvement at Columbus Circle, New York Coliseum Project, New York, New York.

ways. Soon, however, the firm branched out into many new areas of architecture and design, until it eventually became the widely diversified group that it is today.

The company's civil and structural engineering projects include site engineering and infrastructure design at the much-heralded Battery Park City development in Lower Manhattan; collaboration on the Times Square Redevelopment project; modernization, design, and improvements for stations in New York City's subway system; rehabilitation of seven miles of the New England Thruway in New York; the study of alternatives to the controversial Westway project in Manhattan; and replacement designs for some 20 bridges as part of Connecticut's Emergency Bridge Repair Program.

From the beginning company founder Arnold Vollmer has made a

Battery Park City, New York, New York. Photograph by Philip Greenberg. Courtesy, Battery Park City Authority

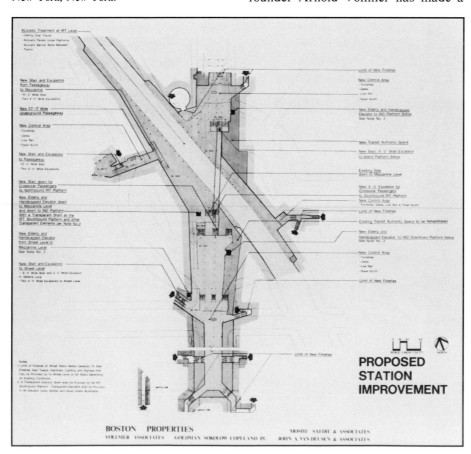

PROPOSED STATION IMPROVEMENT

BOSTON PROPERTIES
VOLLMER ASSOCIATES   GOLDMAN SOKOLOW COPELAND P.C.   MOSHE SAFDIE & ASSOCIATES   JOHN A. VAN DEUSEN & ASSOCIATES

point of stressing aesthetics in the firm's work. In fact, during the 1960s the company was hired by the Connecticut State Highway Department as an aesthetic consultant, reviewing highway and bridge designs submitted by other consultants. Vollmer Associates' landscape architects have since planned and developed aesthetic guidelines for many highways throughout the country. They have also carried out a wealth of projects involving planning and design, building, and/or rehabilitation of parks and recreational facilities of all types. Vollmer Associates also does landscape and site design for commercial projects—ranging from streetscape improvements to master planning and site design for corporate headquarters and new development projects.

The jewel in the crown for Vollmer Associates is said to be the Saratoga Performing Arts Center (SPAC), located in New York's Saratoga Spa State Park. The firm designed the center's semienclosed, 5,200-seat amphitheater, which is the summer home for the Philadelphia Orchestra and New York City Ballet Company and site of many other performances. In addition to designing the amphitheater, Vollmer Associates also completed a feasibility report, survey, preliminary design, contract plans, and construction management for the project. The amphitheater's acoustics have been called the

Nassau Expressway, Queens and Nassau counties, New York.

best of any similar center in the country, and its aesthetic design has also won national acclaim.

Since it opened in 1966, SPAC has helped revitalize Saratoga Springs as a summer resort. More than 20 years after its successful completion, Vollmer Associates' work on SPAC remains a tremendous source of company pride. A related Vollmer accomplishment is the 2,500-seat Niagara Frontier Performing Arts Center in Lewiston State Park, New York, for which the firm did preliminary design work, construction plans, and construction supervision.

In addition to its main office in New York City, Vollmer Associates has branch offices in Norwalk, Connecticut; Paramus, New Jersey; Albany, New York; Boston, Massachusetts; and Collinsville, Illinois. Of the 350 employees in its six offices, more than two-thirds concentrate on traffic studies and highway planning. Outside of New York State, the company has worked on roadways in Maryland, Illinois, North Carolina, Kentucky, Massachusetts, and New Jersey, as well as civil engineering projects in Saudi Arabia.

Vollmer Associates has also served America's highway toll agencies with feasibility studies, traffic studies, assistance with revenue bond financing, revenue projections, operational studies, toll system design, and other services. The company uses these skills to serve such regular clients as the New Jersey Highway Authority, the Kansas Turnpike Authority, the Orlando-Orange County Expressway Authority in Florida, and the Maryland Transportation Authority. In New York Vollmer is the official Economic Consulting Engineer for the New York State Thruway Authority, the longest toll facility in the United States.

In yet another interesting area of expertise, Vollmer Associates is an unparalleled expert on underground New York City. After obtaining a New York Telephone contract in the 1960s

Saratoga Performing Arts Center, Saratoga Springs, New York. Courtesy, Joseph W. Molitor Photography

to plot cables in Manhattan, Vollmer Associates became the top specialist in the city's underground anatomy of phone lines, water mains, electrical cables, steam pipes, sewer lines, and subway tunnels. The firm learned the delicate art of digging around those obstacles, and today it is frequently hired for underground work, such as a 1986 project connecting the IRT subway station at 51st Street and the IND station at 53rd Street. That same year the company was hired as a consultant by 10 of the 12 bidders on a subway improvement project at New York's Columbus Circle—with the other two bidders choosing not to use an engineering consultant.

Company founder Arnold Vollmer sold his interest in Vollmer Associates to the organization's current partners in 1981. Nonetheless, Vollmer remains active, still serving as the firm's ambassador, and still coming to the office daily. Today Vollmer Associates is guided by its senior partners: chairman Daniel W. Greenbaum, Peter E. Shrope, Robert Samson, Gerald V. Nielsten, Karl L. Rubenacker, and Edmund J. Condon. Like Arnold Vollmer, past principal Edward J. Moloney also remains active in the affairs of the company.

EMIGRANT SAVINGS BANK

During the early nineteenth century, savings institutions for the thrifty proved highly successful in the United States. These banks had spread throughout the northeastern United States, conceived to encourage saving among people of limited means.

In the spring of 1850, 18 prominent New York City businessmen, concerned with the financial welfare of the thousands of immigrants arriving in the city, met and invested $200 each to found the Emigrant Industrial Savings Bank. In the 1850s European arrivals, unfamiliar with America's customs and language, were preyed upon by exploiters. The Emigrant Industrial Savings Bank's 18 founders, many of whom had also helped organize the Irish Emigrant Society and were thus aware of the emigrant's problems in New York, wanted to create an institution to safeguard the meager savings of the newly arrived.

The founders leased a small building at 51 Chambers Street as the new bank's home. On the day Emigrant opened its doors, September 30, 1850, savers deposited $3,009—a great sum in those days. Through the nineteenth century and into the twentieth, Emigrant saw to the safety and protection of its depositors, and successfully paid dividends each year to all its customers.

Emigrant Savings Bank's modern history is also a proud one. In 1967 Emigrant dropped the word "Industrial" from its name because the term was no longer relevant to its activities. In 1969 the bank moved its headquarters from 51 Chambers Street to the new 27-story Emigrant Savings Bank building at 5 East 42nd Street.

With a 1970 merger with City Savings & Loan Association, Emigrant proved that it was moving forward in a progressive manner. In 1972 Emigrant opened its first Nassau County office in Long Beach, Long Island. Expanding into Long Island's Suffolk County in 1976, Emigrant became the first New York City-based savings bank to open a branch there, with an office in the Walt Whitman Shopping Mall in Huntington. By then Emigrant had a total of 15 locations in Manhattan, Queens, and Nassau and Suffolk counties.

In early 1979 Emigrant set about to merge with the Prudential Savings Bank. The newly merged Emigrant, with assets exceeding $3 billion, became the fourth-largest savings bank in New York State and the fifth largest in the nation. That addition brought Emigrant to 30 offices in Manhattan, Brooklyn, and Queens, as well as Nassau, Suffolk, and Westchester counties.

Better banking systems and conveniences such as the interbranch computer network and signature validation

An artist's rendering of Emigrant's current headquarters at 5 East 42nd Street.

systems continue to improve Emigrant's service to its nearly one-half-million depositors. The bank has also become a major co-op and home mortgage lender in the greater New York area.

With its recent conversion to a stock savings bank and its corresponding expanded capital base, Emigrant Savings Bank will continue to grow and serve its customers with a modern efficient banking system.

Emigrant Savings Bank was created in 1850 by 18 prominent New York City businessmen who were concerned with the financial welfare of the thousands of immigrants arriving in the city. Pictured here is the bank's first home at 51 Chambers Street. Deposits on the bank's first day totaled $3,009.

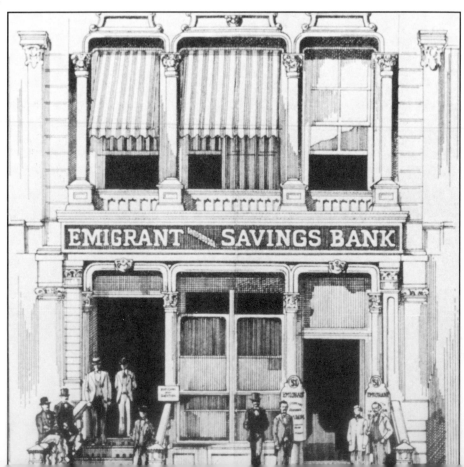

ALBANY SAVINGS BANK

Bankers' hours were different in 1820, when Albany Savings Bank first opened its doors for business. Under its original bylaws Albany Savings Bank would be open for deposits only on Saturday evenings from 6 p.m. to 9 p.m. Withdrawals could be made only on the third Wednesday of January, April, July, and October, if a week's notice had first been given the bank's treasurer. Twice a year depositors were paid interest of 5 percent per annum.

Silversmith Joseph Rice, the first depositor, was one of more than 12,600 Albanians the new bank intended to serve. Rice was joined by 18 other depositors who on that first day deposited a total of $527. Albany Savings Bank, then the second savings bank in the Empire State, grew steadily and successfully, becoming the equal, in quality of its operations and assets, of any bank in the United States. A study in the late 1980s showed Albany Savings Bank very positively in relation to banks with assets of one billion dollars or more. Throughout its history Albany Savings Bank was deeply involved in the economic life of its surrounding region, a region that now embraces an area from Spring Valley in the south, north to Plattsburgh, and from Albany west to Syracuse.

Albany Savings Bank's corporate headquarters, located on one of America's oldest crossroads, was a key element in the renaissance of Albany's urban core when completed in 1974.

By 1988 Albany Savings Bank was looking forward to interstate expansions and had grown from its tiny 1820 staff to nearly 900 employees and 33 branches. In 1820, when patroon Stephen Van Rensselaer became Albany Savings Bank's first chief executive officer, it was a ratification of the institution's soundness and importance. First citizen of Albany, Van Rensselaer would be followed by only 15 other chief executive officers, all influential and prudent men from the top levels of the economic community. Major banking, industrial, mercantile, and political figures would serve as the bank's principal officers and directors throughout its nearly 170-year history.

Now New York State's oldest mutual savings bank, Albany Savings Bank is also among the most stable, while continuing its dynamic growth and progress. Its earnings are strong, with $25 million added to its capital in 1987 alone; its credit cards are successful; and its delinquency rates are well below state and national averages. New mortgage loan closings approximated $300 million in 1987.

In all, nearly 17 decades in operation have witnessed continual progress, steady improvement of Albany Savings Bank's position, and ongoing service to its clients. Joseph Rice and Stephen Van Rensselaer would be pleased to see the product of what each, in his own way, had helped begin.

Chief executive officer Gilbert O. Robert is the 16th man to maintain Albany Savings Bank's enduring position of dependable and healthy growth.

"First citizen" of Albany and first president of Albany Savings Bank was the patroon Stephen Van Rensselaer. To have the approval of this son of Albany's most important family for a project was to give it credibility and recognition.

FAIR-RITE PRODUCTS CORPORATION

The tiny hamlet of Wallkill in Ulster County is home to a creative manufacturing company that supplies critical components to the giants of America's computer and electronics industries. Users of its products include IBM, Digital Equipment, Apple Computer, ATT Information Systems, Zenith, and Motorola, among others.

The firm, Fair-Rite Products Corporation, has fewer than 300 employees, yet is the nation's third-largest manufacturer of its product line.

These products are tiny components made of a material called ferrite (pronounced "Fair-Rite"), made in various shapes that substantially limit the electromagnetic waves emanating from electronic equipment. The components actually are magnetic ceramic materials.

Interference waves from a personal computer would seriously garble TV reception were it not for the Fair-Rité "beads" mounted in the computer. The beads screen and absorb the interference waves before they leave the computer, without impeding the computer's performance.

Thus, home TV and radio operate free from interference that otherwise would be generated by computers and

Ferrite components manufactured by Fair-Rite Products Corporation are available in a variety of sizes and shapes for specific application in the computer and electronic industries to suppress electromagnetic interference waves.

other electronic equipment—such as garage door openers—thanks to ferrite.

Fair-Rite has been manufacturing its components since its founding in 1952 in a small building on the same site the company currently occupies in Wallkill.

Richard G. Parker, president, and Edmund Stanwyck, secretary/treasurer, provided the brains, energy, seed money, and marketing know-how to get the new enterprise off the ground. Parker continues as board chairman and chief executive officer. His wife, Carole Parker, an electrical engineering graduate of Rensselar Polytechnic Institute, is executive vice-president.

The first customers in the 1950s were radio and television manufacturers, and rapid expansion of the TV industry carried the firm to successful business peaks in the 1950s and 1960s. Then the domestic TV industry lost its dominant position to Japan and other Far Eastern countries in the 1970s.

As its primary market flickered and the future looked uncertain, Fair-Rite management made a critical marketing decision that would put the company back on the track. They predicted correctly that the small-computer industry would mushroom in the years immediately ahead, and put their sales and manufacturing emphasis on computer applications of their products. Thus, Parker notes in retrospect, they positioned Fair-Rite for a major role in the growing computer industry.

Ferrite components have been refined in configuration and content, and can be manufactured to specific applications. Their use in impeding EMI (Electro-Magnetic Interference) at high frequencies will continue to grow.

Fair-Rite has developed a manufacturing process that uses high-temperature kilns and sophisticated grinding, burnishing, and molding equipment to produce effective, economical components.

What started as a three-man shop over 35 years ago has grown to become an important manufacturing enterprise with 70,000 square feet of floor space and a branch plant in Illinois in operation since 1966.

NEW YORK CHAMBER OF COMMERCE AND INDUSTRY

The New York Chamber of Commerce and Industry is older than the United States of America itself. Over the course of time it has helped shape New York's—and America's—business profile.

The chamber was founded in 1768 by a small group of merchants and in the succeeding years supported such important ventures as the building of the Erie Canal (1825), the laying of the first successful Atlantic cable (1866), and the construction of New York's first subway (1904). The chamber's illustrious membership rolls have included inventors Cyrus Field, Thomas Edison, and Samuel F.B. Morse; and financiers and industrialists John D. Rockefeller, John Jacob Astor, Andrew Carnegie, and J. Pierpont Morgan. The chamber still numbers the chief executives of some of the nation's largest companies and financial institutions as members. Many small and medium-size businesses are also members, reflecting the growing economic importance of the city's entrepreneurial sector.

Today the New York Chamber of Commerce and Industry is an important advocate for business and provides educational and information programs for its members. The chamber speaks for its members on legislative and regulatory issues. It offers entry to a powerful business network and provides a contact point for new business opportunities. Workshops and seminars keep businesses of all types and sizes up-to-date on issues and growth opportunities.

This portrait was commissioned by the chamber in 1895 to memorialize the completion of laying the first Atlantic cable. Standing in the center is Samuel F.B. Morse, and Peter Cooper is shown on the far left.

The Great Seal of the chamber was struck in 1770 by permission of King George III. The seal disappeared during the occupation of New York City during the Revolutionary War. It was rediscovered in a London antique shop in the 1800s and returned to the chamber.

One of the New York chamber's most important functions is advocacy for its members. At the city, state, and federal levels, the chamber is there to represent its members' concerns. In 1985 and 1986, for example, the organization played a key role in retaining deductibility of state and local income and property taxes on federal returns. In 1987 the chamber's highest priority was a reduction in state taxes. Ultimately, the state enacted a $4.5-billion personal income tax reduction program, phased in over four years.

The chamber is committed to helping small business expand and prosper. Seminars bring entrepreneurs together with corporate customers and lenders. Recognizing the increasingly major role of women in business and as business owners, the chamber's Women's Business Council offers programs tailored to their interests.

On the international front, the chamber publishes a monthly periodical, "World Trade Report," covering overseas business opportunities and trade leads. The organization also helps member companies establish overseas contacts and keeps them informed of changes in regulations, visas, and shipping fees.

The New York Chamber of Commerce and Industry is an affiliate of the New York City Partnership, founded in 1979 by David Rockefeller and business and civic leaders. The Partnership provides a central mechanism for the private sector to address such problems as housing, education, youth employment, public safety, and economic development. Through the Partnership, business and government work together to find solutions and develop workable models for change. The Partnership has become a model for private-public sector cooperative ventures in other cities and regions, as it works to improve the economy and quality of life in New York City.

HERITAGE HILLS OF WESTCHESTER

Heritage Hills of Westchester is the largest, most successful condominium community in the New England area. When completed, its 3,100 homes will be nestled in 1,100 acres of picturesque wooded countryside that span two prominent hills in the town of Somers, New York. The community was begun in 1973, and upon completion will boast a population of more than 5,000.

The community is so well thought out, carefully developed, and impeccably maintained that it almost rates as a bona fide tourist attraction. Much of this appeal is due to the scale of its jewel-like appearance. Heritage Hills presents a sustained level of quality that borders on the uncanny. As one drives through, one wonders how they do it, especially considering its size. The community is so large it has 18-hole and 9-hole private golf courses,

Heritage Hills of Westchester's total planned concept provides its residents with a natural setting of exceptional quality.

which are just a part of its complete recreational package, and its own highway department.

The town of Somers, home of Heritage Hills, dates back to 1699, when it was deeded by the Kitchwan Indians to Dutch colonists who farmed the fertile valleys and grazed sheep on the plush green meadows of the highlands. Somers now consists of approximately 10,000 people in a 32-mile area best known as the Cradle of the American Circus. It was here that Hachaliah Bailey brought the first elephant, Old Bet, to this country in 1815. This event evolved into the famous Barnum & Bailey Circus. An elephant statue in the Somers town square and the Old Elephant Hotel, now the town hall, are tributes to that colorful era.

Success came to Heritage Hills from the project's inception. Within an 18-month period it won three major awards in national competitions. In 1975 the National Association for Home Builders gave it an award less than one year after it opened. The Western Woods Products Association gave the community its design award in 1976. And in July of that year it won the prestigious American Institute of

The talents of professional landscape architects working in conjunction with site planners, architects, and environmental specialists have produced a community designed to work in harmony with its natural environment.

Architects/*House and Home Magazine*'s Homes For Better Living Award.

Much of Heritage Hills' success can be directly attributed to its use of a solid philosophical approach for both its design and the execution of that design. The fact that Heritage Development Group, Inc., employs a serious philosophical approach is, by itself, unique to community developers, regardless of the scale of the community. That Heritage Hills is immense, and that much of its philosophical foundation is based on Henry David Thoreau, makes this project even more unique.

What Heritage has drawn from Thoreau's vision is the concept that a village is something more than a cluster of houses around a green. Heritage is concerned with more than just building basic housing. It is concerned with creating living space that is both functional and enjoyable, requiring that this space be carefully and thoughtfully planned. And further, that the most important factor for any community is the quality, character, and preservation of the environment in which it exists.

Thus, the Heritage Development Group decided at the inception of its Heritage Hills project that all architectural designs would have to harmonize with the existing features of the land. Using a highly detailed master plan that is still the centerpiece of the entire endeavor, the development team carefully thought out all aspects of its project before touching the land itself. This thinking can literally be felt from the moment one enters the community. Every road, every driveway, the setting of each foundation, each design detail takes into account the natural contours

The Elephant Hotel, now the Somers Town Hall, commemorates the colorful beginnings of the American Circus.

of the land. The designers calculated everything, from the views out each window of each home, to how much each home could be seen from any other home.

Even the sequence of construction was meticulously thought out. That way, construction crews could build around natural attributes instead of simply going in with a bulldozer. The crews carefully built around groves of existing trees, leaving the sumptuous underbrush of ferns and wild grasses. Nearly one-third of the land at Heritage Hills has been preserved in its original natural state. Throughout the community additional landscaping supplements these natural features to blend the architecture with the environment.

Another important guideline in the design of Heritage Hills was providing home owners with a variety of architectural plans. Part of this concern has been answered by the actual slopes of the hills. Several different structural designs take advantage of both level sites and the upward and downward slopes of the hillsides to accommodate existing land contours, and each home is sited to maximize its view of the landscape. The designers also imposed a two-story limit in height to lessen the visual impact to the landscape and to assure unobstructed views from adjacent units.

The homes themselves are one-, two-, and three-bedroom town homes in a variety of configurations designed to harmonize with the natural surroundings. The exterior architecture enhances the relationship between buildings and environment by the use of natural materials such as stained cedar siding, shingle roofs, and natural stone walls. The architecture itself is an eclectic mix of New England traditional with California contemporary.

The architectural plans of the homes have continually evolved since the community's inception in response to advancements in building technology and shifts in current tastes. For

Many homes are sited on the slopes of the hills to accommodate existing land contours and maximize views.

example, recent changes in floor plan designs include buyers' preferences for more spacious, well-equipped kitchens and luxuriously appointed bathrooms. Currently there are nine basic designs available in single- and multilevel floor plans. When the project began there were as many as 20 different plans available. Over the years certain design characteristics have become clear favorites, and these preferences have been incorporated into current offerings. As the community continues to evolve, its designers will continue to refine their ideas so that Heritage Hills will be a superb record of home designs and quality life-styles.

In developing a complete community rather than merely building homes, the developers planned Heritage Hills to appeal specifically to buyers who would appreciate quality yet desired an active, carefree life-style

A large part of Heritage Hills' community spirit is based upon its recreational amenities.

free from exterior home maintenance. The only mandatory requirement has been that all residents must exceed the age of 18 to preserve the adult community concept. The result has been a population that runs the gamut in ages and professions, with nearly 70 percent holding full-time jobs. Since all exterior home care is part of the package, Heritage Hills residents have the enviable luxury of more time to devote to their careers and personal interests.

For all this careful planning, the genuine sense of community spirit that exists at Heritage Hills is yet another surprise. The residents feel a sense of belonging and participation that exceeds even the developer's expectations. No doubt part of this community spirit can be traced to the development group's provisions for year-round recreation and activities.

The company's initial concept centered on the creation of a community that offered a total living experience. And a large part of this experience was based on recreational amenities. In order to accomplish this, Heritage went far beyond the addition of a few amenities that could be used as window dressing to attract buyers but would later suffer from overcrowding.

Instead Heritage has built facilities that are more than merely sufficient. Residents can choose from a 9-hole championship golf course with a PGA pro and a full 18-hole champi-

onship course. The main recreation center includes a heated pool, tennis courts, paddle tennis courts, and fully equipped men's and women's gymnasiums with saunas and whirlpools. Satellite recreation areas, located on both the East and West Hills, provide a heated pool and tennis courts. There are miles of country roads for joggers, trails for hikers, and, in the winter, frozen ponds for ice skaters and rolling hills for cross-country skiers.

The Community Clubhouse is the hub of much social activity throughout the year. The facilities include meeting rooms for many of the community's more than 50 clubs and a large central lobby for prefunctions. There is also a private library with a fireplace, a game and billiards room, a full kitchen for culinary clubs and event catering, a photographic darkroom, and a wet pantry. The Heritage Room is also in the clubhouse, with its own stage,

Residents can choose from an 18-hole championship course, a 9-hole course with a PGA pro, and fully equipped men's and women's gymnasiums.

grand piano, and direct access to a large deck for warm-weather gatherings. The lower level of the building houses the arts and crafts studio center, with fully equipped studios for pottery, sculpture, crafts, fine arts, and woodworking. Professional artists regularly offer classes to residents.

The land plan itself is also an amenity. By clustering the homes around two golf courses, residents benefit from acres of open space with spectacular views. The aesthetic value of this open space cannot be underestimated. In fact, the golf courses are equally valuable as aesthetic views and recreational facilities. Other land uses include a very active gardening club.

To ensure the development of the group's total, self-sufficient community concept, a private water-treatment plant was constructed on site to assure residents of the highest-quality service at the lowest-possible cost. The natural beauty of the site has been further preserved by placing all utility lines, power lines, and the community satellite television antenna systems underground. All external equipment is hidden be-

Heritage Hills' two golf courses are equally valuable as aesthetic views and recreational amenities.

hind landscaped foliage. And the professional maintenance crews at Heritage Hills are busy throughout the year with lawn mowing, seeding, mulching, fertilizing, leaf raking, snow removal, and exterior home care.

Once within the peaceful enclave of Heritage Hills, surrounded by the luxurious groves of trees, meandering paths, and spring-fed ponds, one tends to forget that Manhattan is little more than an hour away. In fact, many residents commute to their jobs in Manhattan daily, using Heritage Hills' two shuttle buses to take them to and from the nearby Metro North Commuter Railroad station. The buses also make stops at local shopping areas and recreational facilities. Nearby there are several large corporate presences, including IBM, PepsiCo, and major corporate business parks.

Obviously a project as extensive as Heritage Hills does not come into being without antecedents. In the case of Heritage Hills, the earlier model was another Heritage Development Group project in Southern Connecticut. This project, named Heritage Village, was the first large-scale project in the eastern United States to offer such amenities as nature trails, wildlife preserves, and a wide variety of recreational facilities. In 1982 this project won The Urban Land Institute Award for Excellence in Large Scale Development. The Urban Land Institute Award for developers is like a scientist winning the Nobel Prize. In the previous year this award was won by Walt Disney World.

While Heritage Hills will most likely remain Heritage Development Group's major opus, the company has another unique project already in the works. The Heritage Greylock project in Adams, Massachusetts, is the only planned residential and four-season recreational resort in the United States. Mount Greylock, the highest peak in Massachusetts, is the location of the project. Greylock combines 40 kilometers of Nordic ski trails and 16 alpine ski trails served by ski lifts, with an 18-hole golf course and a 25-acre lake with a full complement of water sports. Many resort areas have evolved over time, adding different features as they went along, but Heritage Greylock is the only one of its size to use comprehensive planning to develop a total integrated package.

While philosophy and comprehensive planning are the hallmarks of Heritage Hills, perhaps the most intriguing aspect is that its creator, the Heritage Development Group, no longer thinks of itself as an organization that buys land and erects houses. In the words of Heritage chief executive officer Henry J. Paparazzo, "We don't think of ourselves as builders of houses anymore. We are developing a community, a place where someone is going to live. We ask ourselves, 'What kind of person are we trying to satisfy? What are their needs?' This is what the individual looks for and has always looked for. The actual physical building is almost secondary to the rest of the package." Considering the quality and scope of Heritage's buildings, this statement is all the more impressive.

Heritage Hills of Westchester is oriented toward today's active adults who are seeking a life-style with freedom from exterior maintenance, a wide variety of amenities, and architectural design within a country setting.

BUSH INDUSTRIES, INC.

In a western New York city long noted for the production of high-quality traditional furniture, a fast-growing company is setting high standards of product design and function in a new furniture industry. Bush Industries, Inc., based in Jamestown, New York, with facilities in Little Valley and Cattaraugus, has grown dramatically over recent years to become one of the nation's leading manufacturers of home and office ready-to-assemble (RTA) furniture.

A corporation that remembers its family roots, Bush Industries has been a public company since April 1985 and is traded on the American Stock Exchange. Its RTA products are available in more than 6,000 retail outlets throughout the United States and include room dividers, wall systems, audio and video cabinets, home enter-

tainment centers, microwave oven carts, personal computer work stations, and desks. Bush recently introduced a line of bedroom furniture as part of its new product strategy of moving into traditional furniture areas.

The company that has evolved into Bush Industries, Inc., had its beginnings as Bush Brothers Products Corporation, an outgrowth of Bush Brothers Plating. In 1959 a 16,000-square-foot building in Little Valley, New York, was acquired to accommodate manufacturing facilities for a line of products that would use Bush Brothers Plating's fabricating and plating facilities. Cousins Robert and Paul Bush joined the family business in the new enterprise that employed six people. The product line consisted of a chrome-plated, tubular Port-a-Rack (a bathroom drying rack) and a line of chrome-plated wall accessories (towel bars, rings, etc.).

Limited growth in the early years led to a total realignment of ownership and responsibilities. In 1967 Paul Bush

It is Bush Industries' goal to become a world-class company through "people working together." President Paul Bush is seen with some of the people who are helping to make that idea a reality.

assumed operating control as he and his father, Stanley, acquired the stock of the company. He began rebuilding the firm internally to establish a foundation for future growth. The product line was expanded to include wood as well as metal.

The year 1968 was the first in a string of growth years. The company expanded its product line to include plastics, with the first plastic parts being tooled and developed in 1971.

The year 1972 saw major changes and substantial growth for the firm. A plastics plant was developed as a source of controlled production and increased profitability. Product innovation became a priority, resulting in the development of the first practical customer-assembled hamper, as well as other bathroom cabinets. These design concepts were patented and have not since been improved upon by a competitor.

The Little Valley facility was expanded, and additional warehouse space was leased in Salamanca, New York. The plastics operation was put into place in leased facilities in Sala-

Oak Elegants Entertainment Center—one of the products that is setting a new standard of style and function in RTA Furniture.

Finishing and packaging operations for Bush's Wood Division are housed in this 78,000-square-foot facility in Little Valley, New York. In Cattaraugus a 65,000-square-foot manufacturing plant fabricates hardwood parts.

manca, and the new division was known as Bush-Hartman Plastics. This division was eventually absorbed into Bush Industries. The beginning of Bush's current product line was a wood-finished plastic TV pedestal table, introduced in 1973. The success of this product showed the potential for furniture designed for home electronics products. That same year saw a change to the beginnings of the management team concept as some key management people were brought into the company. Official recognition of the change in the firm's status came in 1975, when Bush Brothers Products Corporation became Bush Industries, Inc.

In the late 1970s the company was involved in several businesses: bath products, occasional furniture (with a line of chrome and glass tables and shelving), custom molding of plastics, and electronics furniture. In 1979 the wood-fabricating capability was expanded through the acquisition of a 70,000-square-foot building on Elm Street in Salamanca. New woodworking machinery was purchased and installed, and the firm began to grow. The decision was made to consolidate all resources into electronics furniture,

and all other businesses and assets were sold off or phased out. Bush Industries experienced several breakthroughs with the introduction of new products for the electronics furniture industry, and developed its reputation as a leader in product styling and quality. The corporation maintains this product leadership position today.

The company's first computer furniture line—the Home Base series—was introduced in 1983. This grouping, which was the first in the industry to exploit the vertical dimension for storage, was rapidly followed by two other very successful computer furniture lines. The introduction of the first hardwood products (the Oak Classics line of audio/video furniture) to the RTA market was a bold move on the part of Bush Industries. In order to house the hardwood-manufacturing operations, a 65,000-square-foot plant in Cattaraugus, New York, was leased, with finishing operations performed in the Little Valley plant. Customer acceptance of a higher-priced product has been a key element in the growth of the firm, and hardwood products make up an important part of today's product line.

In 1984 Bush Industries embarked on an ambitious expansion and consolidation program with the construction of a new 376,000-square-foot facility in Jamestown, New York, completed in December 1985. The laminated-products-manufacturing operation and

the corporate headquarters are housed in the Jamestown facility, with the Cattaraugus and Little Valley plants comprising the wood operations.

Bush Industries is committed to continued growth and continual improvement based on its traditional values of teamwork, employee involvement, and customer satisfaction, as well as investment in the most modern technology and methods. The company is aggressively expanding its product line for the home and office.

Paul Bush, president and chief executive officer, credits much of the firm's success to its employees. "We wouldn't be where we are if it weren't for the dedication of our people. One of our great strengths is that we are willing to change and grow as individuals, as well as a company. As we have gotten bigger, we have made team building and employee involvement as much a priority as our commitment to excellence."

The corporate mission of Bush Industries is to become a world-class company, able to compete with anyone in the world on the basis of service, product desirability, quality, and value. All of the people of Bush Industries are working together to achieve this goal. One result of the teamwork aspect was Bush's acceptance of the prestigious Partners in Progress Award from Sears, Roebuck and Co. in 1987. Only those suppliers who consistently exceed Sears' standards for quality, manufacturing, service, and supply are recognized as Partners in Progress.

Bush's new 376,000-square-foot facility in Jamestown, completed in December 1985, processes laminated products, from raw materials to packaged goods, under one roof. The company corporate offices are in the forefront of the building.

DELOITTE HASKINS & SELLS

Deloitte Haskins & Sells International (DH&SI), one of the Big Eight accounting firms in the United States, is a worldwide organization. Today nearly 27,000 people, including more than 2,000 partners, work in some 450 DH&SI offices in 62 countries around the globe. The firm's annual worldwide revenues are close to $1.5 billion.

Deloitte Haskins & Sells was founded in New York City in 1895 by Charles Waldo Haskins and Elijah Watt Sells, and was originally named Haskins and Sells. The other branch of the firm's family tree, Deloitte & Company, was founded by William Welch Deloitte in London in 1845. In 1978 both firms changed their names to Deloitte Haskins & Sells, to conform to the name adopted by the international organization of affiliated national firms—Deloitte Haskins & Sells International. The name change was also adopted to emphasize the firm's international presence: It was the first American public accounting firm to open offices abroad.

Of the firm's founders, Haskins was a native of Brooklyn, New York. Sells was a native of Muscatine, Iowa. Englishman Deloitte ran his own accounting practice in London from 1845 to 1897.

Haskins and Sells first met in Washington, D.C., in 1893, when the two men teamed up to perform some important accounting studies at the behest of the United States Congress, thereby establishing a name for themselves. In 1895 Haskins and Sells moved to New York City and formed an accounting partnership. They situated their office in New York's financial district in Lower Manhattan, where the DH&S New York practice office, with its preeminence in serving financial clients, is located to this day. After Haskins died in 1903 at the age of 51, Sells retained the name of the firm and headed it until his own death at 66 years of age in 1924.

Charles Waldo Haskins (above) and Elijah Watt Sells (right), both founding partners whose names are well known today as part of the title of Deloitte Haskins & Sells.

The Deloitte firm had been in business a half-century before Haskins and Sells opened their practice. In New York in 1895 the recognition of accounting as a profession was just beginning, and it was a time of tremendous opportunity. Both Haskins and Sells soon rose to the top ranks of their profession.

When New York State began to regulate the public accounting profession in the latter half of the 1890s, Haskins was named as president of the state's board of examiners for public accountants. In 1897 he helped form the New York State Society of Certified Public Accountants, and soon also became president of that association. Haskins served as the first dean of the New York University School of Commerce, Accounts, and Finance.

During its first few years the accounting firm conducted several extensive investigations for the cities of New York and Chicago. Haskins & Sells also performed accounting studies for the federal government, such as the investigation of records of public authorities in the Philippines and Cuba following the Spanish-American War.

From 1906 through 1907 Sells was president of the American Association of Accountants. A major accounting award, the Elijah Watt Sells Award, was later established. This award has become one of the most widely known accounting honors in the United States. Presented twice yearly by the American Institute of Certified Public Accountants (AICPA), it is conferred for outstanding performance on the semiannual CPA examination. Several people at DH&S have won the award, including Charles G. Steele, the recently retired chairman of DH&S International.

DH&SI has a long-held tradition of professionalism, and its members have garnered many industry awards. Top partners in the firm have been winners of the highest honor conferred by the AICPA: the Gold Medal for distinguished service to the profession. Over the years notable DH&S winners of this medal have included Arthur H. Carter, Arthur B. Foye, and Weldon Powell.

At DH&S service to the profession and service to New York have gone arm in arm for almost a century. These men, prime movers in the field of accounting, have held substantial leadership positions in both arenas. Arthur Carter filled many prominent posts in the accounting fraternity, among them vice-president of the AICPA and three-time president of the New York State Society of CPAs. In the latter capacity, he testified before Congress on the Securities Act of 1933 and the Securities and Exchange Act of 1934, which established the Securities and Exchange Commission and increased the accounting and auditing work required by publicly traded companies. At the time members of Congress had been contemplating using government auditors for all publicly traded companies, and Carter's testimony was instrumental in persuading them of the benefits of using independent accountants instead.

A strong believer in accountants' involvement in matters outside of their profession, Arthur B. Foye held significant international positions in the field of economics in addition to his presidencies of both the AICPA and the New York State Society of CPAs. Foye also served as a trustee of New York University for many years.

Weldon Powell, the first chairman of the Accounting Principles Board of the AICPA, which is located in New York, was one of the profession's most respected authorities on accounting principles and practices. He was the leading figure in the design and implementation of the AICPA's program of developing accounting principles at a critical juncture in the late 1950s and early 1960s.

Other AICPA Gold Medal winners at the firm include partners John W. Queenan, Michael N. Chetkovich, N. Loyall McLaren, Edward A. Kracke, Oscar S. Gellein, Jay A. Phillips, and Elmer G. Beamer. Current DH&S chairman J. Michael Cook was selected for the unique honor of leading

Four generations of leadership at Deloitte Haskins & Sells (from left, standing): Charles G. Steele, John W. Queenan, and Michael N. Chetkovich. Seated is J. Michael Cook.

the AICPA in its centennial year of 1987.

Today, in the United States, Deloitte Haskins & Sells has more than 9,000 people, including approximately 800 partners in more than 100 offices nationwide. The firm's New York practice is one of its most dynamic. The New York executive office serves as a resource center to each of the other practice offices in the United States. At the New York executive office, more than 100 partners and managers coordinate client services, establish firmwide agencies, set technical policies, conduct accounting and auditing research, develop continuing education programs, monitor the entire firm's quality-control system, and manage operations. The New York practice office, the largest DH&SI office in the

country, serves many of the firm's well-known clients, including Merrill-Lynch, First Boston, Equitable Life, and Metropolitan Life.

Since its inception Deloitte Haskins & Sells has led the profession in the worldwide advancement of accounting and auditing standards, and also in the development of innovative tools and techniques. That approach has enabled DH&SI to attract and retain high-caliber professionals at all levels of its operations, dedicated to providing the finest professional services in the most effective and efficient manner.

For more than 90 years Deloitte Haskins & Sells has rendered top professional services to all areas of the business community and to federal, state, and local governmental entities. The firm's concentration on its highly trained staff and its commitment to the latest in innovative and effective techniques, along with its solid financial resources, place it in a strong position for the future.

THE BANK OF NEW YORK

The Bank of New York is a financial institution with a long and distinguished history—one that parallels the history of America itself. In fact, The Bank of New York was the first bank established in New York, and today it is the oldest bank in the United States operating under its original name.

The idea for The Bank of New York's founding came soon after the Revolutionary War, when New York merchants sought to create a financial institution that would meet their pressing financial needs—by providing credit and capital, and by stabilizing the chaotic regional monetary system that then reigned.

On February 23, 1784, just three months after British troops sailed away from New York after the Revolutionary War, a small advertisement appeared in *The New York Packet,* calling on the "Gentlemen of this City to establish a Bank on liberal principles." On the following evening The Bank of New York was launched at a meeting in the Merchant's Coffee House, a famous gathering place for patriots before the Revolutionary War. Young Alexander Hamilton, whose law practice was a recent addition to Wall Street, was enlisted to write the new bank's constitution.

New York's first bankers represented a cross section of the community. Although some of the bank's founders, like William Seton (the bank's first cashier), had Loyalist sympathies, the majority of its founders supported and had fought for independence for their young country. Those on the side of the colonies included the institution's first president, Alexander McDougall, who had been commander of West Point after Benedict Arnold's arrest for treason. Others in the fight against England included Comfort Sands, Gulian Verplanck, Isaac Roosevelt, and Jeremiah Wadsworth. In addition, two early Bank of New York directors were signers of this country's constitu-

This Bank of New York building, completed in 1797, was the first bank building constructed in New York. It was designed by architect George Doolet, whose sophisticated style foreshadowed the style of banking houses that later grew up around it.

tion: Alexander Hamilton and Rufus King. During its early years the bank was generally considered a Federalist institution—that is, its leadership believed in a strong central government and the expansion of American business.

The Bank of New York opened for business at the Walton House in New York City on June 9, 1784. Its charter called for a capital stock of $500,000. Shares of $1,000, payable in gold or silver, were all bought up immediately. The bank's business hours were established from 10 a.m. to 1 p.m. and from 3 p.m. to 5 p.m.

For the next 15 years The Bank of New York served as the center of New York's financial life. Importers of tea, sugar, and other cargoes turned to the bank for financing. If a merchant was found to be "sound, steady, and conservative," he was eligible to receive a "discount" or loan from The Bank of New York.

The institution also played an important role in helping the new nation establish itself on a firm financial basis. After four years on the bank's board of directors, Alexander Hamilton left in 1789 to join President George Washington's cabinet as Secretary of the Treasury. Upon assuming those new duties, Hamilton negotiated the first loan obtained by the new government. The amount of $200,000 was issued by The Bank of New York, against which the treasury drew a series of warrants on the bank. In the years that followed, the institution was also a major lender to the State and City of New York as well as to foreign governments.

Since its founding in 1784 several prominent New York financial institu-

Alexander Hamilton was instrumental in organizing The Bank of New York and wrote its constitution. He served as a director of the bank until 1789, when he left to join President George Washington's cabinet as Secretary of the Treasury.

tions have joined The Bank of New York through merger or acquisition, helping to create a strong financial institution with a long record of steady growth. These institutions include the New York Life Insurance and Trust Company, which joined The Bank of New York in 1922; the Fifth Avenue

Bank, which joined in 1948; Empire Trust Company, which came aboard in 1966; Empire National Bank, which became part of the institution in 1980; and, most recently, the Long Island Trust Company, which became part of The Bank of New York in 1987.

Today The Bank of New York ranks among the 20 largest commercial banks in the United States, with more than $20 billion in assets. Moreover, its parent corporation, The Bank of New York Company, Inc., is one of the country's fastest growing and most

This advertisement from February 23, 1784, proclaims the formation of The Bank of New York.

BANK.

IT appearing to be the disposition of the Gentlemen in this City, to establish a BANK on liberal principles, the stock to consist of specie only; they are therefore hereby invited to meet To-Morrow Evening at Six o'Clock, at the Merchant's Coffee-House, where a plan will be submitted to their consideration.

profitable money-center bank holding companies. The bank's largest business is the providing of credit and other banking services to large U.S. and multinational corporations and to mid-size companies in the greater New York metropolitan area. The bank is also one of the nation's most prominent securities processors, specializing in mutual funds, unit investment trust, government securities clearance, institutional trust and custody, American depository receipts, securities lending, and corporate agency services.

As well as its New York offices, the Bank of New York has subsidiary or affiliate offices in California, Connecticut, Delaware, Florida, and Texas, and in the United Kingdom, Singapore, Australia, and the Cayman Islands.

The Walton House was the first home of The Bank of New York. When the house was built by English merchant William Walton in 1752, it was considered the finest residence in the city. It served as the bank's office until 1787, when the institution moved to new quarters at 11 Hanover Square.

THE PORT AUTHORITY OF NEW YORK & NEW JERSEY

In the past 10 years the New York metropolitan area has witnessed an impressive economic turnaround. The Port Authority of New York & New Jersey has helped fuel that recovery by keeping vital transportation systems moving, and now it expects to do even more. As it entered its 66th year in 1987, the authority unveiled a major capital program to improve and expand its transportation facilities. The plan calls for more than $5.8 billion in expansions and improvements, most of which is to be spent from 1987 through 1991. The program gives us a peek into the Port Authority's future, but first it is also important to study this giant institution's storied past.

On April 30, 1921, the states of New York and New Jersey created the Port Authority to undertake port and regional improvements that neither private investment nor the two states individually were likely to carry out. The move was historic for the entire country because it marked the creation of the first bistate agency empowered under a clause of the United States Constitution that permits compacts between states with congressional consent.

Creation of the Port Authority ended a long period of turf wars between New York and New Jersey, whose quarrels over boundary lines through New York Harbor and the Hudson River once led state police to exchange shots in the middle of the waterway. In addition, the coming of the railroads was a source of bitter litigation between the states, as New Jersey interests saw an advantage in charging one set of freight rail rates to the New Jersey rail heads and a higher set to the New York side.

After virtually a century of contentious rivalry, both sides finally agreed that the port area was, in effect, one community, and that factionalism was detrimental to the port's economic potential. Seeking a governmental forum to administer port affairs, New York and New Jersey found a role model in the Port of London, administered by what was then the only public authority in the world.

The Port Authority's charter defines its operating area as a port district whose boundaries approximate a circle 25 miles in radius centered on the Statue of Liberty and including all or part of 17 counties in both states. The authority is governed by a 12-member board of commissioners, six appointed by New York's governor, six appointed by New Jersey's governor.

Initially given only start-up funds for administration, the Port Authority struggled through its first years until 1930, when the two states gave it control of the Holland Tunnel as a financial cornerstone. From that point on the authority began making landmark contributions to the region. Its bridges and tunnels were built during the late 1920s and on through the 1930s. Three airports were leased from the cities of Newark and New York in the 1940s and made ready for the jet age.

From its early years to the present, the Port Authority has helped the region in diverse and sometimes unexpected ways, involving itself in statewide mass transportation programs, encouraging foreign investment, building industrial parks and containerports, promoting development of the region's 750-mile waterfront, and sharing in marketing and tourism projects.

While the airports, bridges, towers, and tunnels that the Port Authority built—such as the double-decked George Washington Bridge and the World Trade Center—are among the world's engineering marvels, the agency has also been responsible for many inventions, innovations, and discoveries with worldwide and national applica-

tion. These include development of the concept of container shipping and building the world's first containerport; designing the taxiway lighting and signing that have become the standard for airports throughout the world; building the exclusive bus lane, the first reversed highway lane to accommodate peak-hour bus traffic; developing the world's first teleport; pioneering the application of microfiche technology to medical records; building the world's first over-water airplane runways; isolating polyurethane foam as a source of explosive fires; and starting a national campaign to make all plastic furniture fire resistant.

Today, through its facilities—Kennedy, La Guardia, Newark, and Teterboro airports; two heliports; the

Holland and Lincoln tunnels; the George Washington Bridge and Bus Station; the Bayonne, Goethals, and Outerbridge crossings; the Bathgate, Elizabeth, and Yonkers industrial parks; the PATH rail transit system; the Port Newark-Elizabeth, Brooklyn, Red Hook, Howland Hook, and Columbia Street marine terminals; the New York City Passenger Ship Terminal; the Erie Basin Fishport; the World Trade Center and Teleport; and the Port Authority Bus Terminal, Journal Square Transportation Center, Newark Legal and Communications Center, and the New York Union Motor Truck Terminal—the Port Authority is one of the region's most important economic generators.

Bolstered by its ambitious 1987-1991 capital program to build new facilities and rebuild old ones, the Port Authority looks forward to a dynamic future. The five-year program includes a host of important new initiatives, such as upgrading and expanding interstate linkages in the roadway and transit networks; expanding passenger and cargo-handling capacity and improving service at the region's airport system; modernizing terminals, channels, and related facilities of the bistate port; carrying out maintenance and rehabilitation of many vital but aging Port Authority transportation facilities; and stimulating private-sector investment and job creation, especially in business sectors that relate closely to the Port Authority's basic functions or that enhance the region's role as a center of

The Port Authority of New York & New Jersey was created on April 30, 1921, to undertake port and regional improvements that neither private investment nor the two states individually were likely to carry out. Throughout its history the Port Authority has helped the region in a diverse number of ways, involving itself in statewide mass transportation programs, encouraging foreign investment, building industrial parks, and sharing in marketing and tourism projects.

world commerce, and in communities that have not yet fully shared in the region's economic renewal. It is the most ambitious program ever outlined for the Port Authority of New York & New Jersey, and it bodes a continuing bright future to add to the agency's already illustrious past.

BELL AEROSPACE TEXTRON

Lawrence Dale "Larry" Bell started his company in a depression-ridden economy only to turn it into an American success story. An exhibition bears his picture and name in the Smithsonian Institution's air museum in Washington.

The company Bell founded and nurtured in Niagara County, today known as Bell Aerospace Textron, continues to maintain its status on the cutting edge of man's reach for the heavens. A few of the firsts developed at the 53-year-old hotbed of high technology, now headquartered a few miles from Niagara Falls in the Town of Wheatfield, include America's first jet-powered airplane, the world's first commercial helicopter, the world's first supersonic airplane, the world's fastest and highest-flying airplane, the world's first swept-wing and variable swept-wing airplanes, the world's first jet-powered vertical takeoff and landing (VTOL) airplane, and the ascent rocket that lifted Apollo astronauts off the moon. From World War II fighter planes to James Bond-style rocket belts to the gravity sensing systems it manufactures today, Bell has played a key role in the development of many facets of American aviation and space flight.

By 1912 Lawrence Bell had dropped out of high school to enter the aviation business, as a mechanic for two barnstorming exhibition pilots—his brother, Grover F. Bell, and Lincoln Beachy. An accident during a Los Angeles air show that took Grover Bell's life in 1913 gave Lawrence Bell a respect for the dangers of flying. But soon Bell was back in the field as stockboy in a company run by aviation pioneer Glenn D. Martin.

Bell's genius led to his rapid rise in the Martin firm. The company developed the world's first bomber—a Martin exhibition plane equipped with makeshift bombs. At a Martin plant in Cleveland Bell supervised the development of a more sophisticated bomber

plane that was delivered to General Billy Mitchell, used in 1921 to sink the German battleship *Ostfriesland* in an exhibition of air firepower that rocked the aviation world.

In 1928 Bell moved to Buffalo, joining Consolidated Aircraft Co. and rising to the position of vice-president. When Consolidated decided to move to San Diego in 1935, Bell and some associates decided to begin their own company in Buffalo—the Bell Aircraft Corp. Bell built his reputation as an economizer, and the firm survived some lean and hungry years when government contracts went to more established manufacturers.

The company's first breakthrough came with the development of the Bell Airacuda, a combat plane that Bell was awarded an Army contract to produce in 1936. With two 37-millimeter cannons and a top speed of 300 m.p.h., it was the fastest Army plane when the first one flew in September 1937. Expensive and before its time, only 13 were manufactured, but the plane proved to be a springboard for the next Bell success. That was the P-39 Airacobra, the first modern airplane to use the tricycle-style landing gear that would become standard. More than 13,000 Airacobras rolled off Bell assembly lines during World War II, and the versatile plane became a key fighting machine for America and its allies.

Wartime brought prosperity. The Wheatfield plant was built in 1940, adjacent to the Niagara Falls International Airport. Employment soared to 33,000 workers on the Niagara Frontier in 1944 and almost 18,000 more at other facilities in the rapidly expanding Bell empire, including a B-20 bomber factory in Marietta, Georgia, and an Ordnance Division in Burlington, Vermont.

Bell also built the P-59 Airacomet, the nation's first jet-powered plane, designed under such a cloak of secrecy that one general remarked only the

atomic bomb had been kept under tighter wraps. When the first Airacomets were shipped, fake propellers were attached to them to give them a more conventional appearance. Many workers were unaware until months later that they had been building parts and assemblies for a first-of-its-kind aircraft.

At a hastily constructed $50-million plant in Marietta, Georgia, Bell also built 663 B-29 Superfortresses for the war effort.

In 1941 Arthur Young was fortunate enough to catch Lawrence Bell's busy ear long enough to tell him about his idea for a radical new approach to flying called the helicopter. Young showed Bell a model he could fly with electrical controls. Intrigued, Bell put Young and a small staff in a rented garage in Gardenville, a Buffalo suburb,

The Bell Aircraft Corporation plant in Wheatfield turned out P-39 fighter planes by the thousands during World War II.

to work on the project.

Young's inspiration became the world's first commercially licensed helicopter in March 1946. Results of a $12-million investment by Bell, the choppers made early headlines with several rescue missions in the Buffalo area. But the aircraft made its first real inroad in the Korean War, where it was used to move wounded soldiers. Millions of Americans still see the Bell helicopter in reruns of the popular "M*A*S*H" television series. In 1956 alone the company sold $58 million worth of helicopters.

Bell was also moving into other areas, including the development of guided missiles and of a project special to Lawrence Bell—a plane that could fly faster than the fabled sound barrier. This was accomplished on October 14, 1947, in the Bell X-1 by another legend of aviation: Air Force Captain Charles E. "Chuck" Yeager.

Between 1953 and 1956 Bell saw three of its aircraft in succession fly higher and faster than any planes in history. But the death of Lawrence Bell in October 1956 was a sad note in the firm's history. Four years later Textron, headquartered in Providence, Rhode Island, bought the corporation.

Bell was involved in the development of rocket engines that would help make space exploration possible, air cushion vehicles that could glide over land and water, guided missile systems, and vertical takeoff and landing (VTOL) aircraft. Another leap into the space age was Bell's rocket belt, enabling a man to soar over 60-foot obstacles with the assistance of a rocket pack strapped to his back. Bell reaction controls were on the Mercury spacecraft that John Glenn flew on the first American orbit of earth in 1962. Bell's VTOL research led to the design of the deflected-thrust X-14, which is still flying for the National Aeronautics and Space Administration as a research tool for the lunar landing program. A Bell ascent engine propelled astronauts

Bell Aerospace founder Lawrence D. Bell is immortalized in the Smithsonian Institution for his contributions to aviation.

off the surface of the moon after the first lunar landing in 1969.

Today Bell is considered a world leader in the development of precise gravity sensing systems, automatic landing systems for carrier aircraft, microwave landing systems, microwave antennas, precision pointing systems, and tracking radar systems. Key programs include systems for navigation and guidance of the Trident II submarine and a tracking and control radar system that automatically lands carrier-based aircraft in severe sea and weather conditions.

Robert A. Norling, president of Bell Aerospace Textron, says "Our mission is to solve our customers' problems by supplying innovative engineering design solutions and pioneering development of electronic and electromechanical systems in support of our country's defense."

ALBANY INTERNATIONAL CORP.

A modest $40,000 was invested by three ambitious men in 1895 to organize the Albany Felt Company, progenitor of Albany International. Initially a closely held corporation owned by investment banker Selden E. Marvin, Albany patrician scion Parker Corning, and physician's son James W. Cox, Jr., the new company leased property in an industrial neighborhood in Albany. Duncan Fuller, a veteran feltmaker, was engaged as factory superintendent and the new enterprise began, ultimately, to become the world's leading, most competitive manufacturer of paper machine felts and fabrics. From that small first plant on Thacher Street, Albany International eventually would grow to become a firm operating 27 facilities in the United States, Canada, Great Britain, West Germany, Sweden, Norway, Finland, Holland, France, Australia, Brazil, and Mexico.

By 1896 there were 30 employees making felts used to extract excess water from paper stock while imparting a finish to the sheet. The three shareholders increased the firm's paid-in capital to $150,000, and within six years of its founding the successful company outgrew its first facility and acquired a new, six-acre Menands site. The plant erected there required 275,000 bricks and 700,000 board feet of lumber for its construction of buildings that themselves covered two acres, marked from a distance by a 100-foot chimney and housing 150 employees. This new plant also was the first increment of Albany International's ongoing program of robust growth, expansion, and technological advancement.

By 1908 the Albany firm was marketing papermaker felts in Canada, Mexico, Europe, and Japan, and was already outgrowing its factory. The six-acre site permitted additional expansion, allowing all production to be centered there until after World War II

The Albany Felt Plant, circa 1940, was typical of the factories of that time, with machinery requiring considerable labor for its use.

and remaining as corporate headquarters until 1976. In 1988 renovation of the facility will turn the now-old complex into Albany International's headquarters for its global operations, reaffirming the company's New York State origins at a time when many firms were quitting the state.

Expansion of the plant occurred several times between 1908 and 1945, its growth spurred by two world wars and having endured the Great Depression. In 1946 Albany Felt made its first acquisition outside the Albany area, a mill in North Monmouth, Maine, producing flannel for baseball uniforms, as well as industrial textiles.

The year 1951 brought construction of the company's first plant outside

the United States, at Cowansville, Quebec. As foreign sales grew and other facilities were established, Albany Felt was brought ever more directly into the world market. Such continued expansion by the 1960s had made Albany Felt the world's leading supplier of paper machine fabrics, a major manufacturer of a number of industrially utilized fabrics, and, incidentally, the world's largest maker of tennis ball covercloth. Acknowledgment of Albany Felt's now-global role came in 1969, when the firm was renamed Albany International, with Albany Felt as one of its divisions.

By the late 1980s Albany International was a firm that had grown up in its industry, managed by people who had done likewise. Albany International had harnessed the latest innovations in automation and computerization to become a worldwide,

Northeast in many years, and demonstrates the company's commitment to its customers in that region. As the Menands plant gradually shifts equipment across the Hudson River to Rensselaer County, it will become a specialist in certain product lines. As important, nearly nine decades after its construction it will again become corporate headquarters, a cycle of progress fixed in utility and emphasizing the importance of this industrial complex in the Capital District.

With more than 5,000 employees worldwide in 1987 working in a participative corporate environment, up from 1895's Albany work force of 30 employed in a typical nineteenth-century industrial manner, Albany International manufactures a product generi-

Representative of Albany International's modern facilities is this automated high-technology installation, where production has been streamlined by computerization.

cally the same as that it produced close to a century ago while developing fabrics used in a NASA spacesuit. Synthetic, designed fabrics have replaced wool. The high-technology plant rising on the east side of the Hudson River joins Albany International's facilities in other nations to emphasize the company's commitment to the future of New York State and to be the bellwether of the industry it exemplifies.

At its Albany corporate headquarters, Albany International blends the new with the old, an early twentieth-century factory complex built by the muscle power of Capital District laborers now the nexus of the management and technological resources at the company's command, center of an Albany enterprise grown huge. In a sense Albany International has gone full circle, a circle now global, while retaining a strong Empire State identity, where an old industry remains vital because its management understands that technology is the key to its future.

state-of-the-art firm producing paper machine clothing. A 78-acre site was acquired in Rensselaer County, where a major new plant was to open in 1988, encouraged in part by Federal Urban Development Action Grants via the City of Troy and other local and state incentives. The structure, 200,000 square feet of modern space, housed new weaving, needling, and finishing equipment costing $20 million; when fully equipped this new plant represented an outlay of more than $30 million.

A reaffirmation of Albany International's Hudson Valley roots, the establishment of this facility locally saved jobs for New York State and retained for the company workers with years of experience, skills, and knowledge. Albany International's Rensselaer County facility is the first of this industry to be constructed in the

ORANGE AND ROCKLAND UTILITIES, INC.

Typical of many gas and electric companies in the Northeast, Orange and Rockland Utilities, Inc., is a composite of some 14 smaller utilities that were either acquired or merged during this century. One of Orange and Rockland's earliest roots in the New York metropolitan area can be traced to the Nyack and Warren Gas Light Company, a firm capitalized in 1859 by local individuals to manufacture coal gas for street lighting. This early utility company supplied lighting only on moonless nights because, it is said, the moon far outshone the collective lumen level of the gas lamps!

Today Orange and Rockland is poised to meet the challenges of the future while continuing to provide safe, reliable, and affordable energy to its customers in southeastern New York State, northern New Jersey, and northeastern Pennsylvania.

"To achieve tomorrow's goals," says Thomas A. Griffin, Jr., president and chief operating officer, "the company has developed a Master Energy Plan that explores a wide variety of ways in which we can meet our customers' energy requirements into the next century." Orange and Rockland plans to meet future energy needs through a combination of conservation programs, new technologies, energy demand management, and maximizing the produc-

Today Orange and Rockland's Energy Control Center enables the company to constantly monitor its electric system. The Energy Control Center also provides the means to participate in the New York Power Pool, buying and selling power as demand requires.

An Orange and Rockland line crew in 1905. At this time, none of these workers seemed to care about the risks of working with hot wires—none used the sophisticated safety equipment required of today's crews.

tivity of existing electric generating facilities.

O&R was the first utility in New York State to win federal Environmental Protection Agency approval to reconvert a generating facility to low-sulfur, low-cost coal, adding valuable diversity to its oil, gas, and hydroelectric mix for electric generation. These and other methods will enable Orange and Rockland to meet future energy needs while delaying the need for new generating facilities.

Financially, Orange and Rockland has established a solid reputation in the business community—strengthened by its status as the only major utility in the Northeast without nuclear involvement. Under the leadership of chairman and chief executive officer James F. Smith, the firm has earned Double-A ratings from all four major financial ratings services.

But providing electric and gas ser-

vice is only part of the Orange and Rockland story. Because the company has a deep sense of commitment to the communities it serves, it has a wealth of outreach programs that touch on the needs of all its customers, from the elderly, medically disabled, hearing impaired, and financially troubled to the average homeowner who would like to know what steps to take to use energy wisely.

Orange and Rockland has a reputation for being a "good neighbor" to its customers, regularly supporting a variety of community service organizations and programs. Under the direction of former New York State Senator Linda Winikow, vice-president of human resources and external affairs since 1984, the utility has taken firm strides to be an outstanding corporate citizen.

With a firm financial footing, the foresight to prepare now for tomorrow's energy needs, and a strong relationship with the community it serves, Orange and Rockland Utilities, Inc., is ready to step into the next century, confident of its ability to continue its record of outstanding service to its customers.

EMPIRE BLUE CROSS AND BLUE SHIELD

Empire Blue Cross and Blue Shield, the nation's largest private, not-for-profit health insurance company, serves more than 10 million policyholders under various programs, providing hospital, basic medical, major medical, dental, prescription drug, Health Maintenance Organization, and Medicare Supplemental benefits.

Empire Blue Cross and Blue Shield was formed in 1985 through the merger of Blue Cross and Blue Shield of Greater New York and Blue Cross of Northeastern New York. Today the organization serves the 28 eastern counties of New York State, which include the five boroughs of New York City, Nassau, Suffolk, Westchester, Rockland, Orange, Putnam, Dutchess, Ulster, Sullivan, Columbia, Greene, Delaware, Rensselaer, Albany, Schoharie, Schenectady, Montgomery, Saratoga, Fulton, Washington, Warren, Essex, and Clinton.

The organization's roots go back to the early 1930s, when medical care for the working classes was infrequent and expensive. After study by the United Hospital Fund and other hospital groups and health experts, legislation for a group hospital plan was passed in 1934. By the following year Associated Hospital Service (AHS) of New York was opened. The first contracts offered individual coverage for group members. A year later family contracts were offered. By 1949 AHS had enrolled in excess of 4 million customers.

As the Blue Cross system grew it fueled interest in a prepayment plan for doctor services—which came to be known as Blue Shield. In 1940 the Medical Expense Fund was incorporated, and it provided up to $500 per year for services by a participating physician. The following year Associated Hospital Service started its own physician prepayment plan—Community Medical Care, Inc. A merger of the two plans in 1944 formed United Medical Service. In 1949 UMS adopted the Blue Shield insignia; by then it had more than 1.5 million customers.

Growth continued through the 1950s and 1960s. With the inception of the federal Medicare program in 1966, AHS and UMS served as the financial intermediary for the administration of Medicare benefits in New York State.

The early 1970s brought more changes and additions in benefits to keep pace with an evolving medical technology and society. In 1973 AHS started its first Health Maintenance Organization (HMO). In 1974 AHS and UMS merged to create Blue Cross and Blue Shield of Greater New York.

Today's rapidly changing health care marketplace has put new demands on health insurers. Empire Blue Cross and Blue Shield continues to meet this challenge by offering a wide spectrum of health insurance options—including hospital, physician, major medical, dental, prescription drug coverages, Independent Practice Association, Health Maintenance Organization, and managed care products. The corporation's continuous Open Enrollment Policy gives thousands of people

Albert A. Cardone, chairman of the board and chief executive officer of Empire Blue Cross and Blue Shield.

Empire Blue Cross and Blue Shield corporate headquarters is located here at 622 Third Avenue in New York City.

who could not obtain coverage elsewhere the opportunity to purchase health insurance without medical underwriting. Empire Blue Cross and Blue Shield does more than just pay bills. Whether developing new benefit programs, working to reduce health care costs, or bringing affordable health insurance to thousands who would otherwise be without protection, Empire Blue Cross and Blue Shield is a force for progress, concern, and trust in the community.

JAMESTOWN ROYAL

At the turn of the century Jamestown, New York, was emerging as one of the leading wood furniture manufacturing centers of the nation. During the peak of this industry, there were approximately 50 furniture manufacturing companies in Jamestown. Among the finest and most exclusive was Jamestown Royal. It is one of the few that remain in Jamestown today.

Jamestown Royal traces its roots back 75 years to 1913, when the Jamestown Upholstery Company was founded by Clarence Hultquist and Fred Nelson. In 1926 the Jamestown Upholstery Company purchased Royal Upholstery Company, and the two entities were merged to create Jamestown Royal.

Unlike the many Northeast Furniture firms that moved to the sunbelt when the nation's furniture capital shifted south, Jamestown Royal continues to operate at its original location on Crescent Street, which was the heart of Jamestown's furniture district. Over the plant's showroom entrance are the words that have been the company's slogan since its founding: "The Best-Made Line in America."

From the time of its founding, the company has treated furniture making

As a maker of classic furniture, Jamestown Royal has a tradition of elegance and quality that has served it well throughout the years. In the past and today Jamestown Royal uses a small group of craftsmen to make its furniture. This old photo shows the making of nine chairs for the U.S. Supreme Court justices by Jamestown Royal.

as an art form. It has been committed to its slogan and to the motto "Quality First." During world wars, the Great Depression, recessions, and other periods of the twentieth century, Jamestown Royal survived and prospered by dedicating itself to produce the finest-quality hand-made leather- and cloth-upholstered furniture.

Jamestown Royal produces a line of classic styles made by a small group of craftsmen. Each piece is constructed of a heavy hardwood frame, hand-tied springs, plush cushions, and padding, and then covered with the finest upholstery or leather. Many of the styles have a history all their own. Some have been named after famous purchasers, such as the Mamie Eisenhower Chair—a style chosen for use at the Gettysburg farm. Jamestown Royal has also made chairs for the U.S. Supreme Court justices, New York's Governor Thomas E. Dewey, and General Douglas MacArthur.

In the 1950s Lucille Ball, a Jamestown native, and Desi Arnaz furnished their Beverly Hills home with sofas, chairs, and love seats from Jamestown Royal. In fact, the famous couple held a benefit premiere of their first feature film, *Forever Darling,* in Jamestown with a buffet supper in the showroom of Jamestown Royal preceding the show. In the same tradition in 1987, a fund-raising ball for the arts was held in the same showroom.

In 1963 Jamestown Royal was purchased by Leslie H. Johnson, one of the company's leading sales representatives. When Johnson died in 1981, his wife, Ruth, stepped in to manage it, which she did until December 1986, when her son, Peter Johnson, bought the company.

The current management is committed to producing top-quality, classic furniture and to keep Jamestown Royal "The Best-Made Line in America."

This chair was made especially for Thomas E. Dewey, then-governor of New York, by Jamestown Royal.

A classic hepplewhite chair in top-grain leather.

NESTLE FOODS CORPORATION

Whether it is chocolate, coffee, frozen foods, or first-class hotels, Nestle is decidedly a name with international fame, and Nestle Foods Corporation, based in Purchase, New York, is a major part of the Nestle family.

Nestle Foods Corporation is an affiliated company of Nestle Enterprises, Inc. (NEI), which is part of the Swiss parent company Nestle S.A.—the largest food company in the world. Other affiliated companies of Nestle Enterprises, Inc., include Beech-Nut Nutrition Corporation, Hills Bros. Coffee, L.J. Minor Corporation, Nestle Puerto Rico, Inc., Stouffer Foods Corporation, Stouffer Hotel Company, Stouffer Restaurant Company, and Wine World, Inc., the California wine producer.

The Purchase-based Nestle Foods Corporation markets and manufactures products that include Nestle confections and baking products; Taster's Choice coffees, Nescafe coffees, and Nestea teas; Nestle Quik and Hot Cocoa; and Libby's beverages, Cross & Blackwell, Maggi, MJB rices, and Nestle Beich fund-raising confections.

The Nestle legacy traces its roots back to Switzerland in 1866, when Henri Nestle, a German chemist, formulated a unique milk food for infants unable to take mother's milk. Nestle established a business to produce and market his formula, and he subsequently produced sweetened condensed

Nestle Crunch bars, hot cocoa mix, and Nestle Toll House morsels were all introduced in the 1930s and were delivered in trucks like this Lamont, Corliss & Co. delivery truck.

milk. In 1875 Daniel Peter, a chocolate manufacturer in Switzerland, combined the sweetened condensed milk supplied by his neighbor, Henri Nestle, with chocolate, producing the world's first milk chocolate.

In 1900 Nestle opened its first American manufacturing plant, in New York State. The Nestle name has been a key part of New York State business lore for some time. The plant was built in Fulton, New York, to meet a growing demand in the United States for Nestle Milk Food. The Nestle Food Company of New York was then formed in 1905 as a sales agency for Nestle products manufactured in the

United States and in Switzerland.

Nestle came up with many new products in the 1930s, including Nescafe coffee, the Nestle Crunch bar, and Nestle Toll House morsels.

In 1948 The Nestle Company, Inc., was organized for the manufacture and marketing of food products in the United States, and it was headquartered in New York City. The firm moved its headquarters to Colorado, but it only stayed there for two years, returning to New York in 1952. That same year, The Nestle Chocolate Company became a division of The Nestle Company, Inc., and the combined firm moved its American headquarters to White Plains, New York.

In 1985 the company changed its name to Nestle Foods Corporation, which subsequently became part of the expanding network of companies comprised in Nestle Enterprises, Inc.

A symbol of the firm's commitment to the future is the Nestle Foods Corporation headquarters facility in Purchase, New York, which was completed in November 1986. That move brought Nestle people together from various locations in Westchester County and helped them to operate more efficiently as a team.

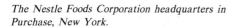

The Nestle Foods Corporation headquarters in Purchase, New York.

SQUIBB CORPORATION

Squibb Corporation, a leading innovator, manufacturer, and marketer of pharmaceutical, medical, and personal care products, remains committed to the lofty standards established by the man who founded the company in Brooklyn, New York, in 1858.

The scope of that commitment has expanded considerably since that time in 1858, when Dr. Edward Robinson Squibb opened a laboratory on the Brooklyn waterfront. The firm he started now provides health care and

Dr. E.R. Squibb resigned as U.S. Navy surgeon in 1858 to found his laboratory on Furman Street in Brooklyn.

personal care products to more than 140 countries. Squibb employs more than 17,000 people and maintains manufacturing, research, or distribution facilities in 47 nations.

Squibb Corporation conducts research, production, and marketing activities for a broad range of pharmaceutical products (cardiovasculars, anti-infectives, anti-inflammatories,

diagnostic agents, consumer health products, medical products, ostomy care, wound care and incontinence supplies, and medical/surgical instruments and supplies).

In the early 1970s Squibb initiated a concerted research program to alleviate cardiovascular disease, particularly in the areas of hypertension and heart failure. In 1979 the firm introduced Corgard (nadolol), the first one-dose-a-day beta-blocking agent for high blood pressure and angina pectoris.

In 1981, following a decade of research, Squibb introduced Capoten (captopril), the first oral angiotensin-converting enzyme (ACE) inhibitor, which blocks the release of a hormone that causes a rise in blood pressure. The label of Capoten, which has proven effective against both hypertension and heart failure, was broadened in 1985 to include first-line therapy in all degrees of hypertension. During 1986 Capoten became the world's third-largest-selling cardiovascular product.

January 1986 marked the U.S. launch of Capozide (captopril/hydrochlorothiazide), a new blood pressure-lowering treatment based on the complementary action of two different types of medications in a single tablet.

In the field of anti-infectives, Squibb was prominent in the development of penicillin production during World War II. Later the firm was a pioneer in introducing antifungal medications such as nystatin and amphotericin B. Squibb's Velosef (cephadrine) capsule is an oral cephalosporin

antibiotic for upper respiratory and urinary tract infections in twice-a-day dosage forms.

In 1981 Squibb discovered a new class of antibiotics with special properties, the monobactams. Azactam (aztreonam), the first compound in this class, has shown remarkable activity against aerobic gram-negative organisms, which thrive in a hospital environment. Azactam has been approved for use in many countries, including the United States, Italy, and Japan.

Princeton Pharmaceutical Products (PPP), a new ethical pharmaceutical marketing and sales organization, was formed in 1986. PPP is dedicated to using the latest technology to provide information about products and services to health care professionals in the most time-effective way. The new organization has geared up a national sales force of 200.

Squibb Mark, a new consumer/multisource product organization, was formed in 1985 to market both Squibb's consumer health products and its patent-expired, branded prescription products. Squibb and Marsam Pharmaceutical Inc. formed a joint company, Squibb-Marsam, Inc., effective January 1, 1986, to develop and market multisource injectable products to hospitals and other institutions.

In the consumer health product area, the Theragran line is one of the leading multivitamin product lines in the United States. The com-

For many years Squibb's main pharmaceutical plant was located at the foot of the Brooklyn Bridge in Brooklyn.

Corporate headquarters from the 1930s to the 1960s was located at Fifth Avenue and 57th Street in New York City. The buildings are (from left) the Sherry-Netherlands Hotel, the Savoy Plaza Hotel, the Squibb Building (with the flag), and the Plaza Hotel.

Squibb tradition rests, dating back to Dr. Edward R. Squibb's work in the nineteenth century. The Squibb Institute for Medical Research was established in 1938, the first industrial-based medical research organization of its kind and a forerunner of what has become a standard component of the pharmaceutical industry. Today Squibb employs more than 1,000 scientists and technicians, with funding for research and development that exceeded $200 million in 1987.

Squibb Corporation has grown immeasurably since Dr. Squibb opened his laboratory, but the philosophy behind it, as stated in its famous trademark, remains unchanged: "The Priceless Ingredient of every product is the honor and integrity of its maker."

Dr. Squibb, on the far left with beard, is seen walking across the Brooklyn Bridge in the 1890s.

pany's many consumer products include Squibb mineral oil, glycerin suppositories, and the Broxodent electric toothbrush.

Squibb-Novo, Inc., a joint company with Novo Industri S/A, Copenhagen, Denmark, markets insulin products in the United States from its headquarters in Princeton, New Jersey. Squibb-Novo now has a complete line of new human insulins for sale in the United States under the Novolin brand name.

In the diagnostic area, Isovue and Isovue-M (iopamidol), nonionic contrast agents to enhance angiogram and myelogram pictures, were introduced for use in the United States on January 1, 1986. The new compound has been found to provide better patient tolerance with less pain than previously used agents.

Squibb's ConvaTec Division is the worldwide leader with its Stomahesive ostomy skin barrier product line, and in two-piece ostomy appliances. In early 1986 it launched its new Durahesive urostomy skin barrier, with a much longer wearing time than products previously available. Also active in the field of wound care with its line of Duo-DERM Hydroactive dressings, Conva-Tec has become a major force in targeted wound management.

Edward Weck Incorporated develops and manufactures a wide variety of products for the physician and surgeon, including hand-held instruments, surgical closures, Argon angiographic catheters and guide wires, and Surgicot operating room supplies.

Research and development has always been the cornerstone on which the

DELAWARE OTSEGO CORPORATION

The Delaware Otsego Corporation, incorporated in 1965, is a holding company that owns eight operating Class III railroads in New York, New Jersey, and Pennsylvania, including the New York, Susquehanna and Western Railway (NYS&W), its major unit.

Delaware Otsego (DO), is a public company whose stock is traded on the NASDAQ National Market System. Its board of directors includes shippers, community development officials, and investors. President and chief executive officer Walter G. Rich has been primarily responsible for the operation and significant expansion of DO properties.

DO's first major step toward the establishment of a regional railroad came in 1980 with the purchase of the NYS&W, a carrier with roughly 74 miles of line in northern New Jersey. This step anchored the DO system in the greater New York metropolitan area.

The second step was the 1982 acquisition from Conrail of some 160 miles of lines in New York and New Jersey. NYS&W negotiated a haulage contract and trackage rights agreement with Conrail, which permitted NYS&W to connect and coordinate operation of the original NYS&W New Jersey trackage (NYS&W's Southern Division) and the New York State lines purchased from Conrail (NYS&W's Northern Division). The acquisition also permitted DO to connect its formerly isolated Central New York Railroad and Lackawaxen and Stourbridge Railroad subsidiaries with other DO lines.

In April 1985 DO began operating a 25-mile rail line extending from New Jersey across Staten Island, New York, formerly a subsidiary of the Chessie System Railroads. In December 1986 this DO subsidiary acquired control of the nine-mile Rahway Valley Railroad in northern New Jersey.

DO owns and operates rail proper-

A New York, Susquehanna and Western Railway stack container train crosses the east branch of the Delaware River at Hancock, New York, en route to Little Ferry, New Jersey.

---

ties and rights extending from the New York-Newark metropolitan area to Syracuse and Utica in Upstate New York. NYS&W interchanges traffic with Conrail at Utica and Binghamton, New York, and Passaic Junction, New Jersey, and with the Delaware & Hudson at Binghamton. DO's new regional, NYS&W, was carefully structured to become a competitor to Conrail in the New York market, which, since 1976,

---

Walter G. Rich, president of Delaware Otsego Corporation.

had been served only by Conrail.

In April 1985 Sea-Land Corporation, the international container steamship company, entered into a long-term lease of 22 acres of NYS&W's Little Ferry (New Jersey) Yard, and constructed a modern container facility on that property. At the same time Sea-Land entered into an operating agreement with NYS&W, Delaware & Hudson, and the Chessie System railroads, which provides for rail transportation between the Little Ferry Yard and Chicago. This agreement represented the first time a regional railroad had successfully concluded an agreement to haul double-stack containerized rail freight.

When DO acquired the NYS&W, it envisioned the development of an industrial corridor along the rail route that would provide for direct rail shipment to on-line customers as well as intermodal transfer terminals that would combine the advantages of rail with the flexibility of motor transport. This approach has met with much success. Little Ferry Yard now handles more than 1,500 carloads and in excess of 40,000 containers of traffic per year.

Several companies have installed in the yard bulk-distribution facilities that transfer plastic, industrial gases, and chemicals. All freight now is terminated at Little Ferry and distributed by truck throughout New York State.

ATLANTIC MUTUAL COMPANIES

On June 27, 1842, the Atlantic Mutual Insurance Company, from its offices near New York's busy waterfront, issued a policy to protect the *A.F. Thorne,* a schooner owned by merchant E.C. Powell. That policy was the company's first—and one of millions to follow.

Atlantic Mutual Companies, as the organization is known today, began as a marine insurer in the days when American clipper ships graced the high seas. And throughout Atlantic's long history, its marine insurance activity has helped America become and continue to be a major maritime power.

Before and during the Civil War, Atlantic protected commercial shipping. Later it was called upon for war risk protection through the Spanish-American War. During World War I Atlantic became a major marine insurer as overseas commerce flourished and marine warfare methods became more sophisticated. In the 1930s and 1940s Atlantic grew to become the national company that it is today. In 1942 Atlantic formed Centennial Insurance Company, a stock subsidiary that brought new diversity, and by 1946 Atlantic had offices in San Francisco, Los Angeles, Seattle, and Portland. By the 1950s Atlantic had expanded to become a carrier of most property and casualty lines of insurance.

The Titantic, *called the "Millionaires' Special" by the press, was four city blocks long and 11 stories high. Protected by the most ingenious safety devices, she was regarded as "unsinkable." Less than five days into her maiden voyage to New York she went down in 12,000 feet of icy water, 300 feet of her hull ripped open by a massive iceberg. Of the $140,000 placed in the American insurance market on the majestic liner's hull, Atlantic Mutual carried $100,000*

Students, historians, researchers, and writers regularly consult Atlantic Mutual's "Disaster Books"—a unique record of vessels, insured by Atlantic Mutual, which were damaged or destroyed at sea.

Today the Atlantic Mutual Companies is comprised of the Atlantic Mutual Insurance Company; its wholly owned subsidiary, the Centennial Insurance Company; and the Atlantic Reinsurance Company. The firms are staffed by the same employees in the same offices. The home office at 45 Wall Street houses Atlantic's executive offices, while day-to-day insurance business is conducted in field offices. At present the Atlantic Mutual Companies has more than 1,500 people working in 30 offices across the United States.

Property, liability, and marine insurance for business and industry are the largest segments of Atlantic's business, accounting for 80 percent of premium income. Atlantic's commercial package provides virtually every kind of property and liability insurance most businesses need, and monoline commercial coverages are also available.

Some 20 percent of Atlantic's business is insurance for the individual or family. Atlantic's Personal Lines Division provides coverages for an individual's auto, home, pleasure boat, other belongings, and personal liabilities.

Atlantic's reputation as a preeminent marine insurance company continues to be its legacy. The firm's marine business encompasses insurance on hulls (commercial watercraft), including "protection and indemnity" (P&I is marine liability), and coverage on all kinds of cargo. The latter accounts for most of Atlantic's marine premiums. Although insurers refer to this business as "ocean marine," coverages can also include transport by air, mail, parcel post, all navigable waterways, and connecting conveyances.

SPECIAL METALS CORPORATION

Special Metals Corporation has been a pioneer in the specialized field of nickel-based superalloy production using vacuum induction melting techniques since 1952, when the firm was founded as the Metals Division of Utica Drop Forge & Tool Company.

The major continuing aim of the New Hartford-based corporation is to use vacuum induction melting as a starting point in the production of cleaner, stronger, and more consistent alloys for critical high-temperature applications.

Producing better turbine blades for military jet engines was the first goal set in 1952 by the then-small division. Since then the goal has been expanded to include commercial and military jet engine turbine disks, shafts, and rings, as well as a variety of products used in oil exploration and nuclear applications, where strength and corrosion resistance in elevated temperature environments are required.

Special Metals Corporation (SMC) also has expanded by acquiring manufacturing divisions in two other locations: the Udimet Division at Princeton, Kentucky, where superalloy powder products are made in a 70,000-square-foot plant, and the Dental Products Division at Ann Arbor, Michigan, where patented silver amalgams and

A superalloy bar being rolled for later use in aerospace or oil exploration industries.

Nitinol orthodontic arch wires are made.

Superalloys, also known as high-temperature alloys, are typically nickel-base materials containing significant quantities of chrome, molybdenum, and cobalt, which are strengthened through a complex reaction involving aluminum and titanium. Because both aluminum and titanium form unwanted oxide and nitride compounds when exposed to air in the molten state, melting in a vacuum is required to achieve the full desired capability of the materials.

Dr. Falih N. Darmara, SMC's founder and later president, developed the first commercial-size vacuum induction melting furnace for superalloy production while serving as assistant to the president of Utica Forge. His development launched a new age of vacuum metallurgy—using a technology that previously had been regarded principally as a laboratory curiosity.

That furnace had a capacity of only six pounds. After testing proved the feasibility of the new technical development, Darmara designed and built a 50-pound vacuum induction furnace. Later he designed one that would produce 200 pounds of a superalloy in one heat.

Darmara's work gave SMC a lead in the development of larger and larger furnaces—a lead it still maintains. Today SMC operates three production vacuum induction melting furnaces, with capacities ranging from 5,000 to 40,000 pounds, in its New Hartford plant. The 20-ton furnace is one of the largest in the world. Eight vacuum arc consumable-electrode furnaces and one electroslag furnace are used to produce the ultimate in homogeneous alloy structure through a sophisticated second melting operation.

Forging capabilities include a press shop in Dunkirk, New York, used to convert ingots to billets, and a heavy-duty rolling mill at New Hartford for

An overhead charger at the Dunkirk, New York, plant. This machine removes 10,000-pound superalloy ingot from furnaces for pressing to billet.

production of bar stock and small diameter billets, supplemented by state-of-the-art cold finish and inspection equipment.

The company's New Hartford plant is its largest. This 263,000-square-foot building houses SMC's principal production and research and development facilities, plus its headquarters and marketing offices.

State-of-the-art peeling and immersion ultrasonic inspection equipment recently has been added in response to industry needs.

Special Metals has always been noted for technical excellence in the superalloy industry. The firm is approved as a materials source by all major gas turbine engine manufacturers. SMC has made production quantities of most domestic and European alloys currently used by industry. Future plans

include a continuance of its bold capital expansion program, which has included several expansions of its New Hartford facilities and the addition of new and more sophisticated production equipment.

SMC's Process Laboratory contains many unique pieces of equipment, including an electron beam melting unit for material cleanliness studies, a centrifugal casting unit capable of melting up to 4,000 pounds of material in a vacuum and casting it into a rotating mold for inclusion elimination, a spinning disk powder production unit, small vacuum induction melting and vacuum arc remelting units, and laboratory-size argon atomizer for powder products.

With the expansion program and growing markets for its products, the future looks increasingly bright for Special Metals Corporation.

A 12,000-pound vacuum induction furnace and electrode molds.

The headquarters of Special Metals Corporation has been located in New Hartford since 1958.

Dr. Darmara's first furnace, the first step in proving the commercial feasibility of vacuum induction melting, resides near the entrance lobby of the building. The furnace, which was used for research until 1979, has been designated a Historical Landmark by the American Society of Metals, the industry's premier trade association.

BOZELL, JACOBS, KENYON & ECKHARDT

Bozell, Jacobs, Kenyon & Eckhardt today is a thriving, multimillion-dollar international advertising agency also offering strategic corporate communications, public relations, and other specialties. This is not surprising considering that it was created in 1986 by the merger of two of the most prestigious and established companies in the business.

Bozell & Jacobs was formed in Omaha in 1921 by two friends and newspapermen, Leo B. Bozell and Morris E. Jacobs. From the outset, the firm provided not only advertising services, but also public relations, a specialization still in its infancy at that time.

An early association with the Nebraska Power Company established Bozell & Jacobs as an expert in communications programs for privately owned utilities, then struggling against public takeover efforts. During the next two decades, B&J remained active in utilities, while steadily increasing its client list, which eventually included Mutual of Omaha, Tenneco, and American Airlines, among others.

Otis Allen Kenyon, an engineer, inventor, and book editor, and Henry Eckhardt, a newspaperman and ad copy writer, were officers of Ray D. Lillibridge, Inc., an ad agency established in New York City in 1899. In 1929, just a few weeks before the stock market crash, they purchased the firm. With the help of some established clients and loyal employees who agreed to pay cuts, K&E survived the Depression, and went on to become a major national advertising agency, representing clients such as RCA, Shell Oil, Nabisco, Ford Motor Company, Lever Brothers, and Pepsi Cola.

Charles D. Peebler, Jr., BJK&E chief executive officer, joined Bozell & Jacobs in 1958 and purchased the firm from Morris Jacobs in 1966. Under his leadership, B&J moved its corporate headquarters to New York City while maintaining full-service offices in major markets throughout the United States. The agency began an acquisitions program that cemented the national and international reputation the firm enjoys. In 1988 BJK&E completed a buy-back from Lorimar Telepictures and is now an employee-owned, independent entity.

Since their respective beginnings, the firms have had a strong tradition of community service. Morris Jacobs referred to his volunteer activities as "paying rent for the space we occupy on earth." Kenyon & Eckhardt provided much of the early advertising work for the Peace Corps, and prepared many materials for the Juvenile Diabetes Foundation and the Fresh Air Fund.

Bozell & Jacobs helped Father Edward Flanagan establish Boys Town, the Omaha home for homeless boys. B&J developed the now famous fund-raising appeal that included a photograph of two young boys and the caption, "He ain't heavy, Father . . . he's my brother."

Charles D. Peebler, Jr., is chief executive officer of BJK&E.

BJK&E is headquartered at 40 West 23rd Street, a beautifully restored 100-year-old building erected for the Stern Brothers department store, appropriate surroundings for a firm so rich in history and tradition. Sitting in his tastefully appointed office, Peebler says, "We've evolved into a full-line communications agency that has a wide range of services and divisions around the world. But we never lost sight of the need to give back to the community."

BJK&E is headquartered at 40 West 23rd Street in a beautifully restored 100-year-old building

KENTILE FLOORS INC.

Anyone selecting vinyl floor tiles for a home or commercial building today has a multitude of choices. Tile that resembles brick, slate, marble, or even ceramic tile is available in a range of colors that can satisfy even the fussiest decorator.

Yet most people do not know that New York City's own David E. Kennedy conceived the idea of floor tiles, and through hard work, perseverance, and vision established an industry. His company, Kentile Floors Inc., today is the second-largest manufacturer of vinyl tiles in the United States, and is well-known as an innovator in tile design and manufacture.

Kennedy felt that cork, with its innate resilience, would make excellent flooring material—and that cut into tiles, installation would be greatly facilitated. In the 1890s he convinced the Armstrong Cork Co., which produced bottle corks, to manufacture tiles and began selling them. Their utility made cork tiles an instant success; they were installed in many of the new buildings of the day, including the New York Public Library's headquarters on Fifth Avenue.

Armstrong then began to sell cork tiles also, bringing on a legal challenge from Kennedy. With his settlement Kennedy set up shop in the East New York section of Brooklyn and went into manufacturing himself, establishing David E. Kennedy, Inc., in 1899.

Kennedy continued developing new products, creating Everlastic Tile from an early version of linoleum, and then asphalt tile, a highly successful product that was used for many years. Business was good, and in the 1920s Kennedy moved to Kentile's present location, a former rope factory on Second Avenue in South Brooklyn.

In 1934 Kennedy's son, David O'D., took over the business upon the founder's death. Under the younger Kennedy's guidance, Kentile gradually moved away from the installation end of the business and concentrated on manufacturing, eventually using only wholesale distributors to sell its products.

The years during World War II saw a shortage of the raw materials needed to make tiles. But thanks to several large government contracts, including providing the flooring for the Pentagon and making cork cartridge plugs for five- and six-inch guns used by the Navy, Kentile survived. For its munitions work Kentile was awarded the government's prestigious "E" award for excellence. Kentile flourished during the postwar building boom, providing flooring for many of the era's large developments, including Long Island's Levittown.

Kentile was instrumental in introducing colors in vinyl tiles, and was the first to feature textured tile. The firm pioneered a manufacturing process

Established by David E. Kennedy in the 1890s, Kentile Floors today is the second-largest manufacturer of vinyl tiles in the United States. Succeeding his father in 1934, David O'D. Kennedy served as president of the firm for 51 years and currently holds the position of chairman. Courtesy, E.R. Bogard, Studio

In keeping with the family tradition of leadership, Andrew G. Kennedy assumed the presidency of Kentile Floors Inc. in 1985. Courtesy, E.R. Bogard, Studio

that created designs such as the "brick look." To accommodate the special needs of computers and other advance electronic equipment in commercial establishments, Kentile created tile that conducts electricity.

Andrew G. Kennedy assumed the Kentile presidency in 1985 from his father, who had held that post for 51 years. David O'D. Kennedy remains the firm's chairman. Together they oversee activities at Kentile's Brooklyn, South Plainsfield, New Jersey, and Chicago facilities, and plan the firm's strategy for challenging its principal competitor: Armstrong.

AMERICAN EXPRESS

In 1841 Buffalo resident Henry Wells launched an express service, carrying a carpetbag full of gold, silver, and securities on a four-day journey from Albany to Buffalo. Wells & Co. prospered, and in 1850 it merged with two competitors—Butterfield, Wasson & Co., and Livingston & Fargo. The new firm was called American Express Company, and Henry Wells became its president.

During the 1850s Wells and William G. Fargo, company secretary, also established the famed Wells, Fargo and Company, and partner John Butterfield launched the legendary Pony Express. American Express, meanwhile, became the nation's foremost express operation, employing 1,500 people in 890 offices and agencies by 1862. Six years later it merged with New York-based Merchants Union Express Company to form the American Merchants Union Express Company. In 1870 Henry Wells passed the reins to William G. Fargo, who guided the firm through a profitable era until his death in 1881. The company dropped the "Merchants Union" from its name in 1873 and again became the American Express Company, with its main headquarters in New York City.

James Congdell "J.C." Fargo, younger brother of William, would lead American Express through 33 years of innovation and diversification. Under his guidance the company developed the famed American Express Money Order in 1882, and nine years later it introduced the renowned American Express Traveler's Cheque. By 1898 the company had shipping offices in France, England, and Germany to handle westbound freight. Soon those offices also became selling agents for

Company headquarters is the American Express Tower in New York City's World Financial Center, a pyramid-topped building with 51 stories.

European railroads and passenger vessels, and by 1909 they were providing rates and itineraries for European tours. In 1915 American Express' entry into the travel business was formalized by the establishment of a Travel Department in New York. Meanwhile, the Rotterdam office was conducting overseas banking transactions, and the freight business was booming. Thus, by the time J.C. Fargo retired in 1914, American Express had become a multinational, multifaceted institution.

George C. Taylor succeeded J.C. Fargo, and he quickly expanded the foreign remittance operations and the Travel Department. These actions proved timely: During World War I the government consolidated all railroad and express companies into a single

In 1915 American Express' entry into the travel business was formalized by the establishment of a travel department in New York. Today American Express serves its travel customers with its charge cards, American Express travelers checks, and travel agency services.

Henry Wells founded American Express Company in 1850, and by 1862 it had become the nation's foremost express operation, employing 1,500 people in 890 offices and agencies. In 1873 American Express Company had its main headquarters in this building in New York City.

government-owned entity, The American Railway Express Company, Inc. George Taylor accepted election as president of this vast government enterprise in 1918, while continuing as president of American Express Company. He led both organizations until 1923.

The government-owned express service had deprived American Express of its founding business, but other valuable businesses remained—money order, Traveler's Cheques, foreign remittances and foreign exchange, travel, a small foreign banking operation, and the international freight business. Frederick P. Small became the next president of American Express, and

during the 1920s the company prospered, following prudent fiscal policies that enabled it to weather the Stock Market Crash of 1929. During the 1930s American Express remained stable and, more remarkably, profitable. By the time Ralph T. Reed became president in 1944, the company was gearing up for the postwar boom.

Throughout the 1950s the firm grew in the areas of travel, travel-related services, financial services, and international banking. Introduction of the American Express Card in 1958 was a milestone, and American Express became a vast and diverse corporation. With the travel boom of the 1960s, use of American Express Traveler's Cheques grew phenomenally, and travel-related services expanded. In 1960 Howard L. Clark, the new president and chief executive officer (the seventh in the company's history), aimed to expand even further in the firm's traditional areas—travel and financial services.

In 1966 American Express acquired W.H. Morton & Co., a major underwriter of government and corporate bonds. American Express also established overseas merchant banking subsidiaries such as London-based Amex Bank Limited. In the Far East, merchant banking subsidiaries were launched to work with Bancom Development Corporation, a Philippine investment banking affiliate. Today American Express Bank Ltd. (formerly American Express International Banking Corporation) has 99 offices in 43 countries.

In 1977 James D. Robinson III became chairman and chief executive officer of American Express. The company has since undergone profound expansion. In 1981 it acquired Shearson Loeb Rhoades Inc., the second-largest securities firm in the United States, and three years later acquired Lehman

The blueprint for the Blue Box showing American Express Company and its principal subsidiaries.

Brothers Loeb Holding Company, to form a subsidiary known as Shearson Lehman Brothers.

In 1983 American Express acquired Trade Development Bank (TDB), a Swiss-based private bank. In 1984 American Express acquired Investors Diversified Services, Inc., and established a new investment services subsidiary, IDS/American Express. In 1985 this subsidiary was renamed IDS Financial Services, Inc.

During the 1980s American Express has greatly enhanced its position as an internationally renowned financial services leader. In addition to the important acquisitions from 1981 through 1984, Travel Related Services Company, Inc. (TRS), the firm's long-established charge card and Traveler's Cheque franchise, has enjoyed dramatic growth. American Express also has diversified into consumer lending, with a nationally chartered bank in Delaware and a state bank in Minnesota, and offerings of personal credit lines and mortgage loans to cardmembers and IDS customers. TRS' subsidiary, First Data Resources Inc., acquired in 1980, has positioned American Express as a major vendor of information-processing services.

In 1986 the company moved to the American Express Tower in New York City's World Financial Center. The pyramid-topped building of 51 stories is an impressive addition to New York City's skyline.

PAN AMERICAN WORLD AIRWAYS

On October 28, 1927, a small trimotor airplane bounced along a dirt runway at Key West, Florida, and took off, heading out over the sea. One hour and 10 minutes later it landed at Havana, Cuba, completing the first scheduled international flight in U.S. airline history—and the first flight of a new airline, Pan American Airways.

Pan Am's founder was a 28-year-old former naval aviator, Juan Terry Trippe. He started with two airplanes, 24 employees, and an unshakable faith in the future of air travel. The goal of his airline, Trippe said, was "to provide mass air transportation for the average man at fares he can afford to pay."

Pan Am's first flights carried only mail, but within three months the fledgling airline was also transporting passengers on a daily schedule between Florida and Cuba. The flights were popular, encouraging Pan Am to acquire additional aircraft, hire more

people, and open new routes—first to other Caribbean islands, then to Mexico and Central and South America.

In 1928, to help survey these new routes, Trippe hired a young pilot who less than a year earlier had thrilled the world by making the first solo, nonstop flight across the Atlantic: Charles Lindbergh. "The Lone Eagle," as he had been dubbed by the press, would serve Pan Am as a technical adviser for more than 45 years.

In 1958 Pan Am led the world into the jet age. Colorful ceremonies preceded the takeoff of Clipper America *on the first scheduled jet flight by a U.S. airline from New York to Paris on October 26, 1958.*

By the end of 1929, just two years after its maiden flight, Pan Am was a major international carrier with a 12,000-mile route system linking the United States and 23 Latin American countries. By 1934 Pan Am was operating 85 aircraft and transporting more than 100,000 passengers annually. Still the airline sought new challenges. On November 22, 1935, the *China Clipper*—a huge flying boat that was the first truly long-range aircraft—took off from San Francisco Bay and headed west. Stopping overnight at island bases, the *China Clipper* landed at Manila six days later, completing the U.S. airline industry's first scheduled transpacific flight.

Less than four years later, in May 1939, Pan Am's *Yankee Clipper*—a Boeing B-314—flew from New York to Lisbon and on to Marseille, inaugurating scheduled transatlantic service. Pan Am flights to Southampton, En-

The eight-passenger Fokker F-7 inaugurated Pan Am's first scheduled passenger flight from Key West, Florida, to Havana, Cuba, on January 16, 1928. The three-engine plane made the 90-mile trip in about one hour, opening a network that later extended throughout the Caribbean to South America, across the Pacific, and finally the Atlantic.

Pan Am founder Juan T. Trippe (right) chats with aviation pioneer Charles A. Lindbergh on the tarmac in Panama. Pan Am began service from Miami to the Canal Zone in February 1929. Lindbergh was a longtime technical adviser to Pan Am, flying many survey flights in the 1930s.

gland, were introduced the following month.

During World War II Pan Am, the nation's only overseas airline, flew more than 90 million miles for the government, carrying high-priority personnel and cargo, ferrying hundreds of bombers and other aircraft to the war zones, building some 50 airports in 15 countries, and training thousands of military pilots, navigators, and mechanics. Through the years Pan Am has also frequently gone to the aid of victims of disasters around the world, flying in supplies, medical help, and emergency equipment and evacuating the injured—often without recompense. Pan Am has flown literally hundreds of these missions of mercy, volunteering its aircraft, personnel, and technical knowledge in response to appeals for help from people of all nationalities.

In 1947 Pan Am inaugurated around-the-world service. Only two decades old, the airline had 19,000 employees and served 62 countries. In 1948 Pan Am introduced a new class of service—now known as economy class—at prices well under the industry's all-first-class level. It was a big step toward Juan Trippe's goal of making air travel affordable to everyone.

In 1950, reflecting the extension of its routes to literally every corner of the globe, Pan American Airways changed its name to Pan American World Airways. Meanwhile, Pan Am began working with the major aeronautics companies to develop commercial jet transport. On October 26, 1958, America entered the jet age when Pan Am's *Clipper America*, a Boeing 707, took off from New York with 111 passengers aboard and flew to Paris. It was the first commercial jet flight by a U.S. airline, the first commercial flight by an American-built jet transport, and the start of daily transatlantic jet service. Soon Pan Am jets replaced the airline's piston-engine planes on all far-flung routes. In one bold stroke Pan Am had slashed flying times in half, and for the first time a traveler could fly to anywhere in the world in just hours.

But as this new chapter opened, another closed. Juan Trippe, who had guided Pan Am for more than four decades and built it into America's leading international airline, retired from the company in 1968. One of the industry's true pioneers, he continued to serve Pan Am as an honorary director until his death in 1981.

With the speed and comfort of the new jets—and the new lower fares initiated by Pan Am—the number of international travelers increased. In 1970 Pan Am alone carried 11 million passengers nearly 20 billion passenger miles. That same year the first Pan Am 747 went into service between New York and London. The 747s soon became the mainstay of the airline's fleet.

Six years later Pan Am introduced

the 747SP—SP for special performance—which enabled Pan Am to offer the first nonstop service between New York and Tokyo, New York and Dhahran, Los Angeles and Sydney, San Francisco and Hong Kong, and other widely separated points. And on May 1, 1976, Pan Am's 747SP *Clipper Liberty Bell* flew east from New York on a record-breaking around-the-world flight. Carrying 96 passengers, it made only two refueling stops—at Delhi and Tokyo—and landed back in New York 46 hours after leaving, beating the previous record by 15.5 hours.

Until the late 1970s Pan Am was exclusively an international airline. Then, with the increased route flexibility resulting from deregulation, Pan Am began to acquire domestic routes within the United States. In 1980 Pan Am's domestic route system expanded when it merged with National Airlines, which served primarily U.S. destinations.

Pan Am is the only major airline based in New York, with its corporate headquarters in the landmark Pan Am Building on Park Avenue and its principal operational hub at New York's John F. Kennedy International Airport.

Today, under the leadership of chairman and chief executive officer C. Edward Acker, Pan American World Airways is a worldwide organization, providing service to 34 U.S. cities and 66 cities abroad, operating a fleet of 112 jet aircraft, and employing more than 20,000 people.

The Worldport, Pan Am's passenger terminal at John F. Kennedy International Airport in New York.

The Hackley School's students and staff pose in front of their Tarrytown facility. Courtesy, Hackley School

PATRONS

The following individuals, companies, and organizations have made a valuable commitment to the quality of this publication. Windsor Publications, The Business Council of New York State, and the New York State Museum gratefully acknowledge their participation in *New York State: Gateway to America.*

Albany International Corp.*
Albany Savings Bank*
American Express*
Arcata Graphics/Buffalo Division*
Atlantic Mutual Companies*
Auburn Steel Company, Inc.*
B.H. Aircraft Company, Inc.
Bankers Trust Company*
The Bank of New York*
Bell Aerospace Textron*
Bozell, Jacobs, Kenyon & Eckhardt*
Brenner Paper Products Co., Inc.*
Bush Industries, Inc.*
Central Hudson Gas & Electric Corporation*
Chase Manhattan Corporation*
Chemical Bank*
Chicago Pneumatic Tool Company*
Consolidated Edison Company of New York, Inc.*
The Crosby Company*
Delaware Otsego Corporation*
Deloitte Haskins & Sells*
Dorsey Millwork, Inc.*
Emigrant Savings Bank*
EMJ/McFarland-Johnson Engineers, Inc.*
Empire Blue Cross and Blue Shield*
Empire Soils Investigations, Inc.*
Empire State Report Magazine
Fair-Rite Products Corporation*
Ferree Plastics, Inc.*
Garden Way, Incorporated*
General Foods*
General Mills, Inc.

Golub Corporation*
Graham Corporation*
Gramco, Inc.*
The Hackley School*
Heritage Hills of Westchester*
Hertlein Special Tool Company, Inc.*
The Hilliard Corporation*
IBM Corporation*
Jamestown Royal*
Jardine Emett & Chandler*
Johnson & Higgins*
Kentile Floors Inc.*
H. Kohnstamm & Co., Inc.*
Ko-Rec-Type*
Lawler, Matusky & Skelly Engineers*
The Lawrence Group, Inc.*
Lovell Safety Management Co., Inc.*
Merrill Lynch & Co., Inc.*
Metropolitan Life Insurance Company*
Ernest J. Milano
Miller Brewing Co.*
Phillip H. Morse
Nestle Foods Corporation*
New Rochelle Precision Grinding Corporation*
New York Casualty Insurance Company*
New York Chamber of Commerce and Industry*
New York State Credit Union League*
New York State Electric & Gas Corporation*
North American Instrument Corporation*
Norton Company/Coated Abrasive Division*
Orange & Rockland Utilities, Inc.*
Pan American World Airways*
Parsons Brinckerhoff Inc.
Peoples Westchester Savings Bank*

Pfizer, Inc.*
Phelps Memorial Hospital Center*
Philip Morris Companies Inc.*
The Port Authority of New York & New Jersey*
Power Line Constructors, Inc.*
Price Waterhouse*
Reader's Digest*
Reliable Automatic Sprinkler Co., Inc.*
The Seamen's Bank for Savings, FSB*
Security Mutual Life Insurance Company*
Special Metals Corporation*
Spence Engineering Company, Inc.*
Squibb Corporation*
Stebbins Engineering and Manufacturing Co.*
Tam Ceramics Inc.*
Ulster County Community College*
Universal Instruments Corporation
V Band Corporation*
Vollmer Associates*

*Partners in Progress of *New York State: Gateway to America.* The histories of these companies and organizations appear in Chapter 10, beginning on page 249.

388

BIBLIOGRAPHY

The literature on New York is voluminous and constantly growing. Highly selective, the following list of books will help readers to learn more about a particular period, topic, or individual. The most extensive bibliography is available in David M. Ellis, James A. Frost, Harold Syrett, and Harry Carman's *A History of New York State* (Ithaca, N.Y.: Cornell University Press, 1967). For the colonial period, see Michael Kammen, *Colonial New York—A History* (New York: Charles Scribner's Sons, 1975). For New York City, see George J. Lankevich and Howard B. Furer, *A Brief History of New York City* (Port Washington, N.Y.: Associated Faculty Press, Inc., 1984). Books dealing with New York's prominent role in the Revolutionary period are listed and evaluated in *New York in the American Revolution A Bibliography* (Albany, N.Y.: New York State American Revolution Bicentennial Committee, 1974), compiled by Milton M. Klein.

GENERAL WORKS

The following books deal with the overall history of the state and metropolis. Readers can trace articles in the annual and decennial indexes of *New York History,* the journal of the New York State Historical Association. The New York Historical Society also published a quarterly for many years after 1917 as well as many volumes of *Collections.* The Buffalo and the Rochester historical societies have also published many books and articles. Because of the state's importance in U.S. history, many national historical journals have printed articles dealing with various aspects of state history.

Carmer, Carl. *The Tavern Lights Are Burning: Literary Journeys Through Six Regions and Four Centuries of New York State.* New York: David McKay Inc., 1964.

Davidson, Marshall. *New York: A Pictorial History.* New York: Charles Scribner's Sons, 1977.

Ellis, David M., et al. *A History of New York State.* Ithaca, N.Y.: Cornell University Press, 1967.

Ellis, David Maldwyn. *New York: State and City.* Ithaca, N.Y.: Cornell University Press, 1979.

Federal Writers' Project of the Works Progress Administration. *A Guide to the Empire State.* New York: Oxford University Press, 1940.

Flick, Alexander C., ed. *History of the State of New York,* 10 vols. New York: Columbia University Press, 1933-1937.

Fox, Dixon Ryan. *Yankees and Yorkers.* New York: New York University Press, 1940.

Klein, Milton M., ed. *New York: The Centennial Years, 1676-1976.* Port Washington, N.Y.: Kennikat Press, 1976.

Kouwenhoven, John. *Columbia Historical Portrait of New York City.* New York: Doubleday and Company, 1951.

Lankevich, George J., and Howard B. Furer. *A Brief History of New York City.* Port Washington: Associated Faculty Press, Inc., 1984.

Lyman, Susan E. *The Story of New York: An Informal History of the City.* New York: Crown Publishers, 1964.

Ritchie, William A. *The Archaeology of New York State.* Garden City, N.Y.: Natural History Press, 1965.

Rosenwaike, Ira. *Population History of New York City.* Syracuse, N.Y.: Syracuse University Press, 1976.

Still, Bayrd, ed. *Mirror For Gotham: New York As Seen by Contemporaries from Dutch Days to the Present.* New York: New York University Press, 1956.

Stokes, I.N.P. *The Iconography of Manhattan Island, 1492-1909,* 6 vols. New York: R.H. Dodd, 1915-1928.

Thompson, Harold. *Body, Boots & Britches: Folktales, Ballads, and Speech from Country New York.* New York: J.B. Lippincott Company, 1939.

Thompson, John H., ed. *Geography of New York State.* Syracuse, N.Y.: Syracuse University Press, 1966.

CHAPTER 1

Bonomi, Patricia. *A Factious People: Politics and Society in Colonial New York.* New York: Columbia University Press, 1971.

Flexner, James T. *Mohawk Baronet: Sir William Johnson of New York.* New York: Harper and Brothers, 1959.

Gerlach, Don R. *Philip Schuyler and the Growth of 1733-1804.* Albany: Office of State History, 1968.

Hamilton, Milton W. *Sir William Johnson: Colonial American, 1715-1763.* Port Washington, N.Y.: Kennikat Press, 1976.

Hunt, George H. *The Wars of the Iroquois.* adison, Wis.: University of Wisconsin Press, 1940.

Kammen, Michael. *Colonial New York—A History.* New York: Charles Scribner's Sons, 1975.

Kenney, Alice P. *Stubborn for Liberty: The Dutch in New York.* Syracuse, N.Y.: Syracuse University Press, 1975.

Kim, Sung Bok. *Landlord and Tenant in Colonial New York Manorial Society 1664-1775.* Chapel Hill, N.C.: The University of North Carolina Press, 1978.

Leder, Lawrence H. *Robert Livingston 1654-1728 And the Politics of Colonial New York.* Chapel Hill, N.C.: The University of North Carolina Press, 1961.

Rink, Oliver A. *Holland on the Hudson An Economic and Social History of Dutch New York.* Ithaca, N.Y.: Cornell University Press, 1986.

Ritchie, Robert C. *The Dukes's Province: A Study of New York Politics and Society.* Chapel Hill, N.C.: The University of North Carolina Press, 1977.

Van der Zee, Henri and Barbara. *A Sweet and Alien Land: The Story of Dutch New York.* New York: Viking Press, 1978.

Wallace, Paul A. *The White Roots of Peace.* Philadelphia, Pa.: The University of Pennsylvania Press, 1946.

CHAPTER 2

Cooke, Jacob E. *Alexander Hamilton A Biography.* New York: Charles Scribner's Sons, 1982.

De Pauw, Linda Grant. *The Eleventh Pillar New York State and the Constitution.* Ithaca, N.Y.: Cornell University Press, 1966.

Flick, Alexander C. *The American Revolution in New York Its Political, Social and Economic Significance.* Albany, N.Y.: University of the State of New York, 1926.

Gerlach, Don R. *Philip Schuyler and the American Revolution in New York, 1733-1777.* Lincoln, Neb.: University of Nebraska Press, 1964.

Graymont, Barbara. *The Iroquois in the American Revolution.* Syracuse, N.Y.: Syracuse University Press, 1972.

Kelsay, Isabel, *Joseph Brant 1743-1807: Man of Two Worlds.* Syracuse, N.Y.: Syracuse University Press, 1984.

Mason, Bernard. *The Road to Independence The Revolutionary Movement in New York 1773-1777.* Lexington, Ky.: University of Kentucky Press, 1966.

Polf, William A. *1777 The Political Revolution and New York's First Constitution.* Albany, N.Y.: New York State Bicentennial Commission, 1977.

Schecter, Stephen L., ed. *The Reluctant Pillar: New York and the Adoption of the Federal Constitution.* Troy, N.Y.: Russell Sage College, 1985.

Spaulding, E. Wilder. *New York in the Critical Period 1783-1789.* New York: Columbia University Press, 1932.

Wallace, Anthony. *The Death and Rebirth of the Senecas: The History and Culture of the Great Iroquois Nation.* New York: Alfred A. Knopf, 1970.

Young, Alfred F. *The Democratic Republicans of New York: The Origins, 1763-1797.* Chapel Hill, N.C.: University of North Carolina Press, 1967.

CHAPTER 3

Albion, Robert G. *The Rise of New York Port, 1815-1860.* New York: Scribner, 1939; repr. 1970.

Andrist, Ralph K. *The Erie Canal.* New York: Harper and Row, 1964.

Bergmann, Frank, ed. *Upstate Literature: Essays in Memory of Thomas F. O'Donnell.* Syracuse, N.Y.: Syracuse University Press, 1985.

Chazanof, William. *Joseph Ellicott and the Holland Land Company The Opening of Western New York.* Syracuse, N.Y.: Syracuse University Press, 1970.

Ellis, David Maldwyn. *Landlords and Farmers in the Hudson-Mohawk Region, 1790-1850.* Ithaca, N.Y.: Cornell University Press, 1946.

————. "The Rise of the Empire State, 1790-1820," *New York History.* (January 1975): 5-27.

Fox, Dixon Ryan. *The Decline of Aristocracy in the Politics of New York, 1801-1840.* New York: Columbia University Press, 1919; repr. 1965.

Frost, James Arthur. *Life on the Upper Susquehanna 1783-1860.* New York: King's Crown Press, 1951.

Gabriel, Ralph Henry. *The Evolution of Long Island: A Study of Land and Sea.* New Haven, Conn.: Yale University Press, 1921.

Hedrick, Ulysses Prentiss. *A History of Agriculture in the State of New York.* Albany, N.Y.: New York State Agricultural Society, 1933; repr. 1966.

Jones, Louis C. *Growing Up in the Cooper Country: Boyhood Recollections of the New York Frontier.* Syracuse, N.Y.: Syracuse University Press, 1965.

McKelvey, Blake. *Rochester the Water-Power City 1812-1854.* Cambridge, Mass.: Harvard University Press, 1945.

McNall, Neil Adams. *An Agricultural History of the Genesee Valley 1790-1860.* Philadelphia, Pa.: University of Pennsylvania Press, 1952.

Mohl, Raymond A. *Poverty in New York 1783-1825.* New York: Oxford University Press, 1971.

Ryan, Mary P. *Cradle of the Middle Class: The Family in Oneida County, New York, 1790 1865.* New York: Cambridge University Press, 1981.

Spaulding, Ernest Wilder. *His Excellency George Clinton: Critic of the Constitution.* New York, 1938; repr. 1964.

Turner, Orsamus *History of the Pioneer Settlement of Phelps and Gorham's Purchase and Morris' Reserve.* Rochester, N.Y.: W. Alling, 1852.

CHAPTER 4

Alexander, De Alva Stanwood. *A Political History of the State of New York, 1774-1882,* 3 vols. New York: Henry Holt and Co., 1906-1909.

Benson, Lee. *The Concept of Jacksonian Democracy: New York as a Test Case.* Princeton, N.J.: Princeton University Press, 1961.

Bridges, Amy. *A City in the Republic: Antebellum New York and the Origins of Machine Politics.* New York: Cambridge University Press, 1984.

Cross, Whitney. *The Burned-over District: The Social and Intellectual History of Enthusiastic Religion in Western New York, 1800-1850.* New York: Harper and Row, 1965.

Ernst, Robert. *Immigrant Life in New York City, 1825-1863.* New York: Columbia University Press, 1949.

Hammond, Jabez. *The History of Political Parties in the State of New York,* 2 vols. Cooperstown: H. & E. Phinney, 1884.

Johnson, Paul E. *A Shopkeeper's Millennium: Society and Revivals in Rochester, New York, 1815-1837.* New York: Hill and Wang, 1978.

Miller, Douglas T. *Jacksonian Aristocracy: Class and Democracy In New York, 1830-1860.* New York: Oxford University Press, 1967.

Mushkat, Jerome. *Tammany: The Evolution of a Political Machine, 1789-1865.* Syracuse, N.Y.: Syracuse University Press, 1971.

Niven, John. *Martin Van Buren The Romantic Age of American Politics.* New York: Oxford University Press, 1983.

Pessen, Edward. *Jacksonian America: Society, Personality, and Politics.* Homeward, Ill.: Dorsey Press, 1967.

Raybeck, Robert. *Millard Fillmore: Biography of a President.* Buffalo, N.Y.: Henry Stewart, Inc., 1959.

Sernett, Milton C. *Abolition's Axe: Beriah Green, Oneida Institute, and the Black Freedom Struggle.* Syracuse: Syracuse University Press, 1986.

Shaw, Ronald E. *Erie Water West: A History of the Erie Canal, 1792-1854.* Lexington, Ky.: University of Kentucky Press, 1966.

Silbey, Joel. *The Transformation of American Politics, 1840-1860.* Englewood Cliffs, N.J.: Prentice-Hall, 1967.

Spann, Edward K. *The New Metropolis: New York City 1840-1857.* New York: Columbia University Press, 1981.

Van Deusen, Glyndon G. *Thurlow Weed: Wizard of the Lobby.* Boston, Mass.: Little, Brown and Co., 1947.

Van Wagenen, Jared, Jr. *The Golden Age of Homespun.* New York: Hill and Wang, 1953.

Wilentz, Sean. *Chants Democratic New York City and the Rise of the American Working Class, 1788-1850.* New York: Oxford University Press, 1984.

Wyld, Lionel. *Low Bridge! Folklore and the Erie Canal.* Syracuse, N.Y.: Syracuse University Press, 1962.

CHAPTER 5

Alexander, De Alva Stanwood. *Four Famous New Yorkers: The Political Careers of Cleveland, Platt, Hill and Roosevelt.* New York: Henry Holt and Co., 1923.

Bass, Herbert J. *"I AM A DEMOCRAT": The Political Career of David Bennett Hill.* Syracuse, N.Y.: Syracuse University Press, 1961.

Benson, Lee. *Merchants, Farmers & Railroads: Railroad Regulation and New York Politics, 1850-1887.* Cambridge: Harvard University Press, 1955.

Callow, Alexander B., Jr. *The Tweed Ring.* New York: Oxford University Press, 1965.

Flick, Alexander C. *Samuel Jones Tilden, A Study in Political Sagacity.* New York: Dodd, Mead & Co., 1939.

Hammock, David C. *Power and Society in Greater New York, 1886-1903.* New York: Russell Sage Foundation, 1982.

McKelvey, Blake. *Rochester The Flower City, 1855-1890.* Cambridge, Mass.: Harvard University Press, 1949.

Mitchell, Stewart. *Horatio Seymour of New York.* Cambridge, Mass.: Harvard University Press, 1938.

Mohr, James G. *The Radical Republicans and Reform in New York During Reconstruction.* Ithaca, N.Y.: Cornell University Press, 1973.

Nevins, Allan. *Grover Cleveland: A Study in Courage.* New York: Dodd, Mead & Co., 1932.

Osofsky, Gilbert. *Harlem: The Making of a Ghetto: Negro New York, 1890-1930.* New York: Harper and Row, 1966.

Riis, Jacob. *How the Other Half Lives.* New York: Charles Scribner's Sons, 1900.

Rischin, Moses. *The Promised City: New York's Jews, 1870-1914.* Cambridge: Harvard University Press, 1962.

Sneller, Anne Gertrude. *A Vanished World.* Syracuse, N.Y.: Syracuse University Press, 1964.

Walkowitz, Daniel J. *Worker City, Company Town: Iron and Cotton-Worker Protest in Troy and Cohoes, New York, 1855-84.* Urbana, Ill.: University of Illinois Press, 1978.

Yans-McLaughlin, Virginia. *Family and Community: Italian Immigrants in Buffalo 1880-1930.* Ithaca, N.Y.: Cornell University Press, 1977.

CHAPTER 6

Chessman, G. Wallace. *Governor Theodore Roosevelt: The Albany Apprenticeship, 1898-1900.* Cambridge, Mass.: Harvard University Press, 1965.

Dubofsky, Melvyn. *When Workers Organize: New York City in the Progressive Era.* Amherst, Mass.: University of Massachusetts Press, 1968.

Gosnell, Harold F. *Boss Platt and the New York Machine.* Chicago, Ill.: University of Chicago Press, 1924.

Howe, Irving. *World of Our Fathers.* New York: Harcourt Brace Jovanovich, 1976.

Kessner, Thomas. *The Golden Door: Italian and Jewish Immigrant Mobility in New York City, 1880-1915.* New York: Oxford University Press, 1977.

McCormick, Richard L. *From Realignment To Reform: Political Change in New York State, 1893-1910.* Ithaca, N.Y.: Cornell University Press, 1981.

Morris, Edmund. *The Rise of Theodore Roosevelt.* New York: Coward, McCann, & Geoghegan, Inc., 1979.

Sayre, Wallace S., and Herbert Kaufman. *Governing New York City Politics in the Metropolis.* New York: W.W. Norton, 1965.

Swanberg, W.A. *Citizen Hearst: A Biography of William Randolph Hearst.* New York: Charles Scribner's Sons, 1960.

Wesser, Robert F. *A Response to Progressivism: The Democratic Party and New York Politics, 1902-1918.* New York: New York University Press, 1986.

——————. *Charles Evans Hughes: Politics and Reform in New York, 1905-1910.* Ithaca, N.Y.: Cornell University Press, 1967.

Yellowitz, Irwin. *Labor and the Progressive Movement in New York State, 1897-1916.* Ithaca, N.Y.: Cornell University Press, 1965.

CHAPTER 7

Bellush, Bernard. *Franklin D. Roosevelt as Governor of New York.* New York: Columbia University Press, 1955.

Burner, David. *The Politics of Provincialism: The Democratic Party In Transition 1918-1932.* New York: Alfred A. Knopf, 1968.

Caro, Robert. *The Power Broker: Robert Moses and the Fall of New York.* New York: Alfred A. Knopf, 1974.

Friedel, Frank. *Franklin D. Roosevelt: The Apprenticeship.* Boston, Mass.: Little, Brown and Co., 1952.

Garrett, Charles. *The La Guardia Years: Machine and Reform Politics in New York City.* New Brunswick, N.J.: Rutgers University Press, 1961.

Ingalls, Robert P. *Herbert H. Lehman and New York's Little New Deal.* New York: New York University Press, 1975.

Morgan, Ted. *FDR: A Biography.* New York: Simon and Schuster, 1985.

Moscow, Warren. *Politics in the Empire State.* New York: Alfred A. Knopf, 1948.

Nevins, Allan. *Herbert H. Lehman and His Era.* New York: Charles Scribner's Sons, 1963.

Smith, Alfred E. *Up To Now: An Autobiography.* New York: Viking Press, 1929.

Ward, Geoffrey C. *Before the Trumpet: Young Franklin Roosevelt, 1882-1905.* New York: Harper & Row, 1985.

Works Progress Administration. *New York Panorama: A Comprehensive View of the Metropolis.* New York: Random House, 1938.

CHAPTER 8

Alba, Richard and Katherine Trent. *New York State Project 2000: Report on Population.* Albany, N.Y.: Nelson Rockefeller Institute of Government at SUNY, 1986.

Auletta, Ken. *The Streets Were Paved With Gold.* New York: Random House, 1979.

Bailey, Robert W. *The Crisis Regime: The MAC, the EFCB, and the Political Impact of the New York City Financial Crisis.* Albany, N.Y.: SUNY Press, 1984.

Carson, Robert B. *Main Line to Oblivion: The Disintegration of the New York Railroads in the Twentieth Century.* Port Washington, N.Y.: Kennikat Press, 1971.

Colby, Peter W., ed. *New York State Today Politics, Government, Public Policy.* Albany: SUNY Press, 1985.

Connery, Robert and Gerald Benjamin. *Rockefeller of New York Executive Power in the Statehouse.* Ithaca, N.Y.: Cornell University Press, 1979.

Dubinsky, David, and A. H. Raskin. *David Dubinsky: A Life With Labor.* New York: Simon & Schuster, 1977.

Freedgood, Seymour. *The Gateway States: New Jersey, New York.* New York: Time Inc., 1967.

Glazer, Nathan, and Daniel Patrick Moynihan. *Beyond the Melting Pot The Negroes, Puerto Ricans, Jews, Italians, and Irish of New York City,* 2nd ed. Cambridge, Mass.: MIT Press, 1970.

Hauptman, Laurence M. *The Iroquois Strug-*

gle for Survival: World War II to Red Power. Syracuse, N.Y.: Syracuse University Press, 1986.

Kennedy, William. *O Albany: An Urban Tapestry*. New York: Viking Press, 1983.

Koch, Edward. *Mayor: An Autobiography*. New York: Viking Press, 1983.

Lowi, Theodore J. *At the Pleasure of the Mayor: Patronage and Power in New York City, 1898-1958*. New York: Free Press of Glencoe, 1964.

McClelland, Peter D., and Alan L. Magdowitz. *Crisis in the Making: The Political Economy of New York State Since 1945*. New York: Cambridge University Press, 1981.

Morris, Charles *The Cost of Good Intentions: New York City and the Liberal Experiment*. New York: Norton, 1980.

Moscow, Warren. *The Last of the Big-Time Bosses: The Life and Times of Carmine De Sapio and the Rise and Fall of Tammany Hall*. New York: Stein and Day, 1971.

Newfield, Jack, and Paul DuBrul. *The Abuse of Power: The Permanent Government and the Fall of New York*. New York: Viking Press, 1977.

Pierce, Neal R. *The Megastates of America: People, Politics, and Power in Ten Great States*. New York: Norton, 1972.

Ravitch, Diane. *The Great School Wars: New York City, 1805-1973*. New York: Basic Books, Inc., 1974.

Shefter, Martin. *Political Crisis Fiscal Crisis The Collapse and Revival of New York City*. New York: Basic Books, Inc., 1985.

Smith, Richard Norton. *Thomas E. Dewey and His Times*. New York: Simon and Schuster, 1982.

Starr, Roger. *The Rise and Fall of New York City*. New York: Basic Books, Inc., 1985.

Zimmerman, Joseph F. *Government and Politics in New York State*. New York: New York University Press, 1981

INDEX

GENERAL INDEX

Italicized page numbers indicate illustrations.